System Center 2016 Virtual Machine Manager Cookbook
Third Edition

Design, configure, and manage an efficient virtual infrastructure with VMM in System Center 2016

Roman Levchenko
Edvaldo Alessandro Cardoso

BIRMINGHAM - MUMBAI

System Center 2016 Virtual Machine Manager Cookbook
Third Edition

Commissioning Editor: Kartikey Pandey
Acquisition Editor: Heramb Bhavsar
Content Development Editor: Devika Battike
Technical Editor: Manish Shanbhag
Copy Editor: Safis Editing, Dipti Mankame
Project Coordinator: Judie Jose
Proofreader: Safis Editing
Indexer: Rekha Nair
Graphics: Tom Scaria
Production Coordinator: Nilesh Mohite

First published: March 2013
Second edition: June 2014
Third edition: February 2018

Production reference: 1190218

Published by Packt Publishing Ltd.
Livery Place
35 Livery Street
Birmingham
B3 2PB, UK.

ISBN 978-1-78588-148-0

www.packtpub.com

`mapt.io`

Mapt is an online digital library that gives you full access to over 5,000 books and videos, as well as industry leading tools to help you plan your personal development and advance your career. For more information, please visit our website.

Why subscribe?

- Spend less time learning and more time coding with practical eBooks and Videos from over 4,000 industry professionals

- Improve your learning with Skill Plans built especially for you

- Get a free eBook or video every month

- Mapt is fully searchable

- Copy and paste, print, and bookmark content

PacktPub.com

Did you know that Packt offers eBook versions of every book published, with PDF and ePub files available? You can upgrade to the eBook version at `www.PacktPub.com` and as a print book customer, you are entitled to a discount on the eBook copy. Get in touch with us at `service@packtpub.com` for more details.

At `www.PacktPub.com`, you can also read a collection of free technical articles, sign up for a range of free newsletters, and receive exclusive discounts and offers on Packt books and eBooks.

Contributors

About the authors

Roman Levchenko is a Microsoft MVP, VMware vExpert, and systems architect working for a leading international IT integrator. He focuses mainly on Microsoft technologies, including Windows Server, System Center, PowerShell, and Azure. Furthermore, he is certified as Microsoft MCSE, MCSA, MCS, MCITP, and VMware VCP6-DCV. As a technical reviewer, he has also participated in the making of some recent and well-known books by Manning. He runs his own blog, and you can follow him on Twitter at @rlevchenko to keep in touch and receive the latest news.

> *I am grateful to everyone with whom I have had the pleasure to work during this project: the team at Packt who found me and offered to take up the writing; Edvaldo Alessandro Cardoso, the author of the previous editions, for being a technical reviewer together with Tomica Kaniski. I have worked nonstop on the book for the last few months and couldn't survive without my family—thanks a ton for your support and love.*

Edvaldo Alessandro Cardoso is a former Microsoft MVP, international speaker, author, evangelist, and a subject matter expert in cloud, virtualization, management, and identity, working for Microsoft as a secure infrastructure architect for Asia Pacific, Greater China, India, and Japan.

He has more than 27 years of experience in the IT industry working with LBDMs, building trust, demonstrating business value, solving complex business problems, and transforming business strategy into technology utilizing existing and innovative technologies. He is a reviewer on this book.

> *It is always a challenge to maintain a work-life balance and I would like to thank my wife, Daniele, and my kids, Nicole, Lucas, and Matheus for their tremendous support, and for always pushing me to achieve my best.*

> *Since the last edition, VMM evolved with some important new features and I would like to acknowledge the great work that Roman Levchenko did by updating the book and getting it to its 3rd edition.*

About the reviewer

Tomica Kaniski is a Microsoft MVP for Cloud and Datacenter Management (since 2010). He is fully engaged with (but not limited to) Microsoft products and technologies. In his spare time, he plays the bass guitar and also likes to read and travel. He currently works in the telecommunications industry for VIPnet d.o.o. in Croatia (A1 Telekom Austria Group/América Móvil company).

> *I would like to thank my family for their patience and constant support.*

Packt is searching for authors like you

If you're interested in becoming an author for Packt, please visit `authors.packtpub.com` and apply today. We have worked with thousands of developers and tech professionals, just like you, to help them share their insight with the global tech community. You can make a general application, apply for a specific hot topic that we are recruiting an author for, or submit your own idea.

About the reviewer

Tomica Kaniski is a Microsoft MVP for Cloud and Datacenter Management (since 2010). He is fully engaged with (but not limited to) Microsoft products and technologies. In his spare time, he plays the bass guitar and also likes to read and travel. He currently works in the telecommunications industry for VIPnet d.o.o. in Croatia (A1 Telekom Austria Group/América Móvil company).

> *I would like to thank my family for their patience and constant support.*

Packt is searching for authors like you

If you're interested in becoming an author for Packt, please visit `authors.packtpub.com` and apply today. We have worked with thousands of developers and tech professionals, just like you, to help them share their insight with the global tech community. You can make a general application, apply for a specific hot topic that we are recruiting an author for, or submit your own idea.

Table of Contents

Preface

System Center 2016 is a comprehensive IT infrastructure, virtualization, and cloud management platform. With System Center 2016, you can easily and efficiently deploy, manage, and monitor a virtualized infrastructure, services, and applications across multiple hypervisors, as well as public and private cloud infrastructures, to deliver flexible and cost-effective IT services for your business.

This book has plenty of recipes to help you design, plan, and improve Virtual Machine Manager (VMM) deployment; integrate and manage the fabric (compute, storage, network controller, gateway, and networking), services, and resources; deploy different types of clusters; configure integration with the operations manager and Windows Azure Pack; and carry out vital tasks quickly and easily.

Who this book is for

This book is essentially intended at system engineers, solution architects, administrators and anyone who wants to learn and master VMM 2016. If you are not familiar with VMM, don't worry. Start from the beginning, and the book will also help you to get insight into the virtualization platform, its management, and other techniques related to the private cloud.

What this book covers

Chapter 1, *VMM 2016 Architecture*, provides an understanding of the VMM modular architecture, which is useful when designing VMM and troubleshooting deployment. This chapter also covers all the requirements that must be satisfied to make a private cloud.

Chapter 2, *Upgrading from Previous Versions*, walks you through all the necessary steps to upgrade the previous version of VMM to the new VMM 2016, covering its database, highly available configurations, and post-upgrade tasks.

Chapter 3, *Installing VMM 2016*, focuses on deploying VMM and its dependencies. It also gives plenty of tips and tricks to install and automate VMM and SQL Server deployments in both Windows Server Core and Full environments.

Chapter 4, *Installing a High Available VMM Server*, dives into more advanced VMM configuration, and provides an understanding of how VMM has become a critical part of the private cloud infrastructure. You will also learn how to make a highly available library server and VMM configuration database.

Chapter 5, *Configuring Fabric Resources in VMM*, discusses building a new fabric in VMM by configuring compute, storage, and networking resources. It starts by adding host groups and ends by creating a hyper-converged cluster with Storage Spaces Direct and Hyper-V. It also covers the deployment of a network controller providing a good starting point for network virtualization implementation.

Chapter 6, *Configuring Guarded Fabric in VMM*, walks you through the recipes to help protect confidential data by deploying new shielded VMs as a part of a Guarded Fabric consisting of Guarded Hosts and a Host Guardian Service. It also discusses how to convert existing VMs to shielded and manage them through VMM.

Chapter 7, *Deploying Virtual Machines and Services*, provides information to help the administrator to create, deploy, and manage private clouds, virtual machines, templates, and services in VMM 2016; it provides recipes to assist you in getting the most of our deployment.

Chapter 8, *Managing VMware ESXi Hosts*, shows you how to manage and make VMware resources available to private cloud deployments. It also covers converting VMware machines to Hyper-V (V2V), deploying virtual machines and templates, all from the VMM console.

Chapter 9, *Managing Clouds, Fabric Updates, Resources, Cluster and the New Features of 2016*, covers other new features of VMM 2016 such as Cluster OS Rolling upgrade and Production Checkpoints. You will also learn how to integrate VMM 2016 with Windows Azure Pack for VM cloud management.

Chapter 10, *Integration with System Center Operations Manager 2016*, guides you through the steps required to complete integration of SCOM 2016 with VMM in order to enable monitoring of the private cloud infrastructure.

To get the most out of this book

This book assumes a medium level of expertise on Windows Server and Hyper-V, basic knowledge on cloud computing and networking, and a moderate experience with PowerShell. To evaluate all the recipes in the book, you will need System Center 2016 Virtual Machine Manager, SQL Server (2016 version is used throughout the book), as a minimum requirement. The book also covers integration with VMware vCenter 6.0; therefore, you need to have it deployed beforehand. Although the recipes provide exceptional step-by-step guides, prepare Windows Azure Pack, Service Provider Foundation, and System Center Operations Manager 2016 media files at least.

Actually, some of the chapters were made in Azure, and you can also use public IaaS services and its free trial to deploy and check some of the explained scenarios. In addition, Azure is required if you plan to protect virtual machines via the Azure Site Recovery service.

Download the color images

We also provide a PDF file that has color images of the screenshots/diagrams used in this book. You can download it here: https://www.packtpub.com/sites/default/files/downloads/SystemCenter2016VirtualMachineManagerCookbookThirdEdition_ColorImages.pdf.

Conventions used

There are a number of text conventions used throughout this book.

CodeInText: Indicates code words in text, database table names, folder names, filenames, file extensions, pathnames, dummy URLs, user input, and Twitter handles. Here is an example: "In addition, it will add the ApplicationFrameworks folder to the library share."

A block of code is set as follow

```
;SQL Server 2016 Configuration File
[OPTIONS]
; SQL Server License Terms
IAcceptSQLServerLicenseTerms="True"
; Setup Work Flow: INSTALL, UNINSTALL, or UPGRADE.
ACTION="Install"
```

When we wish to draw your attention to a particular part of a code block, the relevant lines or items are set in bold:

```
;SQL Server 2016 Configuration File
[OPTIONS]
; SQL Server License Terms
IAcceptSQLServerLicenseTerms="True"
; Setup Work Flow: INSTALL, UNINSTALL, or UPGRADE.
ACTION="Install"
```

Any command-line input or output is written as follows:

```
Set-ItemProperty -Path 'HKLM:SoftwareMicrosoftMicrosoft
System Center Virtual Machine Manager ServerSetup' -Name
VmmServicePrincipalNames -Value "SCVMM/vmm-mgmt01,SCVMM/vmm-
mgmt01.rllab.com"
```

Bold: Indicates a new term, an important word, or words that you see onscreen. For example, words in menus or dialog boxes appear in the text like this. Here is an example: "Launch the SQL Server setup and choose the **New SQL Server failover cluster installation** option."

 Warnings or important notes appear like this.

 Tips and tricks appear like this.

Get in touch

Feedback from our readers is always welcome.

General feedback: Email feedback@packtpub.com and mention the book title in the subject of your message. If you have questions about any aspect of this book, please email us at questions@packtpub.com.

Errata: Although we have taken every care to ensure the accuracy of our content, mistakes do happen. If you have found a mistake in this book, we would be grateful if you would report this to us. Please visit www.packtpub.com/submit-errata, selecting your book, clicking on the Errata Submission Form link, and entering the details.

Piracy: If you come across any illegal copies of our works in any form on the Internet, we would be grateful if you would provide us with the location address or website name. Please contact us at copyright@packtpub.com with a link to the material.

If you are interested in becoming an author: If there is a topic that you have expertise in and you are interested in either writing or contributing to a book, please visit authors.packtpub.com.

Reviews

Please leave a review. Once you have read and used this book, why not leave a review on the site that you purchased it from? Potential readers can then see and use your unbiased opinion to make purchase decisions, we at Packt can understand what you think about our products, and our authors can see your feedback on their book. Thank you!

For more information about Packt, please visit packtpub.com.

1
VMM 2016 Architecture

In this chapter, we will cover:

- Understanding each component for a real-world implementation
- Planning for high availability
- Designing the VMM server, database, and console implementation
- Specifying the correct system requirements for a real-world scenario
- Licensing the System Center VMM 2016
- Troubleshooting VMM and supporting technologies

Introduction

This chapter has been designed to provide an understanding of the underlying **Virtual Machine Manager (VMM)** modular architecture, which is useful to improve the implementation and troubleshooting VMM.

The first version of VMM was launched in far 2007 and was designed to manage virtual machines and to get the most efficient physical server utilizations. It has been dramatically grown from the basic tool to the one of the most advanced tool, with abilities to work even with different type of clouds.

The new VMM 2016 allows you to create and manage private clouds, retain the characteristics of public clouds by allowing tenants and delegated VMM administrators to perform functions, and abstract the underlying fabric to let them deploy the VM's applications and services. Although they have no visibility into the underlying hardware, there is a uniform resource pooling which allows you to add or remove capacity as your environment grows. Additionally, it supports the new Windows Server 2016 capabilities including software-defined storage, networks and shielded VMs (simply put, **Software-Defined Datacenters (SDDC's)**). VMM 2016 can manage private clouds across supported hypervisors, such as Hyper-V and VMware, which can be integrated with Azure public cloud services as well.

The main strategies and changes of VMM 2016 are as follows:

- **Application focus**: VMM abstracts fabric (hosts servers, storage, and networking) into a unified pool of resources. It also gives you the ability to deploy web applications and SQL Server profiles to configure customized database servers along with data-tier applications. However, virtual application deployment based on Server App-V, which was available in older versions of VMM, is no longer existing in VMM 2016. Although, if you upgrade VMM 2012 R2 to VMM 2016, your current service templates with Server App-V will continue to work with some limitations related to scale-out scenarios.

- **Service deployment**: One of the powerful features of VMM is its capability to deploy a service to a private cloud. These services are dependent on multiple VMs tied together (for example, web frontend servers, application servers, and backend database servers). They can be provisioned as simply as provisioning a VM, but all together.

- **Dynamic optimization**: This strategy will balance the workload in a cluster, while a feature called power optimization can turn off physical virtualization host servers when they are not needed. It can then turn them back on when the load increases. This process will automatically move VMs between hosts to balance the load. It also widens and replaces the VM Load Balancing feature that is available for Windows Server 2016 Failover Clusters.

- **Software-Defined Datacenter**: Network virtualization (software-defined networking or simply SDN) was introduced in VMM 2012 SP1 and quickly became popular due to a possibility to define and run multiple isolated networks on a single physical network fabric. It was based on NVGRE abstraction mechanism. VMM 2016 goes beyond and brings Azure's network model closer to your datacenter by introducing network controller as a central point, VXLAN for abstraction from the underlying physical network and integration with software load-balancers and gateways. In addition to SDN, Windows Server 2016 features like **Storage Spaces Direct (S2D)**, **Storage Replica**, and **Quality of Service (QoS)** complement each other and are also supported by VMM 2016.

- **Advanced Security**: Modern data center requires protection for customer's sensitive data from hackers and even technical staff or other persons who can somehow access such data without your permission. To help protect against that problem, VMM supports managing and creating a new guarded fabric with a set of shielded VMs, guarded hosts and hosts with guardian services.

- **Multivendor hypervisor support**: If we compare the list of managed hypervisors in VMM 2012 R2 to VMM 2016, it's been cut. VMM 2016 now manages only Hyper-V and VMware, covering all of the major hypervisors on the market so far. Support for Citrix XenServer has been removed:

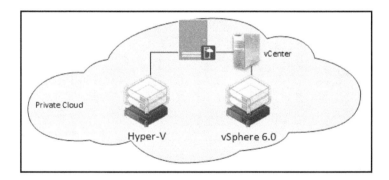

Knowing your current environment – assessment

This is the first step. You need to do an assessment of your current environment to find out how and where the caveats are. You can use the Microsoft MAP toolkit (download it from `http://www.microsoft.com/en-us/download/details.aspx?id=7826`) or any other assessment tool to help you carry out a report assessment by querying the hardware, OS, application, and services. It is important to define what you can and need to address and, sometimes, what you cannot virtualize.

Microsoft MAP toolkit will assess your environment using agentless technology to collect data (inventory and performance), and provide reports. Server Consolidation Report, VMware Discovery Report, Microsoft Workload Discovery and Microsoft Private Cloud Fast Track Onboarding Assessment Report are some of the useful reports that will enable your IT infrastructure planning. For more information, refer to `http://social.technet.microsoft.com/wiki/contents/articles/1640.` `microsoft-assessment-and-planning-toolkit.aspx`.

Currently, Microsoft supports the virtualization of all MS infrastructure technologies (for example, SQL, Exchange, AD, Skype for Business, IIS, and File Server).

Designing the solution

With the assessment report in hand, it is recommended that you spend a reasonable amount of time on the solution design and architecture, and you will have a solid and consistent implementation. The following figure highlights the new VMM 2016 features and others, which have been carried over from older versions, for you to take into consideration when working on your private cloud design:

Deployment	Fabric Management		Cloud Management	Service Management
HA VMM Server	Hyper-V and SOFS Bare-Metal Deployment	Cluster OS Rolling Upgrade	RBAC model, Quotas, Delegations	Service Templates
Upgrade	Nano Server, Hyper-V, VMware	Dynamic and Power Optimization	Integration with Windows Azure Pack	Application Deployment
Custom Properties	Network and IP address Management	Standard and Production Checkpoints	Azure instances management	Template-provisioning for Windows/Linux VMs
PowerShell	Storage Management, QoS, Replica and S2D	Integration with SCOM	Azure Site Recovery protection	Image-Based Servicing
Scalability	Software-Defined Datacenter	Guarded Fabric	Extensibility	PowerShell DSC

Creating the private cloud fabric

In VMM, before deploying VMs and services to a private cloud, you need to set up the private cloud fabric.

There are three resources that are included in the fabric in VMM 2016:

- **Servers**: These contain virtualization hosts (Hyper-V and VMware servers) and groups, PXE, update servers (that is, WSUS), and other servers.
- **Networking**: This contains the network fabric and devices configuration (for example, gateways, virtual switches, network virtualization); it presents the wiring between resource repositories, running instances, VMs, and services.
- **Storage**: This contains the configuration for storage connectivity and management, simplifying storage complexities, and how storage is virtualized. For example, you can configure the SMI-S and SMP providers or a Windows 2016 SMB 3.0 file server.

If you are really serious about setting up a private cloud, you should carry out a virtualization assessment using MAP, as discussed above and work on a detailed design document covering hardware, hypervisor, fabric, and management. With this in mind, the implementation will be pretty straightforward.

System Center 2016 will help you install, configure, manage, and monitor your private cloud from the fabric to the hypervisor and up to service deployment. It can also be integrated with public cloud services(for instance, Azure Site Recovery to protect and replicate your VMs to Azure public cloud).

 Refer to the *Designing the VMM server, database, and console implementation* recipe in this chapter for further related information.

Understanding each component for a real-world implementation

System Center 2016 VMM has six components. It is important to understand the role of each component in order to have a better design and implementation.

Getting ready

For small deployments, test environments, or a proof of concept, you can install all of the components in one server, but as is best practice in production environments, you should consider separating the components.

How to do it...

Let's start by reviewing each component of VMM 2016 and understanding the role it plays:

- **VMM console**: This application connects to the VMM management server to allow you to manage VMM, to centrally view and manage physical and virtual resources (for example, hosts, VMs, services, the fabric, and library resources), and to carry out tasks on a daily basis, such as VM and services deployment, monitoring, and reporting.

  By using the VMM console from your desktop, you will be able to manage your private cloud without needing to remotely connect it to the VMM management server.

It is recommended to install the VMM console on the administrator desktop machine, taking into account the OS and prerequisites, such as a firewall and preinstalled software. See the *Specifying the correct system requirements for a real-world scenario* recipe in this chapter.

- **VMM management server**: The management server is the core of VMM. It is the server on which the Virtual Machine Manager service runs to process commands and control communications with the VMM console, the database, the library server, and the hosts.

  Think of VMM management server as the heart, which means that you need to design your computer resources accordingly to accommodate such an important service.

For high availability, VMM Management Server must be deployed as a HA service on a Windows Server Failover Cluster. Note though that the SQL Server where the VMM database will be installed and the file share for the library share must also be highly available. For more info, check *Planning for high availability* recipe in this chapter and the *Installing a Highly Available VMM* recipe in `Chapter 4`, *Installing a Highly Available VMM Server*.

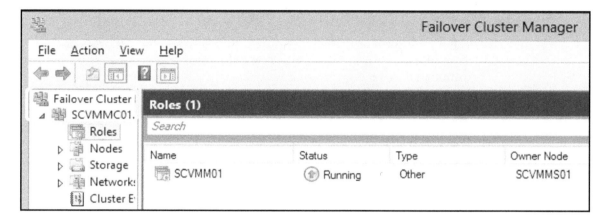

As is the best practice for medium and enterprise production environments, keep the VMM management server on a separate cluster from the production cluster, due to its crucial importance for your private cloud.

- **Database**: The database server runs SQL Server and contains all of the VMM data. It plays an important role when you have a clustered VMM deployment by keeping the shared data. The best practice is to also have the SQL database in a cluster or an availability group.

When running VMM in a cluster, you cannot install SQL Server in one of the VMM management servers. Instead, you will need to have it on another machine.

- **VMM library**: The VMM library servers are file shares, a catalog that stores resources, such as VM templates, virtual hard drive files, ISOs, scripts, and custom resources with a .cr extension, which will all be visible and indexed by VMM and then shared among application packages, tenants, and self-service users in private clouds.

The library has been enhanced to support services and the sharing of resources. It is a store for drivers for Bare Metal deployments, SQL data-tier apps, (SQLDAC), and web deploy packages.

In a distributed environment, you can group equivalent sets of resources and make them available in different locations by using resource groups. You can also store a resource in a storage group that will allow you to reference that group in profiles and templates rather than in a specific virtual hard disk (VHD); this is especially important when you have multiple sites and VMM will automatically select the right resource from a single reference object. This essentially enables one template that can reference an object that can be obtained from multiple locations.

You can also have application profiles and SQL profiles (answer files for configuration of the application or SQL) to support the deployment of applications and databases to a VM after the base image is deployed. Application profiles can be web applications, SQL data-tier, or a general for deploying both application types and running any scripts.

- **Self-service portal**: The web-based self-service portal, was removed from SC 2012. In System Center 2012 SP1/R2, App Controller was being used as a replacement to the self-service portal, however, it was also finally removed in System Center 2016.

The Self-Service Portal's and App Controller's replacement is a Windows Azure Pack.

- **VMM command shell**: VMM is based on PowerShell. Everything you can do on GUI, you can do by using PowerShell. VMM PowerShell extensions make available the cmdlets that perform all of the functions in VMM 2016.

When working with complex environments, or if you need to automate some processess, the PowerShell cmdlets will make your work easier. When doing wizard-based tasks on GUI, save the PowerShell script for future use and automation.

How it works...

As you may have noticed, although VMM management is the core, each component is required in order to provide a better VMM experience. In addition to this, for a real-world deployment, you also need to consider implementing other System Center family components to complement your design. Every System Center component is designed to provide part of the private cloud solution. The Microsoft private cloud solution includes the implementation of VMM 2016 plus the following utilities:

- **System Center 2016 Configuration Manager**: This provides comprehensive configuration management for the Microsoft platform that can help users with the devices and applications they need to be productive while maintaining corporate compliance and control
- **System Center 2016 Data Protection Manager**: This provides unified data protection for the Windows and also VMware environment, delivering backup and restore scenarios from disk, tape, off-premise, and from the cloud
- **System Center 2016 Endpoint Protection**: This is built on the System Center Configuration Manager and provides threat detection of malware and exploits as part of a unified infrastructure for managing client security and compliance to simplify and improve endpoint protection
- **System Center 2016 Operations Manager**: This provides deep application diagnostics and infrastructure monitoring to ensure the predictable performance and availability of vital applications, and offers a comprehensive view of the datacenter, private cloud, and public clouds
- **System Center 2016 Orchestrator**: This provides the orchestration, integration, and automation of IT processes through the creation of runbooks to define and standardize best practices and improve operational efficiency
- **System Center 2016 Service Manager**: This provides flexible self-service experiences and standardized datacenter processes to integrate people, workflows, and knowledge across enterprise infrastructure and applications

There's more...

When deploying System Center, there are some other systems and configurations you need to consider. There are some old components that have also been described here in order to help you to understand your current infrastructure before, for instance, migration to the new VMM from older versions.

Windows Azure Pack

WAP is a free solution to manage resources that integrates with System Center and Windows Server to provide a customizable self-service portal for managing services such as websites, Virtual Machines, SQL or MySQL servers, and Service Bus; it also includes capabilities for automating and integrating additional custom services. For more info see http://www.microsoft.com/en-us/server-cloud/products/windows-azure-pack/.

Service Provider Foundation

Service Provider Foundation (**SPF**) is provided with System Center Orchestrator, a component of System Center since 2012 SP1. Service Provider Foundation exposes an extensible **OData** web service that interacts with **Virtual Machine Manager** (**VMM**). It's main interface for communication between WAP, SCOM, and VMM.

Service Reporting

Service Reporting, an optional component of System Center 2012 R2, enables IT (particularly hosting providers) to create detailed views, for each customer (tenant), of the virtual machine's consumption of the resources (CPU, memory, storage, and networking). For more info see http://technet.microsoft.com/en-us/library/dn251058.aspx.

 Service Reporting has been removed in SC 2016 and is no longer available. Third-party solutions are recommended for billing and utilizing tracking purposes.

Domain controllers

Although the domain controller is not part of the System Center family and it is not a VMM component, it plays an important role in the deployment of a private cloud as VMM requires it to be installed on a domain environment.

 This requirement is for the System Center VMM. You can have the managed hosts on a workgroup mode or even on a trusted domain other than the System Center domain. We will discuss this later in this chapter.

Windows Server Update Service – WSUS

WSUS plays an important role with reference to the private cloud as it is used to update the Hyper-V hosts, library servers, or any other role for compliance and remediation.

 You can use WSUS for other System Center family components as well.

System Center App Controller

The App Controller provides a self-service experience through a web portal that can help you easily configure, deploy, and manage VMs and services across private, third-party hosters (that support Microsoft Hyper-V) and public clouds (Azure). For example, moving a VM from a private cloud to Azure, creating checkpoints, granting access, scaling out deployed services, and so on.

The App Controller has been used as a replacement of the VMM self-service portal since SC 2012 SP1. It was deprecated in the SC 2012 R2 time and finally removed in SC 2016. As noted above, you should plan Azure Pack deployment instead of current App Controller instance.

Microsoft Azure Stack

Azure Stack is a hybrid-cloud platform, bringing core public Azure services to your datacenter. These services are mostly dedicated to Azure PaaS and IaaS and help you out with building unified ecosystems between private and public clouds. Azure Stack is delivered as an integrated system, with software installed on the hardware built by partners like HPE and Cisco. Azure's familiar pay-as-you-go model is mainly being used in Azure Stack and you can stretch the same subscriptions out for both Azure and Azure Stack clouds. If you have unstable or restricted connection to Azure, you may choose to use Azure Stack in disconnected mode with a capacity model pricing package - a fixed fee annual subscription based on the number of physical cores. It's important to note that you can manage WAP VMs from Azure Stack using a special connector, though it's under review and not recommended for production use: `https://aka.ms/wapconnectorazurestackdlc`.

To try Azure Stack for free, you can use its development kit and Azure VM with nested virtualization enabled (this option is tested, but not actually supported) or your own physical resources for a single-server deployment. For more info see `https://docs.microsoft.com/ru-ru/azure/azure-stack/azure-stack-run-powershell-script`.

System Center components scenarios

The following table will guide you through choosing which System Center component is necessary as per your deployment:

Although Configuration Manager (SCCM) is not mentioned in the following table, it plays an important role when it comes to patching Virtual Machine and you can use SCCM **Task Sequence** (**TS**) on a single process to deploy an OS to a **Virtual Hard Disk** (**VHD**). For more info see `http://technet.microsoft.com/en-us/library/dn448591.aspx`.

You should also check Service Management Automation, which will enable Orchestrated offline VM Patching. For more info see `http://blogs.technet.com/b/privatecloud/archive/2013/12/07/orchestrated-vm-patching.aspx`.

Scenarios	Enabling technologies				
	WAP	Operations Manager	Orchestrator	Service Manager	VMM
Fabric provider					
Bare Metal deploy					√
Integration with network and storage			√		√
Host patching					√
Shielded VMs	√				√
Cluster OS Rolling Upgrade					√
Storage QoS and Replica					√
Host optimization / power optimization					√
Software-defined storage (S2D)					√
Software-Defined Networking (SDN)					√

Scenarios	Enabling technologies				
Capacity reporting		√			√
Service provider					
Service templates (offerings)	√				√
Service and VM catalog	√			√	√
Life cycle (create, upgrade, retire)	√		√	√	√
Application and SLA monitoring		√			
SLA and capacity reporting		√		√	
Usage and Metering	√	√			√
Billing and pricing	√	√			√
Service consumer					
Request quote or capacity (cloud)			√	√	√
Request/deploy VM	√	√	√	√	√
Request/deploy service	√	√	√	√	√
Quota enforcement	√				√
Request approvals			√	√	
SDN management	√				√

Planning for high availability

High availability is important when your business requires minimum or no downtime, and planning for it in advance is very important.

Getting ready

Based on what we learned about each component, we now need to plan the **high availability (HA)** for each VMM component.

How to do it...

Start by planning the HA for the core component, followed by every VMM component of your design. It is important to consider hardware and other System Center components, as well as the OS and software licenses.

How it works...

When planning for highly available VMM management servers, you should first consider where to place the VMM cluster. As per best practices, the recommendation is to install the VMM cluster on a management cluster, preferably on some physical servers, if using converged network for your virtual network. However, if you plan to install highly available VMM management servers on the managed cluster, you need to take into consideration the following points:

- Only one highly available VMM management server is allowed per Failover Cluster.
- Despite the possibility to have a VMM management server installed on all cluster nodes, only one node can be active at a time.
- To perform a planned failover, use Failover Cluster Manager. The use of the VMM console is not supported.
- In a planned failover situation, ensure that there are no running tasks on the VMM management server, as it will fail during a failover operation and will not automatically restart after the failover operation.
- Any connection to a highly available VMM management server from the VMM console will be disconnected during a failover operation, reconnecting right after.
- The Failover Cluster must be running Windows Server 2016 in order to be supported.

- The highly available VMM management server must meet system requirements. For information about system requirements for VMM, see the *Specifying the correct system requirements for a real-world scenario* recipe in this chapter.
- In a highly available VMM management deployment, you will need a domain account to install and run the VMM management service. You are required to use **distributed key management (DKM)** to store the encryption keys in Active Directory.
- A dedicated and supported version of Microsoft SQL Server should be installed. For supported versions of SQL Server for the VMM database, see the *Specifying the correct system requirements for a real-world scenario* recipe.

There's more...

The following sections are the considerations for SQL Server and the VMM library in an HA environment.

SQL Server

In an enterprise deployment of VMM, it is recommended that you have a SQL Server cluster to support the HA VMM, preferably on a cluster separated from the VMM cluster. VMM 2016 supports SQL Server Always On Availability Groups. The following link will show you a good example of how to set it up: *See the Configure SQL Server with AlwaysOn AGs* recipe in Chapter 3, *Installing VMM 2016*.

 Although the latest SQL Server versions support basic availability groups (AGs) available in Standard edition, SQL Server Enterprise and advanced AGs are recommended and will be used throughout the book.

VMM library

As it is the best practice in an enterprise deployment, a highly available file server for hosting the VMM library shares is highly recommended as VMM does not provide a method for replicating files in the VMM library, and they need to be replicated outside of VMM.

As a suggestion, you can use the Microsoft **Robocopy** tool to replicate the VMM library files if you have distributed the library type.

Designing the VMM server, database, and console implementation

When planning a VMM 2016 design for deployment, consider the different VMM roles, keeping in mind that VMM is part of the Microsoft private cloud solution. If you are considering a private cloud, you will need to integrate VMM with the other System Center family components.

 You can create application profiles that will provide instructions for installing Microsoft Web Deploy applications and Microsoft SQL Server **data-tier applications (DACs)**, and for running scripts when deploying a virtual machine as part of a service.

In VMM, you can add the hardware, guest operating system, SQL Server, and application profiles that will be used in a template to deploy virtual machines. These profiles are essentially answer files to configure the application or SQL during the setup.

Getting ready

You can create a private cloud by combining hosts, even from different hypervisors (for example, Hyper-V and VMware), with networking, storage, and library resources.

To start deploying VMs and services, you first need to configure the fabric.

How to do it...

Create a spreadsheet with the server names and the IP settings, as seen in the following table, of every System Center component you plan to deploy. This will help you manage and integrate the solution:

Server name	Role	IP settings
vmm-mgmt01	VMM Management Server 01	IP: 10.16.254.20/24 GW: 10.16.254.1 DNS: 10.16.254.2
vmm-mgmt02	VMM Management Server 02	IP: 10.16.254.22/24 GW: 10.16.254.1 DNS: 10.16.254.1

Server name	Role	IP settings
vmm-console01	VMM Console	IP: 10.16.254.50/24 GW: 10.16.254.1 DNS: 10.16.254.2
vmm-lib01	VMM Library	IP: 10.16.254.25/24 GW: 10.16.254.1 DNS: 10.16.254.2
w2016-sql01	SQL Server 2016	IP: 10.16.254.40/24 GW: 10.16.254.1 DNS: 10.16.254.2

How it works...

The following rules need to be considered when planning a VMM 2016 deployment:

- The computer name cannot contain the character string SCVMM (for example, srv-scvmm-01) and cannot exceed 15 characters.
- Your VMM database must use a supported version of SQL Server to perform a VMM 2016 deployment. Express editions of Microsoft SQL Server are no longer supported for the VMM database. For more information, check the system requirements specified in the *Specifying the correct system requirements for a real-world scenario* recipe in this chapter.

 For a full highly available VMM, not only must VMM be deployed on a Failover Cluster (minimum two servers), but the SQL Server must be deployed on a cluster as well (minimum two servers).

- VMM 2016 does not support a library server on a computer that is running Windows Server 2012; it now requires Windows Server 2012 R2 as a minimum, but for consistency and standardization, I do recommend that you install it on a Windows Server 2016.
- VMM 2016 no longer supports creating and importing templates with the Server App-V packages. If you are upgrading from a previous version of VMM that has templates with such applications, you will continue to manage them with VMM, but you will not be able to upgrade the application.

- Hosts running the following versions of VMware ESXi and VMware vCenter Server are supported:
  - ESXi 5.1
  - ESXi 5.5
  - ESXi 6.0
  - vCenter 5.1
  - vCenter 5.5
  - vCenter 6.0
- Upgrading a previous version of VMM to a highly available VMM 2016 requires additional preparation. See `Chapter 2`, *Upgrading from Previous Version* of VMM, for this purpose.
- If you're planning for high availability of VMM 2016, be sure to install SQL Server on a cluster and on separate servers as it cannot physically be located on the same servers as your VMM 2016 management server. In addition, AlwaysOn availability groups can be used for the VMM database.
- The VMM management server must be a member of a domain. (This rule does not apply to the managed hosts, which can be on a workgroup.)
- The startup RAM for the VMM management server (if running on a VM with dynamic memory enabled) must be at least 2048 MB.
- VMM library does not support **DFS Namespaces** (**DFSN**) or **DFS Replication** (**DFSR**). This support is being planned.
- VMM does not support file servers configured with the *case-insensitive option* for Windows Services for Unix, as the network filesystem case control is set to ignore. Refer to the Windows Services for UNIX 2.0 NFS Case Control article available at `http://go.microsoft.com/fwlink/p/?LinkId=102944` to learn more.
- The VMM console machine must be a member of a domain.

There's more...

For a complete design solution, there are more items you need to consider.

Storage providers – SMI-S and SMP

VMM provides support for both Block level storage (Fibre Channel, iSCSI, and **Serial Attached SCSI** (**SAS**) connections) and File storage (on SMB 3.0 network shares, residing on a Windows file server or on a NAS device).

By using storage providers, VMM enables discovery, provisioning, classification, allocation, and decommissioning.

Storage classifications enable you to assign user-defined storage classifications to discovered storage pools for **Quality of Service (QoS)** or chargeback purposes.

 You can, for example, assign a classification of Gold to storage pools that have the highest performance and availability, Silver for high performance, and Bronze for low performance.

In order to use this feature, you will need the SMI-S provider.

VMM 2016 can discover and communicate with SAN arrays through the Storage Management Initiative (SMI-S provider) and **Storage Management Provider (SMP)** provider.

If your storage is SMI-S compatible, you must install the storage provider on a separately available server (do not install on the VMM management server) and then add the provider to VMM management. Some devices come with built-in SMI-S provider and no extra are tasks required in that case. If your storage is SMP-compatible, it does not require a provider installation either.

 Each vendor has its own SMI-S setup process. My recommendation is to contact the storage vendor to ask for a Storage provider compatible with VMM 2016. A list of oficially supported storage arrays is available here: `https://docs.microsoft.com/en-us/system-center/vmm/supported-arrays`.

CIM-XML is used by VMM to communicate with the underlying SMI-S providers since VMM never communicates with the SAN arrays themselves.

By using the storage provider to integrate with the storage, VMM can create LUNs (both GPT and MBR) and assign storage to hosts or clusters.

VMM 2016 also supports the SAN snapshot and clone feature, allowing you to duplicate a LUN through a SAN Copy-capable template to provide for new VMs, if you are hosting those in a Hyper-V platform. You will need to provision outside of VMM for any other VMs hosted with VMware hosts, for example.

Bare metal

This capability enables VMM 2016 to identify the hardware, install the operational system (OS), enable the Hyper-V or file server role, and add the machine to a target-host group with streamlined operations in an automated process.

 As of SC 2016, deploying a bare metal Hyper-V cluster is now a single step. Furthermore, additional cluster hosts can be added to an existing Hyper-V or SOFS cluster using bare metal deployment.

PXE capability is required and is an integral component of the server pool. The target server will need to have a **baseboard management controller** (**BMC**) supporting one of the following management protocols:

- **Data Center Management Interface** (**DCMI**) 1.0
- **Systems Management Architecture for Server Hardware** (**SMASH**) 1.0
- **Intelligent Platform Management Interface** (**IPMI**) 1.5 or 2.0
- Custom protocols such as HPE **Integrated Lights-Out** (**iLO**) or **Integrated Dell Remote Access** (**iDRAC**)

Enterprise and hosting companies will benefit from the ability to provide new Hyper-V servers without having to install the operational system manually on each machine. By using BMC and integrating with **Windows Deployment Services** (**WDS**), VMM deploys the OS to designated hosts through the boot from the VHD(X) feature. The right BMC configuration presence is also a requirement for one of the most interesting features, called OS Rolling Upgrade, which will be discussed in detail later.

Configuring security

To ensure that users can perform only assigned actions on selected resources, create tenants, self-service users, delegated administrators, and read-only administrators in VMM using the VMM console, you will need to create **Run As** accounts to provide necessary credentials for performing operations in VMM (example, for adding hosts).

Run As accounts in VMM

Run As accounts are very useful additions to enterprise environments. These accounts are used to store credentials that allow you to delegate tasks to other administrators and self-service users without exposing sensitive credentials.

By using **Windows Data Protection API (DPAPI)**, VMM provides OS-level data protection when storing and retrieving the Run As account.

There are several different categories of Run As accounts:

- **Host computer**: This is used to provide access to Hyper-V and VMware ESXi hosts
- **BMC**: This is used to communicate with BMC on the host computer, for out-of-band management or power optimization
- **Network device**: This is used to connect to network load balancers
- **Profile**: This is to be used for service creation in the OS and application profiles as well as SQL and host profiles
- **External**: This is to be used for external systems such as System Center Operations Manager

Only administrators or delegated administrators can create and manage Run As accounts.

During the installation of the VMM management server, you will be requested to use **distributed key management** (**DKM**) to store encryption keys in **Active Directory Domain Services** (**AD DS**).

Communications poand protocols for firewall configuration

When designing the VMM implementation, you need to plan which ports you are going to use for communication and file transfers between VMM components. Based on the chosen ports, you will also need to configure your host and external firewalls. See the *Configuring ports and protocols on the host firewall for each SCVMM component* recipe in Chapter 3, *Installing VMM 2016*.

Not all of the ports can be changed through VMM. Hosts and library servers must have access to the VMM management server on the ports specified during setup. This means that all firewalls, whether software-based or hardware-based, must be previously configured.

VM storage placement

The recommendation is to create a big CSV volume. CSV spreads across multiple disk spindles and it will give great storage performance for VMs, as opposed to creating volumes based on the VHD purpose (for example, OS, data, and logs).

 If Storage Spaces Direct is used, It's recommended to make the number of volumes a multiple of the number of servers in your cluster. For example, if you have 4 servers, you will experience more consistent performance with 8 total volumes than with 7 or 9.

Management cluster

VMM 2016 supports management up to 1000 physical hosts and 25000 VMs. Therefore, the best practice is to have a separate management cluster with running VMM components to manage the production, test, and development clusters.

In addition to this, although you can virtualize the domain controllers with Windows 2016, it is not the best practice to have all the domain controllers running on the management clusters, as the cluster and System Center components highly depend on the domain controllers. If it's possible, place one or more DCs on the physical hosts or VMs in the location or fault domains different from the management cluster.

The following figure shows a two-node hyper-converged management cluster, with System Center 2016 components installed in separate VMs to manage the production cluster. All hosts are running on Windows Server 2016 with enabled **Storage Spaces Direct** to provide hyper-converged solutions which help to maximize the server's efficiency and reduce overall costs:

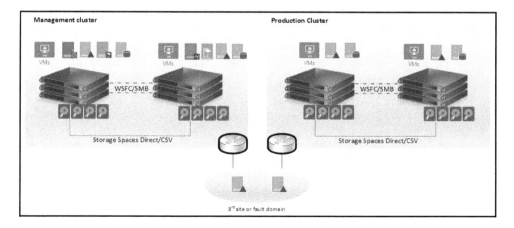

Small environment

In a small environment, you can have all the VMM components located on the same server. A small business may or may not have high availability in place, as VMM 2016 is now a critical component for your private cloud deployment.

Start by selecting the VMM server's location, which could be a physical server or a virtual machine.

You can install SQL Server on the VMM server as well, but as VMM 2016 does not support SQL Express editions, you will need to install SQL Server first and then proceed with the VMM installation.

If you are managing more than 10 hosts in the production environment, my recommendation would be to have SQL Server running on a separate machine.

It is important to understand that when deploying VMM in production environments (real-world scenarios), the business will require a reliable system that it can trust.

The following figure illustrates a real-world deployment where all VMM 2016 components are installed on the same VM and SQL is running on a separate VM.

Note though that this deployment won't allow for converged network if no dedicated network adapter is provided for VMM Management.

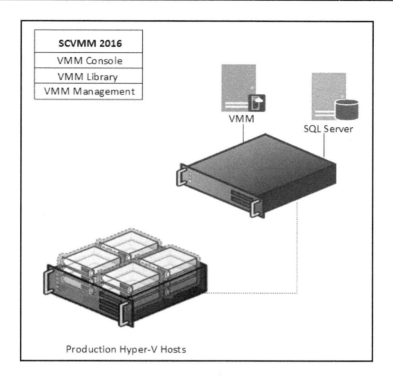

SCVMM 2016
VMM Console
VMM Library
VMM Management

Production Hyper-V Hosts

Lab environments

I would recommend up to 50 hosts in a lab environment with SQL Server and all VMM components installed on a single VM. It will work well, but I would not recommend this installation in a production environment.

 Alternatively, you can leverage a nested virtualization feature in Windows Server 2016. In other words, with nested virtualization, a Hyper-V host itself can be virtualized, so you can make your lab on a single host. Using VMM 2016, you can add a vritualized Hyper-V host to the fabric and manage VMs running on the host. However, a true support of nested virtualization is available only in VMM 1801 semi-annual channel release (for example, enabling and disabling nested virtualization on the VM through VMM console)

Medium and enterprise environments

In a medium-scale or large-scale environment, the best practice is to split the roles across multiple servers or virtual machines. By splitting the components, you can scale out and introduce high availability to the System Center environment.

In the following design, you can see each component and what role it performs in the System Center Virtual Machine Manager environment:

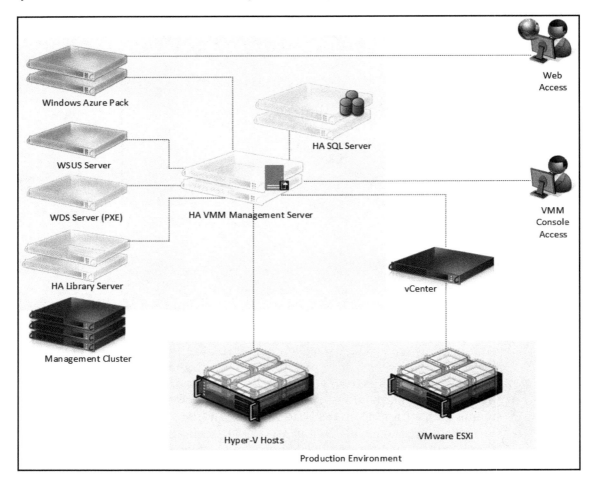

When designing an enterprise private cloud infrastructure, you should take into consideration some key factors such as business requirements, company policies, applications, services, workloads, current hardware, network infrastructure, storage, security, and users.

Private cloud sample infrastructure

Following is a sample of a real-world infrastructure that can support up to 3000 VMs and 64 server nodes running Windows 2016 Hyper-V.

The number of VMs you can run on an implementation like this will depend on some key factors. Do not take the following configuration as a mirror for your deployment, but as a starting point. My recommendation is to start understanding the environment, then run a capacity planner such as a MAP toolkit. It will help you gather information that you can use to design your private cloud.

I am assuming a ratio of 50 VMs per node cluster with 3 GB of RAM, configured to use **Dynamic Memory (DM)**:

- Servers
    - 64 servers (4 clusters x 16 nodes)
    - Dual processor, 6 cores: 12 cores in total
    - 192 GB RAM
    - 2 x 146 GB local HDD (ideally SDD) in Raid 1
- Storage
    - Switch and host redundancy
    - Fiber channel or iSCSI or S2D (converged)
    - Array with capacity to support customer workloads
    - Switch with connectivity for all hosts.

- Network
  - A switch with switch redundancy and sufficient port density and connectivity to all hosts.
  - It provides support for VLAN tagging and trunking.
  - NIC Team and VLAN are recommended for better network availability, security, and performance achievement.
- Storage connectivity
  - **If it uses a fiber channel**: 2 (two) x 4 GB HBAs
  - **If it uses ISCSI**: 2 (two) x dedicated NICs (recommended 10 GbE)
  - **If it uses S2D**: 2 (two) x dedicated 10Gbps NICs (recommended RDMA-capable adapters)
- Network connectivity
  - **If it maintains a 1 GbE connectivity**: 6 dedicated 1 GbE (live migration, CSV, management, virtual machines' traffic)
  - **If it maintains a 10 GbE connectivity**: 3 dedicated NICs 10 GbE (live migration, CSV, management, virtual machines' traffic)

Another way to build private cloud infrastructure is to use hyper-converged solution in which all Storage Spaces Direct, Hyper-V, Failover Clustering and other components are configured on the same cluster hosts. In this model, storage and compute resources cannot be scaled up separately (adding one more host to an existing cluster will extend both compute and storage resources). There are also some requirements for the IT staff who have to carefully plan any management tasks on each storage and compute subsystem to eliminate any possible downtimes. To avoid all these disadvantages and for larger deployments, I'd recommend using a converged solution with separate clusters for SOFS and Hyper-V workloads.

Hosting environments

System Center 2012 SP1 VMM introduced multi-tenancy. This is one of the most important features for hosting companies as they only need to install a single copy of System Center VMM, and then centralize their customer management, each one running in a controlled environment in their own domain. Hosters always want to maximize their compute capacity and VLAN segment hardware so you can't maximize its capacity. Network virtualization moves the isolation up to the software stack, enabling the hoster to maximize all capacity and isolate customers via software-defined networking
VMM 2012 R2 takes advantage of Windows Server 2012 R2 features, VMM 2012 R2 delivers Site-to-Site NVGRE gateway for Hyper-V network virtualization. This capability enables you to use network virtualization to support multiple Site-to-Site tunnels and direct access through a NAT Firewall. The **networking virtualization** (**NV**) uses NVGRE protocol, allowing network load balancers to act as NV gateways. Plus, switch extensions can make use of NV policies to interpret the IP information in packets being sent and communication between, for example, Cisco switches and VMM 2012 R2.

New networking features in VMM 2016

VMM 2016 and Windows Server 2016 continue to improve **Hyper-V Network-Virtualization** (**HNV**) and helps you move to an efficient SDDC solution. VMM 2016 introduces flexible encapsulation which supports both NVGRE (HNVv1) and new VXLAN (HNVv2) to create overlay networks in which original packets from VMs with its MACs, IPs and other data (Customer Address network) are placed inside an IP packet on the underlying physical network (Provider Address network) for further transportation. VXLAN is the default in VMM 2016 and works in MAC distribution mode. It uses a new **Network Controller** (**NC**) as a central management point that communicates with Hyper-V hosts and pushes network policies down to NC host agents running on each host. In short, NC is responsible for the address mapping, and the host agents maintain the mapping database. NC also integrates with Software-Load Balancer (L3 and L4), network layer datacenter firewall and RAS gateways which are also included in Windows Server 2016. Consequently, NC is the heart of SDN in VMM 2016 and should always be considered in a cluster configuration.

Thanks to nested virtualization in Windows Server 2016 (an ability to run Hyper-V server inside a VM), you can evaluate SDN and other scenarios using just one physical machine. The good example of SDN evaluation is available at `https://blogs.msdn.microsoft.com/excellentsge/2016/10/06/deploying-sdn-on-one-single-physical-host-using-vmm/`.

There is also a new way of deploying converged networking that has been introduced in Windows Server 2016 and VMM 2016 to ease and improve SDN deployment. **Switch-Embedded Teaming (SET)** allows you to group up to eight identical adapters into one or more software-based virtual adapters. Prior to VMM 2016 you needed to have two different sets of adapters: one to use with traditional teaming and the one to use with RDMA because of its incompatibility with teaming and virtual switch. SET eliminates this limitation and supports RDMA convergence as well as QoS, RSS, VMQ, and both versions of HNV noted earlier. Furthermore, creating a general Hyper-V virtual switch with RDMA NICs would be also supported:

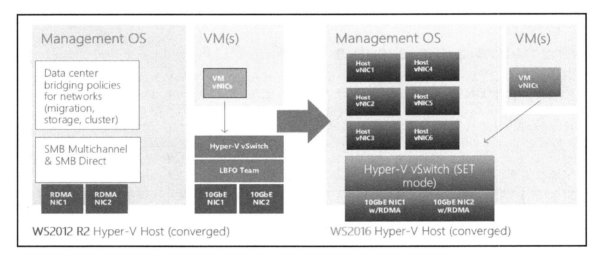

New storage features in VMM 2016

When we discussed possible architectures for management clusters, I referred to a new feature in Windows Server 2016 and VMM 2016, **Storage Spaces Direct** (**S2D**). S2D uses industry-standard servers with local storage which could be direct-attached enclosures or internal disks. S2D provides similar shared storage pools across cluster nodes by leveraging Cluster Shared Volume, Storage Spaces, Failover Clustering and SMB3 protocol for file access (SOFS). Hyper-converged and converged solutions can now be based on software-defined storage running on Windows Server 2016. So, you have a choice: to buy external enterprise SAN or to use S2D. If your goal is a software-defined datacenter, the answer to all questions is very clear - S2D and SDN implementation. The main competitor to S2D is a well-known **VMware Virtual SAN** (**vSAN**) that was first released in vSphere 5.5 and is still present in the newest vSphere 6.6. S2D, just like a vSAN, has special licensing requirements.

 S2D is not available in Windows Server 2016 Standard edition and would require the most expensive Datacenter edition.

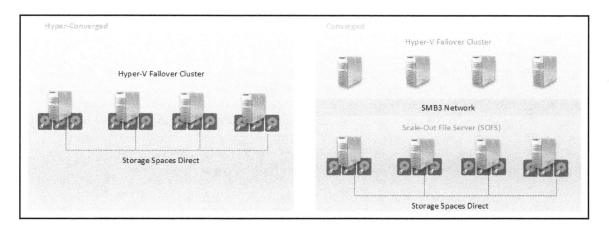

Furthermore, improved Storage QoS in VMM 2016 provides a way to centrally monitor and manage storage performance for virtual machines residing on S2D or another device. Storage QoS was first introduced in 2012 R2 version. You could set maximum and minimum IOPS thresholds for virtual hard disks (excluding shared virtual hard disks). It worked well on standalone Hyper-V hosts, but if you have a cluster with a lot of virtual machines or even tenants, it could be complicated to achieve the right QoS for all cluster resources. The feature automatically improves storage resource fairness between multiple virtual machines using the same file server cluster. In other words, QoS for storage will be distributed between a group of virtual machines and virtual hard disks:

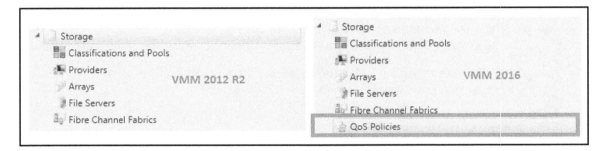

Another feature available only in Windows Server 2016 Datacenter edition is **Storage Replica (SR)**. Previously, we needed to find third-party solutions for SAN-to-SAN replication. And building stretched clusters required a huge amount of money. Windows Server 2016 and VMM 2016 can help to significantly reduce costs and enhance unification in such scenarios. SR is the main component of multi-site clusters or disaster recovery solutions supporting both asynchronous and synchronous replication between any storage devices, including Storage Spaces Direct. Also, you are not required to have identical devices on both sides. However, at the time of writing, only synchronous replication is supported in VMM fabric, and deployment is limited to PowerShell.

Undoubtedly, this is not a final list of new features. Since VMM 2016 is compatible with Windows Server 2016 that brings a lot of major and minor updates in Hyper-V, Failover Clustering and Security, they are also covered in later chapters. New features of VMM 1801 semi-annual channel release will also be briefly covered in next chapters.

See also

For more information, see the following references:

- The *Planning for high availability* recipe
- The Nested Virtualization in Windows Server 2016 page at `https://rlevchenko.com/2015/11/26/nested-virtualization-in-windows-server-2016/`
- The *Configuring ports and protocols on the host firewall for each VMM component recipe* in `Chapter 3`, *Installing VMM 2016*
- The *Deploying hyper-converged cluster with S2D and Hyper-V* recipe in `Chapter 5`, *Configuring Fabric Resources in VMM*
- Rapid Provisioning of Virtual Machines Using SAN Copy Overview: `http://technet.microsoft.com/en-us/library/gg610594.aspx`
- For more on Storage Management Initiative (SMI-S), refer to the following link: `http://www.snia.org/ctp/conformingproviders/index.html`
- For more information on SDN, visit the following link: `https://docs.microsoft.com/en-us/windows-server/networking/sdn/software-defined-networking`
- VMM templates for SDN deployment: `https://github.com/Microsoft/SDN/tree/master/VMM/Templates`

Specifying the correct system requirements for a real-world scenario

In a real-world production environment, you need to specify a system according to the design and business requirements.

Getting ready

When specifying the hardware for your private cloud deployment, take into consideration future growth needs. It is also important to apply the latest OS and software updates.

How to do it...

Use the following tables to carry out an extensive documentation of the hardware and software requirements for your deployment.

Create a document that outlines every solution component, describing the system requirements, before starting to implement.

How it works...

The following table shows the supported OS and servers for SC 2016:

Component	OS/Server supported	Version
VMM server	Windows Server 2016	Server Core, Server with Desktop Experience
VMM database	SQL Server 2012 SP1	Standard, Enterprise
	SQL Server 2014	Standard, Enterprise
	SQL Server 2016	Standard, Enterprise
VMM console	Windows Server 2012	Standard, Datacenter
	Windows Server 2012 R2	Standard, Datacenter
	Windows Server 2016	Standard, Datacenter
	Windows 8.1	x86 and x64
	Windows 10 Enterprise	x86 and x64
VMM library	Windows Server 2016	Standard, Datacenter (full installation or Server Core installation)
	Windows 2012 R2	
Windows Azure Pack	Windows 2012 R2	Standard, Datacenter (full installation with desktop experience)
	Windows Server 2016	
WSUS	Windows 2012 R2, Windows Server 2016 - WSUS 4.0 or later	Standard, Datacenter (full installation with desktop experience)
Managed Hyper-V Host or SOFS	Windows Server 2012 R2, Windows Server 2016	Standard, Datacenter (full installation, Server Core installation or Nano Server[*1])
PXE	Windows Server 2012 R2	Standard, Datacenter (full installation with desktop experience)
	Windows Server 2016	
* Keep in mind that Nano Server is no longer supported for infrastructure roles (Hyper-V, DNS and so on). It's mentioned above to show that existing deployments have support until **Spring of 2018 (April)**. So, plan migration to Windows Server Core or full installation of Windows Server		

Hardware requirements

Following are the hardware requirements to consider when specifying your VMM environment. Although for SMB, POC or demo scenarios you can have SQL installed on the VMM management server, the recommendation is to have SQL Server installed on another server. And you also won't run SQL and Library Servers on the VMM server if you want to manage more than 150 hosts.

Following are the hardware requirements for VMM management server:

Hardware component	Minimum	Recommended
Processor	8 core Pentium 4, 2GHz (x64)	16-core, 2.66 GHz CPU
RAM	4 GB	16 GB
Hard disk space *1	4 Gb	10 GB
*1 Excluding OS partition and SQL Server data (if it's installed on VMM server)		

Following are the hardware requirements for VMM database server:

Hardware component	Minimum	Recommended
Processor	8 core Pentium 4, 2.8 GHz	16-core 2.6 GHz CPU
RAM	8 GB	16 GB
Hard disk space*	50 GB	150 GB
* Excluding OS partition		

Following are the hardware requirements for VMM library server.

Hardware component	Minimum	Recommended
Processor	2 core Pentium 4, 2.8GHz	4 core 2.66 GHz CPU
RAM	2 GB	4 GB
Hard disk space*	As a minimum, I recommend 80 GB, taking into consideration the following table that contains some samples of real image sizes. However, the recommended size will vary depending on business requirements and on the number and size of files stored, especially when working with templates.	
* Excluding OS partition		

The minimum and recommended requirements for a VMM library server will be determined by the quantity and size of the files that will be stored:

Following are the hardware requirements for the VMM console:

Hardware component	Minimum	Recommended
Processor	2 core Pentium 4, 1 GHz CPU	2 core 2 GHz CPU
RAM	4 GB	4 GB
Hard disk space *	10 GB	10 GB
* Excluding OS partition		

Following are the hardware requirements for the Windows Azure Pack.

Before the WAP installation, you need to consider which type of deployment and components you really need. In an express deployment, all core components are installed on the same machine. This type of deployment is recommended for demo and POC scenarios. Distributed deployment is when WAP portals and databases are running on dedicated virtual machines (up to 8, except for VMs for optional resource providers like VM Clouds or Web Sites):

Hardware component	Express/Machine	Distributed/for each machine
Processor	1 CPU	2 CPU
RAM**	8	8 GB
Hard disk space *	40 Gb	40 GB
* Excluding OS partition **dynamic memory is not recommended		

Software requirements

Following are the requirements for VMM management server for SC 2016:

Software Requirement	Notes
Microsoft .NET Framework .NET 4.6	Included in Windows Server 2016 Microsoft .NET Framework 4.6 is available at `https://www.microsoft.com/en-us/download/details.aspx?id=53344`
Windows **Assesment and Deployment Kit** (ADK)	To install the Windows ADK, you need to use the package from `https://developer.microsoft.com/en-us/windows/hardware/windows-assessment-deployment-kit` **Important:** You only need to download and install Deployment Tools and Windows Preinstallation Environment options on the VMM server

Software Requirement	Notes
A supported version of SQL Server (if you're installing SQL on the VMM management server)	See the table for the supported OS's and servers for SC 2016
SQL Server Command Line Utilities	These utilities are required if you plan to deploy services that use SQL Server data-tier applications. You need to download them from the feature pack with the same version as installed SQL Server has. For example, SQL Server 2014 feature pack is available at `https://www.microsoft.com/download/details.aspx?id=42295` Note: If you do not install these utilities, this will not block the installation.
PowerShell 5.0	Included in Windows Server 2016

The following table shows the requirements for the VMM console:

Software requirement	Notes
Windows PowerShell 4.0, 5.0	Included in Windows Server 2012 R2/2016 and Windows 8.1/10
At least Microsoft .NET Framework 4.5	On a computer running Windows 8.1 .NET 4.5.1 is built-in On a computer running Windows 10 .NET has 4.6 version by default and no actions will be required If for some reason, .NET is not installed by default, the VMM setup will install it.

Following are the requirements for core WAP components:

Software requirement	Notes
Microsoft Web Platform Installer 4.6 or later	Required for download and installation WAP components Available at `https://www.microsoft.com/web/downloads/platform.aspx`
IIS 8.0, 8.5, 10	Built-in in Windows Server 2012 R2/2016. WAP wizard configures IIS automatically during setup.
Microsoft .NET Framework 3.5 Service Pack (SP) 1	Available but not installed in Windows Server 2012 R2/2016 by default. The package can also be download at `https://www.microsoft.com/ru-ru/download/details.aspx?id=22`
.NET 4.5 Extended, with ASP.NET for Windows 8	WAP wizard checks and installs automatically.

See also

For more information, see the following references:

- *Deploying Windows Azure Pack for cloud management* recipe in `Chapter 9`, *Managing Clouds, Fabric Updates, Resources, Clusters and new Features of 2016*
- How to install Windows Azure Pack: `https://rlevchenko.com/2014/11/12/step-by-step-installation-of-windows-azure-pack/`

- Service Provider Foundation installation guide at `https://rlevchenko.com/2014/10/29/step-by-step-installation-of-service-provider-foundation-2012-r2/`

- Integrating VMM with WAP page at `https://rlevchenko.com/2015/05/22/windows-azure-pack-how-to-add-and-troubleshoot-vm-clouds-2/`

Licensing the System Center

System Center 2016 is licensed with two versions, Standard and Datacenter. As with System Center 2012 R2, the same capabilities across editions are differentiated only by virtualization rights. All System Center components are included in these two editions. The main difference between SC 2012 R2 and SC 2016 is the licensing model that has been moved from CPU-based to core-based in order to simplify licensing across multi-cloud infrastructures.

Getting ready

The license is required only to manage endpoints. If you have existing **software-assurance** (**SA**) subscription, you can move to the new SC 2016 at any time. SC 2-processor licenses with active SA will be exchanged for a minimum of 8 two-core pack licenses (16 cores) or the actual number of physical cores in use on the server under management.

How to do it...

As part of the private cloud design solution, you need to define which license you will need, based on your solution design and business requirements.

 For updated information about licensing see `https://www.microsoft. com/en-us/cloud-platform/system-center-pricing`.

How it works...

License summary for System Center 2016:

- **Core-Based licensing**: Licensing is based on the number of physical cores on the servers under management, consistent with the Windows Server 2016 model. You need to license all physical cores in the server being managed. Minimum of 8 cores licenses is required for each processor and minimum of 16 cores required for each server. If you have, for example, even one 4-core CPU in server, it would be required to buy eight 2-core packs to license that server. The price of eight two-core packs will be the same as 2-processor licenses for SC 2012 R2.

- **Consistent licensing model across editions**: Core-based licenses for server management. User-based or **operating system environment (OSE)**-based license for client management.
- **For endpoints being managed**: No additional licenses are needed for management servers or SQL Server technology used in the System Center:

System Center 2016 Editions	Datacenter	Standard
Recommendation	For highly virtualized environments	For lightly- or non-virtualized environments
Virtualization rights	Unlimited	2 (two) OSEs
Capabilities	All SC components and all workload types	All SC components and all workload types
License type	one license pack covers 2 cores, minimum of 8 packs required for each server	one license pack covers 2 cores, minimum of 8 packs required for each server

Troubleshooting VMM and supporting technologies

This recipe will take you through the process of troubleshooting VMM and its supporting technologies for a successful VMM deployment.

Getting ready

Having an understanding of the core technologies that VMM depends on to work correctly is the initial step to troubleshooting VMM:

- WS Management (WinRM)
- WMI
- BITS
- DCOM
- WCF

Troubleshooting is never an easy task, but VMM 2016 provides tools and ways to help you find and remediate an issue.

How to do it...

Following are some techniques you can use to troubleshoot:

- **Event logs**

    A good starting point is to look at the event logs. Look for OS- and VMM-related errors or failures. A problem with the **operating system** (**OS**) or one of its core services could result or lead to a problem in VMM.

    For example, if you are running SQL Server on the same server and it did not start, VMM management service will not start either and VMM operations will fail as a direct result of this. You can easily find this by looking for errors in the system or application logs, errors that would indicate, in this example, that the service is not running (for this example, you can also check `Services.msc`).

- **VM manager log**

    When looking for VMM errors, it is recommended that you to look at the VMM log as well. To do so, perform the following steps on the VMM running Windows Server 2016:

    1. On the **Server Manager** window, click on **Tools**
    2. Select **Event Viewer**, expand **Applications and Services logs**, then go to the Microsoft and select the `VirtualMachineManager` log

- **VMM installation-related troubleshooting logs**

    VMM records information about the VMM agent installation. However, if the installation logging is not sufficient to determine the cause of failure, you can enable tracing by using the VMM MPS Reports tool and then restart the installation.

- **VMM server setup logging**

    Installation logs are written, by default, to the `C:\ProgramData\VMMLogs` hidden folder

- **VMM agent installation logging**

  When installing an MSI package, such as installing the VMM agent manually, you can enable logging using the following syntax:

  ```
  msiexec /I MSIPackageName.msi  /L*V path\logfilename.log
  ```

  For example, using the syntax, we can come up with something like the following command:

  ```
  msiexec /I "C:\setup\vmmAgent.msi" /L*V vmmagent.log
  ```

  The local agent installation information is logged in the `C:\ProgramData\VMMLogs` hidden folders.

  Look for the logfile `vmmAgent.msi_m-d-yyy_hh-mm-dss.log`.

In logs, it is common to see errors shown as Carmine errors. Carmine was a VMM project code name during its development process.

- **Troubleshooting WinRM**

  To check if WinRM has remote access, check if:

    - The SID in **RootSDDL** maps to the VMM Servers local group on each Hyper-V host
    - The local group contains the account that VMM management service runs as a service

How it works...

A good understanding of what a successful installation log contains from a POC or a pilot environment is important to identify possible issues, especially if it appears when deploying VMM on a production environment, as you can then compare both logs.

There's more...

Run the following command on the Hyper-V host:

```
winrm id
```

This should produce an output similar to the following output:

```
IdentifyResponse
ProtocolVersion = http://schemas.dmtf.org/wbem/wsman/1/wsman.xsd
ProductVendor = Microsoft Corporation
ProductVersion = OS: 10.0.14393 SP: 0.0 Stack: 3.0
SecurityProfiles
SecurityProfileName =
http://schemas.dmtf.org/wbem/wsman/1/wsman/secprofile/http/spnego-kerberos
```

If the result shows an error, run the following command for a quick configuration of WinRM:

```
winrm qc
```

If prompted, answer Yes. You will receive a response like the following:

```
WinRM already is set up to receive requests on this machine.
WinRM is not set up to allow remote access to this machine for management.
The following changes must be made:
Enable the WinRM firewall exception
Make these changes [y/n]?
WinRM has been updated for remote management.
WinRM firewall exception enabled.
WinRM can now be tested again by typing 'winrm id' as before
```

Now check the listener:

```
winrm enum winrm/config/listener
```

Run the following command on the VMM management server:

```
winrm id -r:http://HyperVHost.yourdomain.local:5985 -u:YOURDOMAIN\AdminUser
```

The result will be similar to the following:

```
IdentifyResponse
ProtocolVersion = http://schemas.dmtf.org/wbem/wsman/1/wsman.xsd
ProductVendor = Microsoft Corporation
ProductVersion = OS: 10.0.14393 SP: 0.0 Stack: 3.0
```

Otherwise you will receive the following error:

```
Error number: -2144108526 0x80338012
The Client cannot connect to the destination specified in the request
```

This could indicate communication issues, so check your network, host firewall, and connectivity.

Most WinRM-related events appear in the system or application event logs. The Service Control Manager often contains the error, as the WinRM service has terminated or restarted for some reason.

To avoid this scenario, conduct the following checks:

- Make sure you installed all of the prerequisites
- Check the firewall rules and make sure the ports are configured correctly
- Open the command prompt (**Run as Administrator**) and type the following command:

```
winrm qc -q
winrm set winrm/config/service/auth @{CredSSP="True"}
winrm set winrm/config/winrs @{AllowRemoteShellAccess="True"}
winrm set winrm/config/winrs @{MaxMemoryPerShellMB="2048"}
```

Verifying WMI providers

You can check if the WinRM can communicate with OS WMI providers by running the following command:

```
winrm enum wmi/root/cimv2/Win32_ComputerSystem -r :http://servername:5985
[-u:YOURDOMAIN\AdminUser]
```

By running the following command, you can check if the WinRM can communicate with Hyper-V WMI providers:

```
winrm enum wmi/root/virtualization/v2/msvm_computersystem
  -r:http://servername:5985 [-u:YOURDOMAIN\AdminUser]
```

Also, to check if the WinRM can communicate with the VMM agent WMI provider, run the following command:

```
winrm invoke GetVersion wmi/root/scvmm/AgentManagement -r:servername [-
u:YOURDOMAIN\AdminUser] @{}
```

If you are using VMM services, do not remove and re-add the host. Instead, evacuate the host before removing or, on the host, uninstall and then re-install the agent manually, then reassociate it in VMM.

Troubleshooting tools

Following are the troubleshooting tools available for use:

- **Windows Management Instrumentation Tester** (`wbemtest.exe`)
  - The `wbemtest.exe` gives you the ability to query WMI namespaces on local or remote servers.
  - Connecting to a namespace locally indicates that it is properly registered and accessible via the WMI service. By connecting to a remote server additionally, it also indicates that WMI connectivity between the two machines is working.
- **WMI Service Control Utility**
  - This tool configures and controls the WMI service, allowing namespace permissions to be modified.
  - To open this tool, in the command prompt type the following:

  `wmimgmt.msc`

  - Then perform the following steps:
    1. Right-click on **WMI Control (Local)**
    2. Select **Properties**
    3. Click on the **Security** tab and then select **Root**
    4. Click on the security button to check the permissions

Background Intelligent Transfer Service (BITS) troubleshooting

BITS transfers files between machines, providing information about the operation's progress. The transfer can be asynchronous.

In VMM, BITS is used for encrypted data transfer between managed computers. Encryption is done by using a self-signed certificate generated when the Hyper-V host is added to VMM.

You can use BITSadmin to verify that BITS is working properly outside of VMM.

BITSadmin is available in Windows Server. Some useful examples of BITSadmin are described at: `http://msdn.microsoft.com/en-us/library/aa362812(VS.85).aspx`.

BTSadmin is deprecated in Windows Server 2016. Administrative tools for the BITS service are now provided by the PowerShell module BitsTransfer:

- Add-BitsFile
- Complete-BitsTransfer
- Get-BitsTransfer
- Remove-BitsTransfer
- Resume-BitsTransfer
- Set-BitsTransfer
- Start-BitsTransfer
- Suspend-BitsTransfer

Data collection tools

The following tools are used to collect data surrounding VMM issues:

- **VMM tracing tools**: VMM tracing tools provide the ability to manage, collect, and view various traces and diagnostic information in a VMM environment:
- **Gathering trace information**: When you face an issue and need to report it to Microsoft, you can gather the trace by performing the following steps:
  1. In the VMM server, open the command prompt with administrative rights and type the following command:

     ```
     logman create trace VMMDebug -v mmddhhmm -o
     $env:SystemDrive\VMMlogs\DebugTrace_$env:computername.E
     TL
     -cnf 01:00:00 -p Microsoft- VirtualMachineManager-Debug
     -nb 10 250 -bs16 -max 512
     ```

  2. Start the trace collection by executing the following command:

     ```
     logman start VMMDebug
     ```

3. Next, try to reproduce the issue, and at the end stop the trace collection by executing the following command:

```
logman stop VMMDebug
```

4. Send the ETL file located in `%SystemDrive%\VMMlogs\DebugTrace_%computername%.ETL` to Microsoft.

5. Delete the debug information by executing the following command:

```
logman delete VMMDebug
```

After gathering the trace, you can use `netsh trace convert` command on the traces. This command converts the ETL binary trace logs into TXT files that can be viewed in any text editor.

To convert the ETL file:

1. Run CMD or PowerShell with administrative privileges.

2. Start conversions by executing the following command:

```
nets  trace convert C:\VMMlogs\yourfilename.etl
```

You will receive a response like the following:

```
Input file:   C:\VMMlogs\VMMLog_VMM01_09242130.etl
Dump file:    C:\VMMlogs\VMMLog_VMM01_09242130.txt
Dump format:  TXT
Report file:  -
Generating dump ... done
```

3. Open the generated TXT-file in Notepad by using the following command:

```
notepad c:\VMMlogs\yourfilename.txt
```

See also

- *Configuring ports and protocols on the host firewall for each SCVMM component* recipe in `Chapter 3`, *Installing VMM 2016*

2
Upgrading from Previous Versions

In this chapter, we will cover the following topics:

- Reviewing the upgrade options
- Checking the VMM system requirements and preparing for the upgrade
- Upgrading to VMM 2016
- Re-associating hosts after upgrading
- Updating the VMM agents
- Performing other post-upgrade tasks

Introduction

This chapter is about guiding you through the requirements and steps to upgrade older VMM versions to VMM 2016. We will start from the VMM 2008 R2 SP1 and end on current VMM 2016.

 There is no direct upgrade path from VMM 2008 R2 SP1 or VMM 2012 to VMM 2016. You must first upgrade VMM 2008 R2 to VMM 2012, and then to VMM 2012 R2. VMM 2008 R2 SP1 -> VMM 2012 -> SCVMM 2012 SP1 -> VMM 2012 R2 -> VMM 2016 is the correct upgrade path.

The main reasons for upgrading might be different:

- Evaluation copy has expired and you need to re-install or upgrade VMM:

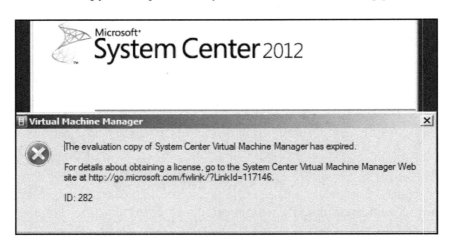

- New functionality and the necessity of managing hosts running on a newer version of Windows Server or ESXi. You can't manage, for instance, Windows Server 2016 hosts in VMM 2012 R2.
- Product life cycle is coming to an end. Knowing the life cycle of your existing VMM helps you plan the upgrade and other infrastructure changes related to a virtualization platform including hosts, libraries, and so on. The following table shows you key dates for VMM versions 2008 R2 through 2016:

Product	End of mainstream support	End of extended support
VMM 2008 R2	Not applicable*	Not applicable*
VMM 2008 R2 SP1	4/8/2014	4/9/2019
VMM 2012	Not applicable*	Not applicable*
VMM 2012 SP1	11/07/2017	12/07/2022
VMM 2012 R2	7/11/2017	7/12/2022
VMM 2016	1/11/2022	1/11/2027
*The latest service pack is required to receive support (see dates for SP1)		

In short, mainstream support is almost complimentary and includes free non-security updates. You can even request design changes or new features with this support type. But when extended support starts, support becomes paid and non-security updates require additional hotfix agreements. Therefore, I'd recommend to plan VMM upgrade before the end of mainstream support.

The following upgrade notes will help you make the right decisions:

- VMM 2012 cannot be directly upgraded to VMM 2016. Upgrading it to VMM 2012 SP1 and then to VMM 2012 R2 is required first.
- VMM 2012 can be installed on a Windows Server 2008 server.
- VMM 2012 SP1 requires Windows Server 2012.
- VMM 2012 R2 requires a minimum Windows Server 2012 (Windows 2012 R2 recommended).
- VMM 2016 requires a minimum Windows Server 2016.
- Windows Server 2012 hosts can be managed by VMM 2012 SP1 and VMM 2012 R2.
- Windows Server 2012 R2 hosts require VMM 2012 R2 or VMM 2016.
- Windows Server 2016 hosts require VMM 2016.
- Self-Service Portal has not been available since VMM 2012 SP1.
- System Center App Controller is completely removed in SC 2016.
- Citrix XenServer support is no longer available in VMM 2016.

 To debug VMM installation, the logs are located in `%ProgramData%\VMMLogs`, and you can use the `CMTrace.exe` tool to monitor in real time the content of files including `SetupWizard.log` and `vmmServer.log`.

As discussed in `Chapter 1`, *VMM 2016 Architecture*, VMM 2016 is a huge product upgrade and there are many improvements. For more details on the new improvements, go through `Chapter 1`, *VMM 2016 Architecture*.

This chapter only covers VMM upgrade.

CRITICAL: If you have previous versions of System Center family components installed in your environment, make sure you follow the upgrade and installation. System Center 2016 has some new components in which the installation order is also critical. It is critical that you follow the following order:

- Service Management Automation
- Orchestrator
- Service Manager
- **Data Protection Manager (DPM)**
- Operations Manager
- Configuration Manager
- **Virtual Machine Manager (VMM)**
- App Controller
- Service Provider Foundation
- Windows Azure Pack for Windows Server
- Service Bus Clouds
- Windows Azure Pack
- Service Reporting

Before we start, I would recommend you to go through `Chapter 1`, *VMM 2016 Architecture*, and pay special attention to the recipe *Specifying the correct system requirements for a real-world scenario*.

Reviewing the upgrade options

This recipe will guide you through the upgrade options for VMM 2016. Keep in mind that there is no direct upgrade path from VMM 2008 R2 or VMM 2012 to VMM 2016.

How to do it...

Read through the following recommendations in order to upgrade your current VMM installation.

In-place upgrade from VMM 2008 R2 SP1 to VMM 2012

Use this method if your system meets the requirements for a VMM 2012 upgrade and you want to deploy it on the same server. The supported VMM version to upgrade from is VMM 2008 R2 SP1. If you need to upgrade VMM 2008 R2 to VMM 2008 R2 SP1, see `https:/` `/technet.microsoft.com/en-us/library/gg318082.aspx`.

Also, keep in mind that if you are running the SQL Server Express version, you will need to upgrade SQL Server to a fully-supported version beforehand as the Express version is not supported in later VMM versions. See `Chapter 3`, *Installing VMM 2016*.

Once the system requirements are met and all of the prerequisites are installed, the upgrade process is straightforward. To follow the detailed recipe, see the *Upgrading to VMM 2016* section.

In-place upgrade means that you can install a new VMM over an existing installation. An uninstallation of an older VMM version is not required. You just run the setup wizard and it does all the tasks for you. An in-place upgrade is only supported in VMM 2008 R2 SP1 to VMM 2012 scenario and not supported for later VMM versions. If you try to upgrade VMM 2012, for example, without its uninstallation, you will receive an error, as shown in the following screenshot:

 You cannot upgrade from the currently installed version of VMM to System Center 2012 SP1 - Virtual Machine Manager. You must first uninstall VMM, and then install System Center 2012 SP1. If you are running System Center 2012, when you uninstall VMM, you can retain the database. When you install System Center 2012 SP1, use the retained database.

 Please also note that the term **in-place upgrade** is used further in this chapter as VMM upgrade on existing machine.

Upgrading VMM on a different computer

Sometimes, you may not be able to do an in-place upgrade to VMM 2012, or even to later VMM versions. In this case, it is recommended that you use the following instructions that are suitable for later VMM versions as well:

1. Uninstall the current VMM, *retaining the database*, and then restore the database on a supported version of SQL Server.

2. Next, on a new server (or on the same server, as long it meets the hardware and OS requirements), install the VMM server prerequisites.

3. Finally, install the new VMM, providing the retained database information on the **Database configuration** dialog and the VMM setup will upgrade the database. When the install process finishes, upgrade the Hyper-V hosts with the latest VMM agents.

 When performing an upgrade from VMM 2008 R2 SP1 with a local VMM database to a different server, the encrypted data will not be preserved as the encryption keys are stored locally. The same rule applies when upgrading from VMM 2012 or VMM 2012 R2 to VMM 2016 and not using **Distributed Key Management (DKM)**.

Upgrading from VMM 2012 to VMM 2012 SP1

To upgrade to VMM 2012 SP1, you should already be running VMM 2012. VMM 2012 SP1 requires a Windows Server 2012 and Windows ADK 8.0. If planning an in-place upgrade, back up the VMM database, uninstall VMM 2012 and App Controller, *retaining the database*, perform an OS upgrade, and then install VMM 2012 SP1.

 Since VMM 2012 SP1 and later VMM support SQL Server 2012, I recommend to upgrade SQL Server to this version in order to simplify migration to VMM 2016 from VMM 2012 SP1 and VMM 2012 R2.

Upgrading from VMM 2012 SP1 to VMM 2012 R2

To upgrade to VMM 2012 R2, you should already be running VMM 2012 SP1. VMM 2012 R2 requires a Windows Server 2012 as minimum OS (Windows 2012 R2 recommended) and Windows ADK 8.1. If planning an in-place upgrade, back up the VMM database, uninstall VMM 2012 SP1 and App Controller, *retaining the database*, perform an OS upgrade, and then install VMM 2012 R2 and App Controller (optional).

Upgrading from VMM 2012 R2 to VMM 2016

To upgrade to VMM 2016, you should be running VMM 2012 R2 with update rollup 9 or later; VMM 2016 requires a Windows Server 2016 and Windows ADK 10. If planning an in-place upgrade, back up the VMM database, uninstall VMM 2012 R2 and App Controller, retaining the database, perform an OS upgrade, and then install VMM 2016 and Windows Azure Pack (optional).

 VMM 2016 configuration database can be placed on SQL Server 2012 with SP1 or later versions. After VMM uninstallation, you need to plan for upgrading SQL Server as well. If you are going to move the database to another SQL instance, set up a supported SQL Server and restore the VMM database on it.

More planning considerations

- **VMware ESX and vCenter**: For VMM 2012, the supported versions of VMware are from ESXi 3.5 to ESXi 4.1, and vCenter 4.1. For VMM 2012 SP1/R2, the supported VMware versions are from ESXi 4.1 to ESXi 5.1, and vCenter 4.1 and 5.0. For VMM 2016, the supported VMware versions are from 5.1 to 6.0 for both ESXi and vCenter.

- **Windows Azure Pack** must be running update rollup 10 or later. Also, you should have update rollup 9 or later applied to VMM 2012 R2 and Service Provider Foundation 2012 R2.

- **SQL Server Express**: It is not supported since VMM 2012. A full version is required. For more details, go through Chapter 1, *VMM 2016 Architecture*.

- **Performance and Resource Optimization (PRO)**: The PRO configurations are not kept during an upgrade to VMM 2016. If you have an Operations Manager (SCOM) integration configured, it will be removed during the upgrade process. Once the upgrade process is finished, you can integrate SCOM 2016 with VMM. SCOM 2012 R2 is not supported by VMM 2016.

- **Azure Site Recovery**: If you have ASR (former Hyper-V Recovery Manager) deployment, you need to re-deploy it after the VMM upgrade.

- **Library server**: Since VMM 2016, VMM does not support a library server on Windows Server 2012. If you have it running and you continue with the upgrade, you will not be able to use it. To use the same library server in VMM 2016, move it to a server running a supported OS before starting the upgrade.

- **Choosing a service account and Distributed Key Management (DKM) settings during an upgrade**: During an upgrade to VMM 2016, on the **Configure service account and distributed key management** page of the setup, you are required to create a VMM service account (preferably a domain account) and choose whether you want to use DKM.
- Make sure to log on with the same account that was used during the VMM installation. This needs to be done because, in some situations after the upgrade, depending on the selected VMM service account, the encrypted data (for example, run as accounts and passwords in templates) will not be available and you will be required to re-enter them manually.
- For the service account, you can use either the local system account or a domain account (recommended). However, when deploying a highly available VMM management server, the only option available is a domain account.

 DKM stores encryption data in Active Directory Domain Services and helps to retain such data after moving VMM to another server, for example. If you don't have DKM configured, encrypted data is being kept locally on VMM server. Also note that DKM is not available in versions prior to VMM 2012.

- **Upgrading to a highly available VMM 2016**: If you're thinking of upgrading to a High Available (HA) VMM, consider the following:
  - **Failover cluster**: You must create and configure a failover cluster prior to the upgrade.
  - **VMM database**: You cannot deploy the SQL server for the VMM database on the highly available VMM management servers. If you're planning on upgrading the current VMM server to a HA VMM, you need to first move the database to another server. For best practice, it is recommended to have the SQL Server cluster separated from the VMM cluster.
  - **Library server**: On a production or High Available environment, you need to consider all of the VMM components to be High Available as well, and not only the VMM management server. After upgrading to a HA VMM management server, it is recommended, for best practice, to relocate the VMM library to a clustered file server. In order to keep the custom fields and properties of the saved VMs, deploy those VMs to a host and save them to a new VMM 2016 library.

- **Distributed Key Management**: You must use DKM for a high availability VMM management server.
- **Service Account**: You must configure the SC VMM service to use a domain account instead of a local account.

How it works...

There are two methods to upgrade to VMM 2016, in-place upgrade and upgrading to another server. Before starting, review the initial steps and the VMM 2016 prerequisites, and perform a full backup of the VMM database.

Check your VMM version and plan upgrade path, uninstall your current VMM (retaining the data), and restore the VMM database to another SQL server running a supported version. During the installation, point to that database in order to have it upgraded. After the upgrade is finished, upgrade the host agents.

VMM will be rolled back automatically in the event of a failure during the upgrade process, reverting to its original installation/configuration.

There's more...

The following table will help you to plan DKM and service account settings during upgrade and not to lose encryption data:

Sign-in account used when upgrading	VMM service account in the current installation of VMM	VMM service account that you define during VMM upgrade	Not using DKM	Using DKM
Any valid administrator account	Local system	Local system	Encrypted data is preserved	Encrypted data is preserved
Any valid administrator account	Local system	Domain account	Encrypted data is not preserved	Encrypted data is preserved

Any valid administrator account	Domain account	Local system	Not supported	Not supported
Same domain account as the VMM service account in current VMM installation	Domain account	Domain account	Encrypted data is preserved	Encrypted data is preserved
Different domain account from the VMM service account in current VMM installation	Domain account	Domain account	Encrypted data is not preserved	Encrypted data is not preserved

Moreover, the names of the VMM services have been changed since VMM 2012. If you have any applications or scripts referring to these service names, update them accordingly:

VMM version	VMM service display name	Service name
2008 R2 SP1	Virtual Machine Manager Virtual Machine Manager Agent	`vmmservice` `vmmagent`
2012 / 2012 SP1 / 2012 R2/2016	System Center Virtual Machine Manager System Center Virtual Machine Manager Agent	`scvmmservice` `scvmmagent`

See also

For more information, see the following references:

- The *Software requirements* section in the *Specifying the correct system requirements for a real-world scenario* recipe in `Chapter 1`, *VMM 2016 Architecture*
- To move the file-based resources (for example, ISO images, scripts, and VHD/VHDX), refer to `https://docs.microsoft.com/en-us/system-center/vmm/library-files`
- To move virtual machine templates, refer to *Exporting and Importing Service Templates in VMM:* `https://docs.microsoft.com/en-us/system-center/vmm/library-vm-templates`

Checking the VMM system requirements and preparing for the upgrade

This recipe will guide you through the steps required to check whether your current VMM installation meets the requirements for an upgrade to a newer VMM. The recipe will also help you with the initial steps that need to be carried out in order to prepare the environment for a VMM in-place upgrade.

Getting ready

Confirm that your system meets the requirements. If you have VMM 2012 R2 and your target is VMM 2016, see the *Supported OS and Servers* section of the *Specifying the correct system requirements for a real-world scenario* recipe in `Chapter 1`, *VMM 2016 Architecture*.

If you have two or more upgrades in a row, check the requirements for each VMM before going to the next upgrade:

- **VMM 2012 and 2012 SP1 requirements**: `https://technet.microsoft.com/en-us/library/gg610562(v=sc.12).aspx`
- **VMM 2012 R2 requirements**: `https://technet.microsoft.com/en-us/library/dn281925(v=sc.12).aspx`

How to do it...

Carry out the following steps to check if your environment meets the system requirements, and to perform the initial steps for an in-place upgrade to a newer VMM:

1. Remove the integration of SCOM with VMM.
2. Remove the integration of VMM with VMware vCenter.
3. Wait for the completion of all jobs running in VMM.
4. Close the VMM console and the VMM command shell. If you have VMM up to 2012 and Self-Service portal installed, close the portal as well.

5. Perform a full backup of the VMM database.
6. The following is applicable for VMM 2012 SP1 and later: if the current VMM database is configured with AlwaysOn Availability Groups, remove it and then initiate a failover to the SQL Server machine on which the VMM database is installed; see the *Upgrading VMM with configured AlwaysOn Availability Groups* section of the *Upgrading to VMM 2016* recipe.
7. If your VMM library is running on another machine, make sure that the OS version meets the minimum requirements. Upgrade the OS if necessary.
8. Update the server by running Windows Update or by implementing the latest update rollup (manually).
9. Verify that there are no pending restarts on the server. Restart the server if necessary.

The job history will be deleted during the upgrade.

Uninstalling previous versions of Windows Automated Installation Kit (WAIK)

VMM 2012 requires WAIK for Windows 7. In VMM 2012 SP1 and later versions, Windows ADK replaced WAIK as a VMM prerequisite. To uninstall WAIK, follow these instructions:

1. In **Control Panel** | **Programs** | **Programs and Features**, select **Windows Automated Installation Kit**.
2. Click on **Uninstall** and then follow the wizard to uninstall the program.
3. Click on **Yes** to confirm, click on **Finish**, and then restart the server.

Checking whether Windows Remote Management (WinRM) is started

It is a prerequisite to have the WinRM service running and set to **Automatic**. The following steps will help you with this:

1. In the **Services** console (`services.msc`), locate and select the **Windows Remote Management (WS-Management)** service. If the **Status** is not showing **Started** and/or the **Startup Type** is showing **Manual**, change the settings by right-clicking on the service and then clicking on **Properties**. This is shown in the following screenshot:

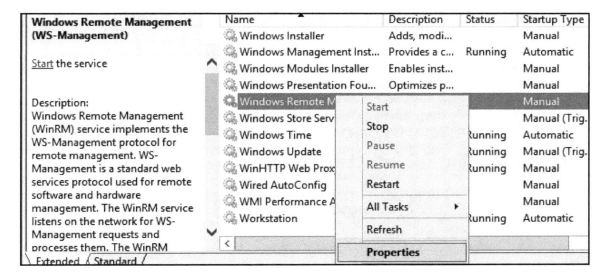

2. On the **Properties** dialog box, change the **Startup Type** to **Automatic**, click on **Start** to initiate the service, and then click on **OK**.

How it works...

If your VMM 2008 R2 does not have the SP1 update applied to it, start by applying it in order for it to be supported for the upgrade to VMM 2012. If you are planning to do an in-place upgrade to VMM 2012 SP1, and if you are running Windows Server 2008 R2, you need to carry it out in two phases and then consider upgrading to VMM 2012 R2 and so on:

- **Upgrade from VMM 2008 R2 SP1 to VMM 2012**: Carry out a VMM database backup, remove VMM 2008 R2 SP1 (choosing to retain data), and then during the VMM 2012 installation, provide the previously-saved database. VMM 2012 will upgrade the database during the installation.
- **Upgrade from VMM 2012 to VMM 2012 SP1**: As VMM 2012 SP1 requires Windows Server 2012, you first need to run an in-place upgrade of the OS to Windows Server 2012 , install the prerequisites, and then carry out the upgrade from VMM 2012 to VMM 2012 SP1.
- **Upgrade from VMM 2012 SP1 to VMM 2012 R2**: As it is recommended Windows 2012 R2 for VMM 2012 R2, you first need to run an in-place upgrade of the OS to Windows Server 2012 R2, install the prerequisites, and then carry out the upgrade from VMM 2012 SP1 to VMM 2012 R2.
- **Upgrade from VMM 2012 R2 to VMM 2016**: VMM 2016 can be running only on Windows Server 2016. So, you need to complete the OS upgrade, install the VMM prerequisites, and then carry out the upgrade to 2016.

 To get more details about Windows Server installation and available upgrade options for different versions and editions, see *Windows Server Installation and Upgrade:* https://docs.microsoft.com/en-us/windows-server/get-started/installation-and-upgrade.

During the upgrade process, if you did not install the command-line utilities for SQL Server beforehand, a warning will be shown in the prerequisites check phase. Although you can proceed without installing these utilities, it is not recommended as they are required to perform some management tasks (see the *SQL Server Connectivity Feature Pack Components* section under the *Installing VMM dependencies* recipe in Chapter 3, *Installing VMM 2016*).

 The Windows Remote Management (WS-Management) service must be started and set to automatic before starting the upgrade, otherwise an error might appear during the prerequisites check.

There's more...

Review the software requirements for VMM Management as given in Chapter 1, *VMM 2016 Architecture*, under the *Specifying the correct system requirements for a real-world scenario* recipe.

Install these prerequisites as well:

- Windows Assessment and Deployment Kit (8.0 for SP1, 8.1 for VMM 2012 R2 and 10 for VMM 2016)
- SQL Server Command Line Utilities (for the supported and installed version of SQL)
- Microsoft SQL Server Native Client

Upgrading to VMM 2016

This recipe will guide you through the tasks required to upgrade VMM 2008 R2 SP1 to VMM 2012, showcasing the possible options and actions. It will then highlight the upgrade path to VMM 2016 in detail.

 For VMM 2012 R2 to 2016, see the *Upgrading from VMM 2012 R2 to VMM 2016* section in this recipe.

Getting ready

Go through the *Checking the VMM system requirements and preparing for the upgrade* recipe after deciding the upgrade method (in-place upgrade or upgrade to another server), and make sure you've installed all of the prerequisites.

If you're planning an in-place upgrade of VMM 2008 R2 SP1 running on a server with an OS other than the supported version, first upgrade the OS, and then carry out the steps to upgrade to VMM 2012, as described in this recipe.

How to do it...

To upgrade to VMM 2016 from VMM 2008 R2, you first need to carry out the following steps in order to upgrade your VMM 2008 R2 SP1 to VMM 2012:

1. On the VMM 2008 R2 SP1 console, click on **General** in the **Administration** view. Next, click on **Back up Virtual Machine Manager** in the **Actions** pane. All of these are depicted in the following screenshot:

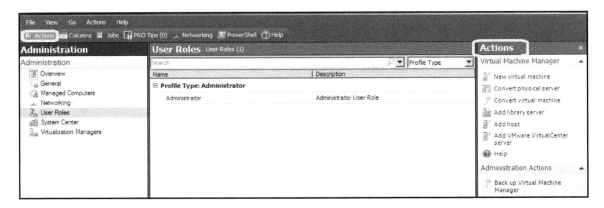

2. In the **Virtual Machine Manager Backup** dialog box, type in the path for the destination folder for the backup file. The folder must not be a root directory and it must be accessible to the SQL Server database.

3. Take note of the backup location as we will need it later during the VMM 2012 upgrade.

4. If you're doing an in-place upgrade and running a full version of SQL Server, go to step 7.

5. If you're upgrading to another server or running SQL Server Express, uninstall SCVMM 2008 R2 SP1, remove all of the components, and choose **Retain Database** during the removal of the SCVMM 2008 R2 SP1 Server service.

6. If you're running SQL Server 2005 Express Edition:
    1. Click on **Start** and in the **Search programs and files** box, or in the **Run** window, type in `services.msc` and press *Enter*. Stop the **SQL Server (MICROSOFTVMM)** service.
    2. Copy **VirtualManagerDB** and **VirtualManagerDB_log** from `C:\Program Files(x86)\Microsoft SQL Server\MSSQL.1\MSSQL\Data` to a backup folder (for example, `C:\backup`).

3. In **Control Panel** | **Programs** | **Programs and Features**, select **Microsoft SQL Server 2005** and click on **Uninstall**, as shown in the following screenshot:

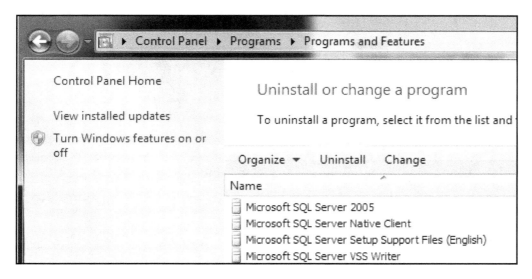

4. On the **Component Selection** page, select the **Remove SQL Server 2005 instance components** checkbox, and also select the **Workstation Components** checkbox.
5. On the confirmation page, click on **Finish** to complete the uninstall process.
6. In **Add or Remove Programs**, select **Microsoft SQL Native Client**, and then click on **Remove**.
7. In the confirmation dialog box, click on **Yes**. Install a full version of SQL Server (it is recommended to install it on another server). See the *Deploying a Microsoft SQL Server for VMM implementation* recipe in `Chapter 3`, *Installing VMM 2016*.
8. Restore the VMM database backup to SQL Server. To do this, open SQL Server Management Studio and select **Restore Database**. On the **Specify Backup** window, click on **Add** and navigate to `C:\backup`. Enter `VirtualManagerDB` as the new name. Select **Restore** and click on **OK**. On successful restoration, a pop up will be displayed. Click on **OK** and close SQL Server Management Studio.

7. Run the VMM 2012 installation wizard and complete the required steps, paying attention to the database and DKM configuration. As a reference, you can use the steps described in the *Upgrading to VMM 2012 SP1 or to VMM 2012 R2* section or steps 6-20 from the *Upgrading VMM 2012 R2 to VMM 2016* section. There are no significant changes in the wizard since VMM 2012.

Upgrading to VMM 2012 SP1 or to VMM 2012 R2

If you are running VMM 2012, you can upgrade to VMM 2012 SP1. As VMM 2012 SP1 requires Windows Server 2012, you will need to upgrade the OS beforehand.

If you are running VMM 2012 SP1, you can upgrade to VMM 2012 R2. As VMM 2012 R2 requires a minimum Windows Server 2012, you don't need to upgrade the OS beforehand, although I recommend that you upgrade the OS to Windows Server 2012 R2.

> You can follow the steps for either VMM 2012 to VMM 2012 SP1 or VMM 2012 SP1 to VMM 2012 R2.

Make sure you take a backup of the VMM database. See *step 2* in the next section, *Upgrading VMM 2012 R2 to VMM 2016*, that provides backup guidance as well.

Next, I would recommend that you uninstall VMM 2012, *retaining the database*, followed by the installation of the VMM 2012 SP1/R2 prerequisites:

Database options

Please select if you want to remove or retain the VMM database when you uninstall the VMM management server.

● Retain database

Choose this option if you plan to reinstall VMM and want to resume managing virtual machines in the same host environment.

○ Remove database

Proceed with the VMM 2012 SP1/R2 installation using the same database. For more details on installing or upgrading VMM 2012 SP1/R2, see the step-by-step guide available at `https://rlevchenko.com/2013/04/14/upgrading-vmm-2012-on-server-2008-r2-to-vmm-sp1/` or refer to *steps 6-20* in the section *Upgrading VMM 2012 R2 to VMM 2016*.

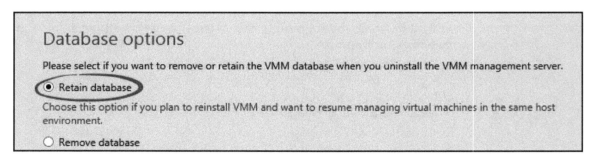

Upgrading VMM 2012 R2 to VMM 2016

Finally, if you are running VMM 2012 R2 with update rollup 9 or later, you can upgrade to VMM 2016. As VMM 2016 requires a minimum Windows Server 2016, you will need to upgrade the OS beforehand. Note that you can choose either Core or Windows Server full installation with desktop experience. The following steps describe in-place upgrading VMM 2012 R2 to VMM 2016 and also highlight VMM database moving required for installation on a different machine as well:

1. First, you need to check if update rollup 9 or later is installed on VMM Server. To determine whether update rollup 9 has been applied, open the **Programs and Features** item in **Control Panel**, then click **View Installed Updates** and in the **Search** box type in `update rollup` and identify the items listed under **Microsoft System Center Virtual Machine Manager Server (x64)**:

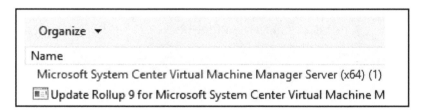

Another way to get the VMM version and related update rollup is to retrieve using PowerShell. Open PowerShell with administrative privileges and paste the following strings:

```
Set-ExecutionPolicy -ExecutionPolicy RemoteSigned -Force
Import-Module VirtualMachineManager
Get-SCVMMServer -ComputerName (Read-Host "VMM Server Name") -
Credential (Get-Credential)|select Name, ProductVersion
```

You will receive the VMM server name and its build number. When you apply the new update rollup or hotfix, the build number might be changed as well. To find *relationships* between VMM version and update rollups, see `https://rlevchenko.com/2017/10/02/build-numbers-for-vmm-2012-r2-and-vmm-2016/`, where you can also find download links for all released update rollups. If UR9 or later is not installed, you need to download and install it before upgrading to VMM 2016.

2. Take a backup of the current VMM configuration. For doing this, open VMM Console, click on **Settings** in the navigation pane, and click on **Backup** in the actions pane. In the **Backup** dialog box, define a path for the destination folder for the backup file. The folder must not be a root directory (for example, C:\ is not allowed) and must be created before doing a backup to avoid an error message:

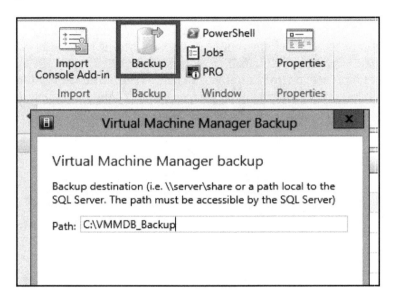

3. If you are going to use SQL Server installed on a different machine than the one that is used for VMM 2012 R2 (current SQL Server is not supported, for example) and you prepared the new one on another machine, follow the steps following:
   1. In the VMM console, click on **Settings** in the navigation pane and expand **General**, and then double-click on **Database Connection**. Take note of the SQL Server name and DB name as we will need them later during the database backup:

2. Press Windows + *R*, type `services.msc`, and check log on account for the VMM service (right-click on **System Center Virtual Manager service** and click on **Properties**). This might be a local account or a domain account. Record this account as well:

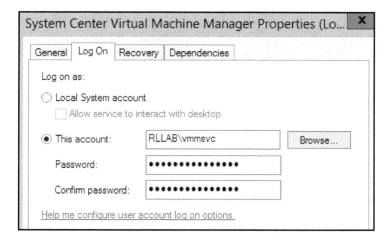

3. Uninstall VMM 2012 R2, remove all of the components, and choose **Retain Database** during the uninstallation.

4. Take a full backup of the VMM database. For doing this, open SQL Server Management Studio, type your credentials in the **Connect To Server** dialog box and recorded SQL server name, expand **Databases**, and then select **VirtualManagerDB**. Right-click on this database and select **Tasks | Backup...**, as shown in the following screenshot:

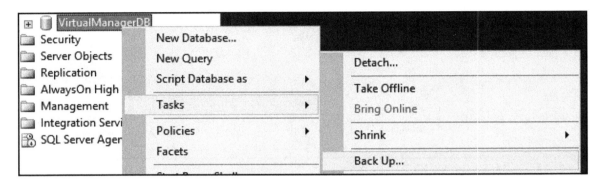

5. In the back up dialog box, add a destination folder for backup files (for example, `C:\VMMDB_Backup`) and verify that backup type is selected to **Full**. Click **OK** to start the backup job.

6. Copy the BAK files to the target SQL Server machine and initiate a restore operation using Management Studio, as shown in the following screenshot. Select **Device**, click **Add**, and define the path for the source backup files. Double-click **OK** to restore database:

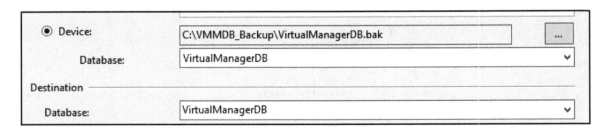

4. Uninstall Windows ADK 8.1. Press Windows + *R*, type `appwiz.cpl`, and press *Enter* to open **Programs and Features** in **Control Panel**, then select **Windows Assessment and Deployment Kit for Windows 8.1** and click on **Uninstall**.

5. Download and install Windows ADK 10. Select only **Deployment Tools** and **Windows Preinstallation Environment (Windows PE)**. Other ADK features are not required for VMM 2016:

> Click a feature name for more information.
>
> ☐ Application Compatibility Tools
>
> ☑ Deployment Tools
>
> ☑ Windows Preinstallation Environment (Windows PE)

6. Browse to the installation media and double-click on `setup.exe`.
7. On the main setup page, click on **Install**.
8. On the **Features to be installed** page, confirm that VMM management and VMM console are selected and click on **Next**.
9. On the **Product registration information** page, enter the VMM product key, and then click on **Next** (if you don't provide a key, VMM 2016 will be installed as a trial version that lasts 180 days).

> If you don't provide key, VMM 2016 will be installed as a trial version that lasts 180 days

10. On the **Please read this license agreement** page, tick the **I have read, understood, and agree with the terms of the license agreement** checkbox, and click on **Next**.
11. On the **Diagnostic and Usage Data** page, read the statement and click on **Next**.
12. On the **Microsoft Update** page, select **On (recommended)** to use Microsoft Update, and click on **Next**.
13. On the **Installation location** page, provide the path for the installation and then click on **Next**.

> I recommend to place VMM program files on a separate drive that is different than the one which is used for OS partition.

14. On the **Database Configuration** page, specify the **Server name** of the SQL server and the **Instance name**; for example, MSSQLSERVER.

15. Select **Existing database** and choose **VirtualManagerDB** (or whichever name the restored database has) from the drop-down menu, as shown in the following screenshot, and click on **Yes** to confirm the upgrade:

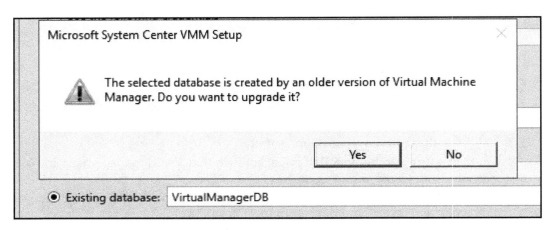

16. On the **Configure service account and distributed key management** page, provide credentials for the service account and DKM path (recommended). As you can see in the following picture, DKM settings are stored in the database. If you had DKM configured in VMM 2012 R2, you can't change its settings during the upgrade to VMM 2016:

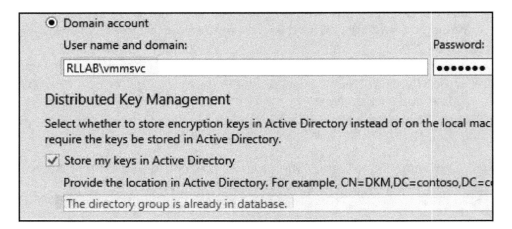

My recommendation is to use the same account as the service account in VMM 2012 R2 (see step 3.2). Also note that you will not be able to change the account after the VMM installation is complete, as this is not supported.

17. On the **Port configuration** page, leave the default port numbers unchanged or provide a unique value for each feature, and then click on **Next**.

 Plan and document the ports before choosing them as you cannot change them again; it would require reinstalling VMM.

18. On the **Library Configuration** page, select **Use an existing library share** if you are doing an in-place upgrade. If you are installing VMM on another machine, you can select **Create a new share** and define its name and location, then click on **Next**.

19. You might find certain issues listed on the page that says **Upgrade compatibility report**. In this case, you can either click on **Next** to proceed with the upgrade, or click on **Cancel** to cancel the upgrade and resolve the issues.

20. On the **Installation summary** page, click on **Install**, and then click on **Close** to finish.

 It's recommended to install the latest available update rollup for VMM 2016 after a successful upgrade. For example, update rollup 1 or later must be installed to reconnect VMM 2016 to SCOM.
Download links are available at `https://rlevchenko.com/2017/10/02/build-numbers-for-vmm-2012-r2-and-vmm-2016/`.

How it works...

Just like all upgrade processes, the VMM upgrade process requires planning. Start by confirming that the current server/VM meets the system requirements for a newer VMM.

Decide the upgrade method, either an in-place upgrade and upgrading to another server. An in-place upgrade will not be successful if the database version is not supported.

Back up the current VMM database. If you're running SQL Express Edition, you will need to uninstall the existing VMM server, retaining the data. You will then need to install a fully-supported SQL version, restore the VMM database, and then start the VMM upgrade process.

> If you are running a small VMM installation, you can install SQL on the same server, as long it is not a HA VMM.

Start the VMM installer and carry out the upgrade steps, reviewing and paying special attention to the database and DKM configuration, and confirming your options in all of the upgrade dialogs. At the end of the process, open the VMM console to confirm the upgrade and update the agent hosts to the newer VMM.

During the migration process, if the database is not compatible, the following pop up dialog (showing an error) will appear:

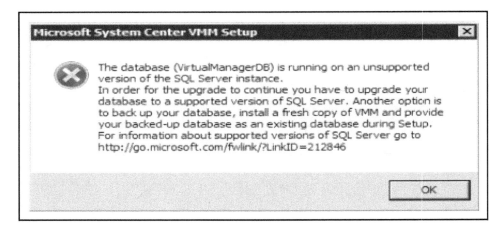

There's more...

Now, let's talk about the VMM upgrade with configured AlwaysOn **Availability Groups** (**AGs**) and the others VMM components.

Upgrading VMM with configured AlwaysOn Availability Groups

If your VMM is configured with AlwaysOn AGs, you need to remove the VMM database from AG before upgrading the VMM. For doing this, open **SQL Server Management Studio**, connect to the server and expand **AlwaysOn High Availability**, select **VirtualManagerDB** under **Availability Databases**, right-click, and then choose **Remove Database from Availability Group...**:

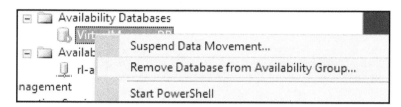

Initiate a failover to the SQL Server on which the VMM database is installed:

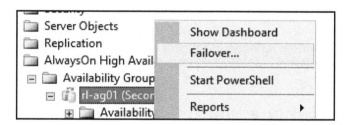

Then, start VMM 2016 installation using the steps described in the previous sections. After successfully upgrading, you will need to configure AlwaysOn AG by adding the VMM database back to the availability group:

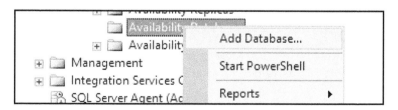

Because the VMM updates SQL security logins only on a primary SQL server, you are required to add the same account after upgrading for every secondary node in the cluster. As you can see in the following figure, this account is identical to the VMM service account; it's not available on the secondary node by default and is mapped to the VMM database as a user with membership to the db_owner. Use the same settings while adding the account to the other nodes in the cluster:

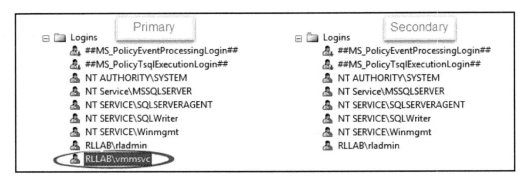

When the account is configured on every secondary node, initiate failover to verify that you can restart the VMM Service on the node different from the primary node. If you are not experiencing any issues after failover and doing a highly available VMM upgrade, you can continue the VMM installation on other VMM nodes.

Upgrading a highly available VMM 2012 R2 to VMM 2016

There are some differences between upgrading standalone VMM and highly available. Since VMM 2016, you no longer need to remove a cluster and create a new one. Using a Cluster OS Rolling Upgrade and its mixed mode, you can upgrade VMM nodes one by one from Windows Server 2012 R2 to Windows Server 2016, and then upgrade VMM 2012 R2 to 2016. See the *Cluster OS Rolling Upgrade* recipe in Chapter 9, *Managing Clouds, Fabric Updates, Resources, Clusters and new Features of 2016* for details.

 If your VMM 2012 R2 is running on Windows Server 2012, you will need to destroy the cluster before upgrading OS to Windows Server 2016.

1. Perform a backup of the current VMM database. You can use the steps from the *Upgrading VMM 2012 R2 to VMM 2016* section.

2. If your VMM is configured with AlwaysOn AGs, you need to remove the VMM database from AG before upgrading the VMM. For doing this, open **SQL Server Management Studio**, connect to the server and expand **AlwaysOn High Availability**, select **VirtualManagerDB** under **Availability Databases**, right-click, and then choose **Remove Database from Availability Group...**:

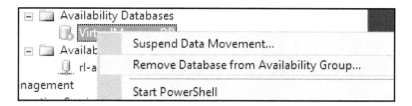

3. Initiate manual failover to the SQL Server on which the VMM database is installed:

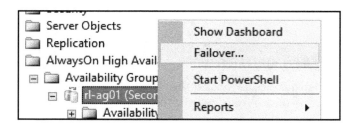

4. Identify the active and passive VMM nodes. For doing this, open **Failover Cluster Manager** (cluadmin.msc), click on **Roles** and note **Owner Node** for VMM HA role, as shown in the following screenshot. **VMM02**, in this example, is the active node:

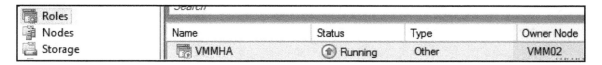

5. Uninstall VMM 2012 R2 from the passive node, retaining the database.

6. Place the passive node into maintenance mode. For doing this, open **Failover Cluster Manager** (cluadmin.msc), click on **Nodes** and right-click on the passive node, then choose **Pause** and **Drain Roles,** then choose **More Actions - Evict** to remove the passive node from the cluster.

You can use PowerShell for this step:
```
Suspend-ClusterNode -Node VMM01 -Drain
Remove-ClusterNode -Node VMM01
```

7. Upgrade OS to Windows Server 2016 on the passive node, and then add the node back to the cluster (`Add-ClusterNode`).
8. Install VMM 2016, confirm high available configuration and upgrade the existing database when prompted.
9. Do failover to the passive node using **Failover Cluster Manager**.
10. Repeat steps *5-8* for the other nodes. Once you've upgraded all the nodes, update the cluster functional level by running the `Update-ClusterFunctionalLevel` command.
11. After upgrading, you will need to configure AlwaysOn AG (if any) for the VMM database. Refer to the *Configure the VMM database with AlwaysOn AGs* recipe in `Chapter 4`, *Installing a Highly Available VMM Server*.

Upgrading a VMM console

Close the VMM Administrator Console and the Virtual Machine Manager Command Shell (if open), and then pick one of the following options:

- **Option 1**: In-place upgrade
- **Option 2**: Uninstallation of the old VMM console

If you picked option 1, you will need to carry out the following steps:

1. Browse to the installation media and run the setup file.
2. On the main setup page, click on **Install**.
3. Go through the installation steps.

If you picked option 2, you will need to carry out the following steps:

1. In **Control Panel | Programs | Programs and Features**, click on **Microsoft System Center Virtual Machine Manager 2012 R2 Administrator Console**, and then click on **Uninstall**.
2. On the confirmation page, click on **Uninstall**.
3. Browse to the VMM 2016 media and double-click on the setup file to run it.

4. On the main setup page, click on **Install**.
5. Go through the installation steps.

Upgrading the VMM Self-Service Portal

As VMM 2012 SP1/R2/2016 does not support the Self-Service Portal, I strongly recommend the removal of the Self-Service Portal and the installation of the Azure Pack instead. See the *Deploying Windows Azure Pack for cloud management* recipe in Chapter 9, *Managing Clouds, Fabric Updates, Resources, Clusters, and new Features of 2016*.

Uninstalling the VMM Self-Service Portal

To uninstall the VMM Self-Service Portal, carry out the following steps:

1. In **Control PanelProgramsPrograms and Features**, click on **Microsoft System Center Virtual Machine Manager 2008 Self-Service Portal**, and then click on **Uninstall**.
2. On the confirmation page, click on **Uninstall**.

Upgrading the App Controller

The App Conroller is deprecated and removed in System Center 2016, and that's why you need to plan the Windows Azure Pack installation. See the *Deploying Windows Azure Pack for cloud management* recipe in Chapter 9, *Managing Clouds, Fabric Updates, Resources, Clusters and new Features of 2016*.

See also

For more information, see the following references:

- The *Deploying a Microsoft SQL Server for VMM implementation* recipe in Chapter 3, *Installing VMM 2016*
- The following recipes in this chapter:
    - *Re-associating hosts after upgrading*
    - *Updating the VMM agents*
    - *Performing other post-upgrade tasks*

Re-associating hosts after upgrading

After upgrading to a new version of VMM, you might need to re-associate the Hyper-V hosts. This recipe will guide you through the steps required to do so.

How to do it...

To re-associate hosts and library servers, carry out the following steps after upgrading VMM:

1. In the **Fabric** workspace on the VMM console, expand **Servers**. Under **Servers**, expand **All Hosts**. In the **Hosts** pane, right-click on the column header and select **Agent Status**.

    If a host needs to be re-associated, the **Host Status** column will display **Needs Attention** and the **Agent Status** column will display **Access Denied**.

   Select the host(s) to re-associate (use the *Shift* or the *Ctrl* key if you need to select multiple hosts), then right-click on the host(s) and click on **Reassociate.**

2. In the **Reassociate Agent** dialog box, type in the account name and password.
3. Click on **OK**. The **Agent Status** column will display **Reassociating**.
4. After the host has been reassociated successfully, it will display **Responding:**

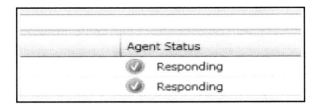

5. On the **Hosts** tab in the ribbon, click on **Refresh**. The **Host Status** will display **OK**.

How it works...

After upgrading to VMM 2016, you will need to re-associate the Hyper-V servers and VMM library servers with VMM. If a host needs to be re-associated, the **Host Status** column will exhibit **Needs Attention** and the **Agent Status** column will exhibit **Access Denied**.

Library agents are treated in the same way as host agents, and therefore, the same procedure needs to be followed for them. Re-associate the VMM library server using the same steps. To view a list of the VMM library servers, in the **Fabric** workspace, expand **Servers**, then click on **Library Servers**.

 After re-association, all the agents will display the status **Update Needed**.

There's more...

DMZ and other untrusted domain hosts will display an **Access Denied** state. They can't be re-associated; they will need to be removed and re-added to the VMM 2016 management.

See also

For more information, see the following references:

- *Updating the VMM agents*
- *Performing other post-upgrade tasks*

Updating the VMM agents

After upgrading to a new version of VMM, you will also need to update the VMM agents running on the Hyper-V server hosts. This recipe will guide you through the steps.

How to do it...

To update the VMM agent of a host, carry out the following steps after upgrading:

1. In the **Fabric** workspace on the VMM console, expand **Servers** and then go to **All Hosts**. In the **Hosts** pane, right-click on the column header and select **Agent Status**.
2. On the **Hosts** tab in the ribbon, click on **Refresh**.

> If a host requires the VMM agent to be updated, it will display **Needs Attention** in the **Host Status** column and **Upgrade Available** in the **Agent Version Status** column.

3. To update the VMM agent, select and right-click on the host, and then click on **Update Agent**.
4. In the **Update Agent** dialog, type in the user credentials, and click on **OK**.
5. The **Agent Version Status** column will exhibit **Upgrading**, which will then change to **Up-to-date** once the update process has completed successfully.
6. On the **Hosts** tab in the ribbon, click on **Refresh**. The **Host Status** for the host will display **OK**.
7. Use the same steps as the ones used before to update the VMM agent on a VMM library server. To view a list of the VMM library servers, in the **Fabric** workspace, expand **Servers**, and then click on **Library Servers**.

> You can use PowerShell to quickly update agents on all managed computers including library servers:
>
> ```
> Get-SCVMMManagedComputer | foreach { Update-
> SCVMMManagedComputer -VMMManagedComputer $_ -Credential
> (Get-Credential) -RunAsynchronously }
> ```

How it works...

After upgrading to VMM 2016, you are required to update the VMM agent on the Hyper-V hosts and VMM library servers. Although this process does not require immediate action after the upgrade (as the previous VMM 2012 R2 agent versions are supported by VMM 2016), take into account that the previous versions do not provide the functionalities that the new VMM agent does. However, in some rare cases (for example, when you have an unsupported VMM agent installed on hosts as shown in the following screenshot), you might need to uninstall agents manually on hosts and then install the agents by using the VMM console:

 Error (408)

Error (408)
vmm2012-02.rllab.com has an unsupported version of the Virtual Machine Manager agent installed.

Recommended Action
Uninstall the Virtual Machine Manager agent using Add or Remove Programs on vmm2012-02.rllab.com, and then try the operation again.

See also

For more information, see the following references:

- *Reassociating hosts after upgrading*
- *Performing other post-upgrade tasks*

Performing other post-upgrade tasks

There are some others tasks that need to be performed after VMM upgrading. This recipe will guide you through them.

How to do it...

To update a VM template, carry out the following steps after upgrading VMM:

1. On the VMM console, in the **Library** workspace, expand **Templates** and click on **VM Templates**.
2. In the **Templates** pane, right-click on the VM template that is to be updated and select **Properties**.

3. On the **Hardware Configuration** page, configure the following:
   - **VLAN ID**: If previously configured in a hardware profile

 In VMM 2012 and later, the VLAN ID will be resolved automatically based on the logical network specified when deploying a VM from a template.

   - **Logical Network/VM Network**: Ensure that the correct network is specified in the hardware profile

How it works...

The VM template settings specifying the VHD file that contains the OS are not preserved during the VMM upgrade. After VMM upgrading, you will have to update the upgraded VM templates to specify which VHD file contains the OS.

There's more...

There are a couple of other tasks that you need to perform if you had driver packages in the previous version.

Re-adding PXE servers

To renew PXE certificates, you need to remove existing PXE servers from the VMM fabric and add them again. Carry out the following steps after upgrading VMM:

1. On the VMM console, in the **Fabric** workspace expand **Infrastructure** and click on **PXE Servers.**

2. In the **PXE Servers** pane, right-click on the PXE Server and select **Remove.**

3. In the **Remove** dialogue box, provide the Run As account or type credentials to remove the PXE server from management, and then click **OK.**

4. Right-click on **PXE Servers** and select **Add PXE Server.**

5. In the **Add PXE Server** dialogue box, specify **Computer Name** and appropriate credentials of the Windows Deployment Server, then click **OK** to add it back to the fabric.

6. Verify that the PXE server appears with an **Agent Status** of **Responding.**

Updating driver packages

After upgrading to VMM 2016, remove any previously-added driver packages and then add them again so that they are correctly discovered. Use the following steps to add the driver packages to the library:

1. Locate a driver package and create a folder in the VMM library share to store the drivers (for example, you could create a folder named `Drivers`).

Do not include other library resources (for example, ISO images, VHD/VHDX files, or scripts with a `.inf` extension) in this folder or else it will not be discovered by the VMM library for indexing.

2. Copy the driver package to a folder within this folder; that is, create a separate subfolder for every driver package.

3. In the **Library** workspace on the VMM console, expand **Library Servers** in the **Library** pane. Select and right-click on the new folder (for example, `Drivers`), and then click on **Refresh** to update the display and show the newly created folder.

Be careful when you delete an INF driver package from a VMM library folder as the entire folder will be deleted.

Relocating the VMM library

If you're upgrading to a HA VMM management server, the best practice is to relocate the VMM library to a cluster file server, create a new VMM library, and move the resources. Carry out the following steps to import physical resources:

1. On the VMM console, in the **Library** workspace on the **Home** tab, click on **Import Physical Resource** and choose one of the following:
   - **Add custom resource** to import a folder and its contents. If you select a folder with a `.cr` extension, it will be imported as a custom resource package. Without a `.cr` extension, only the supported file types will show up in the VMM library.

 You can use Windows Explorer to access the VMM library share in order to access all the files in the folder (if your account has the requisite access rights).

   - **Add resource** to import file(s) of a supported type from another library location.

2. Under **Select library server and destination for the imported resources**, click on **Browse**.
3. Select the library server, library share, and folder location (optional), click on **OK**, and then click on **Import**.

See also

For more information, see the following references:

- *Troubleshooting a VMM Upgrade* (https://technet.microsoft.com/library/dn469631.aspx)
- *Upgrade to VMM 2016* (https://docs.microsoft.com/system-center/vmm/upgrade)
- Build numbers of VMM 2012 R2 and VMM 2016: https://rlevchenko.com/2017/10/02/build-numbers-for-vmm-2012-r2-and-vmm-2016/

3
Installing VMM 2016

In this chapter, we will cover the following topics:

- Creating service accounts
- Deploying a Microsoft SQL Server for VMM implementation
- Installing VMM dependencies
- Configuring **Distributed Key Management** (**DKM**)
- Installing a VMM management server
- Installing the VMM console
- Connecting to a VMM management server by using the VMM console
- Creating Run As Account credentials in VMM
- Configuring ports and protocols on the host firewall for each VMM component

Introduction

Based on what we learned in the previous chapter, you now know that in order to start our System Center 2016 VMM deployment, we should create the service accounts and deploy the SQL database.

As discussed, VMM is required to be an **Active Directory** (**AD**) member server.

In addition, it is up to business requirements and your design to decide where you will deploy the SQL database. However, as previously stated in Chapter 1, *VMM 2016 Architecture*, you should always have SQL installed on a separate server. In this way, you are safe to grow and you will have the scalability and high availability (if installing a SQL cluster) on the database side.

For the purposes of this chapter, we will be referring to the following infrastructure:

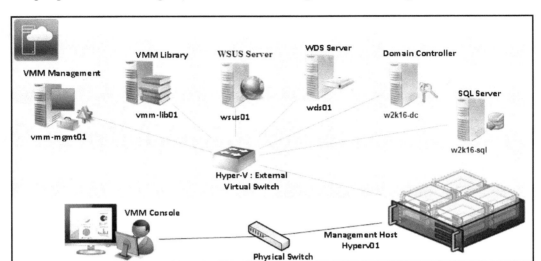

Creating service accounts

Let's start our private cloud deployment. First, we need to create service accounts.

In order to install, configure, and manage SQL, and VMM and its components, we need to create user and service accounts. My recommendation is to keep the account names similar, but the naming convention is up to your business to decide.

Getting ready

To perform this recipe, you need to have domain administrator rights or delegate permissions assigned to your account. You will also need to connect to the domain controller **w2k16-dc** (as shown in the previous infrastructure diagram) by using **Remote Desktop Connection (RDC)**, or use the **Remote Server Administration Tools (RSAT)** to open the **Active Directory Users and Computers (ADUC)**.

 If you do not have the domain admin rights or delegated permissions to execute the following recipe, ask the domain administrator to do it. We are also using `rllab.com` as our domain. Replace it with your own domain.

How to do it...

Carry out the following steps, using the ADUC console to create service accounts:

1. Create the following accounts and groups in your domain; you can name them according to your naming convention:

   - SCVMM Service user account: `RLLAB\vmm-svc`
   - SCVMM Run As user account: `RLLAB\vmm-admin`
   - SCVMM administrators security group: `RLLAB\vmm-admins`
   - SQL Service user account: `RLLAB\sql-svc`
   - SQL Server system administrators' user account: `RLLAB\sql-admin`

 I normally create these accounts under a previously created OU: **Service Accounts**.

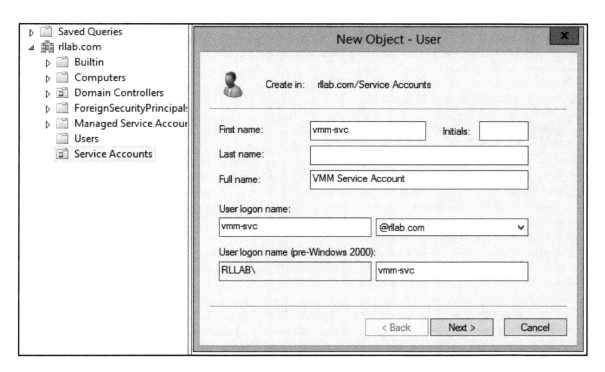

2. After creating the accounts, double-click on the vmm-admins security group.

 Make sure that the **Password never expires** and the **User cannot change password** options are checked for those accounts. Also make sure there is no GPO Applying that changes these settings. Note though that **Group Managed Service Accounts** (**GMSAs**) are not supported by VMM.

3. Select the **Members** tab and then click on **Add**.
4. Enter vmm-svc and click on **OK**.
5. Log in to the VMM management server (vmm-mgmt01) with an account that has local administrator rights (for example, RLLAB\Administrator).
6. Launch **Server Manager** from the Start menu. Click on **Tools** and then click on **Computer Management**.
7. Expand **System Tools**, select **Local Users and Groups** and go to **Groups**, double-click on **Administrators**, and then add vmm-admins.

 Optionally, you can use the following PowerShell commands to create the accounts and add the VMM-Admins group to the local Administrators group on the VMM server:

```
Add-WindowsFeature -Name "RSAT-AD-PowerShell"
$addn=(Get-ADDomain).DistinguishedName
$ouname=Read-host "Enter OU's name (for example, Service
Accounts):"
$vmmsrv=Read-Host "Enter VMM server name:"
$dname=(Get-AdDomain).Name
New-AdUser "VMM Service Account" -SamAccountName "vmm-
svc" -DisplayName "VMM Service Account" -AccountPassword
(ConvertTo-SecureString -AsPlainText "Type account's
password" -Force) -PasswordNeverExpires $true -Enabled
$true -Path "OU=$ouname,$addn"
New-ADGroup -Name "VMM-ADMINS" -GroupCategory Security -
GroupScope Global -Path "OU=$ouname,$addn"
Add-AdGroupMember VMM-ADMINS -Members vmm-svc
Invoke-Command -ComputerName $vmmsrv -Credential (Get-
credential) -ScriptBlock {net localgroup administrators
$args[0]\vmm-admins /add} -ArgumentList $dname
```

8. Repeat steps 5 to 7 for all of the VMM servers: vmm-console and vmm-lib01.
9. Log in to the SQL Server (w2k16-sql) with an account that has local administrator rights (for example, RLLAB\Administrator).

10. Launch **Server Manager** from the Start menu. Click on **Tools** and then click on **Computer Management**.

11. Expand **System Tools**, select **Local Users and Groups** and go to **Groups**, double-click on **Administrators**, and then add `sql-svc` and `sql-admin`.

You can use the domain policy to assign those accounts to the local Administrators group on the VMM and SQL servers. For more information, see `http://social.technet.microsoft.com/wiki/contents/articles/7833.how-to-make-domain-user-as-a-local-administrator-for-all-pcs.aspx`.

How it works...

These accounts will be used to install, configure, and manage SQL Server. They will be used to install, configure, and manage VMM 2016 as well, to configure VMM to communicate with SQL and other System Center components.

They will be used by VMM to manage the Hyper-V hosts as well.

There's more...

At the VMM management server installation, on the **Configure service account and distributed key management** page, you will be required to provide an account for the VMM service account. The account could be either the local system or a domain account (recommended):

- The domain account that you create specifically to be used for this purpose, as per best practice, must be a member of the local `Administrators` group on the computer.
- You are required to use a domain account for the VMM service if you want to use shared ISO images with Hyper-V VMs.
- You are required to use a domain account if you want to use a disjointed namespace.
- You are required to use a domain account if you want to install a highly available VMM management server.

- Changing the account identity of the VMM service after the VMM installation is completed, is not supported. If you need to change it, you must uninstall VMM and then select the **Retain data** option to keep the SQL Server database and the data, and then reinstall VMM by using the new service account.

 If you have a dedicated forest for the VMM environment and another forest for user accounts, you will be required to establish a two-way trust between these cross-forest domains. One-way trusts are not supported by VMM 2016.

If you get the following warning at the end of the installation:

The Service Principal Name (SPN) could not be registered in Active Directory Domain Services (AD DS) for the VMM management server.

Take the following steps in order to register the **Service Principal Name** (**SPN**) and **Service Connection Point** (**SCP**), or else no computers will be able to connect to the VMM management server, including the VMM console:

1. Open a command prompt with administrative rights (**Run As**).
2. Create the SPN for the VMM management server by running the following command:

```
setspn.exe -S SCVMM/vmm-mgmt01.rllab.com rllab\vmm-svc
setspn.exe -S SCVMM/vmm-mgmt01 rllab\vmm-svc
```

3. Check if the VMM Service has the registered SPNs now:

```
setspn.exe -l rllab\vmm-svc
```

   It should return something like this:

```
Registered ServicePrincipalNames for CN=VMM Service
Account,OU=Service Accounts,DC=rllab,DC=com:
SCVMM/vmm-mgmt01
SCVMM/vmm-mgmt01.rllab.com
```

4. Add the SPN values (REG_SZ) to the Registry key:

```
Software\Microsoft\Microsoft System Center Virtual Machine
Manager Server\Setup\VmmServicePrincipalNames
```

You can use PowerShell to complete this registry task:

```
Set-ItemProperty -Path 'HKLM:\Software\Microsoft\Microsoft
System Center Virtual Machine Manager Server\Setup\' -Name
VmmServicePrincipalNames -Value "SCVMM/vmm-mgmt01,SCVMM/vmm-
mgmt01.rllab.com"
```

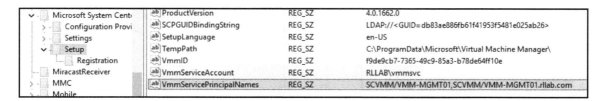

5. Configure the SCP by running the following command:

```
C:\Program Files\Microsoft System Center 2016\Virtual Machine
Manager\setup\ConfigureSCPTool.exe -install
```

To verify VMM SCP, you can check the following object: CN=MSVMM,CN=<VMM hostname>,CN=Computers,DC=rllab,DC=com using ADSI Edit (adsiedit.msc) connected to the Default Naming Context as shown in the following screenshot:

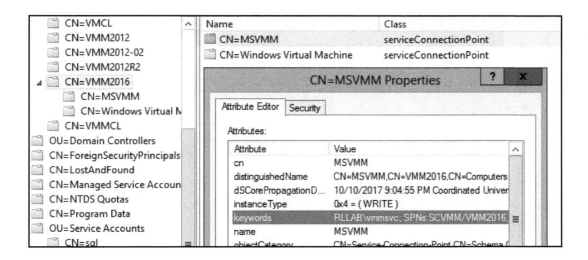

Deploying a Microsoft SQL Server for VMM implementation

In this recipe, we will see how to prepare and install SQL Server for VMM 2016.

> For more information about SQL Server versions supported by VMM 2016, see the *Specifying the correct system requirements on a real-world scenario* recipe in Chapter 1, *VMM 2016 Architecture*.

Getting ready

Assuming that you have already installed the operating system according to the SQL Server requirements of the SQL version you are installing, connect to the SQL Server machine (for example, w2k16-sql).

> Before you install SQL Server on a computer that is running Windows 10 or Windows Server 2016, you must make sure that you fulfill the following minimum requirements: https://support.microsoft.com/en-us/help/2681562/using-sql-server-in-windows-8-and-later-versions-of-windows-operating.

Also before starting, make sure the machine is a member of the domain, and refer to the following Microsoft articles for hardware and software requirements for SQL Server:

- SQL 2012 SP1: msdn.microsoft.com/en-us/library/ms143506(v=sql.110).aspx
- SQL 2014: msdn.microsoft.com/en-us/library/ms143506(v=sql.120).aspx
- SQL 2016: docs.microsoft.com/en-us/sql/sql-server/install/hardware-and-software-requirements-for-installing-sql-server

To provide high availability, it is recommended that you deploy a clustered SQL Server. **Failover Cluster Instance** (**FCI**) leverages a clustering feature in Windows Server in order to provide a single instance of SQL Server that is installed across cluster nodes. Contrary to the **AlwaysOn Availability Groups** (**AlwaysOn AGs**), FCI requires any kind of shared storage between the cluster nodes, including S2D, to be supported by SQL Server 2016 or later versions. This also means that your storage becomes a single point of failure. In addition to, or instead of, the FCI, you can use AlwaysOn AGs which provides replication of databases, improves their availability, and simplifies requirements for your infrastructure.

There are three ways to install SQL Server: through a wizard, a configuration file, or a command prompt. The following recipe will guide you through the process of installing SQL Server by using the configuration file method, which is quite simple to carry out. By using this method, after you have deployed the proof of concept, you will use the same file to replicate the SQL installation onto production or test sites.

How to do it...

The following configuration will install SQL Server 2016 with the following components: Database Engine, Reporting Services, and Full Text:

Reporting Services and Full Text are required by OpsMgr.

1. Log in as RLLAB\SQL-admin or another account that has SQL system admin rights.
2. Create a folder named SqlConf in C:\.
3. Open **Notepad** and copy the following into a new file:

```
;SQL Server 2016 Configuration File
[OPTIONS]
; SQL Server License Terms
IAcceptSQLServerLicenseTerms="True"
; Setup Work Flow: INSTALL, UNINSTALL, or UPGRADE.
ACTION="Install"
; Privacy statement when ran from the command line.
SUPPRESSPRIVACYSTATEMENTNOTICE="True"
```

```
; Microsoft R Open and Microsoft R Server terms
IACCEPTROPENLICENSETERMS="True"
; English Version of SQL Server
ENU="True"
; Setup UI will be displayed, without any user interaction.
QUIETSIMPLE="True"
; Discover and include product updates during setup.
UpdateEnabled="True"
; Microsoft Update will be used to check for updates.
USEMICROSOFTUPDATE="True"
; Specifies features to install, uninstall, or upgrade.
FEATURES=SQLENGINE,FULLTEXT,RS
; Update Location for SQL Server Setup (MU or share)
UpdateSource="MU"
; Setup log should be piped to the console.
INDICATEPROGRESS="False"
; Setup should install into WOW64.
X86="False"
; Specify a default or named instance
INSTANCENAME="MSSQLSERVER"
; Installation directory for shared components.
INSTALLSHAREDDIR="C:\Program Files\Microsoft SQL Server"
; Installation directory for the WOW64 shared components.
INSTALLSHAREDWOWDIR="C:\Program Files (x86)\Microsoft SQL Server"
; Instance ID for the SQL Server features
INSTANCEID="MSSQLSERVER"
; Specifies which mode report server is installed in.
RSINSTALLMODE="DefaultNativeMode"
; TelemetryUserNameConfigDescription
SQLTELSVCACCT="NT Service\SQLTELEMETRY"
; TelemetryStartupConfigDescription
SQLTELSVCSTARTUPTYPE="Automatic"
; Specify the installation directory.
INSTANCEDIR="C:\Program Files\Microsoft SQL Server"
; Agent account name
AGTSVCACCOUNT="RLLAB\sql-svc"
; Auto-start service after installation.
AGTSVCSTARTUPTYPE="Automatic"
; Startup type for the SQL Server service.
SQLSVCSTARTUPTYPE="Automatic"
; Level to enable FILESTREAM feature at (0, 1, 2 or 3).
FILESTREAMLEVEL="0"
; Specifies a collation type
SQLCOLLATION="SQL_Latin1_General_CP1_CI_AS"
; Account for SQL Server service
SQLSVCACCOUNT="RLLAB\sql-svc"
; SQL Server system administrators.
SQLSYSADMINACCOUNTS="RLLAB\rladmin" "RLLAB\sql-admin"
```

```
; Provision current user as a SQL Administrator
ADDCURRENTUSERASSQLADMIN="False"
; Specify 0 to disable or 1 to enable the TCP/IP protocol.
TCPENABLED="1"
; Specify 0 to disable or 1 to enable the Named Pipes protocol.
NPENABLED="0"
; Add description of input argument FTSVCACCOUNT
FTSVCACCOUNT="NT Service\MSSQLFDLauncher"
; Startup type for Browser Service.
BROWSERSVCSTARTUPTYPE="Automatic"
; Specifies which account the report server NT service
RSSVCACCOUNT="RLLAB\sql-svc"
; Specifies the startup mode of the report server service
RSSVCSTARTUPTYPE="Automatic"
```

To enable silent SQL Server installation, you need to switch the parameter QUIETSIMPLE to False and next set the parameter QUIET to TRUE.

4. Save the file as SQLConfigurationFile.ini in c:\sqlconf. Now that you have created the configuration file, let's proceed with the installation of SQL 2016 by using the file.

5. Open the command prompt or PowerShell with administrative rights (Run as administrator).

6. Navigate to **SQL Server Source Media path** and type the following:

```
Setup.exe /SQLSVCPASSWORD="P@ssw0rd1"
/AGTSVCPASSWORD="P@ssw0rd1" /ASSVCPASSWORD="P@ssw0rd1"
/RSSVCPASSWORD="P@ssw0rd1"
/ConfigurationFile=c:\sqlconf\SqlConfigurationFile.ini
```

7. Press *Enter* for the installation to start:

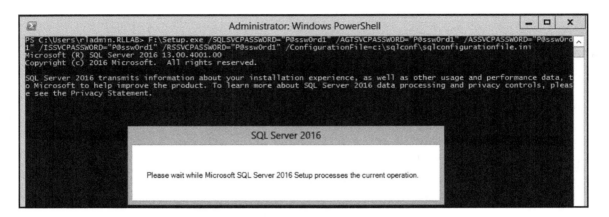

8. You should see a window showing the installation progress (as shown in the preceding screenshot). The installation will proceed without user input.

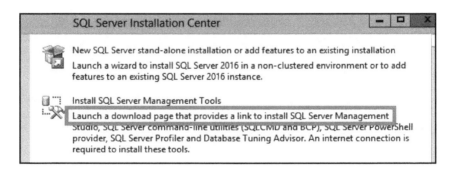

Starting with SQL Server 2016, SQL Management Studio installation has been separated out from the SQL Server installation. Now it's available as a separate package that you need to download and install it manually. See `https://docs.microsoft.com/en-us/sql/ssms/download-sql-server-management-studio-ssms`.

9. Also, I normally open Windows Firewall ports after installation to enable remote use of SQL Services. PowerShell automates this task:

```
New-NetFirewallRule -DisplayName "SQL Database Engine" -Direction
Inbound -Protocol TCP -LocalPort 1433 -Action allow
New-NetFirewallRule -DisplayName "SQL Admin Connection" -Direction
Inbound -Protocol TCP -LocalPort 1434 -Action allow
```

```
New-NetFirewallRule -DisplayName "SQL Browser Service" -Direction
Inbound -Protocol UDP -LocalPort 1434 -Action allow
New-NetFirewallRule -DisplayName "SQL Service Broker" -Direction
Inbound -Protocol TCP -LocalPort 4022 -Action allow
New-NetFirewallRule -DisplayName "SQL Debugger/RPC" -Direction
Inbound -Protocol TCP -LocalPort 135 -Action allow
```

How it works...

The configuration file is a text file with parameters and descriptive comments, which can be useful to standardize SQL deployments. It is processed in the following order:

1. The values in the configuration file replace the default values
2. Command-line values replace the default and configuration file values

For security reasons, it is recommended to specify the passwords at command prompt instead of in the configuration file.

The SQL parameter can install the SQL Server Database Engine, **Reporting Services (RS)**, Replication, Full Text, and **Data Quality Services (DQS)**. The RS parameter will install all RS components and the Tools parameter will install shared components.

In this sample configuration file, RLLAB is the domain and you need to replace it with your own domain.

The following table lists the service account and password parameters:

SQL component	Account parameter	Password parameter	Startup type
SQL Server Agent	/AGTSVCACCOUNT	/AGTSVCPASSWORD	/AGTSVCSTARTUPTYPE
Analysis Services	/ASSVCACCOUNT	/ASSVCPASSWORD	/ASSVCSTARTUPTYPE
Database Engine	/SQLSVCACCOUNT	/SQLSVCPASSWORD	/SQLSVCSTARTUPTYPE
Integration Services	/ISSVCACCOUNT	/ISSVCPASSWORD	/ISSVCSTARTUPTYPE
Reporting Services	/RSSVCACCOUNT	/RSSVCPASSWORD	/RSSVCSTARTUPTYPE

There's more...

There are some tricks that can help you with preparing SQL Server for VMM deployment.

How to easily get the SQL configuration file

You can, optionally, generate the configuration file by using the SQL 2016 wizard. To do this, carry out the following steps:

1. Browse to the SQL Server installation media.
2. Select and double-click on `Setup.exe`.
3. Follow the SQL setup wizard through the **Ready to Install** page, writing down the configuration file path on the **Configuration file path** section.
4. At this point, you can click on **Cancel** to cancel the setup, as we are just looking to generate the configuration file.
5. Browse through the configuration path folder for the generated INI file, as seen in the following screenshot:

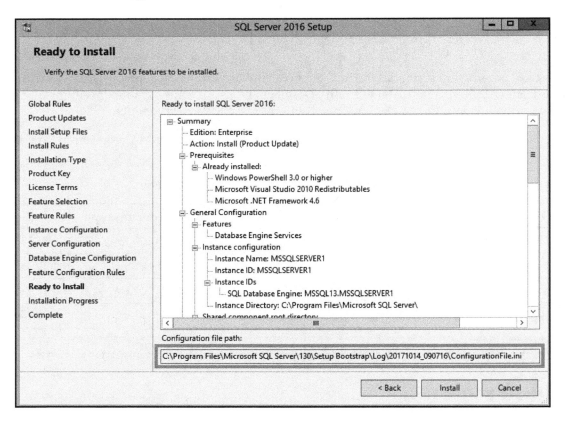

Installing a SQL failover cluster using the configuration file

A SQL failover cluster can also be configured with the configuration file. This approach significantly speeds up the setting up of SQL FCIs by reducing the time for SQL setup and node configuration:

 Before the installation, make sure that your infrastructure meets failover cluster requirements (https://docs.microsoft.com/en-us/sql/sql-server/failover-clusters/install/before-installing-failover-clustering).

1. Launch the SQL Server setup and choose the **New SQL Server failover cluster installation** option as shown in the following screenshot:

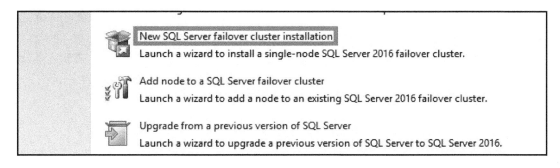

 The Database Engine and Analysis Services are the only components that are cluster-aware. Other features are not cluster-aware and do not have high availability through failover.

2. Proceed with the installation wizard and capture the configuration file. Save the captured configuration as `sqlfciconfiguration.ini` in `c:\sqlconf`.
3. Navigate to SQL Server Source Media path and type the following:
   ```
   Setup.exe /IAcceptSQLServerLicenseTerms=True
   /SQLSVCPASSWORD="P@ssw0rd1" /AGTSVCPASSWORD="P@ssw0rd1"
   /ASSVCPASSWORD="P@ssw0rd1"
   /ConfigurationFile=c:\sqlconf\sqlfciconfigurationfile.ini
   ```

   Press *Enter* for the installation to start.

To enable SQL quiet installation modes, you need to open the configuration file and comment out the UIMODE parameter. Then add the switch /q for silent installation or /qs to show only the installation progress.

4. On the additional SQL node, launch **Add node to a SQL Server failover cluster**, proceed with the wizard, and capture the configuration file. Save the captured file as sqlfcinodeconf.ini in c:\sqlconf:

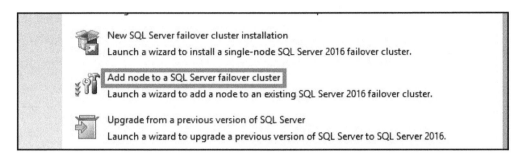

5. Run the following command to add a node to the existing failover cluster:

```
Setup.exe /IAcceptSQLServerLicenseTerms=True
/SQLSVCPASSWORD="P@ssw0rd1"  /AGTSVCPASSWORD="P@ssw0rd1"
/ASSVCPASSWORD="P@ssw0rd1"
/ConfigurationFile=c:\sqlconf\sqlfcinodeconf.ini
```

6. Repeat the previous step on all the additional nodes using the same configuration file.

Configuring SQL Server with AlwaysOn AGs

I would now like to briefly discuss the steps required to enable AlwaysOn AGs on SQL Server Enterprise machines. You can use these steps to extend the standalone SQL Server installation that we discussed in the main *How to do it...* section:

1. Copy the SQL configuration file (*step 3* of *How to do it...*) to the second SQL Server machine (for example, w2k16-sql02) and install a new SQL Server instance using the same steps as we discussed earlier.

2. On each SQL Server, add the failover clustering feature:

```
Install-WindowsFeature Failover-Clustering -IncludeManagementTools
```

3. Next, you need to create a failover cluster and set its witness settings. In the following example, a shared folder on a file server is used:

```
New-Cluster -Name SQLFCI -Node w2k16-sql,w2k16-sql02 -
StaticAddress 10.10.0.200 -NoStorage
Set-ClusterQuorum -NodeAndFileShareMajority\\filesrv\sqlcl
```

> If your SQL Server nodes have unrestricted external access, you can use a new witness type in Windows Server 2016 - cloud witness. For more information, check out this link: https://rlevchenko.com/2017/01/26/whats-new-in-failover-clustering-in-windows-server-2016/.

4. When the failover cluster comes online, you will be ready to enable the AlwaysOn feature on each SQL Server. Run the following command on a SQL machine (for example, w2k16-sql):

```
Enable-SqlAlwaysOn -ServerInstance $env:computername -Force
```

5. Repeat the previous step on the second SQL machine.
6. Open up SQL Server Management Studio, connect to the SQL Server (w2k16-sql, for example), right-click on **Databases** and select **New Database...**, define the **Database Name** (for example, Temp) and ensure that **Recovery Model** is set to **Full**, then click **OK** to create the database.
7. Expand **Databases** and highlight the created database (Temp); right-click on it, select **Tasks** and then **Backup...** ; in the **Backup Database** dialog window, set **Backup type** to **Full**; and click **OK** to start the backup job.
8. To set up AlwaysOn for the database, launch the **New Availability Group** wizard from the context menu of the AlwaysOn **High Availability** (**HA**), specify availability group name (for example, rl-ag01) and select databases as shown in the following screenshot:

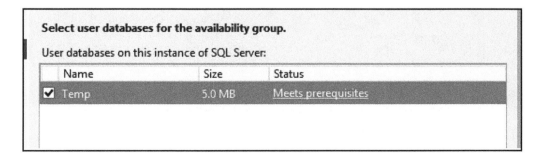

9. Specify instances of SQL Servers to host primary and secondary replicas. Refer to the settings shown in the following screenshot (**Automatic Failover** and **Synchronous Commit** are enabled; **Readable Secondary** is set to **Yes**):

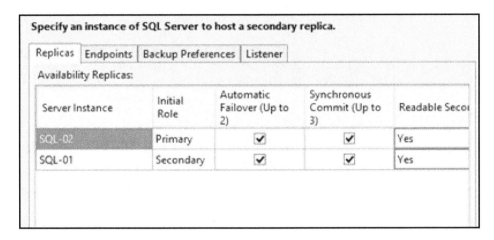

10. Now click on the **Listener** tab to configure the listener for this availability group. A static IP address is preferable. Also ensure that the DNS name and IP address are not in use:

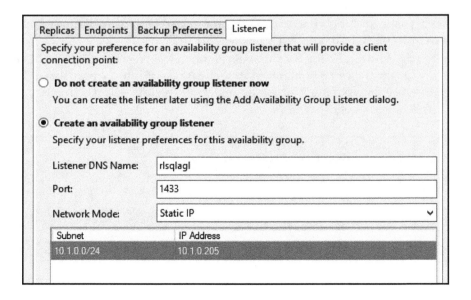

11. On the **Select Data Synchronization** page, you need to specify a network share that will be used to store database and log backups. The SQL Server service account must have read and write permissions on this network share (for example, `\\filesrv\sqlshare`). Then click on **Next**.

12. Review the validation results and summary then click on **Finish** to start the initial replication of the database and the creation of the availability group.

See also

For more information use the following references:

- SQL Server Failover Cluster Installation: `https://docs.microsoft.com/en-us/sql/sql-server/failover-clusters/install/sql-server-failover-cluster-installation`.

- Overview of SQL Server AlwaysOn AGs: `https://docs.microsoft.com/en-us/sql/database-engine/availability-groups/windows/overview-of-always-on-availability-groups-sql-server`.

- Install SQL Server 2016 from the Installation Wizard (Setup): `https://docs.microsoft.com/en-us/sql/database-engine/install-windows/install-sql-server-from-the-installation-wizard-setup`.

- Install SQL Server 2016 from the Command Prompt: `https://docs.microsoft.com/en-us/sql/database-engine/install-windows/install-sql-server-from-the-command-prompt`.

- Configure Windows Service Accounts and Permissions: `http://msdn.microsoft.com/en-us/library/ms143504`

Installing VMM dependencies

Before installing VMM, we need to ensure that the server meets the minimum system requirements and that all of the prerequisite software is installed. For more information, check the software requirements specified in the *Specifying the correct system requirements for a real-world scenario* recipe in `Chapter 1`, *VMM 2016 Architecture*.

As you may have noticed, we use PowerShell cmdlets for almost every task. Windows PowerShell comes installed by default since Windows Server 2008 R2 and provides features that help you to automate all of the IT tasks around private cloud deployment and management, starting with deploying your cloud infrastructure servers, through onboarding virtual machines to that infrastructure, and ending with monitoring your data center environment and collecting information about how it performs.

Getting ready

VMM 2016 has automated almost all of the prerequisites, but you will need to install the Windows **Assessment and Deployment Kit** (**ADK**) for Windows 10 and SQL features (if you are not running SQL on the management server).

> If you are a PowerShell guy (like me), I recommend using the `Test-NetConnection` cmdlet with the `Port` parameter to test or troubleshoot network connectivity between servers. This cmdlet can also be used as a replacement for the Telnet client that is not installed by default starting from Server 2008

To download the Windows ADK for Windows 10, go to:`https://developer.microsoft.com/en-us/windows/hardware/windows-assessment-deployment-kit`.

How to do it...

To install, carry out the following steps:

1. Download and run the `adksetup.exe` file.
2. Select **Install the Windows Assessment and Deployment Kit – Windows 10 to this computer** and click on **Next**.
3. On the **Windows Kits Privacy** page, select **Yes** to join the Customer Experience program and click on **Next**. Then click on **Accept**.
4. Select **Deployment Tools** and **Windows Preinstallation Environment (Windows PE)**, as shown in the following screenshot, and click on **Install**:

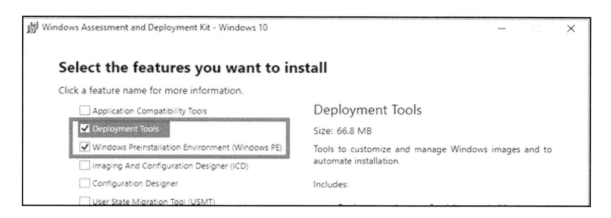

ADK can be installed by using the command line. You can use the following command in the Server Core environment, for example:
`adksetup.exe /quiet /features OptionId.DeploymentTools OptionId.WindowsPreinstallationEnvironment`

How it works...

The ADK for Windows 10, which is a collection of tools that you can use to customize, assess, and deploy Windows operating systems to new computers, is a prerequisite for VMM 2016 and is used for bare metal deployment of Hyper-V servers.

It includes **Windows Preinstallation Environment** (**Windows PE**), Deployment Imaging, Servicing and Management, and Windows System Image Manager.

Right after starting the installation, at the **Windows Assessment and Deployment Kit** page, select **Deployment Tools** and **Windows Preinstallation Environment (Windows PE)** and then follow the wizard to complete the installation.

There's more...

There are more items that you need to install, which will be seen in the following sections.

SQL Server Connectivity Feature Pack components

Download the SQL Server Connectivity Feature Pack and then run the downloaded file to install that package. Note though, that you need the feature pack for the SQL version that the VMM database is running on:

- **SQL Server 2016 Command Line Utilities**: The `sqlcmd` utility allows users to connect to, send Transact-SQL batches from, and output row set information from SQL Server instances. Visit the following site for more information: `https://www.microsoft.com/en-us/download/details.aspx?id=52680`.
- **Microsoft SQL Server Native Client (ODBC Driver)**: This is the single **dynamic-link library (DLL)** containing runtime support for applications using SQL ODBC-only native-code APIs to connect to Microsoft SQL Server 2008, SQL Server 2008 R2, SQL Server 2012, SQL Server 2014, SQL Server 2016, Analytics Platform System, Azure SQL Database, and Azure SQL Data Warehouse. Visit the following site for more information: `https://www.microsoft.com/en-us/download/details.aspx?id=53339`.

The Telnet client

Optionally, you can install the Telnet client, as it is very useful when testing and troubleshooting. An alternative option is to use PowerShell, which is ready for use right out of the box:

1. On the Windows 2016 Start screen, right-click on the tile for **Windows PowerShell**. Next, on the app bar, click on **Run as administrator**.
2. Type the following command and hit *Enter*:

```
Install-WindowsFeature Telnet-Client
```

See also

For more information, use the following references:

- Installing the Windows ADK article is available at:
  `https://docs.microsoft.com/en-us/windows-hardware/get-started/adk-install`

Configuring Distributed Key Management

Distributed Key Management (**DKM**) is used to store VMM encryption keys in an **Active Directory Domain Services** (**AD DS**) container.

When installing VMM, for security reasons (recommended, as it encrypts the information on AD) and when deploying HA VMM (required), choose to use DKM on the **Configure service account and distributed key management** page.

Why do we need DKM? By default, using the Windows **Data Protection API** (**DPAPI**), VMM encrypts some data in the VMM database (for example, the Run As account credentials and passwords), and this data is tied to the VMM server and the service account used by VMM. However, with DKM, different machines can securely access the shared data.

Once an HA VMM node fails over to another node, it will start accessing the VMM database and use the encryption keys conveniently stored under a container in AD to decrypt the data in the VMM database.

Getting ready

The following are some considerations for using DKM in VMM 2016:

- When installing a highly available VMM management server, DKM is required.
- The DKM container should be created in AD before starting with the VMM setup, if you do not have domain administrator rights when installing VMM.
- You must create the DKM container and the VMM service account in the same domain as the VMM management server.
- The installation account requires **Full Control** permissions to the DKM container in AD DS. Also, in the **Apply to** drop-down menu, choose the **This object and all descendant objects** option.
- On the **Configure service account and distributed key management** page, you must specify the location of the container in AD DS (for example, CN=VMMDKM, DC=rllab, DC=com).

 If you do not have the domain admin rights or delegated permissions to execute the following recipe, ask the domain administrator to do it.

How to do it...

Carry out the following steps to configure the DKM:

1. Login as domain administrator on your domain controller (for example, `W2k16-DC`) or use the ADSI Edit console from the administrator desktop if you have installed RSAT.
2. Type `adsiedit.msc` in the **Run** window.
3. When the **ADSI Edit** window opens, right-click on **ADSI Edit** and select **Connect to**.
4. Click on **Select a well known Naming Context** and select **Default naming context**.
5. Click on **OK** and expand **Default naming context**, as shown in the following screenshot:

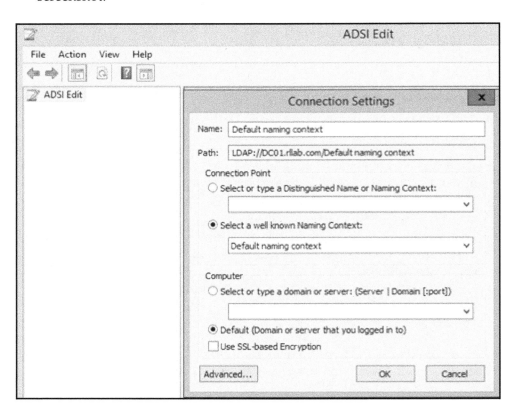

6. Expand `DC=rllab,DC=com`.
7. Right-click on `DC=rllab,DC=com` and select **New**, and then select **Object**.
8. Select container and click on **Next**, as shown here:

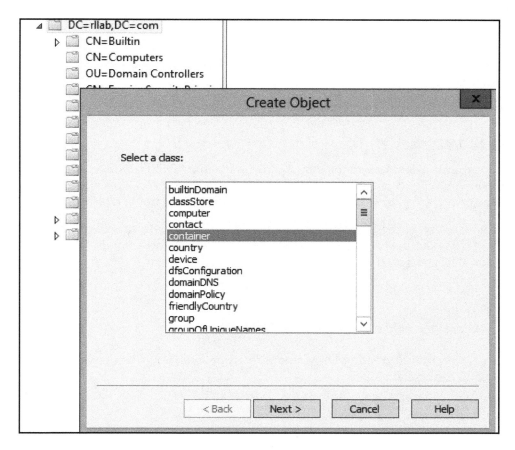

9. In the **Value** textbox, type VMMDKM and click on **Next**.
10. Click on **Finish** and close the **ADSI Edit** window.
11. In the **Active Directory Users and Computers** window, in the top menu, click on **View** and then select **Advanced Features**.

12. Right-click on the **VMMDKM** container and click on **Properties**.
13. Click on the **Security** tab and click on **Add**.
14. Type the name of the VMM Administrators group: `rllab\vmm-admins`.
15. Check the **Read, Write, and Create all child objects** options.
16. Click on **Advanced**.
17. Select **VMM Admins** and click on **Edit**.
18. In the **Apply to** drop-down menu, select **This object and all descendant objects**.
19. Click on **OK**.

How it works...

You can configure DKM before installing VMM by using ADSI Edit or during the VMM setup when you will be asked to enter the location in AD that you would like to use for storing the encryption keys. The location is the **distinguished name** (**DN**) of the container.

If you choose to create the DKM during the VMM setup, the user running the VMM installation (for example, `rllab\vmm-admin`) needs to have the following access rights on the location that you specify during setup:

- Read
- Write
- Create all child objects

> If you are creating DKM under the root level, you will need those rights at the domain level.

The following screenshot shows the permissions configured for the VMM account:

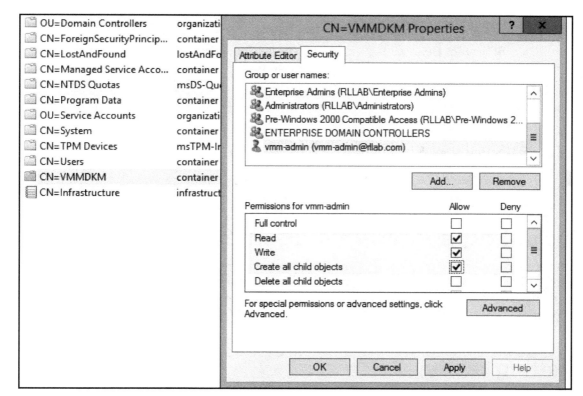

If the user running the setup has the right to create a container in AD DS, VMM setup will check whether there is a DKM container and then do either of the following:

- If there is a DKM container already created in AD, VMM setup creates a new container under VMMDKM and gives the necessary permissions to the VMM service account for this new container
- If there is no DKM container in AD, the VMM setup will create the container

Note that the VMM service account is also selected on this wizard page. For HA VMM installations, the local system account is disabled.

See also

For more information, see the following:

- KB: System Center 2012 Virtual Machine Manager Setup fails to create child objects for DKM. For more information refer to:

  `http://blogs.technet.com/b/scvmm/archive/2012/06/18/kb-system-center-2`
  `012-virtual-machine-manager-setup-fails-to-create-child-objects-for-`
  `dkm.aspx`

- Configuring DKM in VMM:

  `http://go.microsoft.com/fwlink/p/?LinkID=209609`

Installing a VMM management server

As discussed in `Chapter 1`, *VMM 2016 Architecture*, the VMM management server is the core of VMM. In this recipe, we will install the VMM management component. Again, it is important to look at your design first to find out where you are going to deploy this component. This should be the first component to install.

Getting ready

Before you start the installation of the VMM management server, ensure that your SQL server is up and running.

From the VMM server, run the following at Command Prompt:
`Telnet SQL-Server 1433`
If you get a black screen after typing the above and hitting Enter, the communication is established. If you receive the message **Could not open connection to the host**, the connection has failed and you need to look at the SQL services or the firewall rules of your SQL Server and proceed with the VMM installation. You can also use the `Test-NetConnection SQL-Server -Port 1433 PowerShell` command to check the communication between VMM and SQL. If `TcpTestSucceeded` has the value TRUE, VMM can reach SQL Service. Otherwise, the following message will be shown: **WARNING: TCP connect to SQL-Server:1433 failed.**

Get your computer updated by running a Windows update and restart if requested, before continuing with the VMM installation.

Ensure that the following is true:

- The server meets the minimum system requirements.
- You have created the domain account that will be used by the VMM Service (for example, `rllab\vmm-svc`). Do not log in with this account. The VMM service account will be used in the VMMDKM wizard page.
- The installation account (for example, `rllab\vmm-admin`) is a member of the local `Administrators` group. The account you are going to use for VMM is required to be a member of the local `Administrators` group on the computer you are installing VMM in. Add `RLLAB\vmm-svc` as well, which is the account we created previously to be the SCVMM service account.
- You have closed any open applications and that there is no pending restart on the server.
- The computer is a member of the domain. In our case, we are using `RLLAB.COM` as the domain.
- You have created a DKM container in AD DS before installing VMM. Otherwise, if the user account running setup (`RLLAB\vmm-admin`) has the right to create the VMMDKM container in AD DS, you don't need to have created it previously.

 If the setup does not complete successfully, check the logs in the `%SYSTEMDRIVE%\ProgramData\VMMLogs` folder.

How to do it...

Carry out the following steps to install the VMM management server:

1. Login as `RLAB\vmm-admin` or with an account that has administrator rights.
2. Browse to the `VMM setup` folder, right-click on **setup**, and then select **Run as administrator**.

3. On the **Setup** page, click on **Install** and, on the **Select features to install** page, select **VMM management server**, and then click on **Next**, as follows:

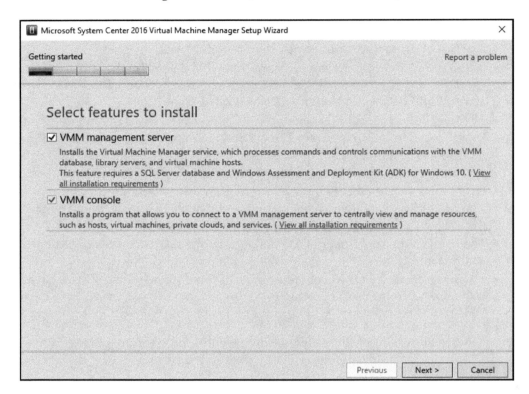

The VMM console option will be selected and installed when you select VMM management server.

4. On the **Product registration information** page, type the key and then click on **Next**.
5. On the **Please read this notice** page, tick the **I have agreed with the terms of this notice** checkbox and then click on **Next**.
6. On the **Diagnostic and Usage Data** page, read the notice, and then click on **Next**.
7. On the **Microsoft Update** page, tick the checkbox **ON (recommended)** to look at the **Microsoft Update Center** for latest updates, and then click on **Next**.
8. On the **Installation location** page, provide the path for the installation and then click on **Next**.

If you plan to install all VMM 2016 components on the same server, my recommendation is to keep the **operating system** (**OS**) partition (`C:`) only for the OS. In this case, you should select another drive for the VMM program files.

9. The server will now be scanned to check whether the requirements have been met and a page will be displayed showing us which requirements have not been met and how to resolve the issue.
10. As we planned our installation and had all prerequisites already installed, the **Database configuration** page will be directly displayed.
11. On the **Database configuration** page, specify the name of the server that is running SQL Server. In our case, it is `w2k16-sql`, as seen here:

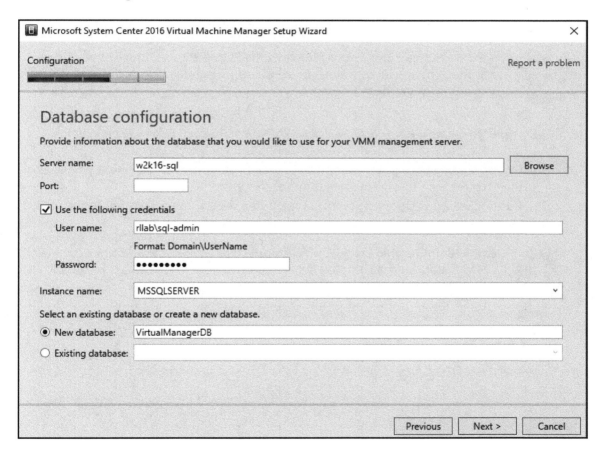

If SQL Server is running on the same server, which is not a recommended approach, you can type `localhost` or the name of the computer (for example, `vmm-mgmt01.rllab.com`). If the AlwaysOn AG is configured, type the listener DNS name.

12. You don't need to specify the port used for SQL communication, unless all of the following conditions are true for SQL:

- SQL Server is running on another server (recommended)
- The SQL Server browser service is not started
- It is not using the default port of `1433`

13. In the **Instance name**, provide the SQL Server instance, or select the default, `MSSQLSERVER`.

If the `Instance name` does not show the SQL instances to select, confirm that the SQL Server Browser service is running and check the inbound firewall rules on the SQL Server.

14. Agree to create a new database (new VMM installation) or to use an existing database (for example, a recover situation) and click on **Next**.
15. On the **Configure service account and distributed key management** page, select the account for Virtual Machine Manager Service.
16. If the selection is Domain account, type in the user domain account, in the format `domain\user`, and the password, and click on **Next**.

You will not be able (as it is not supported) to change the account after the VMM installation is completed. See the *Creating service accounts* recipe in this chapter.

17. In the **Distributed Key Management** section, select **Store my keys in Active Directory** if you have decided to use DKM (recommended approach), shown as follows:

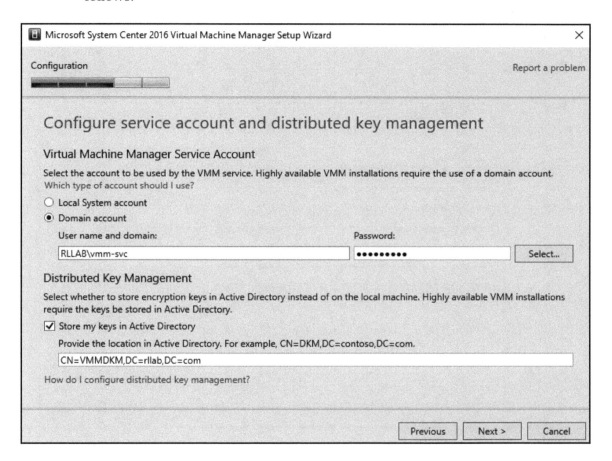

It is strongly recommended that you select to store keys in Active Directory, and it is required when installing a highly available VMM server.

18. On the **Port configuration** page, leave the default port numbers or provide a unique value for each feature, and then click on **Next** as seen here:

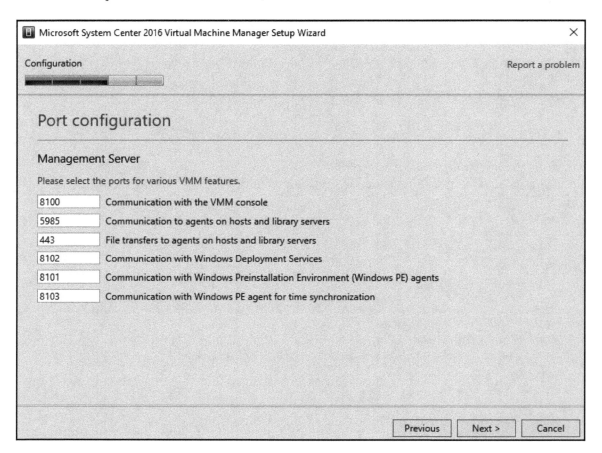

Document and plan the ports before choosing, as you cannot change the ports without reinstalling VMM.

19. On the **Library configuration** page, you can select the **Create a new library share** option if you want to create a new library share or you can select the **Use an existing library share** option if you want to use the existing library share, depending upon your requirements. Click on **Select** to specify the share location:

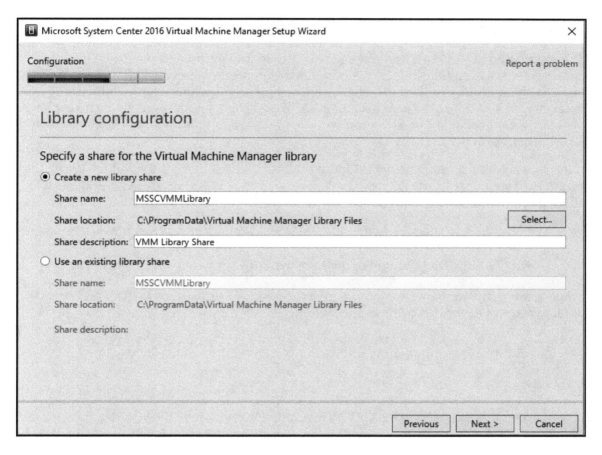

20. Click on **Next** to continue.
21. On the **Installation summary** page, review your selections. Click on **Previous** if you want to change any selections.
22. Click on **Install** to start the installation and an installation progress bar will be displayed.
23. On the **Setup completed successfully** page, click on **Close**.

24. Run **Windows Update** to download and install the latest updates for VMM management server and its console.

Build numbers for VMM 2012 R2 and VMM 2016 are available at:https://rlevchenko.com/2017/10/02/build-numbers-for-vmm-2012-r2-and-vmm-2016/.

How it works...

The installation of VMM Management Server 2016 is straightforward because it has enhancements added that simplify the installation process. When you click on **Install** on the main **Setup** page, this version will install some of the prerequisites for you, if they are necessary. In addition, if you are installing VMM on a cluster node, you will be prompted to make it highly available. For more information, see `Chapter 3`, *Installing a Highly Available VMM Management Server*.

If the user account running the VMM setup (`RLLAB\vmm-admin`) has the right to create the VMMDKM container in AD DS, you don't necessarily need to have created it previously, although it is recommended because of the following:

- VMM setup checks whether the VMMDKM container is present in AD. If it is present, it will create a new container under VMMDKM.
- If the VMMDKM container does not exist, the setup will try to create it.

When creating the container, VMM will give the selected permissions to the VMM service domain account (informed on the same page).

> When installing HA VMM, you cannot select the local system account, as it is not supported in this case.

If your account does not have the **CREATE** permissions option on the SQL database server, or if you are not a database administrator, you can ask them to previously create the VMM database. Alternatively, you can provide an account with permissions to create a database on SQL Server during the installation process by selecting the **Use the following credentials** checkbox and then providing the username and password.

During installation, you will be required to create the VMM library. The default share is `MSSCVMMLibrary` and the folder is located at `%SYSTEMDRIVE%\ProgramData\Virtual Machine Manager Library Files`, which is a hidden folder.

> You will be able to add additional library shares or servers on the VMM console by using the VMM command shell, after the installation.

There's more...

There are many Windows Server Core environments even in my demo infrastructure. See the following recipe to install VMM on Windows Server Core.

Installing VMM 2016 on Server Core

You can install VMM 2016 from a command prompt. This option is particularly useful when you have Server Core environment (Windows Server 2016 without GUI features) or are planning VMM unattended installation. To do this, carry out the following steps:

1. Copy VMMServer.ini from the VMM installation media (root\amd64\setup) to the folder c:\vmmsetup, for example.

2. By default, the entries are commented out in this file. You need to open it, remove the comment symbol (#), and change the required values. In the following example, VMM will be installed using the remote database server (w2k16-sql), DKM (CN=VMMDKM) and domain account for the VMM service:

```
[OPTIONS]
ProductKey=xxxxx-xxxxx-xxxxx-xxxxx-xxxxx
UserName=rlevchenko
CompanyName=rlevchenko
ProgramFiles=D:\Program Files\Microsoft System Center 2016\Virtual
Machine Manager
CreateNewSqlDatabase=1
SqlInstanceName= MSSQLSERVER
SqlDatabaseName=VirtualManagerDB
RemoteDatabaseImpersonation=1
SqlMachineName=w2k16-sql
IndigoTcpPort=8100
IndigoHTTPSPort=8101
IndigoNETTCPPort=8102
IndigoHTTPPort=8103
WSManTcpPort=5985
BitsTcpPort=443
CreateNewLibraryShare=1
LibraryShareName=MSSCVMMLibrary
LibrarySharePath=D:\ProgramData\Virtual Machine Manager Library
Files
LibraryShareDescription=Virtual Machine Manager Library Files
SQMOptIn = 1
MUOptIn = 0
VmmServiceLocalAccount = 0
TopContainerName = "CN=VMMDKM,DC=rllab,DC=com"
```

3. Save `VMMServer.ini` and then run the following command:

```
setup.exe /server /i /f C:\vmmsetup\VMServer.ini /SqlDBAdminDomain
rllab /SqlDBAdminName sql-admin /SqlDBAdminPassword P@ssw0rd1
/VmmServiceDomain rllab /VmmServiceUserName vmm-svc
/VmmServiceUserPassword P@ssw0rd1 /IACCEPTSCEULA
```

4. To verify that the installation is complete, you can check the `SetupWizard` log file in the `%SYSTEMDRIVE%\ProgramData\VMMLogs`:

```
SetupWizard - Notepad
File  Edit  Format  View  Help
11:54:54:LoadedPrerequisiteXmlFile = True
11:54:54:currentInstallItem = Final Configuration
11:54:54:CurrentWorkingInstallItem = Web Deployment Tool
11:54:54:microsoftinstallerinstalldone = True
11:54:54:AfterGrantSetupUserDBAccess = True
11:54:54:appath = C:\Program Files\Microsoft System Center 2016\Virtual Machine Manager\setup
11:54:54:executableinstalldone = True
11:54:54:ProcessingRollback = 1
11:54:54:End of list Property Bag Values.
```

See also

For more information, see the following:

- *Designing the VMM server, database, and console implementation* recipe in `Chapter 1`, *VMM 2016 Architecture*.

Installing the VMM console

After installing the VMM management server, you need to install the VMM console to manage VMM from your desktop.

The VMM console is the GUI interface to the VMM management server. For example, you will be using it to manage the clouds, VMs, fabrics, storage, and other resources.

Getting ready

Before you start the installation of the VMM console, ensure that the VMM management server is up and running. Also, check whether your machine has all the prerequisites for the VMM console installation.

Consult the log files in the %SYSTEMDRIVE%\ProgramData\VMMLogs folder. Check ProgramData if you find issues at the time of installation.

Make sure you log in with an account that is a member of the local Administrators group before starting the installation.

How to do it...

Carry out the following steps:

1. Login as rllab\vmm-admin or with administrator rights.
2. Browse to the VMM setup folder, right-click on **setup, and then select Run as administrator.**
3. On the **Setup** page, click on Install.
4. On the **Select features to install** page, select only **VMM console**, and then click on **Next**, as follows:

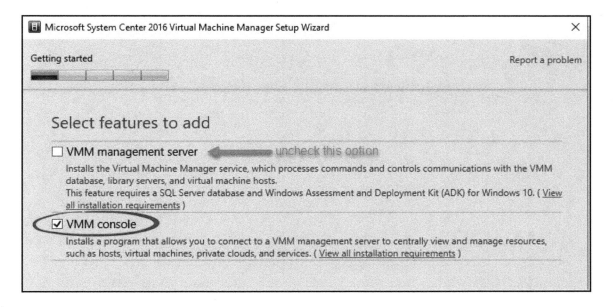

5. On the **Please read this notice** page, tick the **I agree with the terms of this notice** checkbox and then click on **Next**.

6. On the **Diagnostic and Usage Data** page, review the notice, and then click on **Next**.

7. On the **Microsoft Update** page, tick the checkbox **ON (recommended)** to look at the **Microsoft Update** for the latest updates, and then click on **Next**.

8. On the **Installation location** page, provide the path for the installation and then click on **Next**.

9. On the **Port configuration** page, type the port that the VMM console will use to communicate with the VMM management server, and then click on **Next**.

 You already configured this port setting during the installation of the VMM management server. The default port setting is 8100.

10. On the **Installation summary** page, click on **Previous** if you want to change any selections or click on **Install** to proceed with the installation.

 To open the VMM console at the end of the installation, select **Open the VMM console** when this wizard closes.

11. On the **Setup completed successfully** page, click on **Close**.

How it works...

The installation process will install the VMM console on your desktop machine. By doing this, you will be able to connect and perform all VMM-related activities remotely from your computer.

The installation process will scan the computer to make sure the requirements are met, and a page will be displayed showing any prerequisites that have not been met.

Connecting to a VMM management server by using the VMM console

The VMM console is the GUI interface to the VMM management server. You will be using it, for example, to manage virtual machines, services, private cloud, fabric, storage, and resources.

You can use this recipe to configure the VMM console to connect to a VMM management server.

The VMM console will enable you to manage VMM remotely from your desktop without the need of RDP into the VMM server.

How to do it...

Carry out the following steps:

1. In the **Server name** box that is in the **Connect to Server** dialog box of the **Virtual Machine Manager Console** window, type in the name of the VMM management server (for example, `vmm-mgmt01:8100`, where `8100` is the default port).
2. To connect, click on **Specify credentials** and then type the user credentials (for example, `rlab\vmm-admin`) or click on **Use current Microsoft Windows Identity**.

2. Click on **Connect** as shown in the following screenshot:

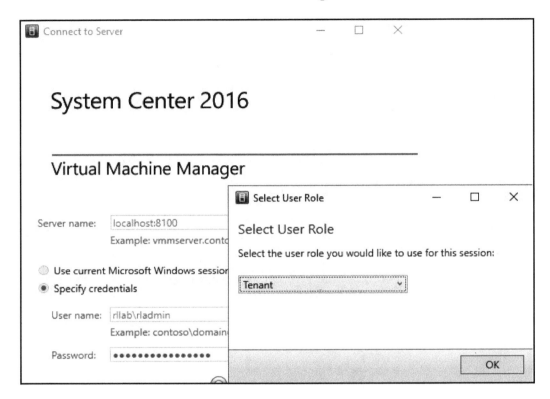

How it works...

You can use the logged Windows login credentials to connect to VMM if the user is allowed to connect, or you can specify an account.

You will need to specify the user credentials on a multitenant environment, or if the user account is not on the same domain as the VMM management server.

If the account has multiple user roles (for example, Tenant Administrator and Self-Service user), you will be prompted to select the user role with which you can log in.

If you have selected **Automatically connect with these settings**, VMM will keep these settings in the registry. You can check or set them by using PowerShell:

```
$path='HKCU:\Software\Microsoft\Microsoft System Center
Virtual Machine Manager Administrator
Console\Settings\Shared'
Get-Item $path
```

For example, this command disables VMM console auto connection:

```
Set-ItemProperty -Path -Name AutoConnect -Value $false
```

See also

For more information, see the following references:

- *Creating user roles in VMM* recipe in `Chapter 7`, *Deploying Virtual Machines and Services*

Creating a Run As account credentials in VMM

This recipe will guide you through the process of configuring security in VMM, by using Run As accounts.

In VMM 2016, the credentials that a user enters for any process can be provided by a Run As account.

Only administrators or delegated administrators have the rights to create and manage Run As accounts.

If within their scope, read-only administrators will be able to read a user's account name related to the Run As account.

How to do it...

Carry out the following steps:

1. In Windows, click on the Start menu and click on the **VMM console**.
2. On the VMM 2016 console, on the bottom-left side, click on the **Settings** workspace.
3. In the **Home** tab, on the top ribbon, click on **Create Run As Account**.
4. In the **Create Run As Account** dialog box, type in the name for the **Run As account** (for example, Hyper-V Host Administration Account).
5. Optionally, enter a description for the account.
6. Provide the user account that will be used by the **Run As account** in the **User name** field (for example, `rlab\vmm-admin`):

You can use a domain user, or group, or a local credential.

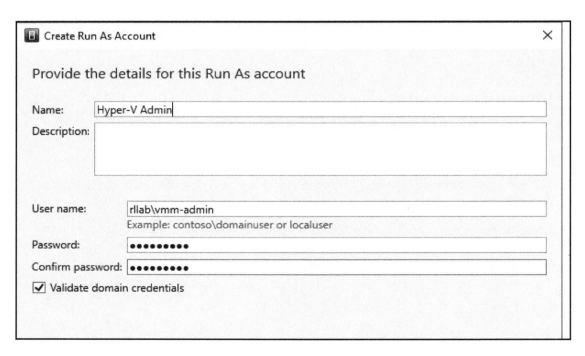

7. Type in the password.

 Unselect **Validate domain credentials** if you are sure that the user and the password are correct.

8. Click on **Finish** to create the account.

How it works...

Creating a Run As account starts by creating the account on the AD that will be used for the association.

A Run As account is an account securely stored in VMM that will be used to perform VMM administrative tasks, such as adding hosts and clusters, and performing bare metal deployments. By using the Run As account, you will not need to provide a username and password while performing tasks that require credentials.

There is no limit to the number of Run As accounts you can have.

There's more...

Administrators and delegated administrators can create, delete, and make a Run As account unavailable temporarily in VMM. They can do the last by disabling the account and then enabling it to have it available again.

 Delegated administrators can only perform these actions within their scope.

Disabling a Run As account

Carry out the following steps to disable a Run As account:

1. In the VMM 2016 console, on the bottom-left side, click on the **Settings** workspace.
2. On the **Settings** pane, click on **Security**, and then click on **Run As Accounts**.

3. On the **Run As Accounts** main pane, click on the enabled **Run As account** to be disabled.

4. In the **Home** tab, on the top ribbon, click on **Disable** and then you will see the **Enabled** status change to a red **X**.

 The account will be unavailable until you enable it again.

Enabling a disabled Run As account

Carry out the following steps to enable a Run As account:

1. In the VMM 2016 console, on the bottom-left side, click on the **Settings** workspace.
2. On the **Settings** pane, click on **Security** and then click on **Run As Accounts**.
3. On the **Run As Accounts** main pane, click on the disabled **Run As account** to be enabled.
4. In the **Home** tab, on the top ribbon, click on **Enable**; you will see the status change to **Enabled**.

Deleting a Run As account

Use the following steps to delete a **Run As account** that is not being used by any VMM running task:

1. In the VMM 2016 console, on the bottom-left side, click on the **Settings** workspace.
2. On the **Settings** pane, click on **Security**, and then click on **Run As Accounts**.
3. On the **Run As Accounts** main pane, click on the **Run As account** to be deleted.
4. In the **Home** tab, on the top ribbon, click on **Delete** and then click on **Yes** to confirm the removal.

Configuring ports and protocols on the host firewall for each VMM component

When designing the VMM implementation, you need to plan which ports you are going to use for communication and file transfers between the VMM components. Based on the chosen ports, you also need to configure the host firewall and external firewalls to enable those ports.

Getting ready

Take note of the following ports to create the firewall exceptions. Depending on your environment, you will need to configure the following exceptions on the host firewall, as well on your external firewall (for example, if you have a DMZ in place).

 Some ports cannot be changed through VMM.

The following table lists the default port settings and the place to change, if it is possible:

Connection from and to	Protocol	Default port	To change the port settings
SFTP file transfer from VMware ESXi hosts	SFTP	22	Cannot be changed
The VMM management server to the load balancer	HTTP/HTTPS	80/443	Load balancer configuration provider
The VMM management server to the WSUS server (data channel)	HTTP/HTTPS	80/8530 (non-SSL) and 443/8531 (with SSL)	These ports are the IIS port bindings with WSUS; they cannot be changed from VMM
The BITS port for VMM transfers (data channel)	BITS	443	During VMM setup

Connection from and to	Protocol	Default port	To change the port settings
The VMM library server to the hosts (file transfer)	BITS	443 (Maximum value: 32768)	During VMM setup
VMM host-to-host file transfer	BITS	443 (Maximum value: 32768)	Cannot be changed
VMware Web Services communication	HTTPS	443	VMM console
SFTP file transfer from the VMM management server to VMware ESXi	HTTPS	443	Cannot be changed
The VMM management server to BMC	HTTPS	443	On BMC
The VMM management server to the in-guest agent (VMM to the virtual machine data channel)	HTTPS (using BITS)	443	Cannot be changed
The VMM management server to the VMM agent on the Windows-Server-based host (data channel for file transfers)	HTTPS (using BITS)	443 (Maximum value: 32768)	Cannot be changed
The VMM management server to Windows file server (RPC)	RPC	135	Cannot be changed
The VMM management server to Windows file server (SMB)	SMB	445	Cannot be changed
The VMM management server to Windows file server	WinRM	80	Cannot be changed
The VMM management server to Windows file server	NetBIOS	139	Cannot be changed
OOB connection IPMI	IPMI	623	On BMC
The VMM management server to the remote Microsoft SQL Server database	TDS	1433	Cannot be changed

Connection from and to	Protocol	Default port	To change the port settings
Console connections (RDP) to virtual machines through Hyper-V hosts (VMConnect)	RDP	2179	VMM console
Remote Desktop to virtual machines	RDP	3389	On the virtual machine
The VMM management server to the VMM agent on the Windows-Server-based host (control channel)	WinRM	5985	During VMM setup
The VMM management server to the in-guest agent (VMM to the virtual machine control channel)	WinRM	5985	Cannot be changed
The VMM management server to the VMM agent on the Windows-Server-based host (control channel - SSL)	WinRM	5986	Cannot be changed
The VMM console to the VMM management server	WCF	8100	During VMM setup
The VMM console to the VMM management server (HTTPS)	WCF	8101	During VMM setup
The Windows PE agent to the VMM management server (control channel)	WCF	8101	During VMM setup
The VMM console to the VMM management server (NET.TCP)	WCF	8102	During VMM setup.
The WDS provider to the VMM management server	WCF	8102	During VMM setup
The VMM console to the VMM management server (HTTP)	WCF	8103	During VMM setup
The Windows PE agent to the VMM management server (time sync)	WCF	8103	During VMM setup

Connection from and to	Protocol	Default port	To change the port settings
The VMM management server to the Storage Management Service	WMI	Local call	Cannot be changed
The VMM management server to the Cluster PowerShell interface	PowerShell	n/a	Cannot be changed
Storage Management Service to SMI-S provider	CIM-XML	Provider-specific port	Cannot be changed

How to do it...

Carry out the following steps:

1. On the server where you need to configure the firewall exceptions, click on **Server Manager** from the Start menu. Next, click on **Tools**, and then click on **Windows Firewall with Advanced Security**.
2. In the Windows Firewall with Advanced Security on Local Computer pane, click on **Inbound Rules**.
3. In the **Actions** pane, under **Inbound Rules**, click on **New Rule**.
4. In the **New Inbound Rule Wizard** window, under **Rule Type**, click on **Port**, and then click on **Next**:

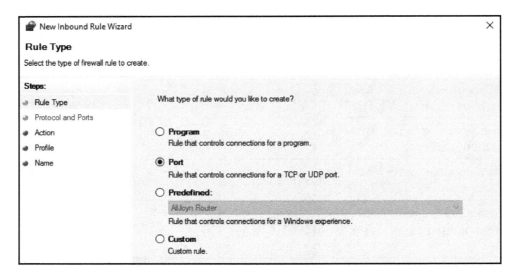

5. In **Protocol and Ports**, click on **TCP**.
6. Click on **Specific local ports** and type the port number (for example, `8100`); then click on **Next**.
7. On the **Action** page, click on **Next**.
8. On the **Profile** page, click on **Next**.
9. On the **Name** page, type the description (for example, `VMM console TCP 8100`).
10. Click on **Finish** to create the rule.
11. Repeat steps 3 to 10 for each port number you need to configure.
12. Close **Windows Firewall with Advanced Security**.

 You can automate this task by using PowerShell. Here is an example of creating one firewall rule:
```
New-NetFirewallRule -DisplayName "VMM Console TCP 8100" -
Direction Inbound -Protocol TCP -LocalPort 8100 -Action
allow
```

See also

For more information, see the following references:

- Configure the Windows Firewall to allow SQL Server access: `https://docs.microsoft.com/en-us/sql/sql-server/install/configure-the-windows-firewall-to-allow-sql-server-access`
- New-NetFirewallRule cmdlet: `https://docs.microsoft.com/en-us/powershell/module/netsecurity/new-netfirewallrule`
- Build Numbers for SC VMM 2012 R2/2016: `https://rlevchenko.com/2017/10/02/build-numbers-for-vmm-2012-r2-and-vmm-2016/`

4
Installing a Highly Available VMM Server

In this chapter, we will cover:

- Installing a highly available VMM management server
- Installing a VMM management server on an additional node of a cluster
- Configuring the VMM database with **AlwaysOn Availability Groups** (**AlwaysOn AGs**)
- Connecting to a highly available VMM management server by using the VMM console
- Deploying a highly available library server on a file server cluster
- Uninstalling a highly available VMM management server

Introduction

Understanding how VMM has become a critical part of the private cloud infrastructure is very important. This chapter will walk you through the recipes to implement a **highly available** (**HA**) VMM server, especially useful in enterprise and data center environments.

VMM plays a critical role in managing the private cloud and data center infrastructure, which means that keeping the VMM infrastructure always available is crucial to preserving the service's continuity and provision, and to monitor VMs to respond to fluctuations in usage.

Before VMM 2012, it was not possible to have an HA VMM management server, which resulted in an unavailable service if a VM stopped responding or if the host server restarted, failed, or needed to be shut down for maintenance or patching.

VMM now allows you to deploy the VMM server on a failover cluster resulting in HA services. You can then plan the failover for maintenance purposes, for example, and it will automatically, in case of a failure, fail over to a running node to ensure that the VMM service remains online.

Keep in mind that the VMM library needs to be made accessible by all cluster nodes as the VMM server requires access to the library irrespective of which cluster node it is running on. This can be achieved by placing the VMM library files on a clustered file server. For more information, see: https://docs.microsoft.com/en-us/previous-versions/windows/it-pro/windows-server-2008-R2-and-2008/cc731844(v=ws.10).

Installing a highly available VMM management server

This recipe will provide the steps to install a highly available VMM management server.

The HA VMM installation is very similar to the standalone installation, and it is integrated into the usual standalone installation.

To install VMM in HA, you just need to start the installation of VMM management in one of the nodes of the cluster and then select **Install**.

Important VMM 2016 highly available notes:

- It is a fault tolerant service feature, but it does not mean that it will increase the scale or performance.
- Of a maximum of 16 nodes, only one VMM management node will be active at any time.
- Connecting to a node name is not allowed. You will have to type the HA VMM service cluster name in the VMM console login when prompted for a VMM server name and port number.
- To run a VMM planned failover, say for server patching, use the failover cluster UI and not the VMM console.

Designing and planning the failover cluster is the first thing to do before beginning the installation of a highly available VMM management server. You can install a VMM management server on a physical cluster or on a guest cluster.

The best practice—and my recommendation—for production hosting and data center operations would be to install the VMM management server on a cluster with dedicated physical servers as you will be running critical solutions.

The following figures show the architecture design for a guest cluster, using a Shared VHDX, VHD Set, and virtual fiber channel:

- **Shared VHDX/VHD Set**: It is a configuration using the shared VHDX or VHD Set stored on a shared storage S2D/iSCSI/FC/File server storage:

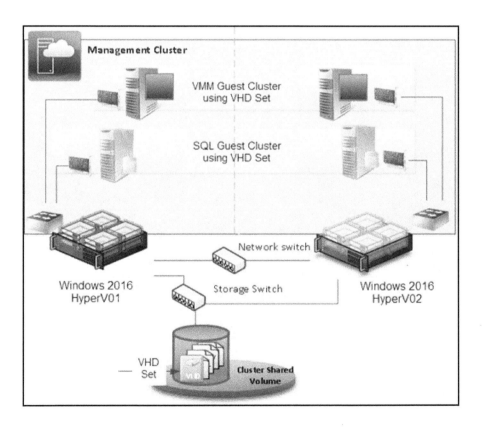

Windows Server 2016 replaces Shared VHDX with **VHD Sets** (**VHDS**). VHDS have the same logic and architecture as Shared VHDX and plus support host-level backup, online resizing, Hyper-V Replica, and application-consistent checkpoints. VHDS are only supported for guest clusters running on Windows Server 2016. However, you can easily migrate existing shared VHDX to new VHD sets: upgrade OS on VM with shared VHDX, turn off the VM with shared VHDX, remove the shared VHDX from the VM (`Remove-VMHardDiskDrive shared.vhdx`), start the conversion of shared VHDX to VHD set. (`Convert-VHD shared.vhdx new.vhds`), attach VHDS to the VM (`Add-VMHardDiskDrive new.vhds`), and then turn on the VM.

- **Virtual fiber channel**: If your storage is fiber channel and does support NPIV, you can use it to create a guest cluster by using virtual fiber channel connectivity directly with the storage:

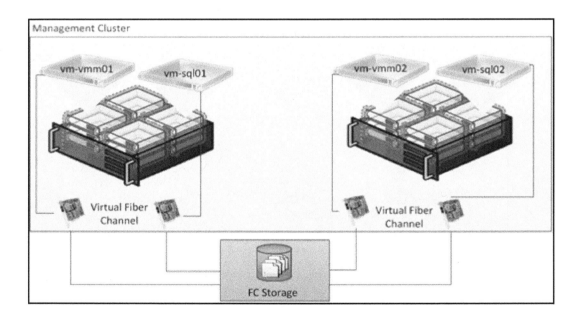

- **No shared storage:** Actually, HA VMM does not require shared storage between VMM cluster nodes. The only thing that you need to plan carefully is a witness. The failover cluster can be deployed with an external disk (as shown in the preceding examples) or file share witness, which must be available for each cluster node and it's needed as a source of extra vote. Witness is highly recommended for clusters regardless of the number nodes in it (starting from WS 2012 R2, dynamic quorum automatically decides when to use witness). In Windows Server 2016, a new witness type has been introduced—**Cloud Witness**. It uses Azure storage accounts for keeping quorum data and is also supported by guest clusters. In the following image, Cloud Witness is used for AlwaysOn AG and VMM cluster:

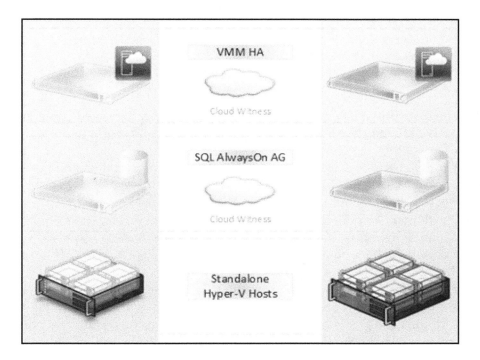

 For more information about Cloud Witness and other new failover cluster features in Windows Server 2016, see: `https://rlevchenko.com/2017/01/26/whats-new-in-failover-clustering-in-windows-server-2016/`

Getting ready

Get your computer ready by running Windows Update and restarting if requested before continuing with the VMM installation.

 I would recommend manually checking that you have the latest Windows Server 2016 build version. See the Windows 10 and Windows Server 2016 update history available at: https://support.microsoft.com/en-us/help/4000825.

Ensure that the server meets the minimum system requirements:

- The failover cluster is created and configured.

 For information on how to create a failover cluster, see: http://technet.microsoft.com/en-us/library/dn505754.aspx.

- The **distributed key management (DKM)** container is created earlier on the **Active Directory (AD)** or using an installation account with permission on the AD container.
- The SQL Server is deployed and ready. The recommendation and best practice is to have a clustered SQL Server. See the *Deploying a Microsoft SQL Server for VMM implementation* recipe in Chapter 3, *Installing SCVMM 2016*.
- The domain account that will be used by the VMM service (for example, rllab\vmm-svc) is created. *Do not log in with this account*. The VMM service account will be used in the VMMDKM wizard page. For HA VMM installations, the local system account is disabled.
- The installation account (for example, rllab\vmm-admin) is a member of the local Administrators group on the computer that you are installing VMM on. Add the RLLAB\vmm-svc account as well, which is the account we previously created to be the SCVMM service account.

- You have closed any open applications and there is no pending restart on the server.
- The computer is a member of the domain. In our case, we are using `rllab.com` as the domain.
- Verify that your machines are ready for VMM 2016 and you installed all the VMM prerequisites. See the *Specifying the correct system requirements for a real-world scenario* recipe in `Chapter 1`, *VMM 2016 Architecture*.

If setup is not completed successfully, check the log files for details. The log files are present in the `%SYSTEMDRIVE%\ProgramData\VMMLogs` folder. Note that the `ProgramData` folder is a hidden folder.

How to do it...

Carry out the following steps to install an HA VMM management server:

1. Log in as `rllab\vmm-admin` or with an account that has administrator rights.
2. Browse to the VMM installation media, right-click on `setup`, and select **Run as administrator**.
3. On the main **Setup** page, click on **Install** and the install process will detect whether it is running on a cluster node and will then ask if you want to make it highly available.
4. Click on **Yes** to start the HA VMM installation.

If you click on **No**, VMM will be installed as a standalone VMM server.

5. Click to select VMM management server and click on **Next**:

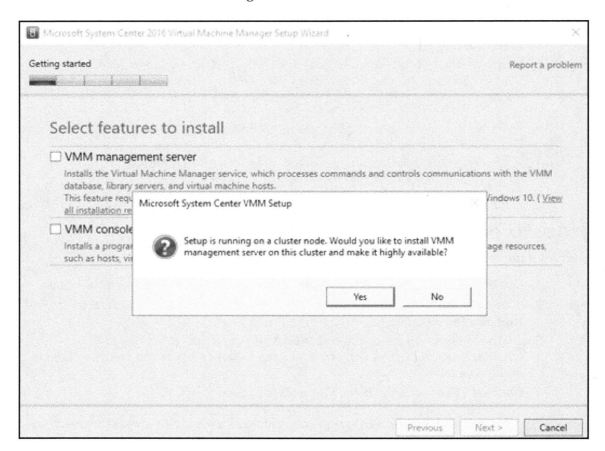

 VMM console is automatically selected when you select a VMM
management server.

6. On the **Product registration information** page, type the VMM key and click on **Next**.

7. On the **Please read this license agreement** page, accept the license and click on **Next**.

8. On the **Diagnostic and Usage Data** page, read the notice, and then click on **Next**.

9. On the **Microsoft Update** page, select **On (recommended)** to use Microsoft Update and click on **Next**.

10. On the **Installation location** page, provide the path for the installation and then click on **Next**.

It is recommended that you keep the OS partition (C:) only for the operation system and allot another drive for the VMM program files.

11. The server will now be scanned to check whether the requirements are met. A page will be displayed showing which requirement has not been met and how to resolve the issue.

12. As we have planned our installation and have had all prerequisites already installed, the **Database configuration** page will be displayed.

As per best practice, and for a full high availability deployment of VMM, it is recommended that you use a clustered SQL Server. See the *Install SQL failover cluster using the configuration file* and *configure SQL Server with AlwaysOn AGs* recipes in Chapter 3, *Installing VMM 2016*.

13. On the **Database configuration** page, specify the name of the server that is running SQL Server. In our case, it is `rlsqlagl01` (**SQL AlwaysOn listener**):

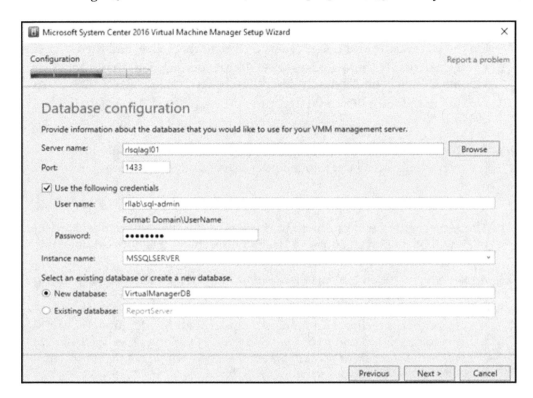

 You cannot have SQL Server on the same machine that will run the highly available VMM management server. SQL Server needs to be available from both cluster nodes.

14. You don't need to specify the port used for SQL communication unless all of the following conditions are true for SQL:

- The SQL Server is running on another server (recommended)
- The SQL Server browser service is not started
- You are not using the default port `1433`

15. In the **Instance name** field, provide the SQL Server instance or select the default, **MSSQLSERVER**.

If the **Instance name** field does not show the SQL instances to select, check whether **SQL Browser service** is running on the SQL Server and the inbound firewall rules on the SQL server are running as well.

16. Specify whether to create a new database or to use an existing database and click on **Next**.

17. In the **Cluster Configuration** page, specify the cluster name, and if required, the network configuration (if the IP is provided by DHCP servers, for example, the network configuration will not be requested):

The cluster name is an AD object name. Make sure the cluster name is a unique name.

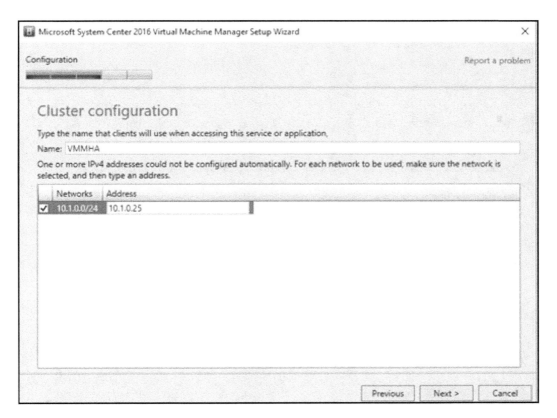

18. On the **Configure service account and distributed key management** page, provide the domain account for the VMM service.

Create a dedicated domain account for VMM as a service account (for example, RLAB\vmm-svc). It is important to know that you will not be able (as it is not supported) to change the account after the VMM installation is completed. See the *Creating service accounts* recipe in Chapter 3, *Installing VMM 2016*.

19. In the **Distributed Key Management** section, define the DKM container that will store your keys in AD as it is required by the HA VMM deployment:

You are required to enter it as the distinguished name of the DKM container (for example, CN=VMMDKM, DC=rllab, DC=com).

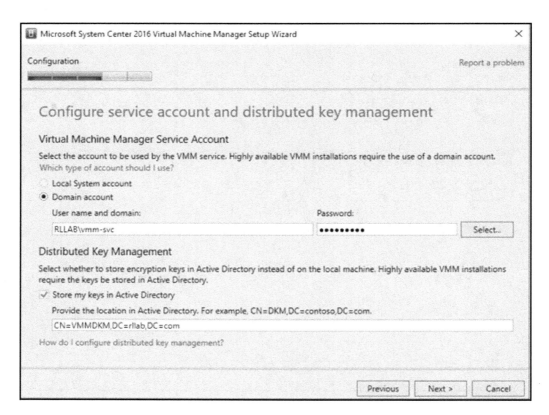

20. On the **Port configuration** page, leave the default port numbers or provide a unique value for each feature, as seen in the following screenshot, and then click on **Next**.

 Document and plan the ports before choosing them as you cannot change the ports without reinstalling VMM.

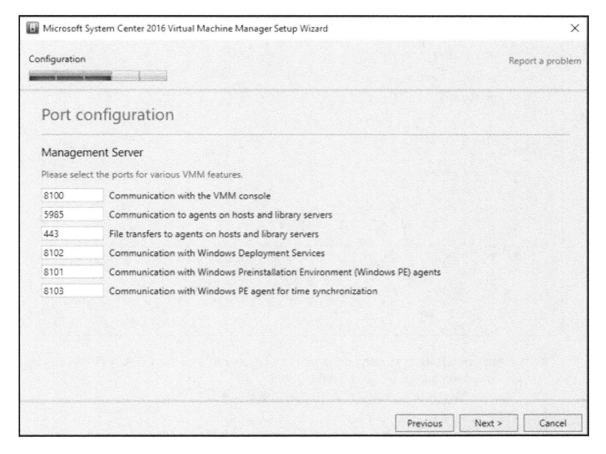

21. On the **Library configuration** page, click on **Next**:

The setup does not create a default library share on an HA VMM installation, as you cannot have a VMM library running on the VMM management cluster.

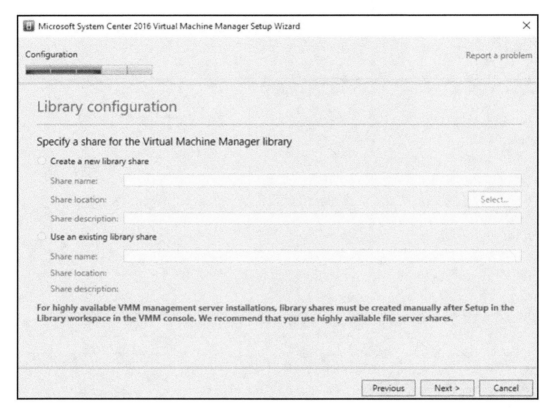

22. On the **Installation summary** page, review your selections. Click on **Previous** if you want to change any selections.
23. Click on **Install** to start the installation and the installation progress will be displayed.
24. On the **Setup completed successfully** page, click on **Close**.

When the installation finishes successfully, you can install VMM in the other cluster nodes. Also, don't forget to update VMM management server/console

How it works...

The installation of VMM management server is straightforward with enhancements added that simplify the installation process. VMM 2016 version will install some of the prerequisites for you, if that is necessary. When you click on **Install** on the main **Setup** page, the setup process will prompt you to install the missing prerequisites.

As we are installing VMM management server on a cluster node, you will be prompted to make the VMM management server highly available. Click on **Yes** to install an HA VMM, or **No** to install it as a standalone VMM running on a cluster.

If the user account running the VMM setup (in our case, RLLAB\vmm-admin) has the right to create the VMMDKM container in AD DS, you don't need to create it previously as the VMM setup checks and creates the VMMDKM container. The DKM allows users and processes running on diverse servers to share data securely. On an HA VMM, if a VMM management service fails over to another node on the cluster, the active node will access the VMM database using the encryption keys stored in the DKM container to decrypt the data that is being held, securely and encrypted, in the VMM database.

If your account does not have the *CREATE* permissions on the SQL database server, or you are not a database administrator, you can ask them to previously create the VMM database. Alternatively, you can provide an account with permissions to create a database on the SQL Server during the install process by selecting the **Use the following credentials** checkbox and then providing the username and password.

When performing an HA VMM installation, although the **Library Configuration** page does appear, click on **Next** as it will not create the default VMM library and you will be required to create an HA library after the installation is complete by using the VMM console.

There's more...

When carrying out a planned failover for VMM, make sure you understand the following points:

- Any connection from the VMM console to the VMM management server will be lost in a failover operation but will reconnect after the failover, as the connection is made through the VMM cluster service name and not to a particular node. Keep that in mind and communicate it to the VMM admin/users beforehand.
- Active running jobs will fail in a failover operation. You will need to restart it manually if it does support restart, otherwise you will need to start the job/task from the beginning.

Finally, the following are some best practices for highly available VMM management server deployment:

- Use a SQL Server cluster for database high availability. AlwaysOn AGs require an additional configuration. See the recipe *Configure the VMM database with AlwaysOn AGs* following this section.
- Give preference, if deploying a highly available production environment, to have the SQL Server cluster on a distinct cluster other than the VMM cluster.
- Use a file server to host the library shares.

Configure the VMM database with AlwaysOn AGs

We used SQL Server with configured AlwaysOn AGs during the highly available VMM deployment. AlwaysOn AG synchronizes databases between SQL Server nodes. Other settings such as SQL logins or user mappings are not synchronized. In addition, VMM installation wizard configures only one SQL Server without adding the VMM database to the availability group. As a result, VMM database is not highly available and the secondary nodes in SQL cluster do not have logins for the VMM service account in the SQL login as shown in the following screenshot. Therefore, you will need to perform the following procedure to complete the configuration of VMM with AlwaysOn AGs:

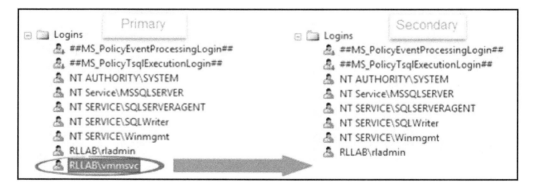

1. Open **SQL Server Management Studio** and connect to the SQL Server on which the VMM database is stored (in our case, w2k16-sql01).
2. Right-click on the VMM database and select **Properties.**
3. Click on the **Options** tab and change the **Recovery Model** from **Simple** to **Full** as shown in the following screenshot:

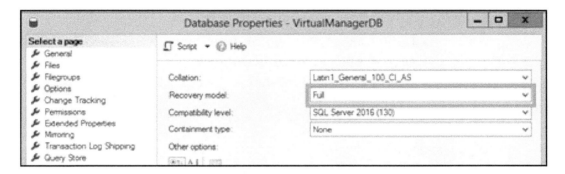

4. Take full backup of the VMM database. Right click on this database and select **Tasks | Back Up...** as shown in the following screenshot:

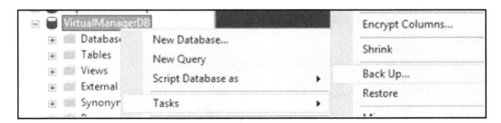

5. In the **Back Up** dialogue box, add destination folder for backup files if needed (for example, C:\VMMDB_Backup) and verify that backup type is selected to **Full.** Click **OK** to start backup job.

6. Now it's time to add VMM database to the availability group. For this, right-click on the availability group and click on **Add Database...** ,then select the **VirtualManagerDB** database and a **Full** data synchronization on the next page to complete the wizard.

7. Connect to the secondary SQL Server node and expand **Security**, then right click on **Logins** and select **New Login...** to create the login for VMM service account. Use the following settings:

   - Login Name: VMM service account (RLLAB\vmm-svc, in our case)
   - User Mapping: VirtualManagerDB
   - Database role membership: db_owner

8. To check that account is configured properly, initiate a failover from the primary node to the secondary node on which we just added the new SQL login. Then, verify that you can successfully restart the scvmmservice (Restart-Service scvmmservice).

9. Repeat the steps 7 and 8 for every secondary SQL server node in cluster.

10. Go to the next recipe to install VMM on additional cluster nodes.

See also

For more information, see the following references:

- *Step-By-Step: Scale-out file shares and continuously available file service*: https://blogs.technet.microsoft.com/canitpro/2013/12/10/step-by-step-scale-out-file-shares-and-continuously-available-file-services/.
- *Install SQL Server with SMB FileShare as a Storage Option*: https://docs.microsoft.com/en-us/sql/database-engine/install-windows/install-sql-server-with-smb-fileshare-as-a-storage-option
- *The Configure SQL Server with AlwaysOn AGs* recipe in Chapter 3, *Installing VMM 2016*.
- The *Configuring distributed key management in VMM* recipe in Chapter 3, *Installing VMM 2016*.
- *What's New in Failover Clustering*: https://rlevchenko.com/2017/01/26/whats-new-in-failover-clustering-in-windows-server-2016/

Installing a VMM management server on an additional node of a cluster

Now that we have our first node running, we are going to deploy the second node of the VMM cluster. This recipe will guide you through adding the additional VMM nodes to an existing VMM management cluster.

You can install VMM management servers on up to 16 nodes on a cluster, but keep in mind that *only one* VMM management service will be active at a time.

The VMM console, in case of a failover, will reconnect automatically to the VMM management server as you are using the cluster service name to connect.

Getting ready

Before we start the installation of an additional node for VMM 2016, close any connections (VMM console and PowerShell) to the primary VMM management node. Also, make sure there are no pending restarts on the current and primary VMM management node.

How to do it...

Carry out the following steps in order to add another VMM node to the VMM cluster:

1. On an additional node of your cluster, log in as `rllab\vmm-admin` or with administrator rights.
2. Browse to the VMM installation media, right-click on `setup`, and select **Run as administrator**.

3. On the main **Setup** page, click on **Install**, and on the **Select features to install** page, select **VMM management server**, as shown in the following screenshot:

The VMM console option will be selected and installed when you select **VMM management server**.

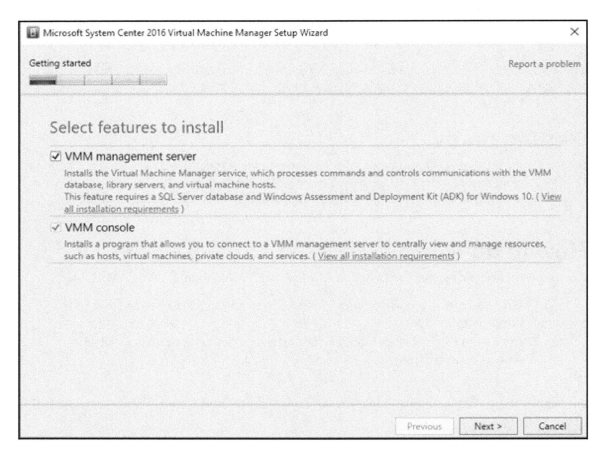

4. Click on **Yes** when the **Highly available VMM already installed** window pops up (as shown in the following screenshot) to proceed with the installation, and then click on **Next**:

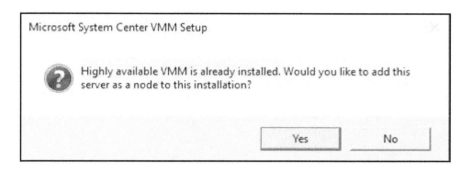

5. On the **Product registration information** page, type the VMM key and click on **Next**.

6. On the **Please read this license agreement** page, accept the license and click on **Next**.

7. On the **Diagnostic and Usage Data** page, read the notice, and then click on **Next**.

8. On the **Microsoft Update** page, select **On (recommended)** to use Microsoft Update and click on **Next**.

9. On the **Installation location** page, provide the path for the installation and then click on **Next**.

 It is recommended that you keep the OS partition (c:) only for the operating system and to have another drive for the VMM program files.

10. The server will now be scanned to check if the requirements are met and a page will be displayed showing which requirement has not been met and how to resolve the issue.

11. In the **Database configuration** page, click on **Next**.

 Because we are installing an additional VMM management server on a cluster node and they both share the same SQL database, this page is only informational.

12. On the **Configure service account and distributed key management** page, provide the password for **Virtual Machine Manager Service**.

13. On the **Port configuration** page, click on **Next**.

14. On the **Library configuration** page, we click on **Next**, as we cannot have a VMM library running on the VMM management cluster:

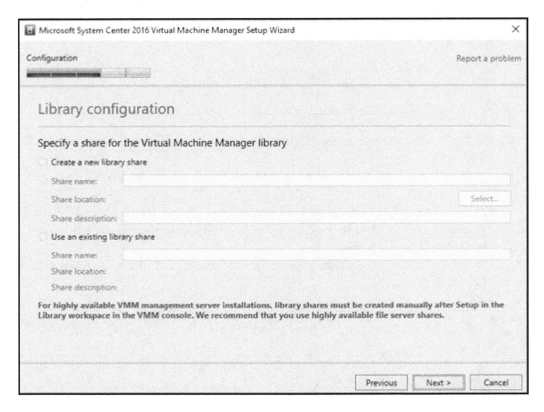

15. On the **Installation summary** page, review your selections. Click on **Previous** if you want to change any selections.
16. Click on **Install** to start the installation, and an installation progress bar will be displayed.
17. On the **Setup completed successfully** page, click on **Close**.

How it works...

With VMM 2016, you can deploy the management server on a cluster.

The installation of an additional node of VMM management server on a cluster is straightforward, with enhancements added that simplify the installation process.

To start, make sure you have the required hardware and software. System Center 2016 only supports Windows 2016 as deployment OS. Check Chapter 1, *VMM 2016 Architecture*, for more information about the hardware and software required for VMM.

VMM 2016 version will install some of the prerequisites for you, if that is necessary. When you click on **Install** in the main **Setup** page, the setup process will prompt you to install the missing prerequisites.

The setup process will detect that you are running on a cluster, and then you will be prompted to choose whether you want to add the installation server to the existing highly available VMM management server or not. Click on **Yes** to confirm the additional node.

On the database page, because you have already informed the SQL Server of whether you want to add the installation server or not during the first VMM node deployment, you will not be prompted to inform it again and the page will be a read-only page.

As for the VMM library, you cannot have a VMM library running on the VMM management cluster. The page will be only for informational purposes.

See also

For more information, see the following references:

- The *Planning for high availability* recipe in Chapter 1, *VMM 2016 Architecture*
- The *Specifying the correct system requirements for a real-world scenario* recipe in Chapter 1, *VMM 2016 Architecture*

Connecting to a highly available VMM management server by using the VMM console

The VMM console is the GUI interface of the VMM management server. You will be using it to manage the cloud, fabric, storage, and resources, for example.

You can use this recipe to configure the VMM console to connect to a highly available VMM management server.

Getting ready

Best practice recommends installing the VMM console on a machine other than the clustered VMM servers. It is recommended that you install it on the management desktop, and from there, connect to the HA VMM cluster as this will prevent a connection loss in case of failure in one of the VMM management nodes.

 Review the *Installing the VMM console* recipe in Chapter 3, *Installing VMM 2016*, for information about installing the VMM console and Chapter 1, *VMM 2016 Architecture*, for system prerequisites.

The VMM console will enable you to manage VMM remotely from your desktop without needing to use RDP into the VMM server.

How to do it...

Carry out the following steps to connect to an HA VMM management server:

1. On a computer on which the VMM console is installed, start the **Virtual Machine Manager** console.
2. On the login screen, in the **Server name** box (as shown in the following screenshot), type the VMM cluster service name, followed by a colon and the port (for example, vmmha:8100):

The default port for VMM console connection is 8100.

3. To connect, click on **Specify credentials** and then type the user's credentials (for example, type the username rlab\vmm-admin) or select **Use current Microsoft Windows session identity**.

You will need to specify the user credentials on a multitenant environment or if the user account is not on the same domain as the VMM management server.

4. Click on **Connect**.

5. If the account has multiple user roles (for example, Tenant Administrator or Self-Service User), you will be prompted to select the user role with which to log in. In this case, select the role, **Tenant**, and click on **OK**:

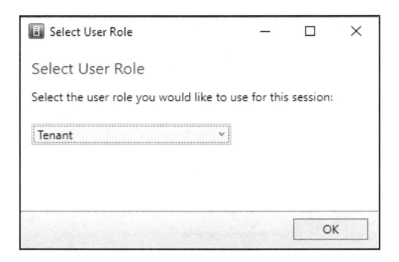

How it works...

After installing the VMM on a cluster, to manage it using the GUI you will need to use the VMM console to connect to the VMM management server.

It is preferable to install the VMM console on the administrator desktop and then follow this recipe to connect to the HA VMM management service by providing the VMM cluster service name (mentioned at the installation of the first VMM cluster node on the **Cluster configuration** page). *Do not type a particular VMM computer server name.*

The VMM console will reconnect automatically to the HA VMM service by using the VMM cluster service name.

See also

For more information, see the following reference:

- *Installing the VMM console* recipe in Chapter 3, *Installing VMM 2016*

Deploying a highly available library server on a file server cluster

Following the deployment of a VMM management server in a cluster and knowing that VMM 2016, when installed in a high availability mode, does not automatically create the VMM library, we now need to deploy the VMM library. Since we are talking about a highly available deployment, the VMM library will have to be HA as well.

In this recipe, we will go through a deployment of a file server cluster to be used as the VMM library. You can use an existing file server cluster as the library as long as it meets the system requirements for SC 2016.

VMM 2016 includes support for designating network file shares on Windows 2012 R2/2016 servers as the storage location for the VMM library.

Getting ready

As a start, make sure your hardware meets the VMM library requirements, as discussed in Chapter 1, *VMM 2016 Architecture*, plus note the following points:

- The hardware must meet the qualifications for Windows Server 2012 R2/2016.
- The storage should be attached to all nodes in the cluster if you are using shared storage.
- The device controllers or appropriate adapters for the storage must be one of these types: **iSCSI**, **Fibre Channel (FC)**, **Fibre Channel over Ethernet (FCoE)**, **Serial Attached SCSI (SAS)**
- **Storage Spaces Direct (S2D)** also can be used for a file server cluster based only on Windows Server 2016 Datacenter. S2D is not available in W2012R2.
- The cluster configuration (servers, network, and storage) should pass all of the cluster validation tests.
- VMM does not support a clustered file share for the VMM library running on the VMM cluster. You need to deploy the cluster file share on another cluster.

- VMM does not support **scale-out file server** (**SOFS**) as library server. Standalone or clustered file servers (recommended) are required. To leverage SOFS storage: right-click on **Library Server** and select **Add Library Shares** and then define unmanaged file share that hosted on SOFS using **Add Unmanaged Share...** button:

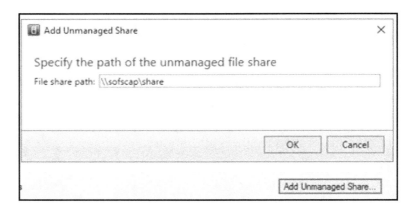

The following figure is a sample design scenario for a highly available VMM library over SMB 3.0 file server deployment:

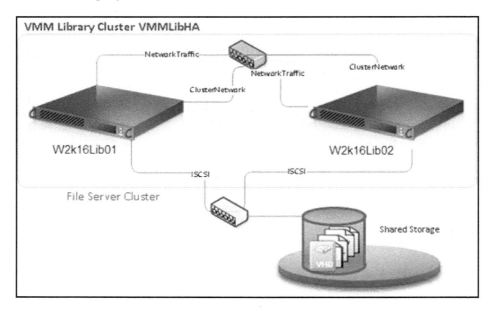

How to do it...

Let's start by setting the file server cluster. Carry out the following steps in order to deploy the HA VMM library.

 For this recipe, I am using two dedicated physical servers for the file server cluster. However, you can set up a Hyper-V guest cluster as well.

First, we will have a look at how to install, validate, and configure the failover clustering feature by using PowerShell:

1. Log in on the first cluster node.
2. Open the Windows PowerShell command prompt with administrator rights and type the following command:

```
Install-WindowsFeature File-Services,Failover-Clustering -
IncludeManagementTools
```

3. Validate and create the cluster by using PowerShell:

```
Test-Cluster -Node w2k16lib01, w2k16lib02
New-Cluster -Name vmmLibHA -Node w2k16lib01, w2k16lib02
```

 w2k16lib01 and w2k16lib02 are the physical server names, and vmmLibHA is the cluster name and DHCP is used.

4. Configure the cluster networks in such a way as to use the ClusterNetwork network and to exclude the NetworkTraffic one, as shown in the following configuration:

```
(Get-ClusterNetwork | ? Address -like 10.16.1.*).Name =
"ClusterNetwork"
(Get-ClusterNetwork | ? Name -notlike Internal*).Name =
"NetworkTraffic"
(Get-ClusterNetwork ClusterNetwork).Role = 3
(Get-ClusterNetwork NetworkTraffic).Role = 1
# Confirm the configuration was successful
Get-ClusterNetwork | Select *
```

`NetworkTraffic` and `ClusterNetwork` are the network names which were previously renamed. You can use any denomination, but remember, for consistency, to rename the cluster networks to match the network names used previously.

5. You can add storage by using the following PowerShell command:

```
Add-ClusterSharedVolume
```

6. This command can be used in the following manner:

```
Get-ClusterResource | ? OwnerGroup -like Available* |
Add-ClusterSharedVolume
```

7. The following screenshot is an example of adding storage using a PowerShell command:

```
                                        Administrator: Windows PowerShell
PS C:\Windows> Get-ClusterResource "disk" | Add-ClusterSharedVolume

Name                                    State
----                                    -----
Cluster Disk 2                          Online
Cluster Disk 3                          Online
```

 I normally rename cluster disks before adding them to CSV. The following command shows how to rename a cluster disk:

```
(Get-ClusterResource | where {$_.Name -eq "Cluster Disk
2"}).Name) = "Data"
```

8. You can also use the GUI to perform these tasks. For more information, refer to http://technet.microsoft.com/en-us/library/hh831478.aspx.

Next, we will need to configure the file server. You will carry out the following steps after installing and configuring the failover cluster:

1. In the **Failover Cluster Management** page, select the main node on the tree, and in the **Actions** menu on the right pane, click on **Configure Role**.
2. When the **High Availability Wizard** starts, click on **Next** to continue.

3. In the **Select Role** page, select **File Server** and click on **Next**.
4. In the **File Server Type** page, select **File Server for General Use**.
5. In the **Client Access Point** page, type the name of the clustered file server (for example, VMMLibFS) and the IP address (for example, 10.1.2.100) if needed and click on **Next**.

6. In the **Select Storage** page, select the disks to be assigned to this clustered file server and click on **Next**.
7. On the **Confirmation** page, click on **Next**.
8. On the **Summary** page, click on **Finish**.

Next, we will create a file share on the cluster shared volume by carrying out the following steps:

1. In the **Failover Cluster Management** window, click on the cluster, expand it, and click on **Roles**.
2. Select the file server, right-click on it, and then click on **Add File Share**.
3. On the **Select the profile** page, select **SMB Share I Applications** and click on **Next**.
4. On the **Share location** page, click on the volume to create the CSV file and click on **Next**.
5. On the **Share name** page, type the share name (for example, VMMLibShare) and click on **Next**.
6. On the **Configure share settings** page, select **Enable continuous availability** and click on **Next**.

 For more info on Windows Server 2016, see Scale-Out File Server for Application Data Overview: http://technet.microsoft.com/en-us/library/hh831349.aspx

7. On the **Specify permissions to control access** page, click on **Customize permissions** to grant full control on the share and the security filesystem to the **SYSTEM** account, **Administrators** and all **VMM administrators**.
8. Click on **Next**.
9. On the **Confirm selections** page, click on **Create** and then click on **Close**.

Next, we will see how to add a VMM library share by performing the following steps:

1. Start the **VMM console**.
2. On the login screen, in the **Server name** box, type the VMM cluster service name followed by a colon and the port (for example, vmmha:8100).
3. In the bottom-left pane, click on the **Library** workspace.

4. Click on the **Home** tab, and then click on the **Add Library Server** option in the ribbon, as shown in the following screenshot:

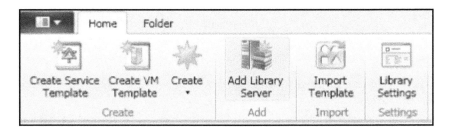

5. In the **Add Library Server** wizard, type a domain account that has administrative rights on the library servers (for example, RLLAB\vmm-admin) and click on **Next**.

 As discussed in Chapter 3, *Installing VMM 2016*, as best practice, it is recommended that you use a Run As account, which you can create by clicking on **Browse**. For more information, see the *Creating Run As account credentials in VMM* recipe.

6. On the **Select Library Servers** page, type the library server domain name (for example, RLLAB.COM).
7. In the **Computer name** box, type the name of the HA file server cluster (for example, vmmLibHA) or click on **Search** to find it in AD.
8. Click on **Add** and then click on **Next**.
9. In the **Add Library Shares** page, select the library shares from the file server cluster to add to VMM (for example, **VMMLibShare**).
10. If you select **Add Default Resources**, the default library resources will be added to the share that is used for services. In addition, it will add the ApplicationFrameworks folder to the library share.
11. We click on **Next** and then, in the **Summary** page, click on **Add Library Servers** to add the selected servers and shares.

How it works...

This recipe guided us through the steps of how to set up a Windows 2016 file server cluster and how to add a VMM library server to VMM management.

VMM does not offer replication for physical files stored in the VMM library or metadata for objects stored in the VMM database. As a recommendation, you should use file server cluster for high availability.

In a clustered file server, when you take the associated file server resource offline, all shared folders in that resource go offline. This means that all shared folders will be affected.

You can set up the file server cluster on a physical server or on a Windows 2016 cluster, by using Hyper-V guest cluster options.

When adding a library server to VMM management, VMM automatically installs the agent on the new library server.

The minimum required permission to the local system (**SYSTEM**) is full control permissions for share and NTFS filesystem level (this is the default setting).

 Make sure you assign the correct access control permissions and assign full control share and NTFS permissions to the **Administrators** group.

See also

For more information, see the following references:

- The failover clustering overview article (`https://docs.microsoft.com/en-us/windows-server/failover-clustering/failover-clustering-overview`)

Uninstalling a highly available VMM management server

When you have a highly available VMM server, to uninstall the high availability completely you will need to uninstall the VMM management server from each node in the cluster.

Before uninstalling VMM management server, ensure that any connections to VMM management server are closed.

How to do it...

Carry out the following steps to remove an additional node of a VMM:

1. On a VMM highly available server node, in the `Programs and Features` folder (**ControlPanel** | **Programs**), click on **Microsoft System Center 2016 Virtual Machine Manager** and click on **Remove features**.
2. On the **Select features to remove** page, click on the **VMM management server** and click on **Next**.
3. On the **Database options** page, click on **Next**.
4. On the **Summary** page, click on **Uninstall** and then click on **Close**.

How it works...

The preceding steps show you how to remove a VMM server installed as an HA VMM server, in which you need to be a member of the local `Administrators` group, or have equivalent rights on the VMM server node that you are removing.

Beforehand, make sure the node is not currently the owner of the HA VMM service in the **Failover Cluster Manager** (**FCM**), moving it to another node in case it is the owner, and then proceed with the removal. Otherwise, the following warning will be shown:

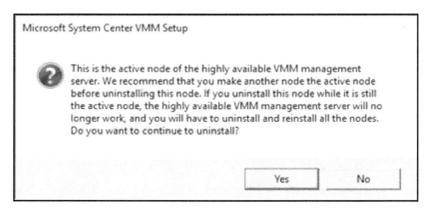

You can also, during the removal steps, select the VMM console to be removed as well.

There's more...

We can uninstall the last node of a highly available VMM management server by using the following steps:

1. On a highly available VMM server node, in the `Programs and Features` folder (**Control Panel | Programs**), click on **Microsoft System Center 2016 Virtual Machine Manager** and click on **Remove features**.

2. In the **Select features to remove** page, click on **VMM management server** and click on **Next**.

3. Click on **Yes** when prompted to uninstall the last node of the highly available VMM management server and click on **Next**.

4. On the **Database options** page, choose whether you want to retain or remove the VMM database.

 By selecting **Retain database**, keep in mind that this database can only be reused for an HA VMM deployment.

5. Click on **Next**.

6. On the **Summary** page, click on **Uninstall** and then click on **Close**.

5
Configuring Fabric Resources in VMM

In this chapter, we will cover:

- Creating Host Groups
- Setting up a VMM library
- Configuring Networks in VMM
- Networking: Configuring Logical Networks
- Networking: Configuring VM Networks, Network Controllers and Gateways
- Networking: Configuring Logical Switches, Port Profiles and Port Classifications
- Integrating and Configuring the Storage
- Creating Physical Computer Profile (Host Profile)
- Provisioning a physical computer as a Hyper-V host: Bare Metal host deployment
- Adding and managing Hyper-V hosts and host clusters
- Deploying a hyper-converged cluster with S2D and Hyper-V

Introduction

This chapter is all about configuring the fabric resources infrastructure that you can use in your private cloud deployment. The following design shows the VMM components infrastructure deployed as VMs on a Hyper-V Server. You can use this as an example for your lab or small deployment.

Note that, on this design sample, there is no guest-cluster implementation; VMM are neither implemented as HA, nor as SQL:

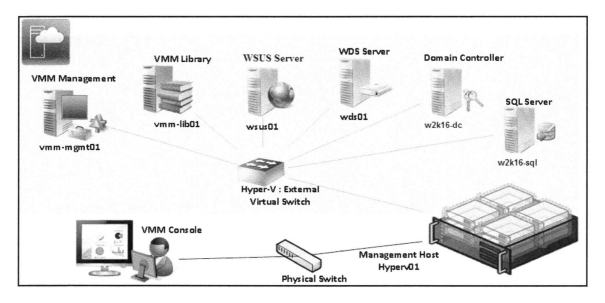

VMM 2016 fabric resources are powerful when configuring resources for private clouds, hosts, VMs, and services. This chapter will give you the necessary guidance to deploy physical servers as Hyper-V hosts and to configure and manage networking, storage, and VMM library resources. These recipes will empower you to get more out of this feature and help you understand the steps required to create the necessary infrastructure for your private cloud deployment.

The fabric resources are the infrastructure needed in order to manage the private cloud, hosts, VMs, or services. The following recipes will guide you when creating those resources.

The following figure illustrates the fabric resources that can be managed by VMM:

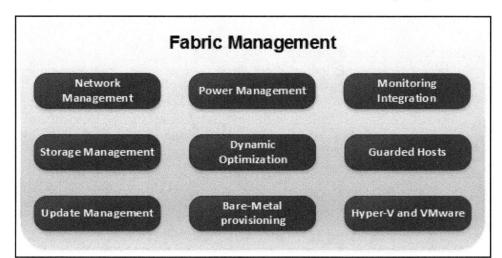

Creating host groups

Based on site location or resource allocation, host groups are designed to group virtual machine hosts.

Getting ready

When you have a host group structure, the following settings and resources will be allocated at the host group level:

- Placement rules
- Host reserve settings (CPU, memory, disk I/O, disk space, and network I/O)
- Dynamic optimization and power optimization settings
- Network resources
- Storage capacity allocation
- PRO configuration
- Custom properties

A host group will also allow you to:

- Assign the groups to delegated administrators and to the read-only administrators roles, and then members of these user roles will be able to view and/or assign fabric resources
- Create a private cloud, assign host groups to it, and then allocate resources from the assigned host groups to that private cloud

 For this recipe, we will create a host group based on site location and system capabilities. You should create it based on your solution design.

How to do it...

Carry out the following steps:

1. Connect to the VMM 2016 console by using the VMM admin account previously created (`rllab\vmm-admin`), and then on the bottom-left pane, click on **Fabric** to open the **fabric** workspace.
2. In the left-hand pane called **Fabric**, expand **Servers**, right-click on **All Hosts**, and then click on **Create Host Group**.
3. Type the name for the host group, for example, `Moscow`.

The following steps will help you create a child host group:

1. In the **Fabric** pane, expand the parent host group for which you want to create the child, right-click on it, and then click on **Create Host Group**.
2. Type the name for the host group, for example, `Hyper-V`.
3. Repeat steps 1 and 2 to create your host group structure.

How it works...

By default, child host groups inherit settings from the parent host group, but it is possible to override those settings in the host properties.

Optionally, you can create a host group by clicking on **All Hosts**, and then on the **Folder** tab, by clicking on **Create Host Group**. VMM will create a new host group initially named **New host group**, with the host group name highlighted. Right-click on that, click on **Rename**, and type in the name you want for the host group.

For guidance, you can create the host group structure based on location, hardware capabilities, applications, server roles, type of hypervisors, business unit, or delegation model.

There's more...

With the host group created, you can then configure its properties.

Moving a host group to another location

Carry out the following steps to change the host group location:

1. In the VMM 2016 console, in the **Fabric** workspace, on the left, expand **Servers** and then expand **All Hosts**.
2. Carry out one of the following actions:
    - Drag and drop the host group to its new location in the tree
    - Click to select the host group and then:
        - Click on the **Folder** tab
        - Click on **Move** in the top ribbon
        - Click to select the target parent host group
        - Click on **OK**

Configuring host group properties

Carry out the following steps to set up the host group properties:

1. In the VMM 2016 console, in the **Fabric** pane, expand **Servers**, expand **All Hosts**, and then click on the host group to configure.
2. In the **Folder** tab, click on **Properties**, on the ribbon, as shown in the following screenshot:

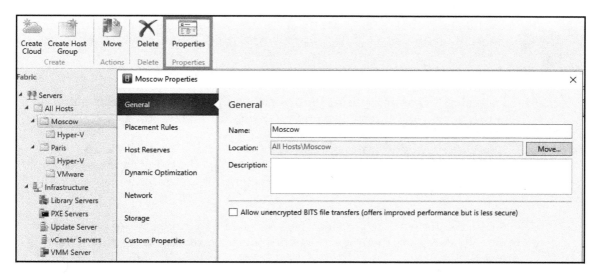

3. Click on the **General** tab and provide the host group name. Optionally, type a description and click on **Allow unencrypted file transfers**; this will improve the transfer performance, but it will be less secure.

4. Click on the **Host Reserves** tab if you want to configure the reserve values (**CPU**, **Memory**, **Disk I/O**, **Disk space**, and **Network I/O**).

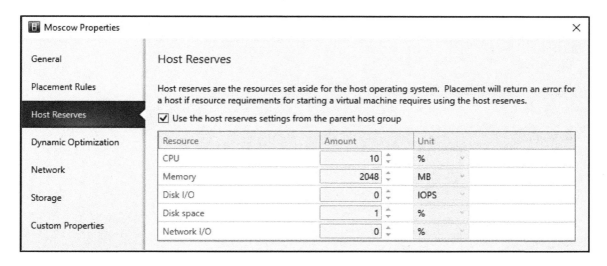

5. Click on the **Placement Rules** tab if you want to specify custom placement rules for this host group.

By default, a host group inherits the placement settings from its parent host group.

6. Click on the **Dynamic Optimization** tab to configure dynamic optimization (aggressiveness and thresholds) and power optimization settings.

As Dynamic optimization provides more functionality, VMM 2016 automatically disables the VM Load Balancing (aka Node Fairness) in-box feature in Windows Server 2016 when Dynamic Optimization is enabled.

7. Click on the **Network** tab to view the associated network resource type and optionally configure the **Inherit network logical resources from parent host groups** setting.
8. Click on the **Storage** tab to view and allocate **storage pools** and **storage units**.
9. Click on **PRO Configuration** (if VMM is integrated with OpsMgr) to configure the host PRO monitor.
10. Click on the **Custom Properties** tab (as shown in the following screenshot) to assign custom properties for **Virtual Machine**, **Virtual Machine Template**, **Host**, **Host Cluster**, **Host Group**, **Service Template**, **Service Instance**, **Computer Tier**, and **Cloud:**

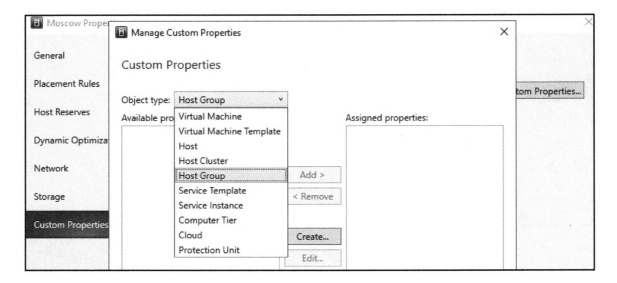

See also

For more information, visit the following references:

- The *How to Allocate Logical Units to a Host Group in VMM* article at
  `http://technet.microsoft.com/en-us/library/gg610686.aspx`
- The *How to Allocate Storage Pools to a Host Group in VMM* article at
  `http://technet.microsoft.com/en-us/library/gg610635.aspx`
- The *Configuring Dynamic Optimization and Power Optimization in VMM* article at
  `http://technet.microsoft.com/en-us/library/gg675109.aspx`

Setting up a VMM library

A default VMM library is configured when you install a VMM management server. However, you can add more VMM libraries later on.

For High Availability, it is recommended that you deploy Highly Available VMM Library. For more information see the *Deploying a HA Library Server with File Server Cluster* recipe in `Chapter 4`, *Installing a Highly Available VMM Server*.

In VMM 2016, the library can store file-based resources, custom resources, templates and profiles, equivalent objects, private cloud libraries, self-service user content, stored virtual machines and services, orphaned resources and update catalogs, and baseline files.

VMM 2016 supports only library servers running on Windows Server 2012 R2 or Windows Server 2016. SOFS is not supported. See the *Deploying an HA Library Server with File Server Cluster* recipe in `Chapter 4`, *Installing a Highly Available VMM Server*.

This recipe will guide you through the process of configuring the VMM library.

Getting ready

The following table shows the configuration that we are going to use in this recipe:

Resource	Name
VMM management server	`vmm-mgmt01.rllab.com`
Library share added during VMM management server installation	`vmm-mgmt01\VMMMLibrary`
Library server and share in Moscow office	`vmm-lib01\VMMMSK-Library`
Second library share in Moscow office	`vmm-lib01\ISO-Library`
Library server and share in Paris office	`vmm-lib02\VMMPAR-Library`

During the VMM setup, you can accept the default `MSSCVMMLibrary` library, provide a new name to be created, or specify an existing share.

 The library server must be on the same domain as VMM, or in a two-way trusted domain.

How to do it...

Carry out the following steps to add a library server:

1. Connect to the VMM 2016 console by using the VMM admin account previously created (`rllab\vmm-admin`) or use an account with VMM administrator rights.
2. On the bottom-left pane, click on **Library** to open the library workspace.
3. Click on the **Home** tab, and then click on the **Add Library Server** button on the ribbon shown in the following screenshot:

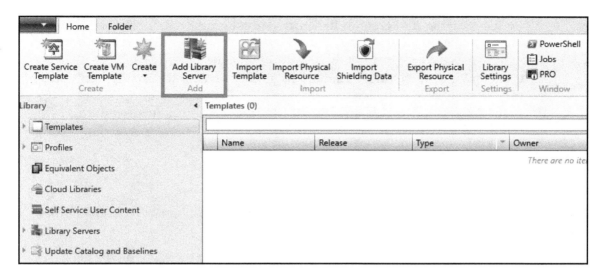

4. When the **Add Library Server** wizard opens, in the **Enter Credentials** page, type a domain account that has administrative rights on the library servers, for example, `RLLAB\vmm-admin`, and then click on **Next**.

You can specify a Run As account. Create one by clicking on **Browse**, or manually type the user credentials in the format *domainusername*.

5. In the **Select Library Servers** page, in the **Domain** box, type the library server domain name, for example, `RLLAB.com`, and then click on **Add**.
6. In the **Computer name** box, type the name of the library server, for example, `vmm-lib01`, or click on **Search** to find the library server in Active Directory.

Although not recommended, if you are sure about the name, you can click on **Skip Active Directory name verification**. By skipping the name verification, you need to manually certify that the computer is a domain member.

7. In the **Add Library Shares** page, select the library shares to add, for example, **VMMMSK-Library**.

8. By selecting the **Add Default Resources** checkbox, the default library resources will be added to the share that is used for services. In addition, it will add the `ApplicationFrameworks` folder to the library share.

9. Click on **Next,** and on the **Summary** page, click on **Add Library Servers** and add the selected servers and shares.

10. In the **Jobs** dialog box, confirm that the library server was successfully added, then close it.

How it works...

The preceding steps guided us through the process of adding a library server and library shares to an existing VMM 2016 installation.

When adding a library server to VMM, it automatically installs the agent on the new library server.

The minimum required permission is the local system account with full control permission in the file share and NTFS file system (the **Security** tab), which is the default setting.

Make sure you assign the correct access control permissions and assign Full Control share and NTFS permissions to the local **Administrators** group.

There's more...

You can also add library shares or file-based resources to a library share.

Adding a library share

Carry out the following steps to add a VMM library share:

1. Connect to the VMM 2016 console by using the VMM admin account previously created (`rllab\vmm-admin`) or use an account with VMM administrator rights.

2. In the library workspace, on the **Library** pane to the left, expand **Library Servers**. Next, select the library server that has a library share to be added.

3. Click on the **Library Server** tab on the ribbon, and then click on **Add Library Shares** (or right-click on the library server and then on **Add Library Shares**).

4. On the **Add Library Shares** page, select the library share and then click on **Next**.

5. On the **Summary** page, confirm the settings and click on **Add Library Shares.**

6. In the **Jobs** dialog box, confirm that the library was successfully added, then close it.

Adding file-based resources to a VMM library share

Carry out one the following steps to add file-based resources to an existing VMM library share and then manually refresh it.

When you add files to a VMM library share, they will not show up until VMM indexes them in the next library refresh.

1. In Windows Explorer, copy the new files to the library share. You can also use **Robocopy** or any other copy method. For more information about using Robocopy, see
http://technet.microsoft.com/en-us/library/cc733145(v=ws.10).aspx.

2. Now, using the VMM console in the library workspace, in the left-hand pane, expand **Library Servers** and then select the library server. Right-click on the library share, click on **Explore**, and start copying the files to the library share.

To manually refresh the VMM library, right-click on the library server or library share and then click on **Refresh**.

3. Click on the **Home** tab, and then click on **Import Physical Resource** or **Export Physical Resource** to import/export file-based resources between library shares.

You can change the library refresh interval by going to the library workspace, in the left-hand pane, under **Library Settings**. The default and the minimum value is one hour.

Creating or modifying equivalent objects in the VMM library

You can mark (create) a similar file type library object in different sites as an equivalent object. This will enable VMM to use any instance of the object when deploying it.

If you have a VHD file that is stored in a library share, for example, in Moscow as well in Paris, and if you mark it as an equivalent object, when you create a new VM template and then specify that VHD for the template, VMM will interpret that as a global object instead of a site-specific object. This allows you to create a single template across multiple locations.

 To mark resources as equivalent, they must be of the same file type (same family name, release value, and namespace).

The following section will guide you through creating and modifying library resources as equivalent objects in VMM.

Marking (creating) objects as equivalent

Carry out the following steps to create an object as equivalent:

1. In the VMM console, in the library workspace and in the **Library** pane to the left, click on **Library Servers** (or if connected using a self-service user, expand **Self Service User Content**, and click on the data path).

2. In the **Physical Library Objects** main pane (or the **Self Service User Objects** pane if connected as a self-service user), click on **Type** on the column header to sort the library resources by type.

3. Next, to select the resources to mark as equivalent, carry out one of the following steps:
   - Select the first resource to mark, press and hold the *Ctrl* key, and then click on the other resources that you want to mark as equivalent
   - Select the first resource to mark, press and hold the *Shift* key, and then click on the last resource

4. Right-click on the objects and then click on **Mark Equivalent**, as shown in the following screenshot:

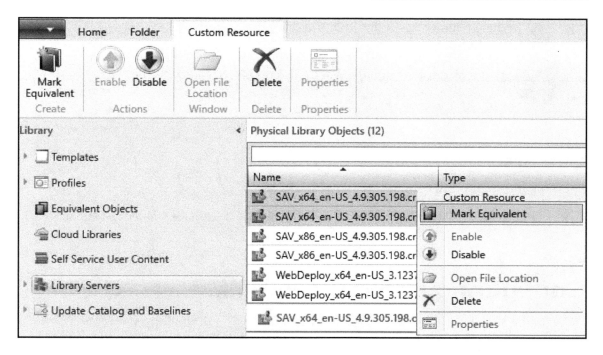

5. In the **Equivalent Library Objects** dialog, type the family name in the **Family** list (for example, W2016STD) and a release value (string) in the **Release** list (for example, 1.0.0).

6. Click on **OK** and verify that the objects show in the **Equivalent Objects** pane. They will be grouped by family name.

 The namespace will automatically be assigned by VMM; a Global namespace if created by an administrator, or a namespace that matches the self-service user name if created by a self-service user.

Modifying equivalent objects

If you need to modify equivalent objects, carry out the following steps:

1. In the library workspace, in the **Library** pane to the left, click on **Equivalent Objects**.

2. In the **Equivalent Objects** main pane, expand the family name and the release value, right-click on the equivalent object, and then click on **Properties**.

3. In the **General** tab, add/modify the values.

 Delete the family name and release values if you need to remove an object from an equivalent objects set. Click on **OK** to confirm.

See also

For more information, see:

- The *How to Import and Export File-Based Resources To and From the Library* article at `http://go.microsoft.com/fwlink/p/?LinkId=227739`

Configuring Networks in VMM

Networking in VMM 2016 includes enhancements such as logical networks, network load balance integration, gateways, and network virtualization, which enable administrators to efficiently provision network resources for a virtualized environment.

How to do it...

First you need to define the model/design you will choose for your network. Planning is the first more important task you need to carry out.

The following should be considered:

- Physical and Virtual Network
- Make sure your hardware (Servers, Switch, Storage) support the network design model
- Will QoS be put in place? Does your physical network device support QoS?
- Is your environment going to support customers/tenants?
- How will you isolate the traffic: physical separation, network virtualization or VLAN?

The diagram below illustrates the steps to configure the network in VMM 2016:

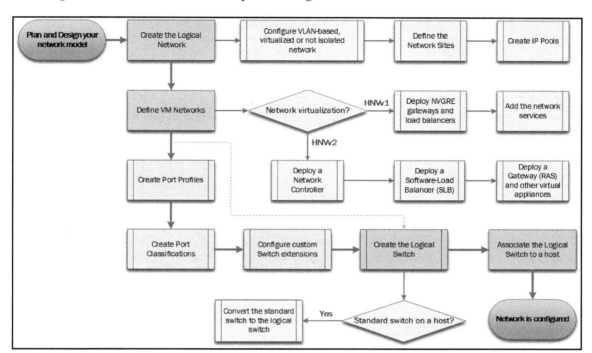

There's more...

I remember the times when we needed to use separate physical network adapters for Hyper-V clusters to organize connectivity for different traffic types such as management, live migration, cluster communication, virtual switch and storage. As a result, these requirements affected the final price of the solution and its efficiency. For example, a cluster network actually does not require a full bandwidth of adapter for sending and receiving heartbeats/metadata within a cluster. Starting with Windows Server 2012, things have been significantly changed by introducing a converged network fabric that makes it possible to use much fewer network adapters in clusters. Data centers now usually have 10 Gb networks and converged networking simplifies the solution and reduces the implementation and running costs. There are many design scenarios for converged networks that we are also going to discuss now.

As VMM 2016 only supports Windows Server 2012 R2 and Windows Server 2016 Hyper-V hosts, Windows Server 2012 won't be mentioned (although some of the scenario described can be used with Windows 2012 as well)

Designing for converged networks

Converged network is a Windows Server 2012 R2/2016 feature that allows the creation of virtual network adapters, meaning that you can partition the physical NIC in many Virtual NIC's. Therefore, different network traffic types mentioned earlier start using the same physical adapters that are usually teamed. NIC teaming, also known as **Load Balancing and Failover** (**LBFO**), is a core element of a converged network fabric. With VMM 2016 and Windows Server 2016, you have two ways to do teaming.

NIC teaming and converged networking can be also configured with only a single NIC in Windows Server 2012 R2 and Windows Server 2016 (for example, to use multiple VLANs). However, you won't have failure protection. I strongly recommend having at least two NICs in a team. Here is a PowerShell example of creation of basic converged networks:

```
New-NetLbfoTeam -Name HV -TeamMembers pNIC1,pNIC2
-TeamingMode SwitchIndependent -LoadBalancingAlgorithm
Dynamic
New-VMSwitch -InterfaceAlias HV -Name VM -
MinimumBandwidthMode Weight  AllowManagementOS 0
Add-VMNetworkAdapter -Name CSV -SwitchName VM -
ManagementOS
Add-VMNetworkAdapter -Name MGM -SwitchName VM -
ManagementOS
Set-VMNetworkAdapterVlan -ManagementOS -
VMNetworkAdapterName "MGMT"
-Access -VlanId 5
Set-VMNetworkAdapterVlan -ManagementOS -
VMNetworkAdapterName "CSV"
-Access -VlanId 10
Set-VMNetworkAdapter -ManagementOS -Name CSV -
MinimumumBandwidthMode 50
Set-VMNetworkAdapter -ManagementOS -Name MGM -
MinimumumBandwidthMode 50
```

Imagine the following scenario: 2 x 10 GB physical network cards are dedicated to virtual Machine and Host management traffic. Those NICs are teamed using Windows 2012 R2 team capability, which will provide fault tolerance and load balancing. The other two NICs are **Remote Direct Memory Access (RDMA)** cards, and will provide SMB Multichannel capabilities and offer great performance, but can't be teamed or used as part of the Virtual Switch.

RDMA delivers low latency network and CPU utilization. RDMA adapters can be based on the network protocols such as iWARP, Infiniband or **RDMA over Converged Ethernet (ROCE)**. Before using any versions of RDMA, an additional network configuration might be required.

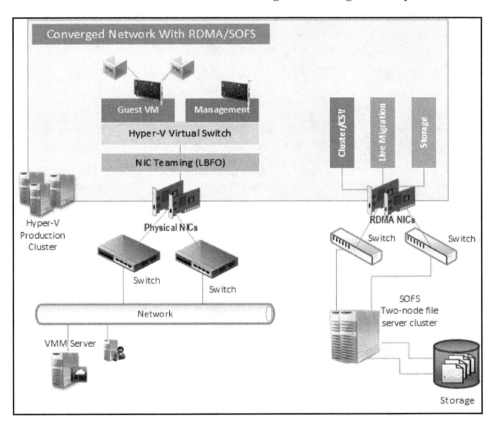

As the Guest VM network is often combined with the management network in flat network environments, you can use just one vNIC for both traffic types. However, it's recommended to have them separated from each other.

Consider the next scenario: 10 Gb single dual-port adapter per host is used, providing fault tolerance and load balancing for any network traffic types, including storage and live migration. You will also need to carefully prioritize the traffic for different networks by using network QoS. VMM port profiles should be used to define the configuration for the virtual NICs: offload settings, security settings and bandwidth settings. Since RDMA data bypasses the Windows Server 2012 R2 protocol stack, physical adapters (team members) won't support RDMA capabilities (if the adapters are RDMA-capable, of course).

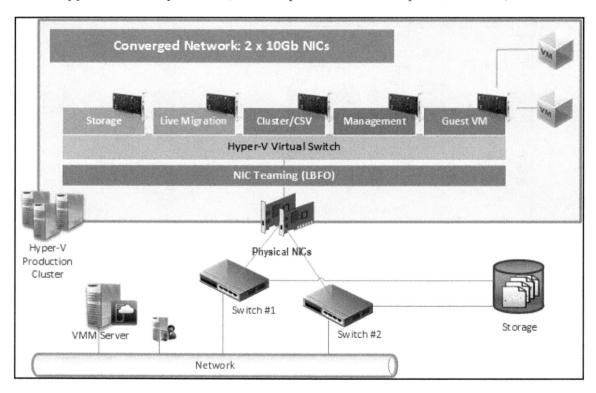

These two scenarios are also supported in Windows Server 2016. However, since RDMA adapters can't be behind a LBFO team or Virtual Switch, having a dedicated pair of RDMA adapters to leverage the SMB Direct and SMB Multichannel features will still be required. Windows Server 2016 solves this problem with Converged NIC and **Switch Embedded Teaming (SET)**.

SET is a NIC teaming that has been integrated to the Hyper-V switch. SET allows you to group up to eight identical adapters into one or more software-based virtual adapters. While native host LBFO can team adapters with different speeds, SET requires Ethernet adapters with the same model, speed and firmware. Also, there is no support for switch dependent (LACP, Static), Active/Passive configurations and Address Hash distribution. SET can be configured only with Hyper-V Port or Dynamic load distribution algorithms. The default values for SET parameters `LoadBalancingAlgorithm` and `BandwidthReservationMode` are Dynamic and Weight respectively. `BandwidthReservationMode` specifies how minimum bandwidth is to be configured on the SET switch. If `Absolute` is specified, minimum bandwidth is bits per second. If `Weight` is specified, minimum bandwidth is a value ranging from 1 to 100. If `None` is specified, minimum bandwidth is disabled on the switch. If `Default` is specified, the mode will be reset to the default settings (to `Weight` if SR-IOV is not enabled and to `None` if SR-IOV is configured). You can define all these settings during the logical switch configuration in VMM 2016 (which will be discussed later in this chapter).

Although VMM 2016 is the best management tool for SET, you can also use PowerShell (as you can't manage SET from Hyper-V Manager/NIC Teaming):

```
New-VMSwitch -Name SET -NetAdapterName "pNIC1","pNIC2"
-MinimumBandwidthMode Weight
-EnableEmbeddedTeaming $True
#To set the Load balancing algorithm
Set-VMSwitchTeam -SwitchName SET -LoadBalancingAlgorithm
Dynamic
#To delete pNIC2 from the SET team
Set-VMSwitch -SwitchName SET -NetAdapterName "pNIC1"
```

Converged NIC can be used with SET or without (one certified RDMA adapter per host) to provide RDMA capabilites through the host-partition virtual NICs to the end services. Consequently, RDMA can now be used in a team with SET and even act as a part of a virtual switch. Therefore, the first scenario described can be simplified to the following:

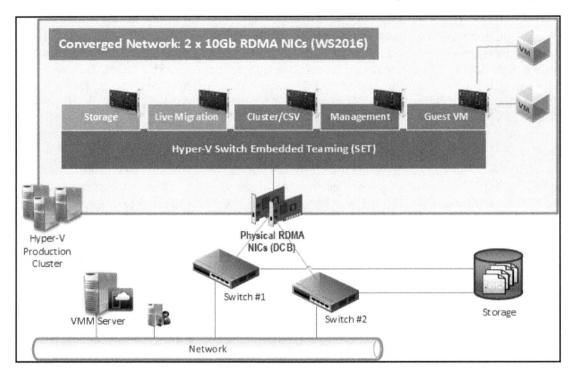

In the diagram above, two physical RDMA NICs are teamed using the new SET feature in Windows Server 2016 in order to make RDMA fully working in a converged network fabric. **Data center Bridging** (**DCB**) is a Windows Server 2016 feature that provides flow control and ability to define traffic classes for the different traffic types in order to configure network QoS. DCB consists of the 802.1 standards that describe **Priority-based Flow Control** (**PFC**) and **Enhanced Transmission Selection** (**ETS**) algorithms. PFC is used to minimize a packet loss when a network is being congested, while ETS provides the bandwidth allocation for traffic classes with different priorities. DCB is limited in Windows Server 2012 R2, as you can see in the comparison chart below, because it works independently of LBFO team. DCB in Windows Server 2016 now operates cooperatively with new SDNv2 QoS and SET, taking out the previous bandwidth management challenges. In most cases, DCB should always be configured for RDMA NICs to enhance the Ethernet protocol and to make RDMA work better.

LBFO and SET Feature comparison						
Feature	LBFO	SET	Feature	LBFO	SET	
Switch Tndependent Teaming			IEEE 802.1X			
Switch Dependent Teaming: Static			IPsecTO			
Switch Dependent Teaming: LACP			LSO			
Dynamic Load Distribution			RDMA			
Hyper-V Port Load Distribution			RSC			
Address Hash Load Distribution			RSS			
Active/Standy mode			SDN-QoS			
Max. team members	32	8	SR-IOV			
VMM Managed			TCP Chimney			
Windows Server UI Managed			VMMQ			
PowerShell Managed			VMQ (filter)			
Works in VMs			VMQ (NIC Switch)			
Different NICs in teams			vmQoS			
Affinity of vNIC/vmNIC to phys.NICs			vRSS			
Checksum offloads (IPv4,IPv6,TCP)			HNV v1 (NVGRE)			
Data Center Bridging (DCB)			HNV v2 (NVGRE/VxLAN)			
VLANs/PVLANs			Custom switch extensions			

You can refer to the following DCB configuration example:

```
Install-WindowsFeature Data-Center-Bridging
New-NetQosPolicy "SMB" -NetDirectPortMatchCondition 445
-PriorityValue8021Action 3
Enable-NetQosFlowControl -Priority 3
#Disable flow control for other traffic classes
Disable-NetQosFlowControl -Priority 0,1,2,4,5,6,7
#Assign QoS to the NIC
Enable-NetAdapterQos -InterfaceAlias "ST-A"
#Allocate 40% of bandwidth to the SMB Direct
New-NetQosTrafficClass "SMB" -Priority 3
-BandwidthPercentage 40 -Algorithm ETS
#Use the same steps to describe other traffic types
```

Networking: Configuring Logical Networks

Logical network is a container that contains elements that define the underlying networking infrastructure. It contains a group of IP subnets and/or VLANs.

In this recipe, we will go through logical network configuration.

Getting ready

A logical network linked to a network site is a user-defined group of IP subnets, VLANs, or IP subnet/VLAN pairs that is used to organize and simplify network assignments. It can be used to label networks with different purposes, for traffic isolation, and to provision networks for different types of **service-level agreements** (**SLAs**).

As VMs move across Hyper-V servers, make sure that the virtual network switches are named exactly the same in all Hyper-V servers (as they are associated with VMs).

To make a logical network available to a host, you must associate the logical network with a physical network adapter on the host.

You cannot associate a logical network with a Hyper-V internal or private vSwitch.

For the purpose of this section, we will be assuming that the physical servers have 4 x 1 GB physical network ports and 2 x 10 Gb ports that are used for storage, live migration and intra-cluster communication, while the 1 Gb ports will be teamed and portioned to create the host management and Guest VM, as shown in the following diagram:

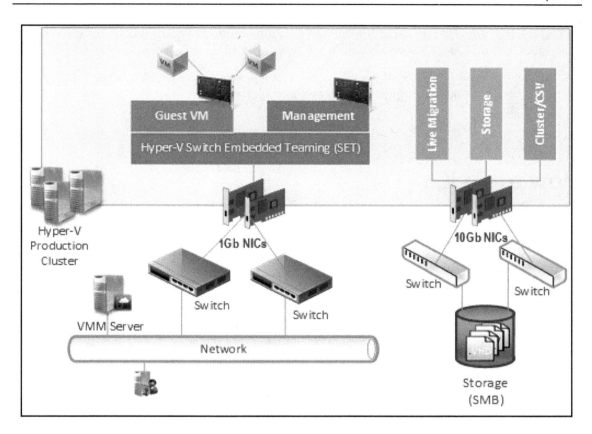

The following table shows the configuration that we will be using for our deployment:

Physical NIC	Teaming	Can it be associated with a logical network?
1 Gigabit NIC #1	SET	Yes
1 Gigabit NIC #2-4		
10 Gigabit NIC #1 (SMB)	-	No
10 Gigabit NIC #2 (SMB)		

In this section, we will create the logical network management which will be used for host management and Guest VM as shown in the preceding diagram.

Some other possible examples of logical networks would include DMZ, backend, frontend, backup and extranet.

How to do it...

Carry out the following steps to create a logical network and an associated network site:

1. Connect to the VMM 2016 console by using the VMM admin account previously created (`rllab\vmm-admin`), and then, on the bottom-left pane, click on **Fabric** to open the fabric workspace.
2. Click on the **Home** tab on the ribbon, and then click on **Fabric Resources.**
3. Expand **Networking** in the **Fabric** pane to the left, and then click on **Logical Networks.**
4. On the **Home** tab, click on **Create Logical Network.**
5. When the **Create Logical Network Wizard** window opens, type the logical network name on the **Name** page (for example, type `Management`) and click on **Next.**

You may type an optional description for the logical network, for example, *Management OS network traffic—Used by Guest VM's, Hosts management, Live Migration and CSV.*

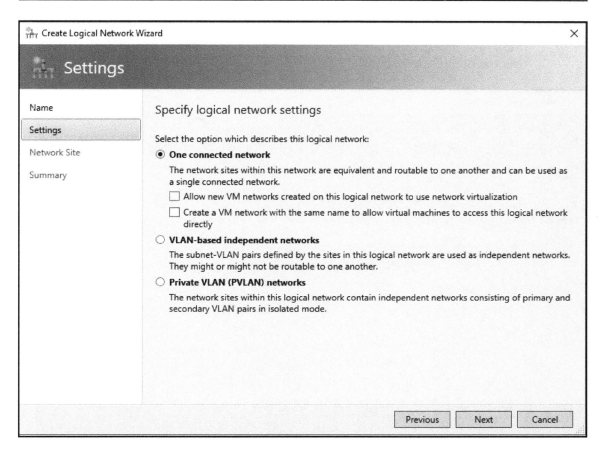

6. Select the option which describes the logical network and click on **Next.**

Check **Create a VM Network with the same name to allow virtual machines to access this logical network directly** to automatically create a VM network for your logical network. If you plan to isolate multiple VM networks using network virtualization, select the **Allow new VM networks created on this logical network to use network virtualization** property.

7. On the **Network Site** page, click on the **Add** button.

8. For **Host groups that can use this network site**, select the host group(s) to make available for this logical network. For example, **Moscow**, as shown in the following screenshot:

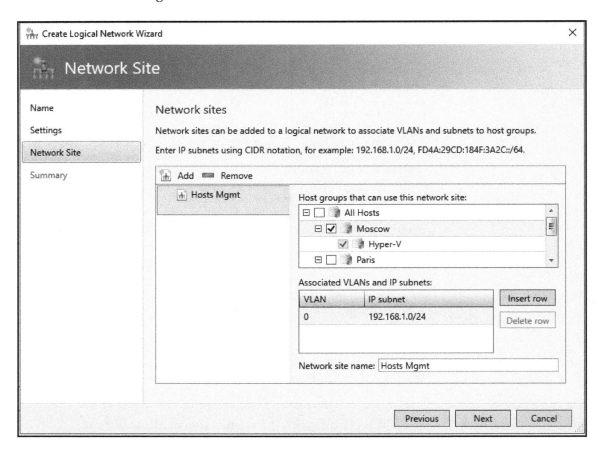

 In case you have a DHCP server to allocate IP addresses and no VLANs configured, you don't need to specify a network site for that logical network.

9. Under **Associated VLANs and IP subnets**, click on **Insert row**.
10. In the **VLAN** column, type the VLAN information, if any.

Leave it blank if there is no VLAN, or type 10, for example, to create VLAN 10. If you selected the **PVLAN** option for logical network, also define secondary VLANs for each primary VLAN.

11. Under **IP subnet**, type the IP address, for example, 192.168.1.0/24.
12. In the **Network Site Name** box, type the network site name, for example, **Hosts Mgmt** and then click on **Next**.
13. On the **Summary** page, click on **Finish**.
14. Repeat steps 6 to 12 to create more logical networks, if required.

 You can use PowerShell to view created logical networks, their network sites, and host groups assigned to them. Use the following one-liner:
`Get-SCLogicalNetworkDefinition|ft Name, LogicalNetwork, HostGroups`

How it works...

The recipe describes the process of creating a logical network, and associating it with a site (normally a physical location), and IP subnet and VLANs (if any).

For VMM to automatically assign static IP addresses, you can create IP address pools from an IP subnet associated with a network site.

When you add a Hyper-V host to VMM, if the physical network adapter is not associated with a logical network, VMM will then automatically create and associate a logical network that matches the DNS suffix of the connection (first one).

Certify that you have at least one physical network adapter available for communication between the host and the VMM management server when associating a logical network with a physical network adapter.

 If working with Full Converged networks, it is recommended that you have a VMM management server outside of the production cluster, on a separated and dedicated cluster.

There's more...

Now, let's create the IP address pool for the **logical network (LN)**, and then associate the LN with a physical network adapter.

Creating an IP address pool

Now that you have created the logical networks, you need to carry out the following steps to create an IP address pool for the logical network:

1. Open the **Fabric** workspace, and then click on the **Home** tab on the ribbon.
2. Click on **Fabric Resources**, expand **Networking** in the **Fabric** pane to the left, and then click on **Logical Networks**.
3. In the **Logical Networks and IP Pools** main pane, click on the logical network to create the IP address pool (**Management**, in our example).
4. On the **Home** tab on the ribbon, click on **Create IP Pool**:

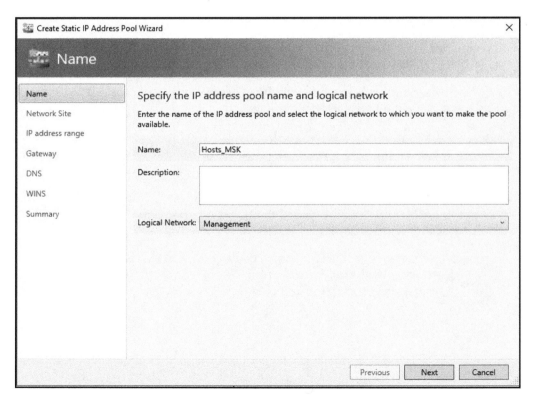

5. When **Create Static IP Address Pool Wizard** opens, on the **Name** page type the name and description (optional) for the IP address pool, for example, `Hosts_MSK`.

6. On the **Network Site** page, click on **Use an existing network site**.

7. Enter the correct IP address range and click on **Next**.

8. Enter the correct gateway and metric and click on **Next**.

9. Enter the correct DNS server address and DNS suffix (if any) and click on **Next**.

10. Enter the correct WINS (if any) and click on **Next**.

11. On the **Summary** page, review the settings and click on **Finish**.

12. Repeat 1-11 steps to create more IP pools for logical networks cluster, Live migration and other. They will be used later in this chapter.

 You can specify one or more IP addresses from the address range in the IP subnet to use to create a **virtual IP** (**VIP**) address, or to reserve one for other purposes.

After completing the Logical Network and IP Pool creation, on the **Fabric** workspace, expand **Networking** and then click on **Logical Networks** to confirm the Logical Networks you just created are listed. The following picture shows all logical networks and their IP pools created in my demo:

Name	Network Compliance	Subnet
⊟ Cluster	Fully compliant	
CLU_MSK	Fully compliant	10.10.25.0/24
⊟ Guest VMs	Fully compliant	
Guest_MSK	Fully compliant	10.10.23.0/24
⊟ Live Migration	Fully compliant	
LM_MSK	Fully compliant	10.10.24.0/24
⊟ Management	Fully compliant	
Hosts_MSK	Fully compliant	192.168.1.0/24
⊟ Storage (SMB)	Fully compliant	
SMB_MSK	Fully compliant	10.10.8.0/24

 To get the list of assigned addresses and their state in an IP Address Pool, you can use the following one-liner:
`Get-SCIPAddress|ft Address, AssignedToType, AllocatingAddressPool, State`

Automating the network configuration

In VMM 2016, you can optionally use the **Global Networking Settings** to automate the creation of a logical network and its association with a physical network adapter, and the creation of external virtual networks. Carry out the following steps in order to configure it:

1. On the VMM Console, in the **Settings** workspace, on the **Settings** pane, click on **General**.

2. Double-click in the **Network Settings** and configure the **Logical Networking** settings from the drop-down menu **Match logical networks by: First DNS Suffix Label, DNS Suffix, Network Connection Name, Virtual Network Switch Name, Disabled**.

3. You can also specify the option to use if the first logical network matching selection fails in the **If the above fails, match by: Network Connection Name, Virtual Network Switch Name, Disabled.**

4. To disable automatic creation of logical networks, uncheck **Create logical networks automatically** and click **Finish** to apply changes:

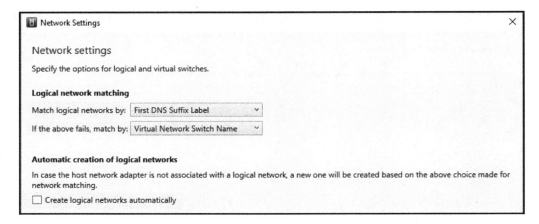

In VMM 2016, the setting **Create logical networks automatically** is enabled by default, which means that when you add a Hyper-V host to VMM, and no Logical Network is assigned with any physical NIC, VMM will automatically create a Logical Network. I always keep this setting disabled to manage networking manually after adding any hosts to fabric.

Associating the VMM Logical Network with the physical adapter

Carry out the following steps to associate the VMM logical network with the physical adapter on the hypervisor host:

 In VMM 2016, if there is no logical network associated to a physical network adapter when adding the Hyper-V host, VMM will by default, create and then associate a logical network matching the first DNS suffix of the connection and a *VM network* configured with *no isolation*.

1. In the **Fabric** workspace, on the **Fabric** pane to the left, expand **Servers** | **All Hosts**, and then expand the host group, for example, **Hyper-V**.
2. In the **Hosts** main pane, select the host to configure, for example, **hv02**.

 In order to proceed with this step, you should have added the Hyper-V server to the host group first. See the *Adding and managing Hyper-V hosts and host clusters with VMM* recipe in this chapter.

3. In the **Host** tab on the ribbon, click on **Properties** (or right-click on the host and click on **Properties**).
4. In the **Host Name Properties** dialog box, click on **Hardware** | **Network Adapters** and select the physical network adapter to be associated.

 Wireless network adapters will not be displayed, as this technology is not supported.

5. If you plan to use this adapter for communication between the VMM and the host, ensure that **Used by management** is checked. **Available for placement** is checked by default, meaning that this adapter can be used by virtual machines.

 At least one adapter for communication between the host and the VMM is required.

6. On the **Logical network connectivity** page, select the **Logical network** to associate with the physical adapter, for example, **Management:**

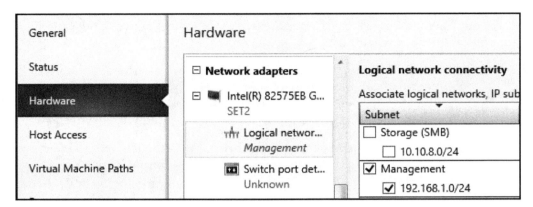

7. Click on **OK** to complete.
8. Repeat these steps on every host of the host group that's using the same logical network.

 Another one-liner can help to quickly get the list of logical networks mapped to the physical adapters on hosts:
```
Get-SCVMHostNetworkAdapter|ft VMHost, Name,
LogicalNetworks
```

See also

For more information, seethe following websites:

- *How to Create IP Address Pools for Logical Networks in VMM:*
  http://go.microsoft.com/fwlink/p/?LinkID=212422
- *How to Configure Network Settings on a Hyper-V Host in VMM:*
  http://go.microsoft.com/fwlink/p/?LinkID=212537
- *How to Configure Global Network Settings in VMM:*
  http://technet.microsoft.com/en-us/library/gg610695.aspx

Networking – Configuring VM Networks and Gateways

A VM network exists on top of a logical network, enabling you to create multiple virtualization networks to isolate and abstract the virtual machines from the logical networks. The types of VM networks in VMM 2016 are as follows:

- **Isolation** (network virtualization):
    - Without the VLAN constraints, isolation enables VM deployment flexibility as the VM keeps its IP address independent of the host it is placed on, removing the necessity for physical IP subnet hierarchies or VLANs.
    - It allows you to configure numerous virtual network infrastructures (they can even have the same **customer IP address (CA)**) that are connected to the same physical network. A likely scenario is either a hosting environment, with customers sharing the same physical fabric infrastructure, or an enterprise environment with different teams that have different objectives also sharing the same physical fabric infrastructure or even on a software house having test, stage, and production environments sharing the physical infrastructure. There are many other different scenarios where the network virtualization will enable each virtual network infrastructure to work as unique, but in fact it will be running on a shared physical network.

- **No Isolation**
    - In **No Isolation** mode, the VM network will act as the associated logical network and you only have one VM network configured with no isolation per logical network.

When creating the Logical Network, click on **One connected network** and then select **Create a VM network with the same name to allow virtual machines to access this logical network directly** and if using network virtualization, check the box for **allow network virtualization**.

- **VLAN-based**:
    - If your environment makes use of a VLAN for network isolation, you can use VMM to manage it.
    - In most cases, **select VLAN-based independent networks**. However, if you are using private VLAN technology, select **Private VLAN (PVLAN) networks**.
- **External networks implemented through a vendor network-management console:**
    - If you have configured the network through a vendor management software console, you can use VMM to import the data settings (for example, for logical networks, network sites, and VM networks) by installing the vendor-specific virtual switch extension manager.
    - If running a multitenant environment, such as a hosted data center with multiple customers, the feature will give you a powerful advantage. Network virtualization is designed to remove the constraints of VLAN and hierarchical IP address assignment for virtual machine provisioning. This enables flexibility in virtual machine placement, because the virtual machine can keep its IP address regardless of which host it is placed on. Placement is no longer limited by physical IP subnet hierarchies or VLAN configurations.
- **Gateways**
    - The likely scenario for this implementation is when you want to configure a VPN tunnel directly on your gateway device and then connect it directly to a VM, by selecting **Remote Networks** when creating the VM network. Note, though, that a gateway device software provider is required on the VMM management server. In the VMM model, the Hyper-V network virtualization gateway is managed via a PowerShell plugin module (which will communicate policy to the gateway). You will need to request from your vendor a PowerShell plugin module to install on the VMM server.

Getting ready

Make sure you've created the logical network in VMM before you start creating the VM Network, as VMM will use it to assign the **provider addresses (PAs)**.

VMM 2016 uses the IP address pools that are associated with a VM network to assign customized addresses to virtual machines by using network virtualization.

How to do it...

Carry out the following steps to create VM network with Isolation:

1. In the VMM console, click on **VMs and Services** in the bottom-left area to open the **VMs and Services** workspace, and then click on the **Home** tab on the ribbon.
2. Click on **Create VM Network**, and in **Create VM Network Wizard**, type the name for the VM network (for example, `CustomerA`) and an optional description.
3. In the **Logical network** list, select a previously-created logical network (following our sample infrastructure, select **Internet**).
4. On the **Isolation** page, click on **Isolate using Hyper-V network virtualization** and click on **Next**.

 If you select **No isolation**, the **VM Subnets and Gateway** page configuration will not appear.

5. On the **VM Subnets** page, click on **Add** and type a name for the VM subnet, for example, `Virtualization`.
6. In the **Subnet** box, type an IP subnet address (for example, `172.16.2.0/24`) followed by the **Classless Inter-Domain Routing (CDIR)** notation.
7. On the **Connectivity** page, if the **No network service that specifies a gateway has been added to VMM** message appears, click on **Next;** otherwise, configure the gateway as per the following:

Do not select any option if you are planning to set up the gateway settings for this VM network later.

- Select the option **Connect to another network through a VPN tunnel** if the VMs will communicate with other networks through a VPN tunnel or if the device will make use of the *Border Gateway Protocol*, then if applicable select and confirm the **VPN Gateway device**.

The VPN Connections wizard will show if the VPN gateway is selected. The **Border Gateway Protocol** wizard will show if selected. Enter the VPN endpoint and bandwidth and other requested information.

- Select the option **Connect directly to an additional logical network** if the VM's will communicate with other VMs in other networks, then select either **Direct routing** or **Network address translation (NAT)**. Select and confirm the **Gateway device.**

8. Click on **Next**, and then on the **Summary** page, click on **Finish**.

To create an IP Pool, select the VM network (for example, **VM-intranet**), right-click on it and click on **Create IP Pool**, and then follow the steps provided in the *Creating an IP address pool* subsection of the *Networking - configuring logical networks in VMM* recipe in this chapter.

9. The following screenshot shows the sample configuration of the VM Network Virtualization with Network Virtualization isolation and Microsoft RRAS as a gateway device (predefined in the **Network Services**, see the next recipe):

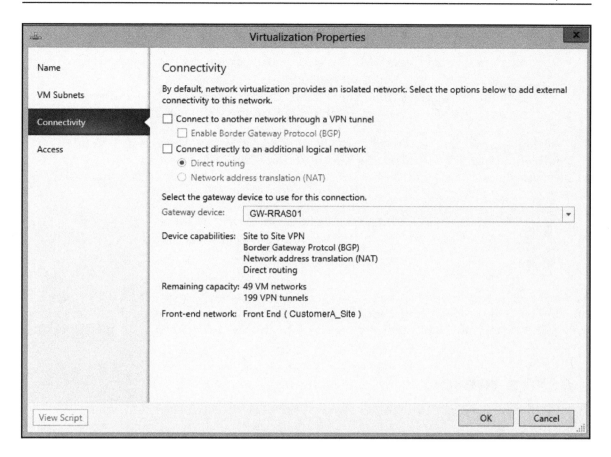

How it works...

You are required to set up the logical network first, since VMM uses it to assign **provider addresses** (**PA**). It will then be visible to the physical network (for example, to hosts, physical switches, gateways). However, it will not be visible to a virtual machine, which will have **customized addresses** (**CA**) assigned by VMM from an IP address pool associated with a virtual network (VM network).

In network virtualization, each virtual machine will be assigned two IP addresses:

- **Customer IP address (CA)**: This address is visible to the VM and is used to communicate with the virtual machine
- **Provider IP address (PA)**: This address is not visible to the VM and is only used by the Hyper-V server to communicate with the VM it hosts

The mechanism that can be used to virtualize the IP address of a VM is called **Network Virtualization with Generic Routing Encapsulation** (**NVGRE**), in which all of the VM's packets are encapsulated with a new header before they get transmitted on the physical network.

 Because the VMs on a specific host can share the same PA, IP encapsulation offers better scalability.

You can assign customer addresses through the DHCP server (it requires DHCPv4 Server Switch Extension), or by using static IP addresses. Then, when creating an IP address pool for a VM subnet, it will automatically provision IP addresses by either of the mechanisms.

There's more...

As of Windows Server 2016, there are two ways to provide network virtualization:

- **Hyper-V Network Virtualization version 1** (HNVv1 or SDNv1) was first introduced in VMM 2012 SP1 and then significantly improved in VMM 2012 R2 by adding support for RRAS multitenant gateway that was used to provide site-to-site VPN tunnels and direct internet access through a NAT to virtualized networks. HNVv1 is based on NVGRE protocol that is described in the RFC 7637 (https://tools.ietf.org/html/rfc7637). HNVv1 is still supported to make it possible to migrate existing HNVv1 deployments to VMM 2016, and also for overall backwards compatibility with Windows Server 2012 R2 environments. Therefore, there are no any features introduced and planned. HNVv1 is available in both Windows Server Standard and Datacenter editions, while new HNVv2 in Windows Server 2016 requires the Datacenter SKU.

Network virtualization gateway can be Microsoft RRAS or non-Windows gateway. See the *Adding a Gateway device, a virtual switch extension or network manager in VMM 2016* recipe for more information.

- **Hyper-V Network Virtualization version 2** (HNVv2 or SDNv2) solves many problems of SDNv1, including complexity of management and limited compatibility of other network solutions. This is partly made possible due to the movement from NVGRE to **Virtual eXtensible LAN** (**VXLAN**) encapsulation protocol which is widely used and also supported by other vendors (RFC 7348: `https://tools.ietf.org/html/rfc7348`) and network devices such as switches, NICs and routers (NICs, for example, support Encapsulation Offloads, reducing CPU load and improving overall performance). VXLAN is the default encapsulation protocol in Windows Server 2016. If you plan to use earlier Windows Server versions as a part of HNV deployment, VXLAN won't be supported as it requires an Azure-inspired networking stack that is only available in Windows Server 2016.

VMM distributed any SDN configuration changes among hosts in HNVv1, so was a highly critical element of SDNv1. However, Windows Server 2016 introduced a **Network Controller** (**NC**) as a new control plane for SDN. This new Windows Server role, that is only available in Datacenter SKU and taken from Azure, communicates with Hyper-V hosts and pushes network policies down to NC host agents running on each host using the *Azure Virtual Filtering Platform* extension in the Hyper-V Virtual Switch. Therefore, VMM is not mandatory for SDNv2. VMM 2016 can now be used as a tool for management and simplified deployment of SDN components.

Since NC is the heart of any SDNv2 deployment, you should always consider NC in high available configuration like all other SDNv2 components, including RAS gateways and software load balancers. Fortunately, they can be running on VMs and share the same physical hosts (for example, you were required to place virtualization gateways in SDNv1 exclusively on dedicated physical hosts; as a result, these hosts became unavailable for virtual machine placement).

SDNv2 is also used in Azure Stack integrated systems (new hybrid cloud platform that helps to deliver some Azure Services to the premises). Azure Stack comes with already-deployed and configured SDNv2.

Deploying a Network Controller using VMM

There are different ways to deploy NC and other SDNv2 components such gateways or load balancers. Microsoft has predefined service templates and even PowerShell scripts that help you to deploy SDNv2 from scratch (refer to `https://github.com/Microsoft/SDN` for more information). This recipe shows how to deploy NC using VMM console and service templates. Carry out the following steps to get started with SDNv2.

1. Open **Active Directory Users and Computers** (Start|**Run**|dsa.msc) and create one domain local group for NC management (for example, **NC-Admins**) and another for NC clients that will have the ability to manage virtual networks (**NC-Clients**, in our demo).

2. Create and add at least one user to each group defined in the previous step (nc.admin domain user, for example). Based on my testing, this domain user must be a member of both groups **NC-Admins** and **NC-Clients**. Otherwise, NC won't work after service deployment.

3. Open VMM 2016 console, and in the **Fabric** pane, click to expand **Servers** and select **All Hosts**, right-click and select **Create Host Group** to create dedicated host group for SDN hosts (for example, *SDN*).

4. The following PowerShell script automates the steps above:

```
Install-WindowsFeature RSAT-AD-PowerShell
New-ADGroup -Name NC-Clients -GroupScope DomainLocal
-GroupCategory Security
New-ADGroup -Name NC-Admins -GroupScope DomainLocal
-GroupCategory Security
New-AdUser NC_Admin -SamAccountName nc.admin
-AccountPassword (ConvertTo-SecureString -AsPlainText
"P@ssw0rd1" -Force) -PasswordNeverExpires $true -Enabled $true
Add-ADGroupMember NC-Admins -Members nc.admin
Add-ADGroupMember NC-Clients -Members nc.admin
New-SCVMHostGroup SDN -ParentHostGroup "All Hosts"
```

5. Create a new VM, install Windows Server 2016 Datacenter, update it with the latest UR and then use sysprep.exe (Start|**Run**|%WINDIR%\system32\sysprep\sysprep.exe) tool to generalize a Windows Server installation. Ensure that you have clicked **Generalize** and **Shutdown** in the **Shutdown Options** as shown in the following screenshot:

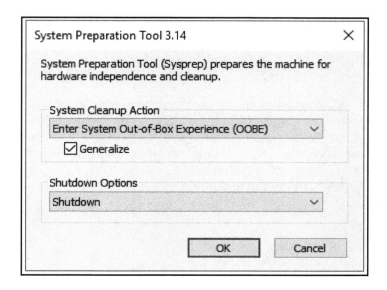

You can also use a cmdline to generalize a Windows Server. The following example uses the same settings as in the picture above:

```
sysprep.exe /generalize /shutdown /oobe
```

6. Import the VHDX file with generalized Windows Server 2016 Datacenter to the VMM Library. See the *Adding file-based resources to a VMM library share* recipe.

7. Create the Logical Network that represents your physical management network. We have already created one in the *Configuring Logical Networks* recipe. If required, refer again to this recipe for more information about adding logical networks to the VMM fabric.

Ensure that the Logical Network is One Connected and has an associated VM network and IP Pool.

8. Create and assign Logical Switch (SET mode) to the hosts where you intend to deploy the NC. See the *Creating a Logical Switch* and *Applying a Logical Switch to host network adapters* recipes to configure Logical Switch in the VMM fabric.

Important: Do not select any of the switch extensions in the **Extensions** page while creating a Logical Switch. NC network service automatically enables Azure VFP switch extension on Hyper-V hosts to which NC is mapped.

9. Before the NC deployment, you are required to have an SSL certificate that will be used for secure communication with NC. You can generate self-signed certificate (`New-SelfSignedCertificate` cmdlet) or use a certificate signed by an existing enterprise CA. Nevertheless, when it comes to security and certificate management, my recommendation is to always use CA (for example, `SVC01\Root-CA` in my demo domain *rllab.com*).

10. Open Notepad and copy the following into a new file:

```
[NewRequest]
Subject = "CN=nc-vm01.rllab.com"
KeyLength = 2048
KeySpec = 1
Exportable = True
ExportableEncrypted=True
ProviderName = "Microsoft RSA SChannel Cryptographic Provider"
HashAlgorithm = SHA256
MachineKeySet = True
SMIME = False
UseExistingKeySet = False
RequestType = PKCS10
KeyUsage = 0xA0
Silent = True
FriendlyName = "NC Certificate"
[EnhancedKeyUsageExtension]
OID=1.3.6.1.5.5.7.3.1
[Extensions]
2.5.29.17 = "{text}"
_continue_ = "dns=nc-vm01.rllab.com&"
```

11. Save the file as `nc_certconf.inf` in the `C:\cert` folder.

12. Now that you have created the file, let's proceed with requesting and submitting the required certificates. Open PowerShell ISE with administrative privileges (**Run as Administrator**), for example, and use the following script:

```
#Request certificate
certreq -new c:\cert\nc_certconf.inf c:\cert\nc_cert.req
#Submit a request
certreq -submit -config SVC01\Root-CA -attrib
"CertificateTemplate:WebServer" c:\cert\nc_cert.req
c:\cert\nc_cert.cer
```

```
#Add certificate to the user personal store
certutil -addstore -f MY C:\cert\nc_cert.cer
#Get a private key
certutil -repairstore MY nc-vm01.rllab.com
#Export PFX and private key
Certutil -privatekey -exportPFX -p P@ssw0rd1 My nc-vm01.rllab.com
c:\cert\nc_srv.pfx
#Delete certificate from the local machine
certutil -privatekey -delstore MY nc-vm01.rllab.com
#Request public CA certificate
certutil "-ca.cert" -config SVC01\Root-CA c:\cert\rootca.cer
```

You could also use a Certificate Request Wizard (Start|**Run**|certmgr.msc), right- click on **Personal**, select **All Tasks**|**Advanced Operations** and then **Create Custom Request...** Make sure that your request includes the server Auth EKU, specified by the OID 1.3.6.1.5.5.7.3.1. In addition, the certificate subject name must match the DNS name of the network controller (nc-vm01.rllab.com, for example).

13. Download templates and custom resources from https://github.com/Microsoft/SDN/tree/master/VMM/Templates/NC. Network Controller Standalone Generation 2 VM.xml is used in this recipe to deploy a standalone NC on VM with Generation 2.

If you plan production deployment, you need to consider to using other available templates, for example, Network Controller Production Generation 2 VM.xml which deploys three-node NC (HA deployment).

14. At this step you need to copy the generated certificates to the custom resources (.cr) folders that you downloaded in the previous step. Copy the c:\cert\nc_srv.pfx to the ServerCertificate.cr folder, the c:\cert\nc_cert.cer file to NCCertificate.cr and c:\cert\rootca.cr to the TrustedRootCertificate.cr folder.

15. Import NC custom resources (.cr) folders to the VMM Library (for example, to the precreated NC folder). See the *Adding file-based resources to a VMM library share* recipe in this chapter.

16. Return to the VMM console, and in the **Library** pane, in the **Home** tab, on the top ribbon, click on **Import Template**.

17. In the **Import Package Wizard** dialog window, provide the path to the downloaded NC service template (xml file) and click **Next.**

18. On the **Configure References** page, map service template parameters to the library resources (imported `.cr` folders with certificates, sysprepped vhdx and capability profile) as shown in the picture, then
change **Name** and **Release** version if required and click **Next:**

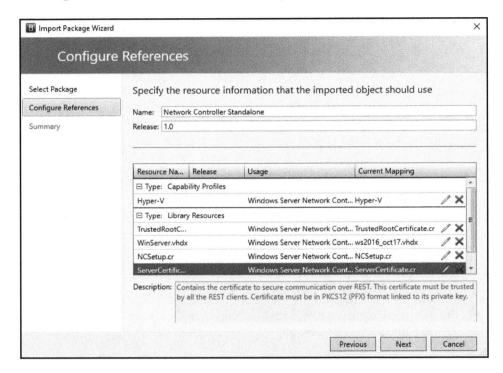

19. On the **Summary** page, press **Import** to confirm the settings and import **NC service** template. Once done, in the **Jobs** pane, ensure that the job **Import Template** is completed.

20. I prefer to customize the template before the deployment. Moreover, if you don't provide a valid product key, then deployment will stop at the Product Key page during NC VM provisioning. For doing this, in the **Library** pane, click on **Service Templates** and select the network controller service template, right-click and select **Open Designer**. In the new window, double-click on the computer tier, and then click **OS Configuration | Product Key** to change a product key and click **Time Zone** to define time settings if necessary. If you plan to place a NC VM on a cluster, switch to **Hardware Configuration | Availability** and check **Make this virtual machine highly available** and click **OK.**

By default, the NC service template is configured to randomly generate VM and computer names using the NC-VM## format (NC-VM01, NC-VM02 and so on) defined in **OS Configuration | Identity Information.** If you change it to a hard coded name (NC, for example), computer tier cannot be scaled out.

21. In the **Virtual Machine Manager Service Template Designer** window, click **Save and Validate** and then **Configure Deployment.**

22. In the **Select name and destination** dialog box, type the **Name** of service instance and its **Destination** (target host group, for example, *SDN*), then select the management logical network we created earlier and click **OK:**

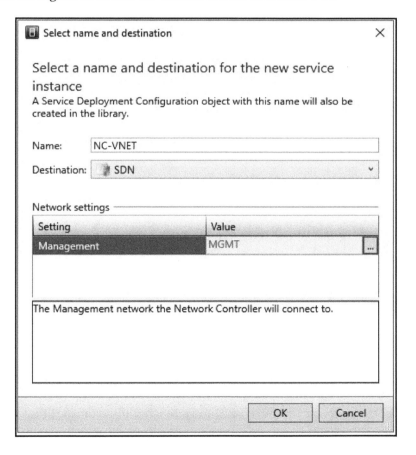

23. In the **Deploy Service** window, configure deployment settings and click **Refresh Preview** to find a suitable host for deployment and to verify initial requirements for the NC service instance.

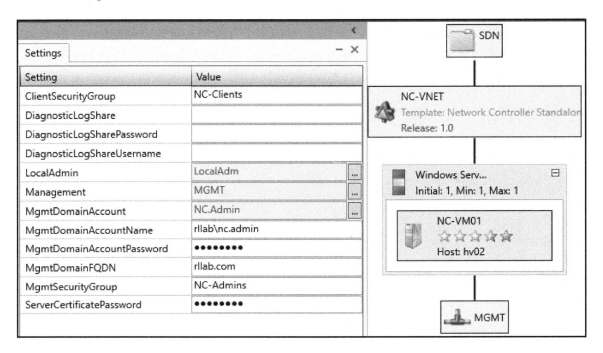

DiagnosticLogShare, DiagnosticLogSharePassword, DiagnosticLogShareUsername are optional settings. You are required to defined other settings with values that we used in the previous steps (**NC-Clients** as **ClientSecurityGroup** and **NC-Admins** as **MgmtSecurityGroup**, for example). Note that **LocalAdmin** username should be **.\Administrator** (create RunAs if it's not created) and **MgmtDomainAccount** is a member of NC management security group defined in the **MgmtSecurityGroup**.

24. In the **Home** tab, on the top ribbon, click on **Deploy Service**, and in the **Deploy Service** window dialog box, confirm the service deployment by pressing **Deploy** button. **Create the Service Template** job will be created that you can monitor in the **Jobs** pane.

25. Once the deployment is finished, switch to the **VMs and Services** pane and click on **Services** in the **Home** tab, on the top ribbon. Verify that you have a running service **NC-VNET** as shown in the following screenshot.

Name	Status	All VMs Accessible	VM Status	User Role	Job Status
⊟ NC-VNET	OK	Yes	Running	Administrator	Completed
⊟ Windows Ser...	OK	Yes	Running		
NC-VM01....	Running		Running	Administrator	Completed

I strongly recommend to manually check NC installation logs located in the folder `C:\NCInstall` on the NC's VM. In addition, check from the VMM server that you can download `servers.json` from the following URL: `https://nc-vm01.rllab.com/networking/v1/servers`

26. Now it's time to add the network controller to VMM 2016. Refer to the next recipe that has some information about adding gateways as well.

Adding a Gateway device, a virtual switch extension or network controller in VMM 2016

Carry out the following steps to configure a gateway device or network controller to provide support for the VM network.

Some provider software is included in VMM 2016, for example, providers for Microsoft RRAS Gateway and Network Controller. If your provider software is not included, it is required that you previously installed the provider on the VMM management server, and if the network service requires a certificate, make sure it is imported.

1. In the **Settings** workspace, on the **Settings** pane, click on **Configuration Providers** and confirm that the gateway provider is installed (*Microsoft Network Controller*, for example).

2. Click on the **Fabric** workspace and then in the **Home** tab, click on **Fabric Resources**.

3. In the **Fabric** pane, click to expand **Networking** and then select **Network Services**, which include gateways, vSwitch extensions, **top-of-rack** (**TOR**) switches, network managers or new network controller (as a part of SDNv2 deployment).

4. In the **Add Network Service Wizard** window, type the gateway name and description (optional) and click on **Next**.

5. On the **Manufacturer and Model** page, select the provider manufacturer and model or leave default, *Microsoft Network Controller*, for example, if adding an NC and click on **Next**.

6. On the **Credentials** page, provide the Run As Account and click on **Next**.

Alternatively, you can click on **Create Run As Account** to create a new **Run As Account**. If adding an NC, provide a user that is a member of the NC management group (`nc.admin`, for example).

7. On the **Connection String** page, type the gateway connection string in accordance with the vendor predefined syntax (for example, the connection string for the Microsoft RRAS Gateway looks as follows: *VMHost=hvcluster.rllab.com;GatewayVM=gwcluster.rllab.com*) and click on **Next**. The following screenshot shows a connection string for NC:

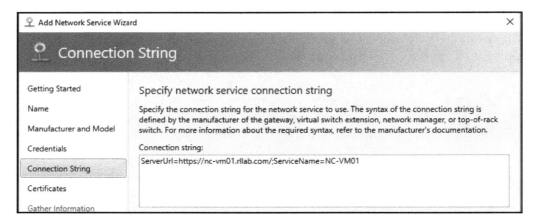

8. On the **Certificates** page, if your gateway requires a certificate, *select the check box* to confirm that the certificate can be imported to the trusted certificate store, as shown in the following screenshot, and then click on **Next.**

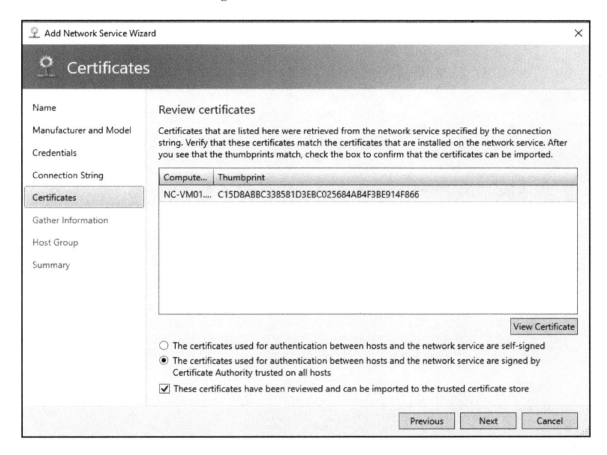

9. On the **Gather Information** page, click on **Scan Provider** to carry out a simple validation check. The test results for the NC are shown in the following screenshot:

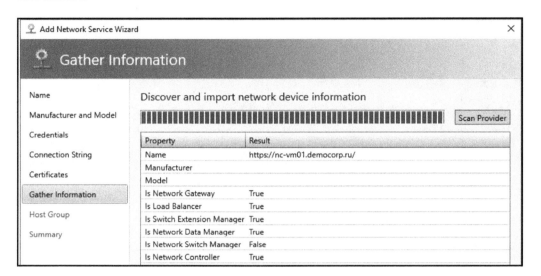

If test results are **False** for all properties except **Is Network Switch Manager** while adding a network controller, for example, it's because the NC is not working properly. VMM won't add a network service that failed the test. Check your deployment, logs and configuration and then try again.

10. On the **Host Group** page, select the host groups that will have the network service available to them (*Moscow*, for example).

The host group on which the network controller service instance was deployed must be part of this network service's scope. In our example, the NC was deployed on the *SDN* host group that is a child of the *Moscow* host group. So, I need to select the *Moscow* host group to make available the NC to Hyper-V hosts in Moscow site.

11. On the **Summary** page, click on **Finish**.

12. If adding a *gateway device*, under **Network Services**, select the gateway, right-click and select **Properties.** Click on **Connectivity**, and enter the following information:
    - Select **Enable front end connection**, then select the network adapter of the gateway and the network site with external connectivity
        - Select **Enable back end connection**, then select the network adapter of the gateway and the network site with internal connectivity

 If you need to allow VPN connectivity, make sure the network site has a route to/from the external network and a static IP address pool.

13. Make sure **Hyper-V Network Virtualization** is enabled for the logical network and that the network site has a static IP address pool.

The sample configuration of gateway connectivity is shown in the picture below (HA RRAS Gateway is used):

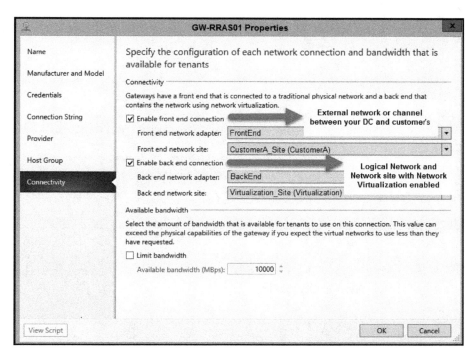

You can use predefined service templates to reduce the deployment time of highly available RRAS gateways (SDNv1). These templates, and quick-start guides are available at `http://go.microsoft.com/fwlink/p/?LinkId=329037`.

Validating a Network Controller deployment

Carry out the following steps to validate an NC deployment, and understand the new options in VMM 2016 for Logical Networks when NC is configured in the VMM fabric.

1. In the **Fabric** pane, under **Networking**, right-click on **Logical Networks** and select **Create Logical Network**

2. In the **Create Logical Network wizard** window, type the network name and optionally a description (for example, *HNVv2*), then select checkboxes **Allow new VM networks created on this logical network to use network virtualization** and **Managed by Microsoft Network Controller** and click on **Next**:

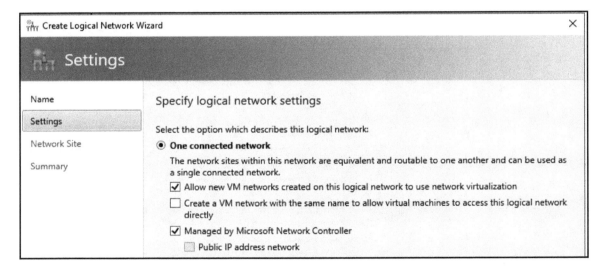

3. On the next page, create a new network site and define VLANs with IP Subnet (for example, *VLAN 20 and* `10.10.20.0/24` *as a subnet*), and then click **Next** and **Finish**:

This logical network is the HNVv2 PA network that will be used by VMs to communicate with each other. Ensure that all SDN hosts have a physical connectivity to this network.

4. Right-click on the created Logical Network and select **Create IP Pool**, then use an existing network site and define gateway (for example, 10.10.20.1) and DNS servers.

 See the *Creating an IP address pool* recipe for more information if required.

5. In the **Networking** pane, click **Port Profile** and select Hyper-V switch profile that is already connected to the Hyper-V hosts (for example, *SET*) and associate it with created network site HNVv2_0 and click **OK:**

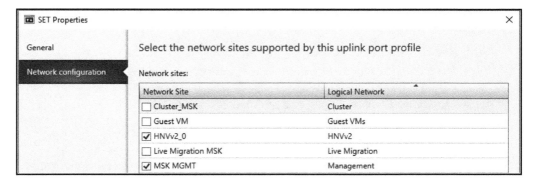

6. Right-click on the **Logical Network** and select **Create VM Network**, type a name (for example, *VNET*) and optional description, verify that *HNVv2* logical network is selected and click **Next.**
7. On the next page, select **Isolate using Hyper-V Network virtualization** and click **Next**
8. On the **VM Subnets** page, add a new VM subnet that using a CIDR notation type a subnet name (for example, *VSUB and* 172.16.1.0/24), and click **Next.**
9. On the **Connectivity** page, accept the default settings and click on **Next** and then **Finish** to create a VM network.

10. Switch to the **VMs and Services** pane, right-click *VNET* VM network and select **Create IP Pool** and define gateway and DNS parameters (for example, `172.16.1.1` and `10.10.20.25` respectively)

11. Create two test VMs, connect their adapters to the *VNET* VM Network and then place them to the different Hyper-V hosts. When VM deployment is finished, try to get them to ping each other (ensure that Windows Firewall does not block ICMP packets).

You can use the same virtual hard disk image as we used for NC deployment to provision VMs. See `Chapter 7`, *Deploying Virtual machines and Services*, for more information about creating VMs.

See also

For more information, see the following references:

- *Software-Defined Networking Overview:*
  https://docs.microsoft.com/en-us/windows-server/networking/sdn/software-defined-networking
- *Deploy and manage SDN in the VMM Fabric:*
  https://docs.microsoft.com/en-us/system-center/vmm/deploy-sdn
- *Deploying SDN on One single physical host using VMM*:
  https://blogs.msdn.microsoft.com/excellentsge/2016/10/06/deploying-sdn-on-one-single-physical-host-using-vmm/
- *Deploy a SDN infrastructure using scripts*:
  https://docs.microsoft.com/en-us/windows-server/networking/sdn/deploy/deploy-a-software-defined-network-infrastructure-using-scripts

Networking: Configuring logical switches, port profiles and port classifications

VMM 2016 allows you to configure port profiles and logical switches. They work as containers for network adapter capabilities and settings, and by using them, you can apply the configuration to selected adapters instead of configuring those settings on each host network adapter.

How to do it...

Let's start by creating the port profiles, and then we will create the port classification, followed by the Logical Switch. Carry out the following steps to create port profiles for uplinks:

1. In the VMM console, in the **Fabric** workspace and on the **Fabric** pane, under **Networking**, click on **Port Profiles**.
2. On the **Home** tab on the ribbon, click on **Create**, and then click on **Hyper-V Port Profile**.
3. In the **Create Virtual Network Adapter Port Profile** window, on the **General** page, type the port profile name and optionally a description.
4. Click on **Uplink port profile**, select the load balancing algorithm and the team mode, and click on **Next:**

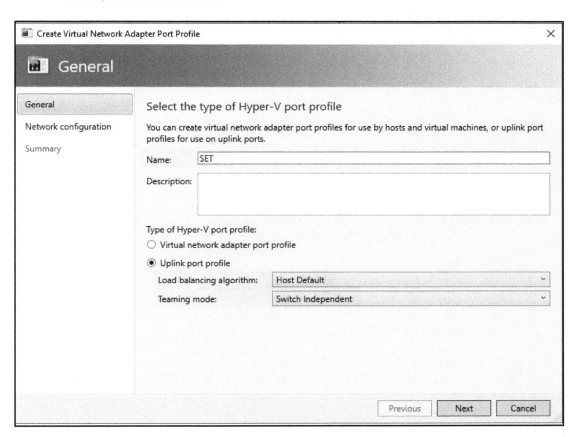

5. On the **Network configuration** page, select the network site (which could be more than one). Network sites must have at least one host group in common (in our case, all network sites are assigned to the Moscow host group). Otherwise, you will receive an out-of-scope error. Sample configuration is shown in the following screenshot:

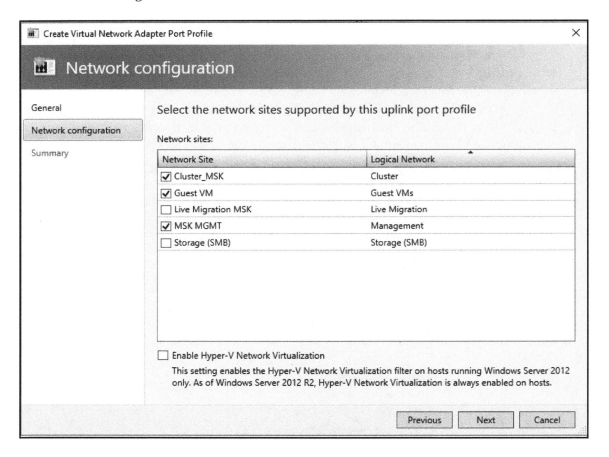

6. Optionally, to enable network virtualization support for it, click on **Enable Windows Network Virtualization.**

 This setting requires a logical network with the **Allow new VM networks created on this logical network to use network virtualization** setting checked.

7. Click on **Next**, and then on the **Summary** page, click on **Finish**.
8. Repeat 1-8 steps to create additional port profiles (for example, *SET-10G*).

How it works...

Profiles are useful features that can be used to apply settings or capabilities to an entire data center instead of configuring each adapter's settings. With uplink port profiles you describe how physical adapters should be configured, NIC teaming settings and network sites (and hence logical networks) that must be associated with the adapters.

After creating a *Hyper-V port profile*, the profile will need to be assigned to a logical switch. Make it available through the assigned logical switch, which can then be selected to be applied to a network adapter in a host. This will make the network consistent across the Hyper-V hosts.

There's more...

Before creating the Logical Switch, you also need to check virtual adapter port profiles, port classification, and optional switch extensions and managers.

Creating port profiles for VM adapters

VMM 2016 makes use of virtual port profiles to define the configuration for the virtual NICs: offload settings, security settings and bandwidth settings. There are already some pre-existing configured virtual port profiles (for example *Host Management, Cluster, Live Migration, iSCSI, High Bandwidth Adapter)*, but you can create a customized one. Carry out the following steps to create native port profiles:

1. In the VMM console, in the **Fabric** workspace and on the **Fabric** pane, under **Networking**, click on **Port Profiles**.
2. On the **Home** tab on the ribbon, click on **Create** and then click on **Hyper-V Port Profile**.
3. In the **Create Virtual Network Adapter Port Profile** window, on the **General** page, type the port profile name and optionally a description.
4. Click on **Virtual network adapter port profile**, and then click on **Next**.

5. On the **Offload Settings** page, select the settings you want to enable (if any), such as **virtual machine queue, IPsec task offloading, Single-root I/O virtualization and new RDMA**, then click on **Next:**

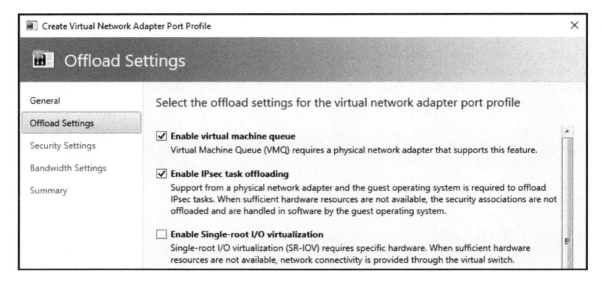

6. On the **Security Settings** page, select the settings you want to allow/enable (if any), such as **MAC spoofing, DHCP guard, router guard, guest teaming**, and **IEEE priority tagging**, and click on **Next:**

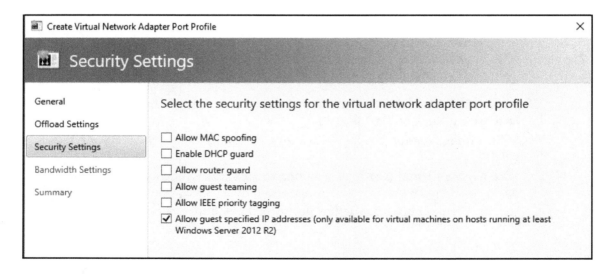

7. On the **Bandwidth Settings** page, if you want to configure the bandwidth settings, specify **Minimum bandwidth (Mbps)** or **Minimum bandwidth weight**, and **Maximum bandwidth (Mbps):**

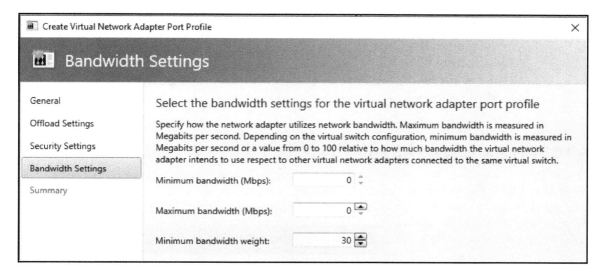

 It is best practice to set up the weighted configuration. The total weight of all adapters and the virtual switch default should stream to `100`. You can use the following PowerShell one-liner to check the default bandwidth weight:

```
Get-SCVirtualNetworkAdapterNativePortProfile | ft Name,
MinimumBandwidthWeight
```

8. On the **Summary** page, click on the **Finish** button.
9. Repeat steps 1-8 to create more virtual port profiles that will describe settings, for example, of Guest VMs virtual network adapter.

Creating a Port Classification

Carry out the following steps to create port classifications:

1. In the VMM console, in the **Fabric** workspace, on the **Fabric** pane, click on **Networking** and then click on **Port Classifications**.
2. On the **Home** tab on the ribbon, click on **Create** and then click on **Port Classification**.
3. In the **Create Port Classification Wizard** window, type the port classification name and optional description and click on **OK**.

Creating a logical switch

VMM 2016 has updated the wizard for creating logical switches. The updates include embedded teaming (SET) uplink mode, ability to create new uplink port profiles and define virtual network adapters in the wizard instead of creating virtual NICs individually on each host in VMM 2012 R2 fabric. Any logical switch that was created in VMM 2012 R2 had the Weight bandwidth mode by default, and there was no option to change that behavior. VMM 2016 provides an ability to set or disable the minimum bandwidth mode as well. I would say that **Logical Switch** wizard has become more logical and even simpler, providing new features and refined steps for setting it up. To get started with logical switches, carry out the following steps:

1. In the VMM console, in the **Fabric** workspace, on the **Fabric** pane, click on **Logical Switches**.
2. Right-click on it and then click on **Create Logical Switch**.
3. On the **Getting Started** page, click on **Next.**

4. In the **Create Logical Switch Wizard** window, type the logical switch name, an optional description, and select type of teaming in **Uplink Mode** (**Embedded Team** is a SET, *Team* is a LBFO/stand-alone teaming, **No Uplink Team** - a teaming won't be used for physical adapters), then click on **Next**:

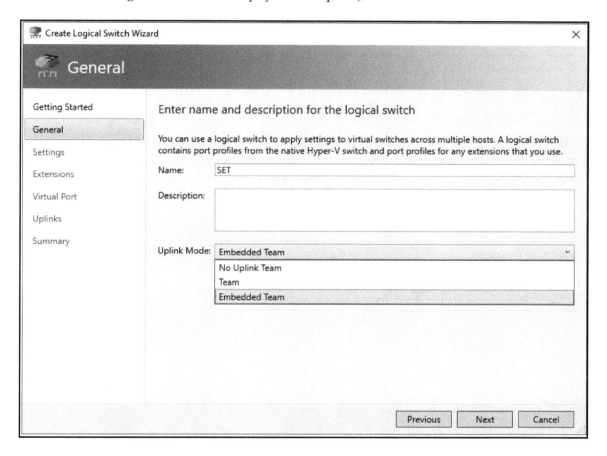

5. As mentioned earlier, VMM 2016 allows you to define a minimum bandwidth mode for logical switch. **Weight** mode is recommended and selected by default. If the network adapter has SR-IOV support and you want to enable it, click on **Enable Single Root I/O Virtualization (SR-IOV)**. If Network Controller is configured in your fabric and you plan to use this switch with SDN, check also **Managed by Microsoft Network Controller** and then press **Next:**

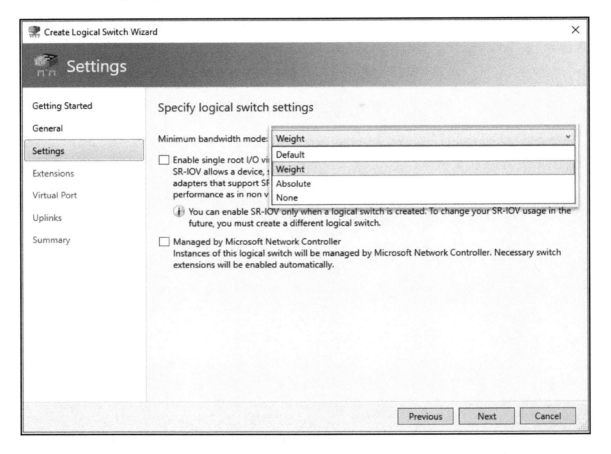

You can refer to the *Designing for Converged Networks* section in this chapter to get more details about the minimum bandwidth modes.

6. If you are using the virtual switch extensions, or your switch is not managed by NC, select the extensions on the **Extensions** page, making sure they are in order as to be processed, and click on **Next:**

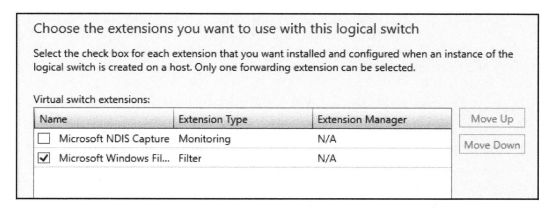

 The Windows Server 2012R2/2016 Hyper-v Extensible Switch allows you to add extensions to the Virtual Switch which can capture, filter or forward traffic.

7. On the **Virtual Port** page, click on **Add** to add port classifications which are associated or not to a VM network adapter port profile, and click on **Next:**

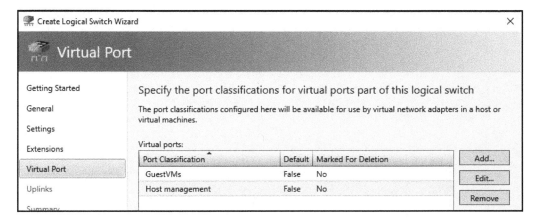

8. On the **Uplinks** page, click on **Add** to create **New Uplink Port** profile or to use **Existing Uplink Port** profile, then, if necessary, add virtual network adapters by pressing **New virtual network adapter**. In my case, I defined the virtual NICs for GuestVMs and management as shown in the following screenshot. If you don't see the required network sites in the list, check the supported network sites by the port profile (**Fabric | Networking | Port Profiles |** double-click on the **Port Profile | Network Configuration**). Check **This virtual network adapter will be used for host management** and **Inherit connection settings from host network adapter** if you have an existing DHCP server in the management network, for example. Otherwise, select **Static** and define the corresponding IP Pool:

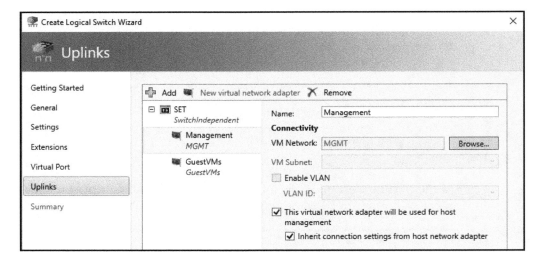

Only one virtual network adapter can be marked as used for host management.

9. On the **Summary** page, review the switch configuration and click on **Finish**.
10. Repeat 1-9 steps to create one more logical switch if required.

Configuring the Network Adapter for VMs and host management

Carry out the following steps to configure the network adapter:

1. In the **Fabric** workspace, on the **Fabric** pane, expand **Servers | All Hosts** and select a host group; then select a host in the **Hosts** main pane.
2. Right-click on the host and click on **Properties**, and then click on the **Hardware** tab.
3. In **Network Adapters**, select the physical network adapter to configure. For VMs, click on **Available for placement**. For management, click on **Used by management**.

> If a logical switch and an uplink port profile were previously configured for the network adapter, when you click on **Logical network connectivity**, the result connectivity will display.

4. Do not change individual settings if you are planning to use a logical switch and uplink port profiles. Instead, apply the configuration to the virtual switch on the hosts (see the next recipe).
5. Click on **OK** to finish.

Applying a logical switch to host network adapters

A logical switch helps to ensure that logical networks, VLANs, IP subnets, and other network settings such as port profiles, are consistently assigned to host network adapters. Carry out the following steps to add Logical Switch to hosts:

1. In the **Fabric** workspace, on the **Fabric** pane, expand **Servers | All Hosts** and select a host group; then select a host in the **Hosts** main pane.
2. Right-click on the host and click on **Properties**, and then click on the **Hardware** tab.

3. In Virtual Switches, click on **New Virtual Switch** and select **New Logical Switch** to add an existing logical switch. If you have two or more logical switches in the fabric, define the right one in the **Logical switch** drop-down menu, then check adapters that you plan to use with the Logical switch in **Physical adapters** and, if required, add more adapters by pressing **Add**, and then review the list of **Virtual adapters** that will be automatically created and click on **OK:**

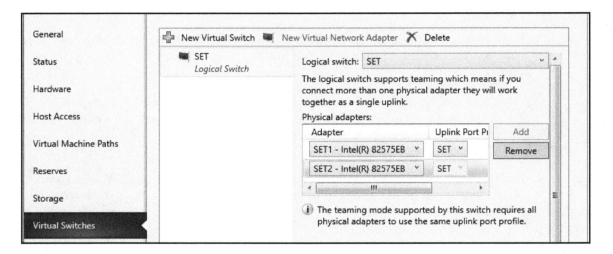

 The host might temporarily lose network connectivity when VMM creates the switch and virtual network adapters.

4. In the **Jobs** workspace, check that the job **Change properties of virtual machine host** is completed:

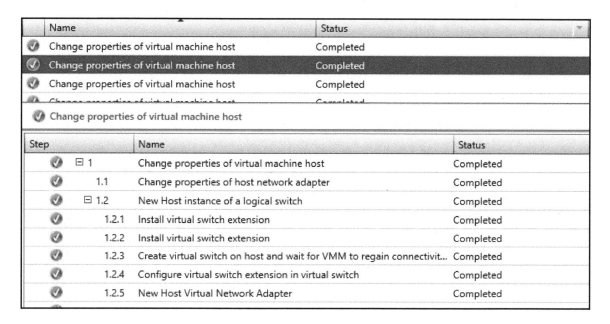

 New Host Virtual Network Adapter subtasks in the job indicate processes of creating virtual NICs that you defined the switch creation (see the *Creating a Logical Switch* recipe)

5. Repeat the first two steps, and in **Virtual Switches,** additionally check that the **Logical switch** and **Virtual Network Adapters** (Management and Guest VMs, in our case) are successfully added:

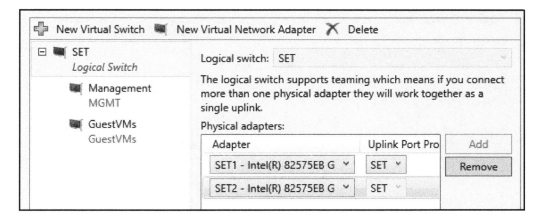

After applying the logical switch, you can check that host network settings are compliant with the logical switch (**Fabric | Networking | Logical Switches** and switch to **Home | Show | Hosts**) or use the following one-liner:

```
Get-SCVMHostNetworkAdapter|? {$_.UplinkPortProfileSet -
like "SET"}|ft Name, LogicalNetworkCompliance,
LogicalNetworkComplianceErrors
```

Converting a standard switch to a logical switch

When you add new Hyper-V hosts with existing virtual switches, VMM categorizes them as standard switches and we did not have any options in VMM 2012 R2 to convert them to logical switches that could simplify network configuration on newly-added hosts. VMM 2016 allows you to convert existing virtual switches on Hyper-V hosts to the logical switch with just one click. Carry out the following steps to convert switches:

1. In the **Fabric** pane, select **All hosts** and double-click on the host on which you want to convert a standard switch, then navigate to **Virtual Switches** and select the virtual switch (for example, **Switch_Ext**). As shown in the following screenshot, if logical switches don't match virtual switch settings, the **Convert to Logical Switch...** button will be greyed out. Create a new logical switch or change an existing one in order to make this option available:

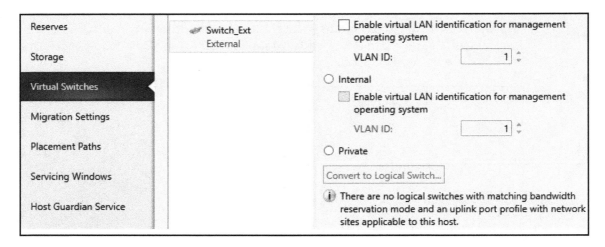

Minimum bandwidth mode (weight/absolute and etc), SR-IOV, **Uplink Mode**, and Load Balancing algorithm settings must be the same in the logical switch as they are in the virtual switch on Hyper-V host.

2. In the **Fabric** pane, under **Networking**, select **Logical Switches** and double-click on the targeted logical switch, on the **Settings** page change the bandwidth mode to **Absolute** (as my standard switch **Switch_Ext** is configured with **Absolute** mode), and then change other settings if required (SR-IOV and uplink mode).

3. Switch back to the host **Virtual Switches** and ensure that the **Convert to Logical Switch...** button is active:

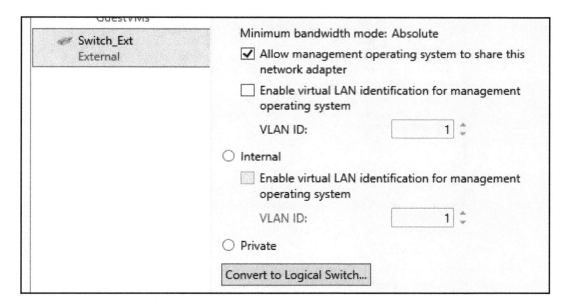

 VMM does not support conversion of **Embedded Team Standard Switch** to **Logical Switch**. Create and deploy SET through VMM instead.

4. Press **Convert to Logical Switch**, and in the **Convert a Standard Switch to a Logical Switch** dialog box, define a **Logical switch** and **Uplink port profile** and click on **Convert:**

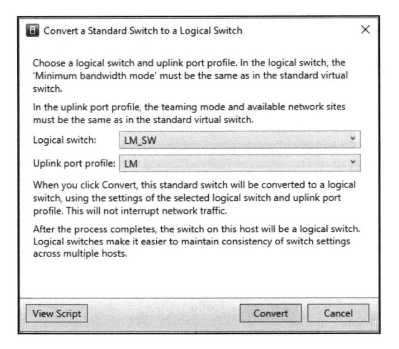

5. In the **Jobs** pane, make sure that the job **Change properties of virtual machine host** is completed.

6. Switch back to the host **Virtual Switches** (refer to step 1 if required) and verify that the switch was converted to the logical switch (**LM_SW**, in my case) as shown in the following screenshot:

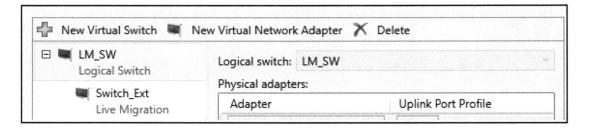

See also

For more information, visit:

- *Overview of RDMA and SET:*
  https://docs.microsoft.com/en-us/windows-server/virtualization/hyper-v-virtual-switch/rdma-and-switch-embedded-teaming
- *Set up the VMM networking fabric:*
  https://docs.microsoft.com/en-us/system-center/vmm/manage-networks

Integrating and configuring the storage

VMM 2016 supports **block-level storage devices** and **file storage** solutions:

- **Block-level storage devices**
  - These expose **logical unit numbers** (**LUNs**) for storage, using fiber channel, iSCSI, and SAS connection mechanisms. You can integrate these arrays with VMM using a storage provider, meaning that you will be able to manage the arrays through the VMM console.
  - The supported storage providers in VMM 2016 are as follows:
    - **SMI-S CIM-XML**: VMM 2016 uses SMAPI to interconnect with the SMI-S compliant server. This in turn uses the Microsoft standards-based **Storage Management Service** (**SMS**) to communicate with the SMI-S external storage.

 If your storage is SMI-S compatible and provider is not embedded, install the SMI-S provider on a server accessible by the VMM management server over the network by an IP address or by a **fully qualified domain name** (**FQDN**). If using FQDN, confirm that the DNS is resolving.

  - **SMP**: VMM uses SMAPI to directly connect with the SMP storage devices.

For a complete list of supported storage providers, see `https://social.technet.microsoft.com/wiki/contents/articles/16100.system-center-2012-vmm-supported-storage-arrays.aspx` (VMM 2012 R2) and `https://docs.microsoft.com/en-us/system-center/vmm/supported-arrays` (VMM 2016).

- **File storage:** In VMM 2016, you can use SMB 3.0 network shares for storage, which can reside on a file server running on Windows Server 2012 and later or on a vendor **Network Attached Storage** (**NAS**). VMM allows you to control and manage file server, SOFS and new Storage Spaces Direct (**S2D**) that is based on SMB 3.0 as well.

See the *Deploying a hyper-converged cluster with Hyper-V and S2D* recipe for more information about managing S2D clusters in VMM 2016.

Getting ready

My first recommendation is to find out whether your storage is compatible with VMM 2012 R2, or better, with VMM 2016. If your storage is not supported, it still recognizes the local storage and remote storage that is on the storage array. However, you might not be able to perform storage management operations such as logical unit creation or removal and assignment of storage through VMM to hosts/clusters. For the unsupported storage, you will need to perform these operations in the vendor storage console.

The steps below describe the workflow to automate storage deployment in VMM 2016:

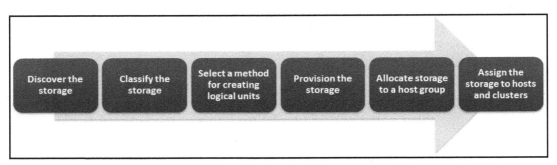

You need to create a Run As account with rights to access the SMI-S provider before configuring it. In this recipe, I will assume that you have an iSCSI storage array and that you have installed its storage provider.

 Contact your storage vendor to obtain the storage provider and installation steps. You also need to ensure that your storage device supports VMM 2016. For example, Dell Equalogic PS series, which was supported in VMM 2012 R2, has not received support for VMM 2016 yet (at the time of writing).

You should also keep in mind that dedicated physical NICs are highly recommended for SAN. The following diagram shows a sample of network configuration that you can use as a reference. In this example, 2 x 10Gb network ports are teamed using SET, while the other two are dedicated for storage and configured with MPIO:

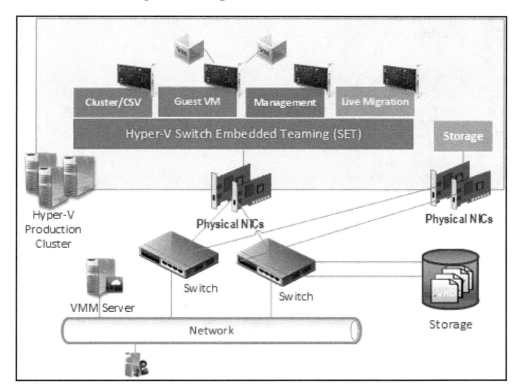

How to do it...

The following steps will help you add/discover the storage in VMM 2016:

1. In the VMM console, in the **Fabric** workspace, on the **Fabric** pane to the left, right-click on **Storage** and then click on **Add Storage Devices**.
2. In the **Add Storage Devices Wizard** window, on the **Select Provider Type** page, choose **SAN and NAS devices discovered and managed by a SMI-S provider** or **SAN devices managed by a native SMP provider**.
3. If you chose the SMI-S provider, in the **Specify Discovery Scope** page, on the **Protocol** list, choose between **SMI-S CMXML** and **SMI-S WMI**. Then type the FQDN or IP of the storage provider and the port number to connect to it, and then select a Run As account by clicking on **Browse** and then click on **Next**.

 If prompted to import a certificate, click on **Import** in the **Import Certificate** dialog box to continue a storage discovery.

4. If you chose the SMP provider, click on **Import** to refresh the list. VMM will then discover and import the storage device information. If you are using SSL, check whether the certificate contains a CN value that matches the value used in VMM, or disable CN check by adding a DWORD value of 1 in the HKEY_LOCAL_MACHINE/SOFTWARE/Microsoft/Windows/CurrentVersion/Storage Management/DisableHttpsCommonNameCheck registry.
5. Once the discovery completes, click on **Next**, and then on the **Select Storage Devices** page, select the **Classification** column for each storage pool that requires classification, then under the **Host Group** column, choose the desired host group and click on **Next**.
6. On the **Summary** page, click on **Finish**.

How it works...

Storage automation through VMM 2016 is only supported for Hyper-V servers.

In VMM 2016, there are three possible types of storage management: **SMI-S provider**, **SMP provider**, and **Windows-based file server storage** (FS/SOFS/S2D).

VMM 2016 makes use of the Microsoft Storage Management service to enable the storage features and communicate with the storages through either SMI-S or SMP providers. This is required to be previously installed on a server other than VMM management and Hyper-V hosts.

 Some storage devices have embedded providers and, therefore, no additional configuration is required.

By making use of the storage providers and automating the process, VMM allows you to assign and add storage to Hyper-V hosts and clusters, for example.

The following are the steps to automate the storage in VMM. To install the storage provider, discover and classify the storage, create the logical units (provision), assign the storage to hosts groups, and then as CSV, assign it to Hyper-V hosts/clusters.

Windows-based file server storage makes use of network shares for storage, and it does support SMB 3.0.

Install the **Multipath I/O (MPIO)** feature for iSCSI storage, and set the **Microsoft iSCSI Initiator** service to start automatically.

For fiber channel storage support, each Hyper-V host must have a HBA zoned correctly.

In addition to that, if the storage pool does support thin provisioning in VMM 2016 by creating a logical unit, you will be able to select the **Create thin storage logical unit with capacity committed on demand** option.

To view the added/discovered storage, click on **Arrays**, and the following settings will be shown: array name, total and used capacity, managed storage pools, provider name, port, and status.

There's more...

After configuring the storage provider, you will be able to carry out tasks such as bringing storage pools and assigning classifications.

Creating an iSCSI session on a host

Carry out the following steps to create the iSCSI sessions on each Hyper-V server connected to the storage:

1. On each Hyper-V server, confirm that **Microsoft iSCSI Initiator Service** is started and set to **Automatic**.
2. In the VMM console, in the **Fabric** workspace, on the **Fabric** pane to the left, expand **Servers**, click on **All Hosts**, right-click on the Hyper-V to configure, and then click on **Properties**.
3. In the **Properties** dialog box, click on the **Storage** tab, and if the storage is not listed, click on **Add** in **iSCSI Arrays** to add it.
4. In the **Create New iSCSI Session** dialog box, select the iSCSI storage in the array list and then click on **Create** if choosing the automatic setup. For manual/customized settings, click on **Use advanced settings** and select the target portal, target name, and the IP address of the initiator, and then click on **Create**. The array will appear under **iSCSI Arrays**.

 VMM creates the iSCSI session by matching the host initiator IP address subnets with the iSCSI target portal IP subnets.

Bringing the storage pools under management and assigning classifications

Carry out the following steps:

1. In the VMM 2016 console, in the **Fabric** workspace, on the **Fabric** pane to the left, expand **Storage**, click on **Arrays**, right-click on the array, and then click on **Properties**.
2. In the **Array Name Properties** dialog box, in the **Storage Pools** tab, in the **Storage Pools** section, select the storage pool.
3. In the **Classification** section, select a previously-created classification. You can create a new one by clicking on **Create classification** and typing the classification name (for example, GOLD). Click on **OK** to confirm.

Configuring the allocation method for a storage array

To configure new logical units that will be allocated while rapidly provisioning VMs through the SAN copy technology, carry out the following steps:

1. In the VMM console, in the **Fabric** workspace, on the **Fabric** pane to the left, expand **Storage**, click on **Arrays**, right-click on the array, and then click on **Properties**.
2. Click on the **Settings** tab, and then in the **Storage array settings** window, choose between **Use snapshots** (default) and **Clone logical units**.

Creating logical units (LUN)

Carry out the following steps:

1. In VMM 2016 console, in the **Fabric** workspace, on the **Fabric** pane to the left, expand **Storage**, click on **Classifications and Pools**, and then select the storage pool.
2. On the **Home** tab, click on **Create Logical Unit.**
3. In the **Create Logical Unit** dialog box, type the logical name (for example, VMs), an optional description, and the logical unit size.

 If the storage pool supports thin provisioning, you can click on **Create thin storage logical unit with capacity committed on demand**.

4. To format the disk, in **Format new disk**, click on **Format this volume as NTFS volume with the following settings**.
5. In the **Mount point** section, choose **Assign the following drive letter** and select the drive letter (**V**, for example), or choose **Mount in the following empty NTFS folder** and then select an empty folder by clicking on **Browse**; or do not assign a drive letter or path.
6. Click on **OK** to confirm.

Allocating logical units and storage pools to a host group

Carry out the following steps:

1. In the **Fabric** workspace, on the **Fabric** pane, click on **Storage**, and then on the **Home** tab, click on **Allocate Capacity** and select the host group from the **Host groups** list.

> If you are logged as a delegated administrator, right-click on the host group, click on **Properties**, and click on the **Storage** tab.

2. Click on **Allocate Logical Units**, select each logical unit to be allocated to the host group, and click on **Add**.

> Optionally, select the **Display as available only storage arrays that are visible to any host in the host group** check box.

3. Click on **OK** to complete.

See also

For more information, see the following references:

- The *Storage fabric overview in VMM 2016* article at: `https://docs.microsoft.com/en-us/system-center/vmm/manage-storage`
- The *How to Configure Hyper-V virtual fibre channel in the VMM* article at `http://docs.microsoft.com/en-us/system-center/vmm/storage-fibre-channel`

Creating physical computer profile – host profile

Host profile or physical computer profile is the configuration settings that can be used to deploy new physical servers as well as clusters using Bare Metal deployment. In this recipe, the following network settings will be configured during host provisioning:

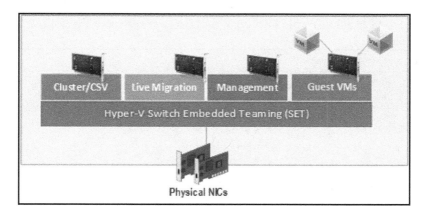

Getting ready

I assume that you already have networking fabric configured in the VMM, as we will use four physical adapters allocated to the logical switch named *SET-1G* in order to get converged networks on host after bare-metal deployment.

Although you are not required to use **Consistent Device Naming (CDN)**, if the physical server that is going to be provisioned does support CDN, you will have first to configure the CDN in the BIOS. This will allow the OS to read the information from the BIOS at the deployment time, and then when configuring the network in the host profile you will be able to provide the name in the configuration settings, which will then allocate the networking settings to the correct physical NIC.

My next recommendation is to use VHDX format as an image containing the OS. As VMM 2016 has a limited list of supported OSes, you can install Windows Server 2012 R2 or Windows Server 2016 on any hosts that you plan to manage in VMM. In this recipe, I will use sysprepped Windows Server 2016 DC image.

How to do it...

Carry out the following steps:

1. Connect to the VMM 2016 console by using the VMM admin account previously created (`rllab\vmm-admin`), and then on the bottom-left pane, click on **Library.**
2. In the **Library** tab, click on **Create** and select **Physical Computer Profile.**
3. In the Wizard, type a name (e.g. `W2016-HyperV`) and an optional description.
4. Select **VM Host** as a role and click on **Next** as shown in the following screenshot:

 If you plan to deploy file servers using Bare-Metal deployment, add another host profile with selected **Windows File Server** role in the **Profile Description** window.

5. In the **OS Image** window, type the path to the sysprepped virtual hard disk containing the operating system and check **Do not convert the virtual disk type to fixed during deployment** to use a dynamic disk.
6. Now, you need to add the physical network adapters to the profile. In the **Hardware Configuration** window, click on **Add** to add a physical or virtual network adapter.

 The number of physical NICs that you need to add, depends on the physical server that will receive the profile. For this exercise, we will use four NICs defined in the host profile W2016-HyperV and connected to the logical switch SET-1G. Management, Cluster and Guest VM networks will be defined as virtual network adapters.

7. To add the NIC1, click on **Add** and select **Physical Network Adapter.**
8. Now, expand the **Physical NIC #1** and click on **Physical properties.**
9. Although not required, you can provide the CDN, if the physical server that is going to be provisioned supports it, or you can select **Physical network adapter's CDN is unknown**.

> The CDN should be enabled on the Physical server BIOS beforehand.

10. Select **Connect this physical NIC to the following logical switch** and select a previously-created logical switch (in our example, select *SET-1G*).
11. Select the port profile for the **Apply the uplink port profile** that we created for the switch earlier in this chapter. In our example, the port profile name is the same as switch's name – SET-1G:

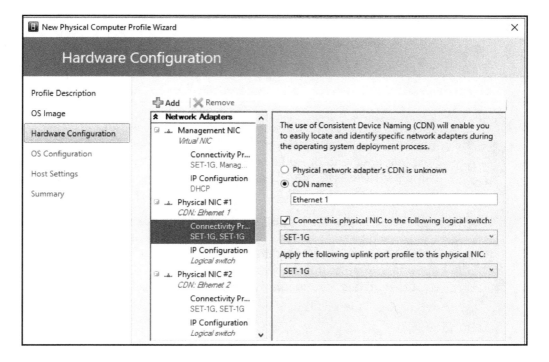

12. Repeat steps 7-11 to add the NIC2-NIC4.
13. Now, click on the **Management NIC** and, based on the diagram described at the start of this section, select **Create a virtual network adapter as the Management NIC**:

TIP

This is to configure how the physical host will communicate with VMM server.

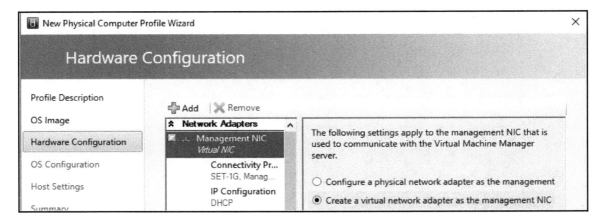

This configuration will depend on your network design and on the number of physical adapters. You can choose to have a dedicated NIC for host management, or you can use a Virtual NIC. In our example, we'll be using a **virtual NIC** (**vNIC**) as shown in the diagram in the introduction of this section. A vNIC will be the most common scenario

14. Expand **Physical Properties** and select **Host Management** port classification.

This vNIC will be assigned to the *SET-1G,* switch as there are no other options available. If there were more physical NICs assigned with other logical switches, you would have the option to select:

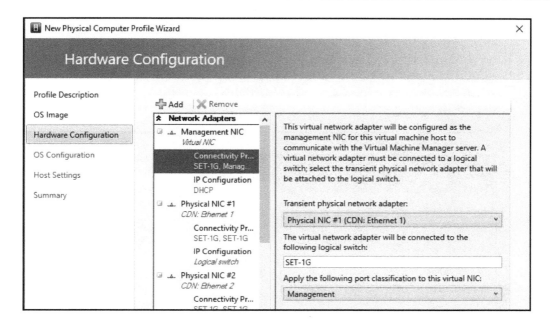

 On the **IP Configuration** window, you can select whether to acquire an IP address through a DHCP Server or to assign a static IP address from the logical network that you specify.

15. Expand **IP Configuration,** select **Management** from **Create this virtual NIC on this virtual network (VM network)**, and choose how to acquire an IP address for management:

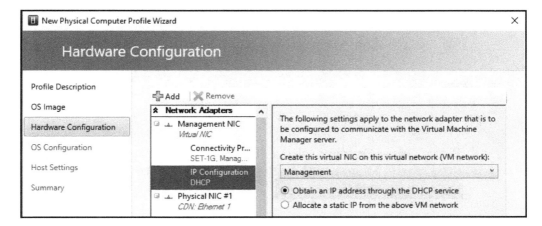

16. You will need to create all the Virtual NICs as per our diagram as shown at the start of the secion: Live Migration, Cluster/CSV and Guest VM. To do that, click on **Add** and select **Virtual Network Adapter** and configure it as you did for the virtual Management NIC, but selecting **Live Migration, CSV** or **GuestVMs**, when applicable on the **Create this virtual NIC on this virtual network (VM network)** option:

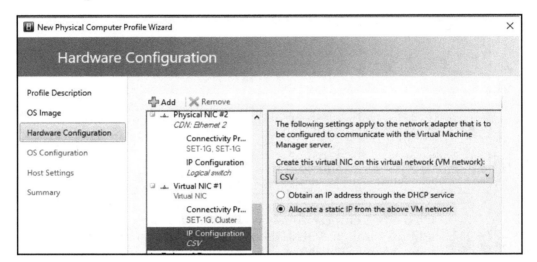

 The Host Profile Network Adapter should now show four Physical NICs and 3 three virtual network adapters.

17. Now, let's configure the Disks. Below **Disk and Partitions**, for the first disk, select the disk partition: **Master Boot Record (MBR)** or **GUID Partition Table (GPT)**.

 To add a new disk or a new partition, click on **+ Add**, and then choose **Disk** or **Partition**

18. Below **Driver Options**, select **Filter drivers with matching PnP IDs** or **Filter drivers with all matching tags specified below.** In our example, we use a DL360 tag, so all drivers that have a DL360 tag will be applied to the host during the deployment:

19. Below **General Settings**, inform the **domain** the host will join, **RunAs account** for domain join, **Identity Information**, **Product Key**, **Time Zone** and commands (scripts, if any).

20. In the **Host settings** window, input the path to store files related to the VM's that will be stored on the host.

The placement will determine the most suitable location, if not specified. You won't be able to select the drive C:\. It will not be available for placement. Also note the Host setting window is not available for File Server host profiles.

21. In the **Summary window**, click on **Finish.** The host profile is now complete.

How it works...

After making sure the network is configured (logical switches), we can start creating the Host profile, which will contain reference to a sysprepped virtual hard disk comprising the OS, the OS configuration settings, and the networking configuration.

To start creating the Host Profile, open the VMM Library tab and select **Create Physical Computer Profile**, provide the name, select **VM Host or File Server** as the server role and provide the OS and network settings.

When configuring the settings, you can choose whether to convert the virtual hard disk type to fixed during deployment or not.

During the bare metal process, VMM will check for the availability of free space on the physical server and it will fail if the hard disk free space is smaller than the sysprepped hard disk containing the operating system with the error:
VHD_BOOT_HOST_VOLUME_NOT_ENOUGH_SPACE

In the Bare metal deployment process, there is a feature called **Deep Discovery** that will get the physical NIC information for correct assignment. If the server is powered off, VMM automatically turns it on during Deep Discovery.

Although not required, you can provide the CDN, if the physical server that is going to be provisioned supoorts it, or you can select **Physical network adapter's CDN is unknown**.

The CDN should be enabled on the Physical server BIOS beforehand.

See also.

For more information, see the following references:

- *How to add profiles to the VMM Library:* `https://docs.microsoft.com/en-us/system-center/vmm/library-profiles`
- *How to Add Driver Files to the VMM Library:* `http://technet.microsoft.com/en-us/library/gg610589.aspx`

Provisioning a physical computer as a Hyper-V host – Bare metal host deployment

In this recipe, we will go through the steps to use VMM 2016 to discover a physical computer, install an operating system, add the Hyper-V role, and then add the machine to a host group with streamline procedures in a highly automated operation called **Bare Metal deployment**.

Getting ready

Before starting a Bare metal deployment, a one-time configuration of the environment is required, and then when that is completed, you can start provisioning physical servers.

To deploy a Hyper-V server, you will need to run the **Add Resources** Wizard, which will then discover the physical computers pre-configured for PXE, and then you will configure settings such as host group, physical computer profile, and custom settings, before starting to deploy the physical server.

Go through the following steps to prepare the infrastructure for a Bare-Metal deployment:

1. **Deploy a PXE Server**: Install a new server (for example, **wds01**) with **Windows Deployment Services** (**WDS**) to provide PXE services. Configure both the deployment server and transport server options.

 You can use an existing PXE server if it is provided through Windows Deployment Services.

2. **Configure a PXE server in VMM 2016**: Add the PXE server to VMM 2016 management by using the VMM console. Although this task is straightforward, you can refer to steps 4-6 in the *Re-adding PXE servers* recipe in Chapter 2, *Upgrading from Previous Versions*.

3. **DHCP Server**: The Hyper-V servers must be configured to start from the network, by executing a PXE boot, which will also require a **Dynamic Host Configuration Protocol** (**DHCP**) server.

 If a DCHP server is running on the WDS server, WDS must be configured to not listen on port 67 and DHCP option 60 must be added to all DHCP scopes. Ensure that **Do not listen on port 67** and **Configure DHCP option 60 to 'PXEClient'** are selected on the DCHP tab in the WDS server properties.

4. **Add a base image for the operating system installation**: Using the Windows Server 2016 VHDX file, you can add a base image for the operating system installation to the VMM library and optional hardware driver files. See *How to Add Driver Files to the VMM Library* (http://technet.microsoft.com/en-au/library/gg610589.aspx).

5. **Create a Run As account**: You need to create a Run As account for the host add operation. We created that before in Chapter 2, *Upgrading from Previous Versions* (**vmm-admin**).

6. Create **Domain Name System** (**DNS**) entries and Active Directory computer accounts for the computer names that will be provisioned.

 This optional step is recommended to environments with multiple DNS servers where replication can take some time to complete.

7. **Create a host profile**: See the previous recipe for any details.
8. Make sure the physical network infrastructure is configured.

> If you are using Deep Discovery during the search for the physical computers, VMM will show more detailed information about the computer.

How to do it...

First, we will perform the initial configuration of the physical server:

1. As VMM installs Hyper-V server role during bare-metal deployment, ensure that machine BIOS is configured to support virtualization technology. Intel VT or AMD-V should be turned on as well as **Execute Disable Bit** (**EDB**) (XD bit, Intel Systems) or **No Execution Bit** (NX bit, AMD systems).

> Hyper-V in Windows Server 2016 requires SLAT-compatible CPU. Check CPU specification or use *systeminfo.exe* to get Hyper-V compatibility report.

2. Enable booting from a network adapter for access to the **Pre-boot Execution Environment** (**PXE**).
3. Upgrade the firmware and configure the BMC board by:

   - Enabling the out-of-band management protocol that could be IPMI (Version 1.5 or 2.0), DCMI (Version 1.0), SMASH (Version 1.0) or custom protocols (ILO, iDRAC and etc.). For example, my HP DL360 has configured iLO and it's accessible from the VMM management server.
   - Configuring the network settings, which include **Host Name**, **Domain Name**, **IP Address**, and **Subnet** (you should be able to ping this IP from the VMM management and console).
   - Enabling system services.
   - Configuring login credentials to allow VMM 2016 remote access. In our example, I also created a Run As account with iLO credentials to make BMC available to VMM/WDS servers.

4. Create DNS entries with the server's name and AD computer objects that will be assigned to the hosts when they are deployed.

The next step is to discover the physical server and deploy it as a managed Hyper-V host in VMM 2016:

1. In the VMM console, in the **Fabric** workspace, click on **Servers**, on the **Fabric** pane to the left.
2. Click on **Add Resources** on the **Home** tab, and then click on **Hyper-V Hosts and Clusters**.
3. On the **Resource location** page, select **Physical computer to be provisioned as virtual machine hosts** and click on **Next**, as shown in the following screenshot:

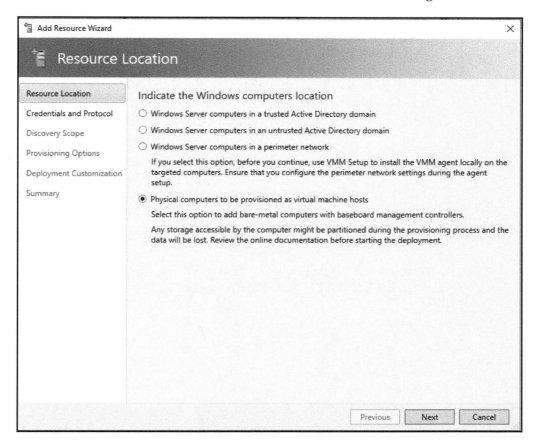

4. On the **Credentials and protocol** page, select the Run As account (with BMC access permissions) by clicking on **Browse** (for example, select **bare-metal**), and click on **OK**.

5. In the **Protocol** list, select the out-of-band management protocol previously configured (for example, **Intelligent Platform Management Interface (IPMI)**) and click on **Next**.

Select **Intelligent Platform Management Interface (IPMI)** to use **Data Center Management Interface (DCMI)**.

6. On the **Discovery scope** page, type the IP scope and click on **Next**.

If you use the IP address, the machine immediately reboots into PXE and deep discovery will be started. I would recommend to provide an IP range even if you have just one machine. The behavior is slightly different. VMM will scan machine first and give you information about that machine (serial number, model and so on), so you can verify IP address/machine before a deep discovery and prevent machines from unexpected restarts.

7. By specifying an IP subnet or an IP address range, select the server(s) to be installed as Hyper-V host in the **Target resources** page, and click on **Next**.

Make sure that you select the correct server(s) and document the IP addresses of the BMCs by creating a spreadsheet to track them, or use IPAM server (recommended).

8. On the **Provisioning options** page, in the **Host group** list, select the target host group for the new Hyper-V host(s), for example, **Moscow\Hyper-V**.

9. Once deep discovery is completed, you will get the following window:

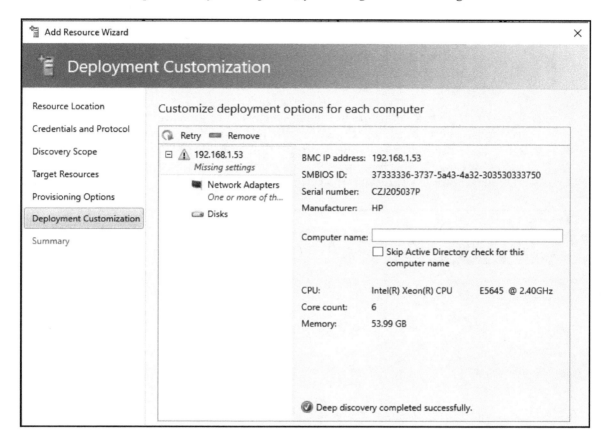

10. On the **Deployment customization** page, type the server name (for example, `HV03`) and review the computer information.

 Although not recommended, you can skip AD validation by clicking on **Skip Active Directory check for this computer name**. By skipping the validation, if the computer already exists, it will be overwritten by the deployment process.

11. Click on **Network Adapters** in the list on the left to provide missing settings. For example, if you have adapters with Static IP assignment or if the host profile settings do not match machine configuration, you are required to provide the correct settings for each adapter. In our example, we need to define settings for virtual adapters as shown in the screenshot:

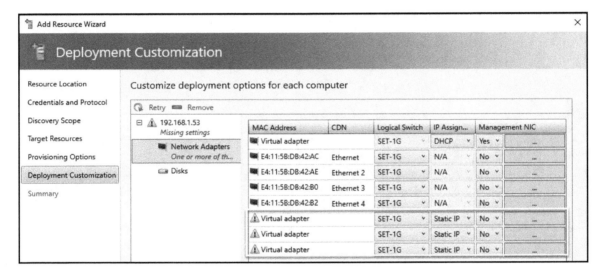

12. Click the **Configure** button (**...**) on the right side, review port classification and VM network, change them if required, and then specify a name for the virtual adapter (for example, *Cluster*).

13. To define IP assignment, click **Configure a static IPv4 address for this network adapter** and **Obtain an IPv4 address from the IP pool corresponding to the selected subnet** as shown in the following screenshot:

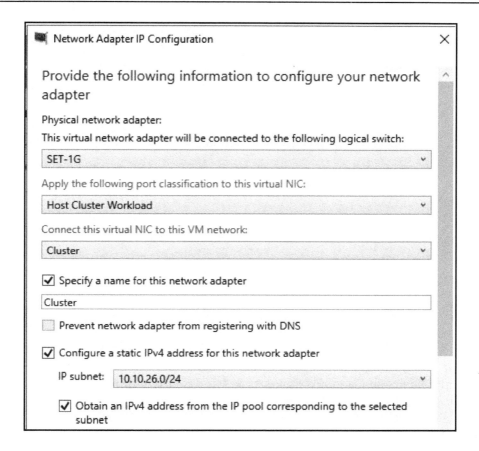

To assign a specific IP address from the selected IP subnet, clear the
Obtain an IP address corresponding to the selected subnet check box. In
the **IP subnet** list, click the IP address range that you want. In the **IP
address** box, enter an available IP address that falls in the subnet.

14. Repeat the previous step for other virtual adapters (for example, Live Migration
    or GuestVMs), and then ensure that you don't have any warning messages for
    Network Adapters in the list.

15. Once you have provided network settings for adapters, verify disk settings by clicking on **Disks**, then click the **Specify which disk the OS should be applied to** and select the desired disk for the OS deployment:

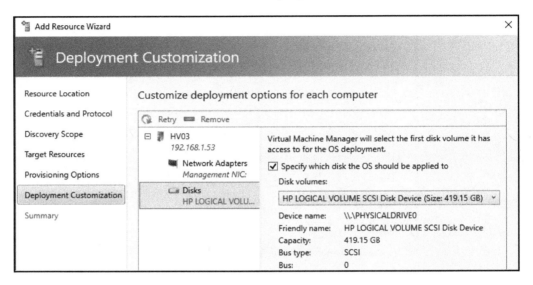

When all this is done, you can click on **Next** and on the **Summary** page, click **Finish** to start the deployment. The **Create a new host from physical machine** job will be started. Make sure that all steps in the job have a **Status** of **Completed**,and then verify that logical switch and virtual network adapters are configured on the host:

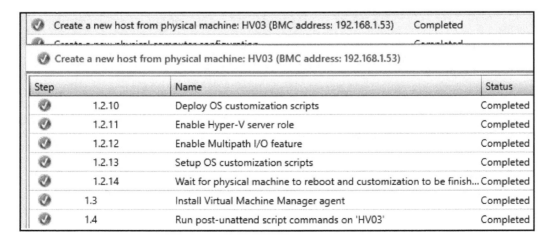

How it works...

The bare-metal provisioning feature in the VMM simplifies deployment of physical bare-metal machines as Hyper-V hosts and clusters.

Going forward, bare-metal provisioning in VMM 2016 is also used to create file servers/clusters or add bare-metal nodes to existing clusters. Cluster OS upgrade does rely on this feature and provides easier cluster migration.

To start, you need a PXE server (it can be an existing one) provided through **Windows Deployment Services** (**WDS**). Then, you need to add it to VMM management server.

On each physical server, in the BIOS, configure virtualization support and boot from PXE and the BMC. This will require you to have a working DHCP server in place.

Then, create the DNS entries for each server; add the required resources to the VMM library. These resources include a generalized Windows Server VHD/VHDX file that will be used as the base image, and optional driver files to add to the operating system during installation.

Create host profiles (which include image location, hardware, and OS settings) in the VMM library.

CDN can be configured in the host profiles, and if supported by the physical server (Hyper-V), it will identify and associate physical NICs to the correct logical switches.

Use VMM to discover (scan) the physical computers, to configure deployment and settings, and to start the deployment of the OS and Hyper-V role configuration. VMM will use BMC commands during this phase to power the servers off/on.

If you decide to assign IP addresses from a VMM IP address Pool to the Hyper-V hosts (on management network), be prepared to manually enter the MAC address of the physical NIC that is used for PXE or use the VMM deep discovery feature to retrieve the information. CDN provides the physical NIC's name, but not the MAC addresses.

When they restart, the PXE server will respond to the boot request with a customized image (Windows PE). The Windows PE agent will then prepare the server by downloading and applying the OS image and specified driver files from the library and by adding the Hyper-V server role; then, it restarts the server.

Multipath I/O feature will be enabled during bare-metal provisioning as well.

On the **Deployment customization** page, a small amount of wait time (in minutes) for the Deep Discovery to complete is normal, and when it is complete, VMM will show a success message.

After the host deployment, if a post-deployment task is required, right-click on the host and click on **Run Script Command** to run a script.

See also

For more information, see the following references:

- *Provision a Hyper-V host or cluster from bare-metal:* http://docs.microsoft.com/en-us/system-center/vmm/hyper-v-bare-metal
- *System requirements for Hyper-V on Windows Server 2016:* http://docs.microsoft.com/en-us/windows-server/virtualization/hyper-v/system-requirements-for-hyper-v-on-windows

Adding and Managing Hyper-V hosts and host clusters

In VMM 2016, you can add Hyper-V hosts/clusters running on the same domain as the VMM, on a trusted domain, or in a disjointed namespace. You can also add Hyper-V hosts (not clusters) running on an untrusted domain and on a perimeter network (for example, DMZ). Using Bare metal as we described before, physical computers with no OS can be added as well.

If you want to manage a standalone host that is in a workgroup, use the method to add a host in a perimeter network.

Getting ready

Make sure virtualization support is enabled in the BIOS. If the Hyper-V role is not installed, VMM will install it as part of the setup.

The following steps will guide you through how to add a Hyper-V host or a Hyper-V cluster in a trusted Active Directory domain.

How to do it...

Carry out the following steps to add a trusted Hyper-V host or cluster:

1. In the VMM console, click on the **Fabric** workspace, and then on the **Fabric** pane, click on **Servers**.
2. On the **Home** tab, click on the **Add Resources** button on the ribbon, and then click on **Hyper-V Hosts and Clusters**.
3. On the **Resource location** page, click on **Windows Server computers in a trusted Active Directory domain** and click on **Next**.
4. On the **Credentials** page, specify an existing Run As account, for example, **Hyper-V Host Administration Account** (created in Chapter 2, *Upgrading from Previous Version*) or manually type the user credentials, for example, rllab\vmm-admin.

 To create a Run As account at this point, click on **Browse**, and in the **Select a Run As Account** dialog box, click on **Create Run As Account** and enter the requested information.

5. Click on **Next**, and in the **Discovery scope** page, select between the following options:
   - **Specify Windows Server computers by names**: Type the IP or server name/cluster name (one per line). Click on **Next**.

 By typing just part of the name, the wizard will list the servers that match.

- **Specify an Active Directory query**: And then type an AD query, or click on **Generate an AD query** to create it. Click on **Next**:

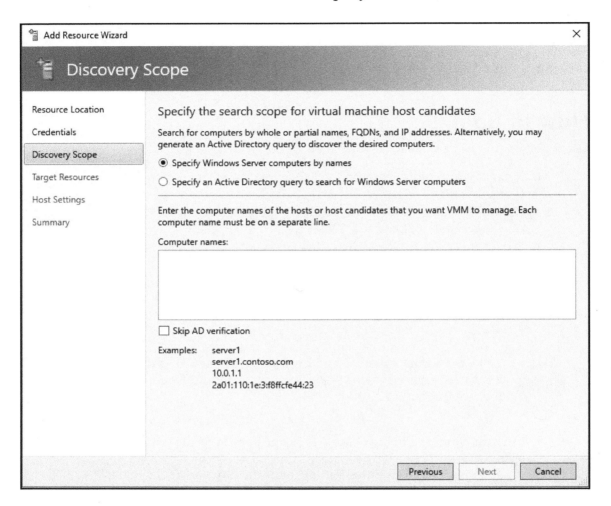

6. On the **Target resources** page, select the computer(s) or cluster name(s).

 If the Hyper-V role is not enabled, a message will be displayed stating that the role will be installed and the server will restart. Click on **OK**. Click on **Next**, and on the **Host settings** page, select the host group from the **Host group** list. Click on **Reassociate this host with this VMM environment** if the host was associated with another VMM server.

7. When adding a standalone host, type the local host path to store VM files (for example, D:\VMS), click on **Add**, click on **Next**, and then click on **Finish**.

 A machine will be rebooted one or more times during Hyper-V role installation

How it works...

When adding a standalone server or cluster in a trusted domain environment, and the domain is not the same as VMM, make sure that there is a two-way trust factor in place.

Use **Group Policy** (**GPO**) to configure WinRM, which is the only supported method for WinRM Service settings, but consider this:

- The GPO settings that VMM supports are **Allow automatic configuration of listeners**, **Turn On Compatibility HTTP Listener**, and **Turn On Compatibility HTTPS Listener**, and this is only for hosts that are in a trusted domain
- WinRM Client settings through GPO are unsupported
- It may not be possible to install VMM Agent if you enable other WinRM settings by GPO

 The use of the VMM service account to add or remove Hyper-V hosts is not recommended, as it could impose security risks.

When installing a standalone server, you will be required to provide a local VM path (if it does not exist, it will be created). If left empty, the default will be used (%SystemDrive%\ProgramData\Microsoft\Windows\Hyper-V). When installing a cluster, the path will be located on shared storage.

 Using the OS drive to store VM files is not recommended.

There's more...

You can also add Hyper-V hosts that are not on the same domain or that are on a perimeter network.

Adding Hyper-V hosts in a disjointed namespace

Carry out the same steps to add a trusted Hyper-V host or cluster, considering the following points:

- On the **Credentials** page, type the domain account credentials (for example, `poc\vmm-admin`)
- On the **Discovery scope** page, type the FQDN of the host (for example, `hyperv03.poc.local`) and check the **Skip AD verification** checkbox

> VMM checks the domain for the SPN. If it does not exist, and if the VMM service account has permission to perform `setspn`, it will be created.

You will be required to add the SPN manually if the account does not have permission.

At the command prompt, with administrator rights, type the following command (of the format `setspn -A HOST/<FQDN> <NetBIOSName>`):

```
setspn -A HOST/hyperv03.poc.local hyperv03
```

Adding Hyper-V hosts in a perimeter network

Carry out the following steps to add a standalone Hyper-V server that is in a perimeter network (for example, DMZ) to be managed by VMM:

1. Create the following spreadsheet for documentation purposes:

Hyper-V server (Hostname)	Encryption key	Location folder	IP address

> Keep this spreadsheet in a secure place.

Installing the agent on the standalone server

Carry out the following steps to install the VMM agent on a standalone Hyper-V server:

1. Connect to the standalone server, and from there, browse to the VMM setup folder. Right-click on **setup**, and then click on **Run as administrator**.
2. On the **Setup** menu, click on **Local Agent**. Click on **Optional Installation** and click on **Next**. And then, on the **License** page, click on **Next**.
3. On the **Destination Folder** page, enter the installation path and then click on **Next**.
4. On the **Security File Folder** page, check the **This host is on a perimeter network** checkbox and type in and confirm a complex security key.

> Take note of the security key.

5. Specify the location for the storage key by clicking on **Change**, and then copy the security file to a folder on the VMM console.
6. If you require it, select **Use a CA signed certificate for encrypting communications with this host** and type the thumbprint.

> To obtain the thumbprint, select **Computer account** in the **Certificates** snap-in. Double-click on the certificate and select and copy the Thumbprint field value on the **Details** tab.

7. Click on **Next**, and on the **Host network name** page, choose whether VMM will communicate with the host by using a local computer name or IP address.
8. Click on **Next**, and if you chose **Use IP address**, select an IP address from the list.
9. In the **Configuration settings** page, confirm the port settings (5986 and 443) and click on **Next**; then click on **Install**.

Adding perimeter hosts to VMM

Carry out the following steps to add a Hyper-V server on a DMZ to VMM:

1. In the VMM console, in the **Fabric** workspace, on the **Fabric** pane, click on **Servers**.
2. On the **Home** tab, click on **Add Resources** in the ribbon, and then click on **Hyper-V Hosts and Clusters**.
3. On the **Resource location** page, click on **Windows Server computers in a perimeter network** and click on **Next**.
4. On the **Target resources** page type the hostname or the IP, encryption key, and path for securityFile.txt, for each host. Select the target host group and then click on **Add**.
5. Click on **Next**, and in the **Host settings** page, type the local host path to store VM files in (for example, D:\VMS), click on **Add**, and then click on **Next**.
6. On the **Summary** page, click on **Finish**.

> For a detailed host status view in VMM, right-click on the host, click on **Properties**, and check the status for overall health, host agent health, and Hyper-V role health. If you find an issue, click on **Repair all**.

See also

For more information, see the following references:

- *Add existing Hyper-V hosts and clusters to the fabric*: http://docs.microsoft.com/en-us/system-center/vmm/hyper-v-existing

Deploying a hyper-converged cluster with S2D and Hyper-V

In this recipe, we will discuss how to create clusters in VMM 2016. This is best illustrated through a real-world example that I will refer to.

Suppose, you have four identical servers with local-attached storage—two SSDs and four HDDs on each server, and two other dedicated HDD disks are used for system partitions. How can you make a shared storage from all of this? The right answer is S2D. S2D can group up local disks to one storage pool available for each cluster node. It requires internal disks or direct-attached storage enclosures and does automatic storage caching and tiering configuration depending on the types of drives present in your systems. Fault tolerance and storage efficiency for virtual volumes in a pool are achieved through the different resiliency types such as parity, mirror or mixed. S2D can be considered in two deployment models: hyper-converged and converged.

As we already discussed in Chapter 1, *VMM 2016 Architecture, hyper-converged* model allows you to share the same servers between storage and compute resources. Therefore, Hyper-V and S2D are configured on the same cluster. In the converged model, S2D and Hyper-V clusters are separated from each other and **Scale-out File Server** (**SOFS**) is used on top of S2D to provide remote file access via SMB 3.0 to Hyper-V cluster nodes.

Whether you are going to use hyper-converged or converged model, VMM 2016 will make it easier to deploy and manage S2D and Hyper-V clusters.

 Storage Spaces Direct is only included in Windows Server 2016 Data center. VMM 2016 server must also be running on Windows Server 2016 Datacenter in order to manage S2D and Storage Replica.

Getting ready

Before you start creating a hyper-converged cluster, there are some requirements that you need to look at. These may also be applied to the S2D converged model:

- At least two identical servers are required. In this recipe, we will use four servers with the same hardware, firmwares and configuration.

 While Hyper-V cluster can consist of a maximum of 64 nodes, S2D supports up to 16 nodes. If you plan to scale up compute resources to over 16 nodes, you may consider the converged model instead.

- There must be a minimum of four drives per server. S2D supports SATA, SAS or NVME drives connected via internal or external storage enclosures. These disks must not be presented as part of RAID arrays, as RAID controllers are not supported. S2D requires simple HBA and not partitioned disks.

If your all drives, including dedicated drives for OS, are connected via the same storage enclosure and, therefore, RAID is not available, you can use disk mirroring for system partitions to provide basic fault tolerance. See the *Configuring Disk Mirroring for Windows Server 2012* for more information, see `https://wp.me/a2WWs4-1wC`.

- S2D automatically binds and configures some of the disk drives as cache devices to maximize storage performance. Whether to use cache or not, S2D decides on the basis of drive types present. As shown in the following screenshot, if you have two or three drive types, S2D will select the fastest ones for cache purposes. Typically, two dedicated drives per server are required for cache at least. In all-flash deployments, cache won't be used by default.

Drive types present	Minimum number required	Cache drives
All NVMe (same model)	4 NVMe	None, Write-only (if configured manually)
All SSD (same model)	4 SSD	None, Write-only (if configured manually)
NVMe + SSD	2 NVMe + 4 SSD	NVMe, Write-only
NVMe + HDD	2 NVMe + 4 HDD	NVMe, Read + Write
SSD + HDD	2 SSD + 4 HDD	SSD, Read + Write
NVMe + SSD + HDD	2 NVMe + 4 Others	NVMe, Read + Write for HDD, Write-only for SSD

It's recommended to have capacity drives in multiples of the number of cache devices (ratio 2:1, for example, could be a good start point).

- At least two 10 Gbps NICs per server, preferably RDMA-capable, are recommended for S2D intra-cluster communication.

Networking requirements are the most critical for S2D as it uses *Software Storage Bus* that spans cluster nodes and allows to see all disks across all servers in the cluster, so it makes disks visible to the storage spaces layer used to create virtual volumes in which data is synchronously replicated to the multiple cluster nodes depending on volume's resiliency type.

- The hosts should meet the requirements for a failover clustering and should be running Windows Server 2016 Datacenter with the latest updates.
- The hosts must all be part of the same domain to be added as cluster nodes.
- The hosts should be configured with SET switch to leverage RDMA capabilities.

I normally create SET switch with virtual NICs for SMB, Live Migration CSV or management traffic types. Refer to the *Designing for converged networks* recipe for more details.

- The VMM management server must either be in the same domain as the hosts or on a trusted domain. My VMM is also outside of hyper-converged cluster and running on the dedicated and separate cluster.
- The hosts that are going to be added as cluster nodes need to be in the same host group.
- Domain account is required for creating a cluster. The account must have administrative permissions on cluster hosts and should have Create Computer objects and Read All Properties permissions in the Computers container. Use its credentials to create Run As account in the VMM.

For the purposes of this section, we will be using the configuration established in the *Networking: Configuring Logical Networks* recipe. The servers have local-attached two SSDs and four HDDs, drive configuration is the same for all cluster nodes (types, size, firmware).

 I would also recommend to make sure that you have the latest firmwares and OS drivers for server hardware components. Use HP Service Pack, for example, to check and update HPE Proliant servers.

How to do it...

Carry out the following steps to create cluster using VMM:

1. In the VMM console, click on the **Fabric** workspace, and then on the **Fabric** pane, click on **Servers**.
2. On the **Home** tab, click on the **Create** button on the ribbon, and then click on **Hyper-V Cluster**.

 To create separated SOFS cluster, you need to select **File Server Cluster** and on the **General Configuration** page select **Storage attached directly to each cluster node (Storage Spaces Direct)** as a storage configuration for a new file cluster.

3. On the **General Configuration** page, type the cluster name (for example, HV-CL01) and select the host group from the **Host group**, click **Enable Storage Spaces Direct** to automatically configure S2D, and then click on **Next**.

I will use the host group named *S2D* with the existing Hyper-V servers. See the **Adding and Managing Hyper-V hosts and host clusters** recipe for more details.

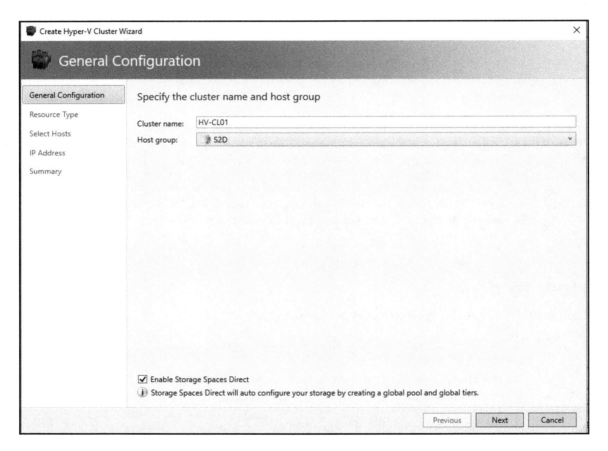

S2D will create one storage pool containing all eligible disk drives. Cache and tiers will also be configured automatically.

4. On the **Resource Type** page, specify an existing Run As account, for example, `clu-admin` and select **Existing servers running a Windows Server operating system** as a type of resources that you want to use for cluster. Although you can select **Skip Cluster Validation,** it's not recommended, as a cluster without a validated configuration won't be supported by Microsoft.

 Select **Physical computer to be provisioned** to create cluster from bare-metal machines. See the *Provisioning a physical computer as a Hyper-V host* recipe in this chapter to prepare your environment for bare metal provisioning, then use the steps in this recipe. They will be the same as for existing Hyper-V hosts.

5. On the **Select Hosts** page, define the hosts that are going to be added as cluster nodes as shown in the following screenshot:

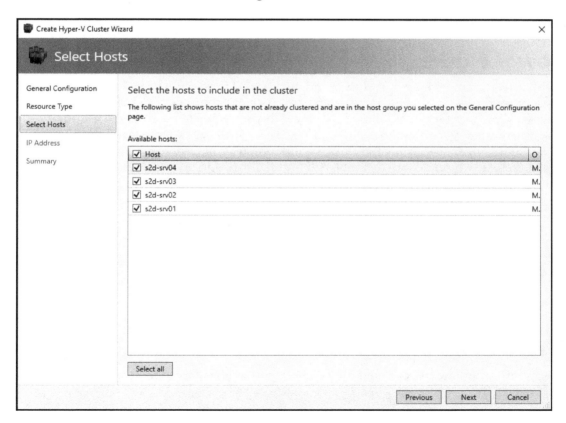

6. On the **IP address** page, type a static IP address (for example, `10.10.25.50`) for **cluster name object (CNO)** or select a static IP pool.

7. On the **Summary** page, review the settings and click on **Finish**.

8. Monitor the **Install Cluster** job in the **Jobs** pane. Once it's completed, review the cluster validation report (see the *Information 25353* event):

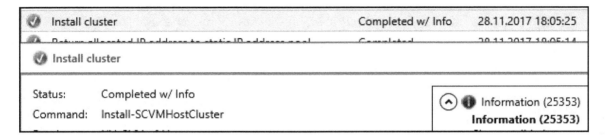

How it works...

VMM 2016 can create Hyper-V cluster and enable S2D from already-managed Hyper-V hosts, or by provisioning new hosts from bare-metal machines. During the cluster creation process, VMM verifies whether the hosts meet the prerequisites such as the required operating system versions and the domain. For each host, VMM enables the failover clustering feature. VMM runs the cluster validation tests and then, if tests are not failed, it creates a cluster. If you chose to enable S2D, VMM 2016 adds the file server, storage replica and Data Deduplication features, turns on Direct-Attached S2D on cluster, and then discovers and creates one global storage pool with cache and tiering settings, depending on drives present.

 When you add a new node to the hyper-converged cluster, VMM 2016 enables S2D and automatically discovers and adds suitable disks to the S2D storage pool. If you remove a node from the cluster, its disks will be removed from the storage pool as well.

There's more...

After configuring the hyper-converged cluster, you will be able to manage S2D storage pool and create CSV.

Managing the storage pool

Carry out the following steps:

1. In the VMM 2016 console, in the **Fabric** workspace, on the **Fabric** pane to the left, expand **Storage**, click on **Arrays**, right-click on the S2D storage array (`HV-CL01`, for example), and then click on **Manage Pools** as shown in the following screenshot:

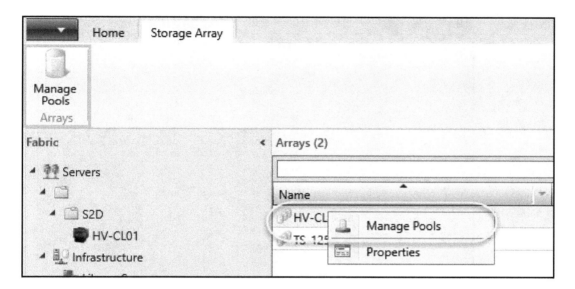

 I would recommend to refresh storage provider before doing any changes. Click on **Providers**, right-click on a provider and select **Refresh.** Monitor the job named Reads Storage Provider in the **Jobs** pane.

2. In the **Manage Pools of Storage Array** dialog box, click on **Edit** to review or modify pool settings.
3. On the **General** tab, change the pool's name and its classification if required.

 Click on **New** to create a classification for the pool, and in the **New Classification** dialog box, type a name and its optional description and click on **Add.**

4. On the **Physical Disks** tab, review the drives that are members of S2D storage pool and remove some of them from the pool, if required. For doing this, highlight disks that you would like to remove and click on **Uncheck Highlighted.** The removed disks will be placed in the Primordial pool holding claimed and available disks for storage spaces pools:

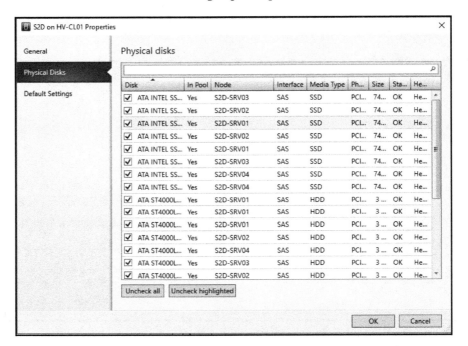

 See the `https://rlevchenko.com/2017/12/02/s2d-disks-dont-show-up-in-the-disk-manager/` if you want to get back drives from the pool and make them available for disk management in OS (`diskmgmt.msc`).

5. On the **Default Settings** tab, interleave settings are shown. You can change its default value (256 Kb), though it's not recommended.

 Interleave represents the amount of data written to a single column of drives per stripe. If you have a three-way mirror, for example, column-to-disk correlation is 1:3 and S2D duplicates the column's data onto three disks.

Creating cluster shared volumes

Carry out the following steps to create the virtual disks and CSV:

1. In the VMM console, click on the **Fabric** workspace, and then on the **Fabric** pane, expand **Servers** and right-click on the cluster, for example, HV-CL01, then select **Properties**.

2. In the **Cluster Properties** dialog box, select **Shared Volumes** tab, and then click on the **Add** button.

3. When the **Create Volume** wizard opens, in the **Storage Type** page, type a volume name (for example, Volume01_VM), select the storage pool and classification for this volume as shown in the screenshot, and then click **Next**:

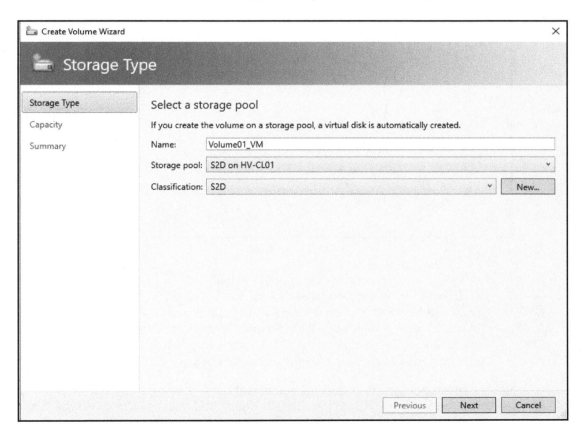

4. On the **Capacity** page, define the volume's size and choose the file system (for example, *ReFS*) and select **Configure advanced storage and tiering settings** as shown in the following screenshot:

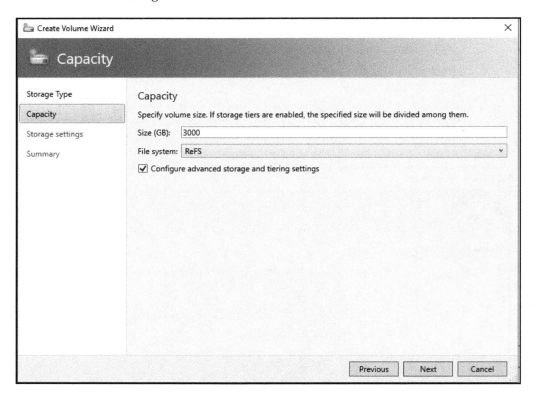

ReFS is the recommended file system for S2D, though it does not support the data deduplication feature in Windows Server 2016. If your workloads (for example, VDI) require deduplication, create a volume with the NTFS file system and set deduplication settings (*Hyper-V, Virtualized backup server, General Purpose file server*). However, data deduplication supports ReFS in Windows Server 1709 semi-annual channel release.

5. On the **Storage settings** page, define the **Storage tier count** (for example, 1) and review resiliency and capacity settings for tiers, and then click on **Next**. In this recipe, all volumes don't use tiering as we have only two types of drives:

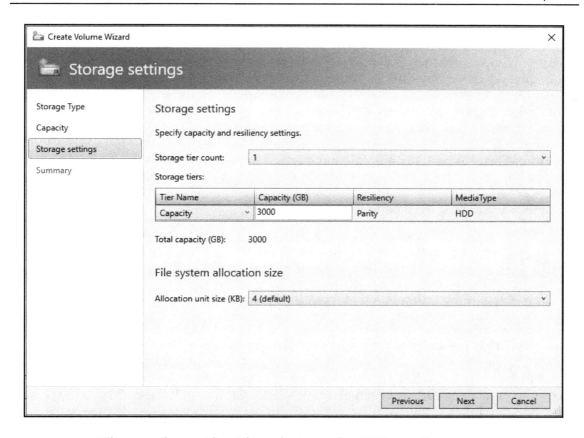

When you have at least four cluster nodes, S2D uses the parameter *ResiliencySettingName* (with values either *Mirror* or *Parity*) for tiers to define their resiliency types. Capacity refers to the dual-parity and Mirror represents a three-way mirror resiliency. To get the current resiliency settings for storage tiers, use the following one-liner: `Get-StorageTier -FriendlyName Capacity| ft FriendlyName, ResiliencySettingName, PhysicalDiskRedundancy`

And if you would like to change default resiliency type for a storage tier: `Get-StorageTier -FriendlyName Capacity|Set-StorageTier -ResiliencySettingName Mirror`

Then open the VMM console and refresh storage provider to receive the new resiliency settings.

6. On the **Summary** page, review the settings and click on **Finish** to create the shared volume.

Setting storage QoS policies

Storage QoS was introduced in Windows Server 2012 R2 and enabled an ability to set minimum and maximum IOPS thresholds at the virtual disk level. It meant you had to define storage QoS policy for each VHD and, therefore, it was quite difficult to provide the right QoS in large environments with huge numbers of VMs. Moreover, you simply couldn't predict a real storage performance as there was no guaranteed number of minimum IOPS for VHDs. To meet those challenges, storage QoS in Windows Server 2016 introduces a way to centrally monitor and manage storage performance for virtual machines by providing storage QoS cluster resource as a policy manager, and storage resource fairness to ensure that targets receive a minimum number of IOPS and fairly distributes available storage performance to them.

> VMM 2016 can only manage storage QoS of VHDs which are residing on the S2D hyper-converged clusters and SOFS. You should also keep in mind that VHDs must reside on CSVs in order to be managed by new storage QoS. However, an ability to apply storage QoS to all managed clusters was added to the VMM 1801 semi-annual channel release.

There are two storage QoS policy types in the VMM 2016-**All virtual disk instances share resources** (single-instance or aggregated) and **Resources allocated to each virtual disk instance** (multi-instance or dedicated). If you applied the same aggregated policy to two VMs with one connected VHD to each VM, for example, VMs will share the minimum and maximum number of IOPS between these two VHDs. However, if these VMs were assigned to the dedicated policy, they would use exactly the same IOPS values as defined in the policy.

> One thing in common, if a VM has multiple VHDs assigned to the same storage QoS policy, the VM will share IOPS across the VHDs regardless of policy type.

Carry out the following steps to create new Storage QoS policy:

1. In the VMM console, click on the **Fabric** workspace, and then on the **Fabric** pane, expand **Storage** and right-click on the **QoS Policies**, and then click **Create Storage QoS Policy**.
2. On the **General** page, type a policy name (for example, *Silver*) and an optional description, and then click on **Next**.
3. On the **Policy Settings** page, specify the policy type, and then define the minimum and maximum values for IOPS and **Maximum bandwidth (MB/s)** as shown in the screenshot:

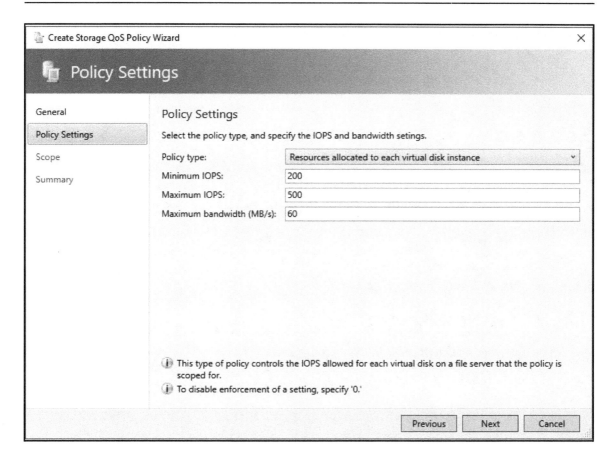

 Value 0 for IOPS or bandwidth settings means unlimited performance.

4. On the **Scope** page, select the managed storage arrays (for example, *HV-CL01*) on which to apply the policy settings and click on **Next**.
5. On the **Summary** page, verify the settings and click on **Finish**.
6. Apply the created Storage QoS to the VHD, for example, during a VM creation process from a template.

To create a new Storage QoS, you can use PowerShell as well:
`New-SCStorageQoSPolicy -Name "Silver" -Description "Storage QoS (Gold)" -PolicyType "Dedicated" -IOPSMinimum "200" -IOPSMaximum "500" -BandwidthLimitMBPS "60"`

See also

For more information, see the following references:

- *Overview of Storage Spaces Direct:*
  http://docs.microsoft.com/windows-server/storage/storage-spaces/storage-spaces-direct-overview
- *Understanding the cache in Storage Spaces Direct:*
  http://docs.microsoft.com/windows-server/storage/storage-spaces/understand-the-cache
- *Manage Storage Spaces Direct in VMM:*
  http://docs.microsoft.com/en-us/system-center/vmm/s2d
- *Manage Storage Replica in VMM:*
  http://docs.microsoft.com/en-us/system-center/vmm/storage-replica
- *Test your S2D with VMFleet and Diskspd:*
  https://rlevchenko.com/2017/12/22/deploying-vmfleet-to-test-s2d-performance/

6
Configuring Guarded Fabric in VMM

In this chapter, we will cover the following recipes:

- Deploying the host guardian service
- Configuring additional HGS cluster nodes
- Deploying guarded hosts
- Defining guarded fabric settings in **Virtual Machine Manager** (**VMM**)
- Deploying shielded VMs
- Converting existing VMs to shielded

Introduction

It must be difficult to find customers who have never thought about moving their enterprise workloads to the cloud. Some of them decide to build hybrid clouds, while others migrate all of their resources in order to make an all-in-the-cloud model. However, almost everyone is concerned about security and it often becomes an obstacle on their road to cloud. *How can you be sure that your data is kept securely and that only you have access to it?* Since a VM is just a set of files that can be copied by bad guys from the cloud's provider and then simply used on other systems, your competitors may be able to get access to that data and steal your client's database, personal data, administrator credentials, confidential data, and so on. More simply, compromised backup admins can restore your VM and do anything with your confidential data. Cloud providers, thus, are required to provide a solution to eliminate all these risks and also to protect themselves from unexpected data theft by disgruntled employees.

This chapter is all about a new guarded fabric consisting of the following components:

- **Shielded VMs**: These are protected VMs from compromised or malicious fabric administrations. In these VMs, **virtual trusted platform module (vTPM)** is used to encrypt disks, Secure Boot is enforced on live migration traffic as well as saved state, replica, and checkpoints; files are also encrypted. All other insecure paths are also blocked, for example, VM console connection, PowerShell Direct, and some of the integration components, such as data exchange service and guest services. Using VMM 2016, you will be able to convert traditional VMs to shielded and create new shielded VMs.

- **Host Guardian Service** (HGS): This is a new role in Windows Server 2016 that attests Hyper-V hosts health and manages encryption keys used to unlock shielded VMs. HGS cannot be configured from the VMM console and requires a manual deployment. Once it's deployed, you can then define HGS attestation and key protection URLs and code integrity policies (ensure that the host is running only on trusted code) in VMM console to use them with guarded hosts.

- **Guarded Hosts (also known as HGS clients)**: Guarded hosts are Hyper-V hosts attested for by HGS and on which protected VMs (shielded VMs) can run. VMM 2016 automates deployment of guarded hosts. You can provision new hosts from bare-metal or configure existing hosts in the VMM fabric as guarded. Before deploying HGS and guarded fabric, you need to choose the HGS attestation type, which can be TPM-trusted and AD-based. The main differences between these attestations are shown in the following table:

Attestation mode	Pros and cons
TPM-trusted (TPM-based)	• Requires a certified hardware with TPM 2.0 and a UEFI with firmware version 2.3.1 as minimum and enabled secure boot. • Offers the strongest protection, as hosts are approved based on their TPM identity. • **Code integrity policies (CIP)** can be applied to hosts to define the binaries allowed to run in both user and kernel mode. If you have identical Hyper-V hosts, only a single policy is needed. • More configuration steps required.

Admin-trusted (AD-based)	• No special requirements for hosts. You can use existing hosts that do not have TPM 2.0. • Approval of guarded hosts is based on membership in a special AD security group. • Requires less time to configure. • Provides the same shielded VM features as TPM-trusted does. • Fabric admins are responsible for ensuring the health of guarded hosts as CIPs are not used.

HGS cannot work in both attestation modes at once. You are required to choose the right one before deploying guarded fabric. However, you can start with AD-based mode and your existing servers, and then effortlessly switch mode to TPM-trusted when the required hardware is available. For example, the following cmdlet switches AD-based to TPM-trusted:

```
Set-HGSServer -TrustTPM
```

For the purpose of this chapter, we will be referring to an infrastructure with AD-based attestation mode as shown in the following figure:

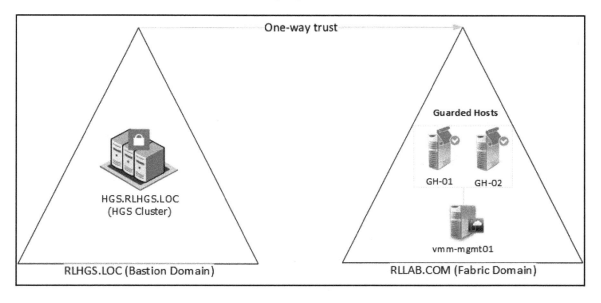

Deploying the host guardian service

This recipe will guide you through the steps required to deploy an HGS and provide initial steps that need to be carried out in order to prepare the environment for an HGS. First things first, review the following short list of requirements:

- As HGS plays a critical part in guarded fabric, clustered configuration is highly recommended. At least three virtual or physical machines are required. However, you can start with just one HGS and add additional nodes later.
- HGS nodes supports both Windows Server 2016 Datacenter and Standard editions. Server Core is the recommended installation type, as it has a smaller disk footprint and a reduced attack surface.
- Machines that you want to use for HGS must not be members of your fabric domain. By default, a new bastion domain and forest are created during HGS provisioning. Using HGS in the existing domain is possible, but not recommended.
- Hardware requirements actually depend on the number of guarded hosts. Based on the official statements, HGS node with eight cores and 4 Gb RAM can handle up to 1000 Hyper-V hosts.
- Signing and encryption certificates are required. In this recipe, they will be requested from enterprise certificate authority. Self-signed certificates are possible, but their usage in production environments is not recommended.
- Your OS must be up-to-date, as some new functionality comes through cumulative updates available through Windows Update.

How to do it...

As already mentioned, HGS cannot be configured from the VMM console and requires steps that needed to be done on an HGS server (HGS-01 in my demo).

1. The first step is to request signing and encryption certificates that play a part in the decryption of shielded VM keys. To do this, I'm using my **Certificate Authority (CA)** through which the certificate is added to the HGS machine as a Trusted Root CA template named HGS and the following code:

Ensure that the machine from which you make requests has the read and enroll permissions on the certificate template (HGS, in my case). Otherwise, requests will fail with the following error: **The permissions on the certificate template do not allow the current user to enroll for this type of certificate**.

```
#Signing certificate
Get-Certificate -SubjectName "CN=rlevchenko.com"
-CertStoreLocation cert:\LocalMachine\My -Template "HGS"
#Enryption certificate
Get-Certificate -SubjectName "CN=rlevchenko.com"
-CertStoreLocation cert:\LocalMachine\My -Template "HGS"
#Export signing certificate and its private key
Export-PfxCertificate -Cert (Get-ChildItem -Path
Cert:\LocalMachine\my\809FE7B7837580FB204E089BC8E001CD97B2E750)
- FilePath c:\certs\hgs_sign.pfx
-Password (ConvertTo-SecureString -String "P@ssw0rd1" -Force -
AsPlainText) -Force
#Export encryption certificate and its private key
Export-PfxCertificate -Cert (Get-ChildItem -Path
Cert:\LocalMachine\my\1424F501458AB279D1F799E96A2504ABA0C45DAB)
- FilePath c:\certs\hgs_encr.pfx -Password
(ConvertTo-SecureString -String "P@ssw0rd1" -Force -
AsPlainText) -Force
```

In this example, the HGS certificate template is actually a copy of the default WebServer template with an enabled **Allow private key to be exported** setting in the **Request Handling** tab of template properties.

2. Log in to the HGS server, run PowerShell with administrative privileges, and use the following one-liner to install HGS server role:

```
Install-WindowsFeature HostGuardianServiceRole
-IncludeManagementTools -Restart
```

The server will be automatically restarted after installation. Also, don't confuse this server role with **Host Guardian Hyper-V Support** role (HostGuardian) that is only used on guarded hosts.

3. After a successful restart, you need to configure an HGS server role. In the following example, I'm using `rlhgs.loc` as the name of the bastion domain that will be created and configured automatically for HGS services:

```
$adsafePassword = ConvertTo-SecureString -AsPlainText
'P@ssw0rd1' -Force
Install-HgsServer -HgsDomainName 'rlhgs.loc' -
SafeModeAdministratorPassword $adsafePassword -Restart
```

4. Once the machine is restarted, log in as the domain administrator (in my case, `rlhgs\administrator`), copy certificates created in step 1 to the `c:\certs\` folder, and then initialize the HGS cluster using the following code:

```
$certpassword= ConvertTo-SecureString -AsPlainText 'P@ssw0rd1'
-Force
Initialize-HgsServer -HgsServiceName 'HGS' -
SigningCertificatePath  'c:\certs\hgs_sign.pfx' -
SigningCertificatePassword $certpassword -
EncryptionCertificatePath 'c:\certs\hgs_encr.pfx' -
EncryptionCertificatePassword $certpassword -
TrustActiveDirectory
```

 Do not provide a FQDN as a HGS cluster name (`hgs.rlhgs.loc`, for example). Use a NetBIOS name instead (HGS, in my case).

5. At this step, you need to ensure that the DNS name resolution between the HGS forest and your fabric forest is working. Log in to one of your DNS servers in the fabric forest and use the following one-liner to configure the conditional forwarder zone:

```
Add-DnsServerConditionalForwarderZone -Name rlhgs.loc -
ReplicationScope "Forest" -MasterServers 10.10.23.101
```

 `10.10.23.101` is the address of my HGS server that is a member of `rlhgs.loc`.

6. To allow the HGS to locate the fabric domain controllers and validate group membership of the guarded hosts, you need to create a one-way forest trust. To do this, run the following commands on the HGS server:

Add-DnsServerConditionalForwarderZone -Name rllab.com -

```
ReplicationScope "Forest" -MasterServers 192.168.1.201

netdom trust rlhgs.loc /domain:rllab.com
/uD:rlevchenko@rllab.com /pD:Rllab2017 /add
```

 192.168.1.201 is the address of my fabric domain controller with AD-integrated DNS. Netdom parameters /uD and /pD describe credentials of the fabric administrator (rllab\rlevchenko).

7. Although it's an optional step, I would highly recommend that you configure HGS IIS web sites with SSL certificates to enable secure HTTPS communication between Hyper-V hosts and HGS. In this recipe, an SSL-certificate obtained from CA is used. You can refer to the following commands:

```
#Obtain certificate
Get-Certificate -SubjectName "CN=hgs.rlhgs.loc" -
CertStoreLocation cert:\LocalMachine\My -Template "HGS"

Export-PfxCertificate -Cert (Get-ChildItem -Path
Cert:\LocalMachine\my\53ed0d54fc77939598c692a69c186fcfd562dd8b)
- FilePath c:\certs\hgs_ssl.pfx
-Password (ConvertTo-SecureString -String "P@ssw0rd1" -Force -
AsPlainText) -Force

$sslpwd = ConvertTo-SecureString -String "P@ssw0rd1" -Force -
AsPlainText

#Set HGS server settings
Set-HgsServer -Http -Https -HttpsCertificatePath
'C:\certs\hgs_ssl.pfx' - HttpsCertificatePassword $sslpwd
```

8. As HGS was initialized with AD-based attestation, we need to create a new global AD group in the fabric domain and add desired Hyper-V hosts that will run shielded VMs. In addition, note a SID value for this group:

```
#Create new group
New-ADGroup -Name GuardedHosts -GroupCategory Security -
GroupScope Global
#Add hosts to the group
Add-ADGroupMember GuardedHosts GH-01,GH-02
#Get group's SID
(Get-ADGroup GuardedHosts).SID.Value
```

9. Return to the HGS server and register the group (GuardedHosts, in this recipe) with HGS services. To do this, note the group name and its SID value and run the following code:

```
Add-HgsAttestationHostGroup -Name GuardedHosts -Identifier
"S-1-5-21-229858842-1213098622-3796074901-1282"
```

10. Finally, ensure that HGS is configured properly by running the built-in diagnostic tests Get-HgsTrace -RunDiagnostics -Detailed, as shown in the following screenshot:

```
Administrator: Windows PowerShell

Windows PowerShell
Copyright (C) 2016 Microsoft Corporation. All rights reserved.

PS C:\Users\Administrator> Get-HgsTrace -RunDiagnostics -Detailed
Overall Result: Pass
    HGS-01: Pass
        HGS Service Configuration: Pass
            Code Integrity Policies Installed: NotApplicable
            Baseline Policies Installed: NotApplicable
            Authorized Hosts Added: NotApplicable
            Authorized Host Groups Added: Pass
        Hardware: Pass
            Provisioned Memory: Pass
            Memory Usage: Pass
        HTTPS: Pass
            Key Protection Administration Certificate Validation: Pass
            Bindings without SSL Certificates: Pass
            Attestation Server Certificate Subject Verification: Pass
            Key Protection Server Certificate Subject Verification: Pass
        Certificates: Pass
            KPS Certificate Permissions: Pass
            Attestation Certificate Permissions: Pass
            Attestation Signing Certificates Valid: Pass
            Attestation Signing Certificates Registered: Pass
```

How it works...

When a user requests to start a shielded VM, the Hyper-V host sends attestation requests to the HGS that decides whether the host is compromised or not. Depending on the attestation mode, HGS validates that the host belongs to a special security group (GuardedHosts, in this recipe) or uses the TPM present on hosts to identify the current health level of their boot path and whether the host meets the code integrity policy. Assuming attestation succeeds, the health certificate is sent to the host, and then the host provides this certificate to **key protection service** (**KPS**) and, if the certificate is validated by the KPS, the host receives the decryption keys needed to unlock and start the VM.

HGS attests hosts on their startup and every eight hours thereafter.

HGS plays a critical role in a guarded fabric and you must consider at least three virtual or physical machines for HGS services. VMM is not used for deployment and you prepare HGS with your own hands by providing certificates and information of a trusted security group created in the fabric domain. When the TPM-based mode is used, you provide additional host information to HGS, such as code integrity policies, TPM identifiers, and baselines.

 When you add the **Host Guardian Service** role, **Active Directory Domain Services** (**AD DS**), BitLocker drive encryption, Web Server (IIS), and failover clustering server roles will be automatically installed as well.

There's more...

Once you have deployed the first HGS, you can configure additional HGS cluster nodes.

Configuring additional HGS cluster nodes

This recipe shows how to add an additional HGS node to the cluster (HGS.rllab.loc, in my demo scenario). Before adding one, ensure that the primary node has a healthy state and then carry out the following steps to add a new HGS machine to an existing cluster:

 I will use the machine name HGS-02 that has the same configuration (OS and hardware) and is connected to the same network as the primary node HGS-01.

1. Log in to the node (HGS-02, in my case) that you want to add to the HGS cluster and install the HGS server role using PowerShell:

   ```
   Install-WindowsFeature HostGuardianServiceRole -
   IncludeManagementTools -Restart
   ```

2. Once the host is restarted, you need to promote the node to the HGS server:

```
$adsafepass=ConvertTo-SecureString -AsPlainText 'Pass1' -Force
$admpasswd=ConvertTo-SecureString -AsPlainText 'Pass1#!' -Force
$creds=New-Object System.Management.Automation.PSCredential
("administrator@rlhgs.loc", $admpasswd)
Install-HgsServer -HgsDomainName 'rlhgs.loc' -
HgsDomainCredential $creds -SafeModeAdministratorPassword
$adsafepass -Restart
```

Ensure that you can resolve the bastion domain's name from the node (`rlhgs.loc`, in this example), and then provide valid domain administrator credentials.

3. Log in to the node as an HGS domain administrator and initialize the node to join the existing HGS cluster:

```
Initialize-HgsServer -HgsServerIPAddress 10.10.23.101
```

`10.10.23.101` is the address of the primary node that we already deployed. Wait while the server is initialized and then check the logs located at `C:\Windows\Logs\HgsServer` to verify that Initialize Host Guardian Service completed (check the last string in the log file)

4. Signing and encryption certificates are automatically replicated from the first node within 10 minutes. However, the SSL certificate required for HTTPS communication is not replicated and you may request a new one or use an existing certificate. Copy the SSL certificate to the folder `c:\cert` on the node and run the following code:

```
$sslpwd = ConvertTo-SecureString -String "P@ssw0rd1" -Force -
AsPlainText
#Set HGS node settings
Set-HgsServer -Http -Https -HttpsCertificatePath
'C:\cert\hgs_ssl.pfx' -HttpsCertificatePassword $sslpwd
```

You can refer to step 7 in the *Deploying the host guardian service* recipe for more information about requesting an SSL-certificate.

5. Once all certificates are replicated and SSL is set, run HGS diagnostic tests to verify the node configuration:

```
Administrator: Windows PowerShell

PS C:\Users\Administrator.rlhgs> Get-HgsTrace -RunDiagnostics -Detailed
Overall Result: Pass
    HGS-02: Pass
        HGS Service Configuration: Pass
            Code Integrity Policies Installed: NotApplicable
            Baseline Policies Installed: NotApplicable
            Authorized Hosts Added: NotApplicable
            Authorized Host Groups Added: Pass
        Hardware: Pass
            Provisioned Memory: Pass
            Memory Usage: Pass
        HTTPS: Pass
            Key Protection Administration Certificate Validation: NotApplicable
            Bindings without SSL Certificates: NotApplicable
            Attestation Server Certificate Subject Verification: NotApplicable
            Key Protection Server Certificate Subject Verification: NotApplicable
        Certificates: Pass
            KPS Certificate Permissions: Pass
            Attestation Certificate Permissions: Pass
            Attestation Signing Certificates Valid: Pass
            Attestation Signing Certificates Registered: Pass

Traces have been stored at "C:\Users\Administrator.rlhgs\AppData\Local\Temp\HgsDiagnostics-
```

Make sure that the root CA issued the SSL certificate and is in the trusted root certification authorities: `Get-ChildItem -Path Cert:\LocalMachine\Root -Recurse | ? Subject -like "*Root-CA*"`

6. Repeat steps 1-4 on other additional HGS nodes (for example, `HGS-03`)

See also

- *Initialize HGS using TPM-trusted attestation*: https://docs.microsoft.com/en-us/windows-server/virtualization/guarded-fabric-shielded-vm/guarded-fabric-initialize-hgs-tpm-mode.

- *Guarded Fabric and Shielded VM Planning Guide for Hosters*:
  https://docs.microsoft.com/en-us/windows-server/virtualization/
  guarded-fabric-shielded-vm/guarded-fabric-planning-for-hosters.

- *Troubleshooting the Host Guardian Service*:
  https://docs.microsoft.com/en-us/windows-server/virtualization/guarded
  -fabric-shielded-vm/guarded-fabric-troubleshoot-hgs.

Deploying guarded hosts

Once HGS nodes are configured, you are ready to deploy Hyper-V hosts that will be attested by HGS to run the safeguarded VMs. This recipe will guide you through the steps required to implement guarded hosts in your production fabric. Before beginning, check that your Hyper-V hosts meet the following requirements:

- Unlike HGS, your Hyper-V hosts must be running on Windows Server 2016 Datacenter, as host guardian Hyper-V support is only available in this edition.
- If TPM attestation mode is used, Hyper-V hosts must meet the TPM requirements mentioned previously (such as TPM 2.0, UEFI 2.3.1). Refer to the introduction section in this chapter for more information about attestation modes.
- At least one host is required to test shielded VMs. In this recipe, I will use two up-to-date Hyper-V hosts (GH-01 and GH-02) in my fabric domain, in order to verify that live migration of shielded VMs works as well.
- If AD-based attestation mode is used, add your Hyper-V hosts to the trusted security group (GuardedHosts, in my demo) and register the SID of the group with HGS if it's not done yet.
- Ensure that you have configured HGS and it's passed all diagnostic tests.
- Make sure that Hyper-V hosts trust the HGS SSL certificate.

 See the *Deploying the host guardian service* recipe for more information.

How to do it...

Carry out the following steps to deploy guarded hosts:

1. On the VMM 2016 console, click on **Settings** and select **General.** Next, click on **Host Guardian Service Settings** and specify the mandatory **Attestation Server URL** and **Key Protection Server URL,** as shown in the following screenshot. When TPM is used for attestation, you will also need to add **Code Integrity Policies** to restrict the software that can run on guarded hosts. If you have already made VHD for shielded VMs, specify the path for the **Shielding Helper VHD** (which will be described later in this chapter) and then click on the **Finish** button:

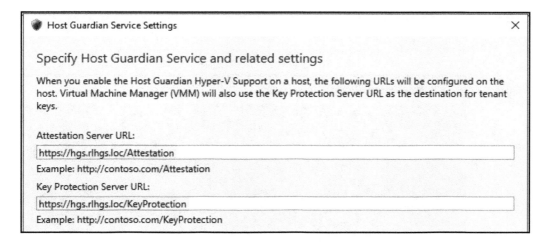

To get URLs for HGS services, you can use the following one-liner running on one of the HGS nodes:
`(Get-HgsServer).Values.AbsoluteUri|Sort-Object`

2. In the **Fabric** workspace on the VMM console, expand **Servers**. Under **Servers**, expand **All Hosts**. In the **Hosts** pane, right-click on the Hyper-V host (`GH-01.rllab.com`, in my case) and select **Properties**.

If you are doing bare-metal provisioning, change the **OS Configuration** | **Host Guardian Service** settings of the physical computer profile to enable deployment of the Host Guardian Service Hyper-V Support role and apply HGS settings/policies.

3. In the host properties dialog box, navigate to the **Host Guardian Service** page and check **Enable Host Guardian Hyper-V Support and use the URLs configured as global settings in VMM.** If VMM is used to manage code integrity policies defined in the HGS settings, click on **Use a Code Integrity policy to restrict software that can run on the host** and choose the right policy for the host, click on **OK** and then **Yes** to apply the changes.

If the host is a part of the cluster, suspend the node and drain roles before applying HGS client settings. Once the host is restarted, take it out of maintenance.

4. Right-click on the host and select **Connect via RDP**, provide credentials (rllab\rlevchenko, in my case), and check that the host passed attestation by running the Get-HgsClientConfiguration PowerShell cmdlet, as shown in the following screenshot:

```
Administrator: Windows PowerShell

Windows PowerShell
Copyright (C) 2016 Microsoft Corporation. All rights reserved.

PS C:\Windows\system32> Get-HgsClientConfiguration

IsHostGuarded              : True
Mode                       : HostGuardianService
KeyProtectionServerUrl     : https://hgs.rlhgs.loc/KeyProtection
AttestationServerUrl       : https://hgs.rlhgs.loc/Attestation
AttestationOperationMode   : ActiveDirectory
AttestationStatus          : Passed
AttestationSubstatus       : NoInformation
```

5. In addition, run diagnostic tests to check host health by executing the following cmdlet:

```
Get-HGSTrace -RunDiagnostics -Detailed
```

Ensure that the overall result is **Pass**.

6. Repeat steps 1-5 to add additional guarded hosts (GH-02, for example).

When TPM attestation mode is used and you have changed code integrity policies, use the **Apply Latest Code Integrity Policy** button to update HGS clients.

How it works...

VMM 2016 is used to automate the configuration of guarded hosts. You can deploy them from bare-metal machines or already managed hosts in the VMM fabric by providing global HGS settings, such as attestation and key protection URLs and optional code integrity policies (if HGS and the hosts are TPM-compatible). These settings are then distributed to the hosts, while enabling the **Host Guardian Hyper-V Support** role. Once hosts are restarted, you verify their health using cmdlets of module HGSClient.

 If you modify attestation and key protection URLs outside the VMM console (using PowerShell, for example), you need to update them in VMM and then re-configure the hosts by re-selecting the **Enable Host Guardian Hyper-V Support and use the URLs configured as global settings in VMM** checkbox.

Optionally, you can also specify a shielding helper VHD. Refer to the next recipe to get more information about creating a shielding helper VHD and updating HGS settings through the VMM management console.

 VMM checks the host's attestation status every time you add/refresh the host.

There's more...

To shield existing VMs, you should have a shielding helper VHD.

Preparing shielding helper VHD

Shielding helper VHD is a special disk prepared with shielded VM tools and not related to the template disks, which are used for creating shielded VMs. You are required to prepare this VHD in order to enable support for converting existing machines into shielded machines. Carry out the following steps to prepare your helper VHD:

1. On any Hyper-V host that it is not a part of the guarded fabric (HV03, for example), install Shielded VM Tools:

```
Install-WindowsFeature RSAT-Shielded-VM-Tools -Restart
```

In this chapter, the separate host HV03 will also be used to prepare VMs before moving them to the guarded fabric.

2. Once the host is restarted, create a new VM with a blank VHD, start it, and install Windows Server 2016 using attached ISO media. When the OS is installed, verify its working state and shutdown the VM. You don't need to sysprep the VM:

```
New-VM -VMName HelperVM -Generation 2 -MemoryStartupBytes
2048Mb -NewVHDPath D:\vms\rlevchenko\HelperVM\helper.vhdx -
NewVHDSizeBytes 40Gb
Set-VM -VMName HelperVM -ProcessorCount 2
Add-VMDvdDrive -VMName HelperVM -Path
D:\vms\rlevchenko\HelperVM\ws2016.iso
Get-VM -VMName HelperVM | Start-VM
Get-VM -VMName HelperVM | Stop-VM
```

3. Indicate a path for VM's VHD and then use the following command to make shielding helper VHD from the VHD that we created in the previous step:

```
Initialize-VMShieldingHelperVHD -Path
'D:\VMs\rlevchenko\HelperVM\Helper.vhdx'
```

4. Once the command is completed, copy the VHD to the VMM library and then delete the VM created in step 2:

```
#Copy the VHD to VMM library
Copy-Item D:\VMs\rlevchenko\HelperVM\Helper.vhdx
\\librsrv01\VMMLibrary\VHDs\
#Delete helper VM
Remove-VM -VMName HelperVM -Force
```

5. Log in to the VMM server and update the VMM library shares by using the following command:

```
Get-SCLibraryShare | Refresh-LibraryShare
```

6. In the VMM 2016 console, click on **Settings** and select **General.** Next, click on **Host Guardian Service Settings**, use the **Browse** button to select the Helper VHD (Helper.vhdx, in this recipe) from your library share, and then click on the **Finish** button to apply the new settings to the VMM server. As an alternative, you can complete this step using PowerShell, as shown in the following example:

```
$ShieldingHelperVhd = Get-SCVirtualHardDisk -Name
Helper.vhdxSet-SCVMMServer -ShieldingHelperVhd
$ShieldingHelperVhd -RunAsynchronously
```

 The process of converting existing VMs to be shielded will be described in the next section, which is devoted to the deployment of shielded VMs.

See also

- *Authorize guarded hosts using TPM-based attestation*:
  https://docs.microsoft.com/en-us/windows-server/virtualization/
  guarded-fabric-shielded-vm/guarded-fabric-tpm-trusted-attestation-
  capturing-hardware.

- *Troubleshooting Guarded Hosts*:
  https://docs.microsoft.com/en-us/windows-server/virtualization/guarded
  -fabric-shielded-vm/guarded-fabric-troubleshoot-hosts.

- *Guarded Fabric Diagnostic Tool*:
  https://docs.microsoft.com/en-gb/system-center/scom/deploy-overview?
  view=sc-om-1801

Deploying shielded VMs

This section describes how to deploy shielded VMs in VMM 2016. You will also learn about template disks and shielded data files, which are used to create shielded VM templates.

How to do it...

Before you start, verify that HGS and guarded hosts are configured and that you have set global HGS settings in VMM (see the previous recipes for details).

Preparing and protecting a template disk

The first thing you need to do is prepare an OS gold image (VHDX) that will be used to create shielded VMs in VMM. Because shielded VMs are not regular VMs and BitLocker is used, the image must meet additional requirements:

- Must be a GPT disk (this is needed for Gen2 VMs to support UEFI)
- The logical disk type must be basic (as BitLocker does not support dynamic disks)
- The logical disk must have at least two partitions (one is dedicated to Windows installation, another is active and contains the bootloader)
- The filesystem must be NTFS (usually it's set by default)
- You can install and generalize OS that support Gen2 and Secure Boot template (Windows 8, Windows Server 2012 and later)

Carry out the following steps to create and protect a template disk for shielded VMs:

1. Create a new VM, install an OS (Windows Server 2016 Standard, for example), apply the latest updates for the OS, do the usual OS setup steps (enable Remote Desktop or disable IE Enhanced Security, for instance), and then generalize the image by using sysprep: `Sysprep /generalize /shutdown /oobe`

> As this VHDX will be signed and used with shielded VMs, create a copy of the VHDX to simplify servicing tasks (updating and so on).

2. Now, log onto the server with the shielded VM RSAT tools installed (`HV03`, in my case). If you haven't installed them yet, use the following command (note that the server will automatically be restarted): `Install-WindowsFeature RSAT-Shielded-VM-Tools -Restart`.

3. You are required to obtain a certificate to sign VHDX. Although a self-signed certificate is suitable for demo purposes, I will request the certificate from my CA:

```
Get-Certificate -SubjectName "CN=sign.rlevchenko.com"
-CertStoreLocation cert:\LocalMachine\My -Template "Sign"
#Export the certificate
Export-PfxCertificate -Cert (Get-ChildItem -Path
Cert:\LocalMachine\my\EF19A28D32AA64827070D3B33D1B52F0C96B70FE)
-FilePath c:\cert\sign.pfx -Password (ConvertTo-SecureString -
String "P@ssw0rd1" -Force -AsPlainText) -Force
#Import to the machine store
Import-PfxCertificate -CertStoreLocation Cert:\LocalMachine\My
-FilePath C:\cert\sign.pfx -Password (ConvertTo-SecureString -
AsPlainText "P@ssw0rd1" -Force)
```

Keep in mind that CA must be trusted by you and your tenants. In this recipe, my own PKI is used, as there aren't any public tenants.

4. Once RSAT tools are installed and the certificate is added, run the template disk wizard (press *WIN+R* and type `TemplateDiskWizard.exe`).
5. On the **Certificate** page, press the **Browse** button, select the certificate that was created before, and then click **Next**.
6. On the **Virtual Disk** page, select the VHDX (our gold image created earlier) and click on **Next**.
7. On the **Signature Catalog** page, type a friendly disk name (for example, `SH_WS2016STD`) and its version (`1.0.0.0`, in my case) and then press **Next.**
8. On the next page, review the settings and click on **Generate** to begin the template creation process; this can take a while depending on the disk size.

The wizard enables BitLocker on the template disk, performs template hash calculation, and creates a Volume Signature Catalog that is stored in the VHDX metadata

9. On the **Summary** page, verify that the template generation is completed, click **Close**, and locate the template disk (note its path).
10. Copy the template disk to the VMM library by using the following command:

```
Copy-Item D:\VMs\rlevchenko\template_disk.vhdx
\\libr01\vmmlibrary\vhds
```

11. On the VMM console, navigate to the **Library** pane and select the file share that contains the template disk (`template_disk.vhdx`, for example). The disk must have a small shield icon. Double-click on the disk and provide information about the operating system, family name, and release version, as shown in the screenshot:

Physical Library Objects (6)

Name	Type	Shielded	Family Name	Operating System
Blank Disk - Large.vhd	VHD	No		None
Helper.vhdx	VHDX	No		Unknown
Blank Disk - Small.vhdx	VHDX	No		None
Blank Disk - Small.vhd	VHD	No		None
Blank Disk - Large.vhdx	VHDX	No		None
template_disk.vhdx	VHDX	Yes	Windows Server 2016 (Shielded)	Windows Server 2016 Standard

When you add resources to the VMM library outside of the VMM console, you will need to refresh the library: `Get-SCLibraryShare | Refresh-LibraryShare`.

Creating and importing a shielded data file

This recipe describes the process of creating a special file that keeps shielded VMs secret, such as guardian metadata, tenant certificates, or local administrator passwords. Carry out the following steps to define a new shielded data file:

1. As tenants can connect to their shielded VMs through a remote desktop connection, you need to obtain an RDP certificate to satisfy that they are connecting to the right endpoint. In most cases, this certificate is issued from the tenant's PKI (although self-signed certificates are also possible). Use the following example to obtain the certificate from your certification authority:

```
Get-Certificate -DNSName '*.democorp.ru' -CertStoreLocation
cert:\LocalMachine\My -Template "RDP"
Export-PfxCertificate -Cert (Get-ChildItem -Path
Cert:\LocalMachine\my\8E23434F29BA067CDCE4E489FB77DDAEC93B9CCF)
-FilePath c:\cert\rdp_cert.pfx -Password (ConvertTo-
SecureString -String "P@ssw0rd1" -Force -AsPlainText) -Force
```

Make sure that you are requesting a wildcard certificate as the same shielded data file is usually used for multiple tenant VMs. In the preceding example, I'm using the certificate template *RDP* that is actually made from the built-in template *Workstation Authentication* (**Allow private key to be exported** is ticked, **Subject Name** is set to **Supply in the request**, Server Authentication is defined in the Application Policies).

2. The template disk created in the previous recipe is generalized and requires an answer file to specialize the tenant's shielded VMs. In particular, the RDP certificate, as well as your product key or scripts, might also be defined in the answer file. On a machine that is not a part of the guarded fabric, run the following:

```
Install-Module -Name GuardedFabricTools -Force
$LocalAdmPassword = ConvertTo-SecureString -AsPlainText
"P@ssw0rd1" -Force
$RDPCertPassword = ConvertTo-SecureString -AsPlainText
"P@ssw0rd1" -Force
New-ShieldingDataAnswerFile -AdminPassword $LocalAdmPassword -
RDPCertificatePassword $RDPCertPassword -RDPCertificateFilePath
C:\cert\rdp_cert.pfx -ProductKey UserSupplied -StaticIP -Path
C:\sh_data\unattend.xml
```

Make sure that your machine has internet access, so as to be able to download and install the GuardedFabricTools module. In this example, the tenant's VM will be configured with the following settings: a static IP, a user supplied product key (in a VM template, for example) and an RDP certificate.

3. Once the answer file is created, it's time to get the volume signature catalog file that was added during the template disk creation process. The VSC is used to match the right template disk during a shielded VM provisioning. To do this, run the following code on any machine with the VMM console and PowerShell module:

```
$disk=Get-SCVirtualHardDisk -Name "template_disk.vhdx"
$VSC = Get-SCVolumeSignatureCatalog -VirtualHardDisk $Disk
$VSC.WriteToFile("C:\sh_data\templateDisk.vsc")
```

If you haven't created a template disk yet, see the *Preparing and protecting a template disk* recipe for more details. In addition, if tenants have their own template disks, a VSC file can be generated without VMM, using the following command: `Save-VolumeSignatureCatalog -TemplateDiskPath templateDisk.vhdx -VolumeSignatureCatalogPath templateDisk.vsc`.

4. Obtain the guardian metadata to authorize a hosting fabric to run a shielded VM:

```
$rlhgsmetadata = Get-SCGuardianConfiguration
$rlhgsmetadata.InnerXml | Out-File c:\sh_data\rlhgs.xml -
Encoding UTF8
```

HGS Global Settings should be configured in VMM. Refer to the *Deploying guarded hosts* recipe for more details.

5. Finally, on the machine with Shielded VM Tools installed, run `%systemroot%\System32\ShieldingDataFileWizard.exe` to create the shielded data file. On the wizard's first page, click on **Browse** and provide a name and location of the data file that will be created (for example, `c:\sh_data\shdatafile.pdk`), select **Shielded data for Shielded templates**, and then choose **Shielded** as the type of VM in the guarded fabric, as shown in the following screenshot:

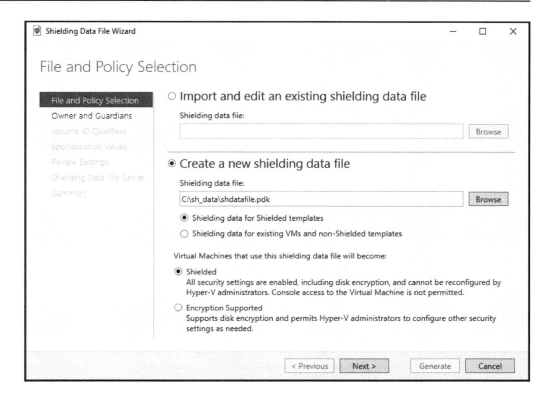

 Select the **Shielding data for existing VMs and non-Shielded templates** if you want to create a shielding data file for converting existing VMs to shielded ones. You won't need to provide VSC and answer files for this type of shielding data.

6. On the **Owner and Guardians** page, click on **Manage Local Guardians** and then press the **Create** button. In the **Create a New Guardian** dialog box, type a guardian name (LocalGS, for example), ensure that **Self-signed Guardian** is selected, and click on **Next.** On the next page, click **Create** and then **Close**

7. In the **Manage Local Guardians** dialog box, click on **Import** and provide the guardian metadata file created in step 4 (C:\sh_data\rlhgs.xml, in my case). Review the guardian details, type a friendly guardian name (HGS_rllab, for example), and then click **OK** twice.

8. On the **Owners and Guardians** page, select the local guardian you have just created from the drop-down menu (LocalHGS, in my case) and then select your or the host provider's guardian that has just been imported (HGS_rllab, in my demo), as shown in the following screenshot:

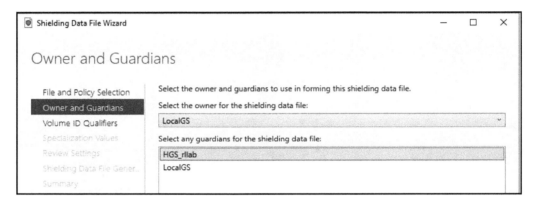

 The local guardian represents you as an owner of the VM, while the guardians that were imported by using their metadata are actually representatives of the fabric in which the shielded VMs are authorized to run.

9. On the **Volume ID Qualifiers** page, click on **Add** and then **Browse** to select the volume signature catalog file that we created earlier (templateDisk.vsc, in my case), review the certificate details and click on **OK**.

10. On the **Specialization Values** page, click on **Browse**, provide the answer file that will be used to specialize your VMs, and then click on **Add** to select the RDP certificate that is described in the answer file and will be installed onto the VM:

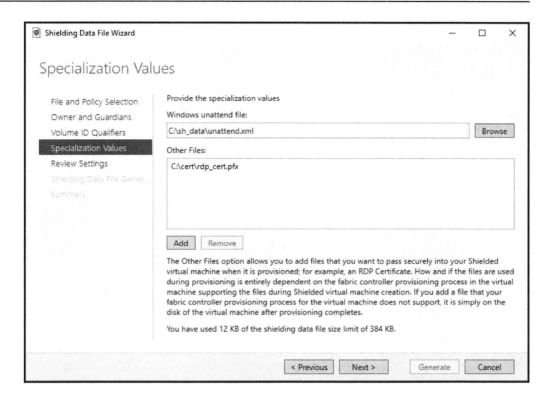

Add script files if they are defined in the answer file. Also, keep in mind that any files you specify in the **Other Files** field will automatically be copied to `C:\temp\` on the VM that is created.

11. On the next page, review the settings and click on **Generate.** Once the shielded data file generation is completed, check the summary and close the wizard.

12. On the VMM console, click on **Library** and select **Import the shielding data** in the ribbon, press the **Browse** button to locate your PDK file (`shdatafile.pdk`, in my case), provide a friendly name and its optional description, and then click on **Import**. Optionally, you can complete this step by using PowerShell:

```
New-SCVMShieldingData -Name "TenantA" -VMShieldingDataPath
"\\hv03\c`$\sh_data\shdatafile.pdk" -Description "Shielding
data file for TenantA"
```

Navigate to the **VM Shielding Data** under **Profiles** in the **Library** pane to check and manage all imported shielded data files.

Creating a shielded VM template

The creation of new VMs and templates will be discussed in the Chapter 7, *Deploying Virtual Machines and Services*. However, I would like to partly describe it now, in order to fully verify our guarded fabric deployment, assuming that you have already finished the recipes above in this chapter and VMM networking is configured (logical networks, IP pools, and so on). Carry out the following steps to create a shielded VM template:

1. On the VMM console, click **Library**, and then **Create VM Template** in the ribbon to add a new template.
2. In the **Create VM Template Wizard** window, select **Use an existing VM template or a virtual hard disk stored in the library** and press **Browse**.
3. In the **Select VM Template Source** dialog box, select the shielded template disk (template_disk.vhdx, in my environment) and then click **OK**.

Right click the column headers and toggle the shielded VM template to quickly find the right shielded resources by sorting them out using that column.

4. On the **Identity** page, type the **VM Template Name** (TenantA_Shielded, for example) and its optional description, then press **Next**.
5. On the **Configure Hardware** page, specify the hardware as well as availability properties for the VM and ensure that at least one network adapter is configured, as tenants use remote management tools including RDP to access their VMs:

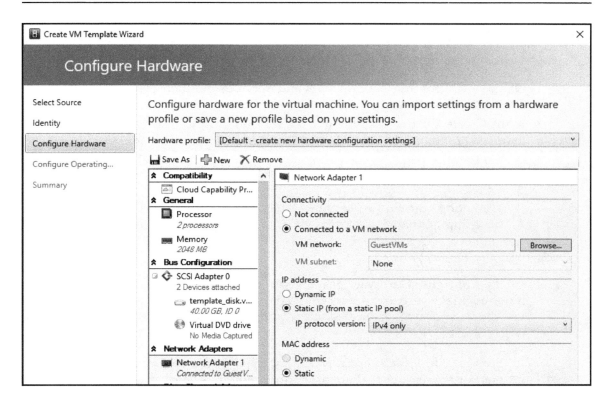

 If your answer file uses a Static IP, ensure that the VM network adapter is connected to a VM network and **Static IP (from a static IP pool)** is selected.

6. On the **Configure Operating System** page, specify the OS of the VM, provide a valid product key and set a desired time zone, then click on **Next** twice to create a VM template. Once a template is created, it will be shown in **VM templates.**

 Make sure that the template is available for the tenant administrator role. Otherwise, tenants won't be able to create VMs from the template.

Deploying a shielded VM from a template

Carry out the following steps to deploy shielded VMs from VM templates:

1. On the VMM console, click on **VMs and Services** and then **Create Virtual Machine** in the ribbon at the top.
2. In the **Create Virtual Machine** wizard, click on **Browse**, select a shielded VM template (TenantA_shielded, in my case), and then click on **Next**.
3. On the **Identity** page, type a VM name (sh_vm01, for example) and its optional description.

 If you don't provide a VM name, VMM will generate a VM name based on the computer name, the format of which is defined in the template.

4. On the **Configure Hardware** page, review the settings and change them if required. Make sure that the network adapter is connected to the VM network and the static IP pool is selected. It's required because we have an answer file with a static IP defined.

 See the *Creating and importing a shielded data file* recipe for details about answer file settings that are used throughout this chapter.

5. On the **Configure Operating System** page, verify the settings (especially the product key value) and click on **Next**.
6. On the next page, click on **Browse** and select the shielding data file (*TenantA*, in my case) and click on **Next**.
7. On the **Select Destination** page, select whether to deploy the VM to the cloud or to place the VM on a host. If you haven't got a cloud yet, select the host group (Moscow/Hyper-V, in my case) and click on **Next**.
8. On the **Select Host** page, once VMM has finished calculating ratings for each host in the selected host group, choose a suitable host (GH-01, in my environment) and click on **Next**:

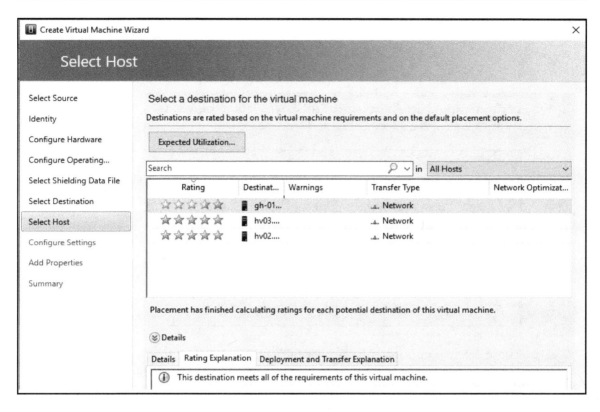

9. On the **Configure Settings** page, verify the storage location for VM files, change a randomly generated computer name if necessary, set the **Address pool** and **IP address** for the network adapter, and then click on **Next**.

10. On the **Add Properties** page, select the actions that describe the VM's behavior when the server starts or stops. I usually use **Turn on the virtual machine if it was running when the physical server stopped** (no delays) and default **Save State** respectively.

11. On the **Summary** page, review and confirm the settings by pressing the **Create** button. Normally, I also tick **Start the virtual machine after deploying it**.

12. In the **Jobs** pane, ensure that the **Create virtual machine** job is completed successfully. This might take a while, depending on your network and host performance. Once the job is finished, check that the VM (Sh_VM01, in my case) is running and has a special shielded icon, as shown in the following screenshot:

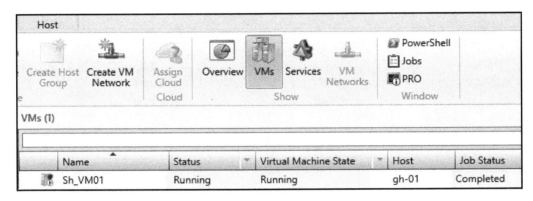

13. These are two optional steps to verify the basic shielded VM features (console access and BitLocker). Right-click on the VM and select **Connect and View** and then **Connect via Console**. *Can't use a console because this option is greyed out?* It's normal for shielded VMs. Let's try the same from the Hyper-V host (GH-01, in my case). Open Hyper-V Manager and select the shielded VM. Notice that there is no video preview for this machine and, if you attempt to connect to the VM, the following message will be shown: **You cannot connect to a shielded virtual machine using a Virtual Machine Connection.** Use a Remote Desktop Connection instead:

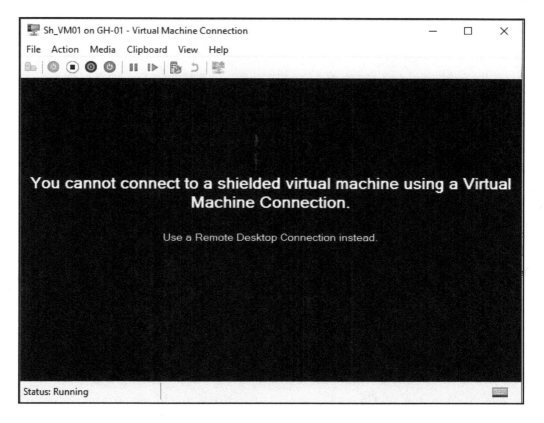

14. On the host running the shielded VM, shutdown the VM, locate its VHD, and then attach it (right-click on the VHD and select **Mount**). Open the diskmgmt.msc and try to open a primary partition, for example. Again, you won't be able to do this, as BitLocker was used (thanks to vTPM) for that partition. The **Access is denied** message shows every time you try to access a BitLocker encrypted drive. Once finished, detach the VHD, and start the VM.

On the host running the shielded VM, open a PowerShell and try the following command to open a PowerShell Direct session: Enter-PsSession -VMName Sh_VM01. *So, was it successful?*

Converting an existing VM to a shielded VM

In the previous recipes, you learned how to configure VMM to work with guarded fabric and create shielded VMs. So, to complete this recipe, you must already have VMM with defined HGS settings, including the shielding helper VHD that is used for shielding existing VMs in the VMM fabric. If you have a Gen2 VM with Secure Boot enabled and Windows 8/2012 at least, carry out the following steps to convert this VM to shielded:

 Keep in mind that only VMs running on guarded hosts can be converted. If a VM is running on a general Hyper-V host, migrate this VM to the guarded host.

1. On the VMM console, select **VMs and Services** and right-click on the VM that you want to convert to shielded (Exis_VM01, in my case), then click on **Shut Down** to take the VM offline.
2. Right-click on the VM and select **Shield.** In the new dialog box, select or import the shielding data for existing VMs and non-shielded templates and press **OK.**

 The creation of shielding data for existing VMs and non-shielded templates is straightforward. See the *Creating and importing a shielded data file* recipe for more information.

3. Once the job **Change properties of virtual machine** is completed, check that the VM is now shielded and then start the VM if needed.

 VMM attaches helper VHD to the VM during the shielding process to encrypt an existing OS volume. Once it's finished, VMM removes a temporary VM and detaches helper VHD from the converted VM.

How it works...

You can deploy either encrypted or shielded VMs, in addition to the standard/unprotected VM in the guarded fabric. Encrypted VMs have BitLocker-enabled volumes, while shielded VMs provide additional security benefits, such as a disabled VM console and some integration services, reaching a comprehensive security for VMs. Before deploying shielded VMs in VMM, you prepare the following components:

- A signed template disk used by tenants to protect sensitive data during the shielded VM's deployment. This disk is encrypted by BitLocker, keeps a **Volume Signature Catalog** (**VSC**) with the disk's hash, and is signed with a provided certificate. Consequently, tenants can be completely sure that the disk has not been modified by someone.

 VMM 2016 supports only Windows-based secure template disks. However, you can shield Linux VMs in the VMM 1801 semi-annual channel release.

- A shielding data file to protect the VM's configuration and consisting of:
  - **Answer file**: An unattended file used to specialize and configure VMs in order to meet tenants' requirements
  - **Volume signature catalog file**: This contains information about the template disks that tenants trust
  - **Guardian metadata**: Used to describe guarded fabric on which tenants can run their shielded VMs
  - **Local administrator password**: This is a password for the local administrator specified while creating an answer file
  - **Other files**: RDP and other certificates, script files that are used during the VM's provisioning
- A helper VHD to encrypt OS volumes during the shielding of existing VMs

These files should then be imported to VMM before you start deploying shielded VMs or converting existing VMs to shielded ones. As for traditional VMs, you need to define a VM template to simplify creating multiple shielded VMs. When you create a VM from the template, you will be asked to select a shielded data file and a suitable guarded host to deploy the VM. VMM does the host's verification and won't allow you to place the VM on a non-suitable host. Once deployment is finished, you can access the VM through RDP and verify that it has BitLocker-enabled volume with an encryption key that is stored in the vTPM present and shown in the `tpm.msc` of the shielded VM.

See also

- Deploy a Shielded VM using PowerShell:
  `https://docs.microsoft.com/en-us/windows-server/virtualization/guarded-fabric-shielded-vm/guarded-fabric-create-a-shielded-vm-using-powershell`.

- *Shielded VMs - Generate an answer file by using the New-ShieldingDataAnswerFile function*:
  `https://docs.microsoft.com/windows-server/virtualization/guarded-fabric-shielded-vm/guarded-fabric-sample-unattend-xml-file`.

- *Trusted Platform Module Technology Overview*: `https://docs.microsoft.com/en-us/windows/device-security/tpm/trusted-platform-module-overview`.

Deploying Virtual Machines and Services

7

In this chapter, we will cover:

- Creating private clouds
- Creating hardware, guest OS, application, and SQL profiles
- Creating user roles in VMM
- Creating and deploying virtual machines
- Creating virtual machine templates
- Creating and deploying service templates
- Rapidly provisioning a virtual machine by using SAN Copy

Introduction

A private cloud is a collection of resources (for example, host groups of servers running common or diverse hypervisors, storage, and networking) and settings that provide virtualization infrastructure for **cloud users** (for example, tenants and self-service users), and it is deployed within your organization boundaries using your own hardware and software.

This chapter guides you through private cloud deployment and management, VMs, and services in VMM 2016, providing recipes to assist you to get the most out of the deployment.

Creating private clouds

This recipe provides guidance on how to create a private cloud from host groups running diverse hypervisors, such as Hyper-V, VMware ESXi host, or from a VMware resource pool in VMM 2016.

By using VMM 2016 and deploying a private cloud, you will be able to offer a unique experience for creating VMs and services, which will in turn lead towards the consumerization of IT.

A private cloud deployment allows **resource pooling**, where you can present a comprehensive set of fabric resources but limit it to quotas that can be increased or decreased, providing fully optimized elasticity without affecting the private cloud's overall user experience. In addition to this, you can also delegate the management to tenants and self-service users who will have no knowledge of physical infrastructures, such as clusters, storage, and networking.

A private cloud can be created using the following resources:

- Host groups that contain Hyper-V and VMware ESXi
- VMware resource pool

Getting ready

First, start by configuring the fabric resources in VMM:

- **Network**: Refer to the recipes on networking in `Chapter 5`, *Configuring Fabric Resources in VMM*
- **Storage**: Refer to the *Configuring storage with VMM* and *Deploying a Hyper-converged cluster with S2D and Hyper-V* recipes in `Chapter 5`, *Configuring Fabric Resources in VMM*
- **Library servers and shares**: Refer to the *Setting up a VMM library* recipe in `Chapter 5`, *Configuring Fabric Resources in VMM*
- **Create the host groups**: Refer to the *Creating host groups* recipe in `Chapter 5`, *Configuring Fabric Resources in VMM*
- **Add the hosts**: Refer to the *Adding and managing Hyper-V hosts and host clusters with VMM* recipe in `Chapter 5`, *Configuring Fabric Resources in VMM,* and the *Adding VMware ESXi hosts or host clusters to VMM* recipe in `Chapter 8`, *Managing VMware ESXi Hosts*

In this recipe, we will create a private cloud that we will name RLCLOUD. It will be created from the resources of previously configured host groups.

 Shielded VMs are described separately. Refer to `Chapter 6`, *Configuring Guarded Fabric in VMM* for more details about deploying such VMs.

How to do it...

Carry out the following steps to create your own private cloud:

1. Connect to the VMM 2016 console by using the VMM admin account that was previously created (for example, `rllab\vmm-admin`), and then in the bottom-left pane, click on **VMs and Services** to open the **VMs and Services** workspace.
2. Under the **Home** tab on the ribbon, click on **Create Cloud**.
3. In the **Create Cloud Wizard** window, type the private cloud's name.

4. Using the drop-down menu **Shielded VM Support** to specify whether the cloud will support shielded VMs, type a description (optional), and then click on **Next**:

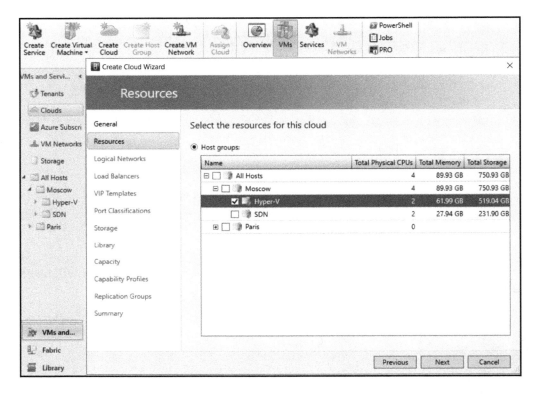

5. In the **Resources** page, select between the following options:
   - Select **Host groups**, then select the host group(s) that will be added to this private cloud (for example, **Moscow**), and then click on **Next**
   - Select **VMware resources pools**, then select a **VMware resource pool** from the drop-down list, and then click on **Next**

6. On the **Logical Networks** page, select the logical network(s) that will be made available to this private cloud (for example, **Guest VMs**, which was created in the *Networking - configuring logical networks in VMM* recipe in Chapter 5, *Configuring Fabric Resources in VMM*) and then click on **Next**.

Only logical networks that are associated with physical network adapters will be listed. Make sure you have configured the logical network and assigned it to the physical network beforehand.

7. On the **Load Balancers** page, if you have a load balancer deployed and integrated with VMM, select it and click on **Next**.

Only associated load balancers will be displayed.

8. On the **VIP Templates** page, select the VIP template(s), if any, that will be available to this private cloud (for example, **HTTPS traffic**) and click on **Next**.
9. On the **Port Classifications** page, select each port classification that you want to make available to the cloud.
10. On the **Storage** page, if you do have a storage managed by VMM and if there are storage classifications for storage pools assigned to selected host groups, select the storage classification that will be available to this private cloud (for example, **GOLD**) and click on **Next**.

For more information on storage classification, check the *Configuring storage in VMM recipe* in Chapter 5, *Configuring Fabric Resources in VMM*.

11. On the **Library** page, provide the stored VM path by clicking on **Browse**, and in the **Select Destination Folder** dialog box, click on the library server and then select a library or a folder in the share to be used as the location for self-service users to store VMs in (for example, **CloudVMs**); then click on **OK**.
12. In the **Read-only library shares** section, click on **Add**, select the library share(s) for read-only resources, click on **OK** to confirm, and then click on **Next**.

13. On the **Capacity** page, configure the capacity limits and then click on **Next**. You can manually set quotas for the **Virtual CPUs, Memory (GB), Storage (GB), Custom quota (points)**, and **Virtual machines** dimensions, as shown in the following screenshot:

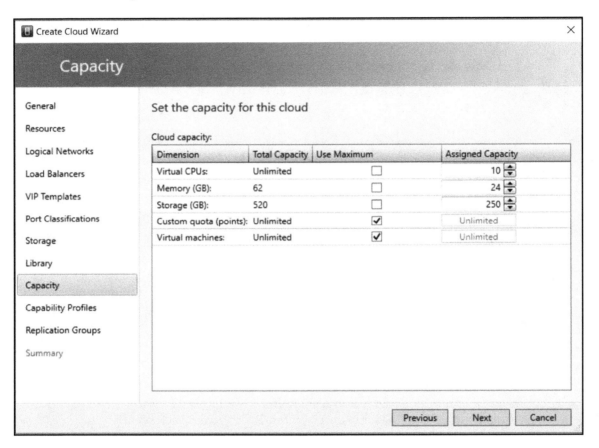

To use quotas, deselect **Use Maximum**. See the *Creating an application administrator (self-service user) role* subsection in the *Creating user roles in VMM* recipe of this chapter.

14. On the **Capability Profiles** page, select the VM capability profile(s) that matches the hypervisor running on the selected host group(s)—for example, **Hyper-V**—and click on **Next**.

Built-in capability profiles embody the minimum and maximum configured values for a VM, for each hypervisor that is supported.

15. On the **Replication Groups** page, select the storage replica groups for the cloud, if any, and click on **Next**.

Refer to `https://docs.microsoft.com/en-us/system-center/vmm/storage-replica` for more details about storage replica in VMM.

16. On the **Summary** page, click on **Finish.**

How it works...

Configure the fabric resources, such as storage, network, library, host groups, and hosts that will be available in the private cloud beforehand. Configure library paths and set the capacity for the private cloud, which can be created from host groups containing a unique mix of hypervisors, such as Microsoft Hyper-V and/or VMware ESXi hosts, and also from a VMware resource pool (which needs to be under VMM management).

You cannot use VMM to manage/assign storage classifications for ESXi hosts' storage.

In the **Library** workspace, you can create custom capability profiles to limit the resources being used by the private cloud's VMs.

On the **Capacity** page, you can set the capacity limits manually by deselecting the option **Use Maximum**.

To verify if the private cloud library was created, check whether it is listed under **Cloud Libraries** in the **Library** workspace. If you configured read-only library shares, they will be listed together with a **Stored Virtual Machines and Services node**.

Self-service users require store and redeploy permissions to save a VM on a library share, which must be located on a different share other than the read-only resource location, which cannot be a child path of the user role data path. The self-service user role data path is configured when creating/modifying the user role.

The self-service user can log on to the VMM console directly.

When creating the private cloud, VMM creates the read-only library shares and stored VM path.

There's more...

After creating the private cloud, you need to assign users who will have access to managing it.

Assigning the private cloud to a user role

Now that you've created the private cloud, you can assign it to a user role(s). Carry out the following steps to do so:

1. In the VMM console on the bottom-left pane, click on the **VMs and Services** workspace and then expand **Clouds**.
2. Select the created private cloud (for example, **RLCLOUD**).
3. Under the **Home** tab in the ribbon, click on **Assign Cloud** and select the user role by choosing one of the following options:
    - **Use an existing user role**: This option is enabled only if you have created any user roles previously
    - **Create a user role and assign this cloud**: Click on **OK** to continue and follow the steps to create and assign the user role to the private cloud

See also

For more information, see the following references:

- Chapter 5, *Configuring Fabric Resources in VMM*
- The *Creating an Application Administrator (Self-Service User) role* subsection in the *Creating user roles in VMM* recipe in this chapter

Creating hardware, guest OS, application, and SQL profiles

Profiles are resources that are used to deploy VMs. For example, a SQL profile provides instructions for SQL Server instance deployment and customizations. An application profile provides instructions to install Web and other applications.

Getting ready

You can create the following types of profiles in VMM to be used in a VM template:

Profile type	Purpose
Hardware	To configure hardware settings (for example, memory, network adapters, and DVD drives)
Guest OS	To configure common OS settings (for example, computer name, domain name, product key, and time zone)
Application	To provide directives for Web Deploy and SQL Server data-tier (DACs) applications, and for running scripts when deploying VMs as a service
SQL Server	To provide directives for a SQL customization when deploying a VM as a service

How to do it...

Carry out the following steps to create a hardware profile:

1. In the VMM console, click on the **Library** workspace.
2. Expand **Profiles** on the left pane, click on **Hardware Profiles**, and then right-click and select **Create Hardware Profile**.
3. In the **New Hardware Profile** dialog box on the **General** page, type the hardware profile name, for example, **rllab_std (2vCPU, 2Gb RAM)**, and then select the **VMs Generation (typically, Generation 2)**.

4. Click on **Hardware Profile** on the left pane, configure the hardware settings, and click on **OK** to finish.

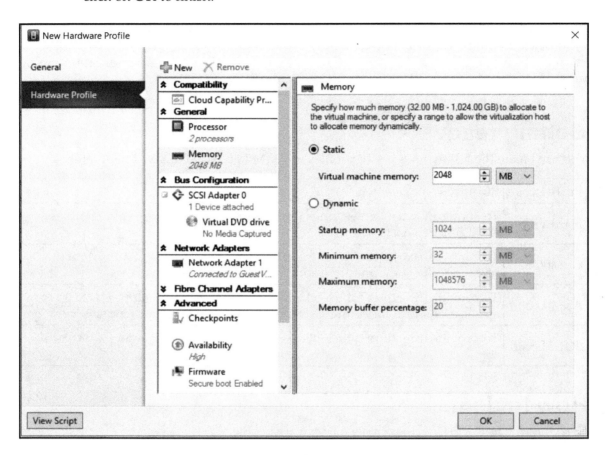

How it works...

Use this recipe to create the profiles that will contain the settings and specifications that VMM will use when deploying a VM.

To start creating a profile, expand **Profiles** in the **Library** workspace; click on **Create**, select the profile you want to create, and provide the settings to be used when deploying the VM.

When deploying the VM to a private cloud, the capability profile must be supported by the private cloud.

When creating an application profile, you can add one or more application scripts, but only after adding and configuring an application with the appropriate settings.

You can also create an application profile to deploy SQL Server DAC packages or scripts to an existing SQL server in the **Compatibility** list, by selecting **SQL Server Application Host**.

There's more...

The following sections will guide you through creating guest OS, application, and SQL Server profiles.

Creating a guest OS profile

1. In the **Library** workspace, click on **Guest OS Profiles** by expanding **Profiles** on the left pane, and then right-click on **Guest OS Profiles** and select **Create Guest OS Profile**.

2. In the **New Guest OS Profile** dialog box, type the guest OS profile name (for example, W2016 Standard), and select OS type from the **Compatibility** drop-down menu **(Windows**, by default).

> Guest OS profile settings will vary depending on the **Compatibility** value selected (**Windows, Windows (Shielded)** or **Linux**).

3. Click on **Guest OS Profile** on the left pane and configure the settings (product key or server roles, for example), and click on **OK** to finish.

> You can provide a pattern for the computer name. For example, if you type W2016-SRV###, the computers will be named W2016-SRV001, W2016-SRV002, W2016-SRV003, W2016-SRV004, and so on.

Creating an application profile

Carry out the following steps to create an application profile:

1. In the Library workspace, click on **Application Profiles** and select **Create Application Profile**.

2. In the **Application Profile** dialog box, type the application profile name (for example, First_DC), select the compatibility type (in most cases, **General** is a good choice as it provides all profile features for every kind of application, whether it's a web app or just script), and then type its optional description.

3. Click on **Application Configuration** in the left pane and then on **OS Compatibility**, and select the supported OS (**Windows Server 2016 Standard** and **Windows Server 2016 Datacenter**, in my case). VMM prevents you from deploying apps to incompatible OSes while creating services.

4. If there is an application package, click on **Add**, select the application type, and then provide the application package.

5. If there is a script, click on **Add** and then select the script to add to the application profile and click on **OK** to finish.

To add a custom resource to the VMM library, create a folder with a .cr extension, place content in the folder (scripts, for example), and then copy the folder to a VMM library share. VMM discovers and imports the folder into the VMM library as a custom resource. In addition, you can use Get-SCCustomResource and Set-SCCustomResource cmdlets to manage CRs.

Creating a SQL Server profile

1. In the **Library** workspace, click on **SQL Server Profiles** and select **Create SQL Server Profile**.

2. In the **New SQL Server Profile** dialog box, type the SQL Server profile name (for example, RLLAB_SQLENT).

3. Click on **SQL Server Configuration** and then on Add: SQL Server Deployment.

4. Select **SQL Server Deployment - Deployment 1**, and type the SQL instance name and the account (**Run As account**) to be used when installing it. Also provide a valid SQL Server product key.

5. Select **Configuration** and provide information about the configuration (for example, security mode or SQL Server configuration file).

6. Select **Service Accounts** and provide the SQL Server service **Run As account** and click on **OK** to finish.

 See the *Deploying a Microsoft SQL Server for VMM implementation* recipe in `Chapter 3`, *Installing VMM 2016* for more details about SQL Server deployment.

See also

For more information, see the following references:

- *VMM 2012/2016 SQL Server Profile* article available at `http://blogs.technet.com/b/scvmm/archive/2011/09/27/vmm-2012-sql-server-profile.aspx`
- *Add profiles to the Library* article available at `https://docs.microsoft.com/en-us/system-center/vmm/library-profiles`

Creating user roles in VMM

User roles in VMM 2016 are used to define the objects and management operations that specified users can create/manage/perform in VMM.

These user roles are as follows:

- **Administrator**: The members of this group can perform tasks/actions on all objects managed by VMM. In addition to this, only administrators can add WSUS servers to VMM.
- **Fabric (delegated) administrator**: The members of this group can perform tasks/actions within their assigned scope (host groups, private clouds, and/or library servers). They can create delegated administrators with a subset of their scope.
- **Read-only administrator**: The members of this group are able to view the status and properties of objects or jobs within their assigned scope (host groups, private clouds, and/or library servers) and to specify the **Run As accounts** that they can view.
- **Tenant administrator**: The members of this group can create/manage self-service users (specifying the tasks/actions they can execute on VMs and/or services), VM networks, and VM services.

- **Application administrator (self-service user)**: The members of this group can create, deploy, and manage their own VMs and services, such as specifying private clouds to have a VM or service deployed, granting access to logical and physical resources in the VMM library, and configuring quotas and PRO tips settings. Only administrators and delegated administrators (within their scope) have the rights to create application administrator roles, which can only view a simplified placement map (containing only their VMs/services) on a VM or service deployment operation.

Getting ready

If the self-service user role has more than one private cloud within its scope, users select the appropriate cloud before placement runs.

When creating a self-service user role, you will be required to configure quotas, which only apply to the VMs deployed. They do not apply to the VMs in the library.

 The quota is applied individually to each member of the user role.

Quota types supported	Description of what can be consumed
Virtual CPUs	The maximum number of VM CPUs
Memory (MB)	The maximum amount of VM memory
Storage (GB)	The maximum amount of VM storage
Custom quota (points)	For backward compatibility, an arbitrary value that can be assigned to a VM template based on its anticipated *size*
Virtual machines	The number of VMs

How to do it...

Carry out the following steps to add a user to the built-in administrator user role:

1. In the VMM 2016 console, click on **Settings** and then expand **Security**.
2. Click on **User Roles** and then click on the main pane, right-click on the **Administrator user** role, and select **Properties**.

3. In the **Administrator Properties** dialog box, click on **Members** and then on **Add**.

4. In the **Select Users**, **Computers**, or **Groups** dialog box, type an AD user account or group (for example, `rllab\rlevchenko`), and then double-click **OK**.

 To delete a user, on the **Members** page select the user or group and click on **Remove**. The preceding steps can also be used to add users to other user roles.

How it works...

The built-in administrator user role is created when you install VMM, and then the user account that you used to run the VMM setup and all the domain users in the local **Administrators** group are added to the built-in administrator user role.

To add users or groups to roles, or remove them from roles, you can use this recipe, noting that only administrators can add/remove users to/from the administrator user role.

You can also use this recipe to create the new tenant administrator role if you are an administrator or delegated administrator (with rights). Tenants can have quotas on VMs and resources.

There's more...

There are more user roles that can be created.

Creating a delegated or read-only administrator user role

Carry out the following steps to create an optional delegated or read-only user role:

1. In the VMM 2016 console, in the **Settings** workspace, click on **Create User Role** on the ribbon.

2. In the **Create User Role Wizard** window, type the name (for example, `vmm-delegated-admin`) and the optional description, and click on **Next** to continue.

3. To create a delegated or read-only admin, on the **Profile** page select either of the two options:

- **Fabric Administrator**: Select this to create and add a user as a delegated administrator
- **Read-Only Administrator**: Select this to create and add a user as a read-only administrator

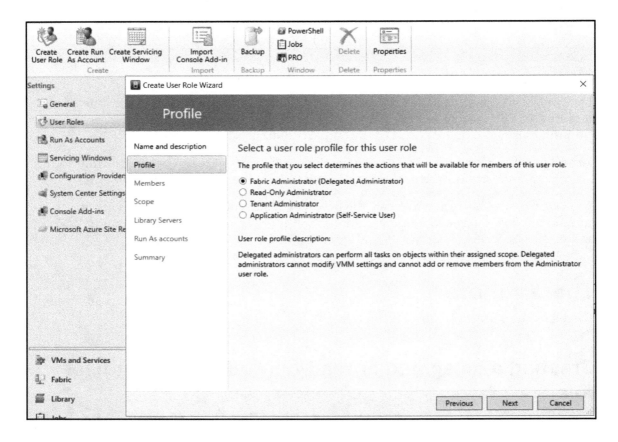

4. Click on **Next** and then on the **Members** page to add the user account(s) or group(s), click on **Add**, and then click on **Next**.

5. On the **Scope** page, select the private cloud(s) or host group(s) (for example, **RLCLOUD**) that can be managed by this role and then click on **Next**.

6. On the **Library servers** page, select one or more library servers. Click on **Add**, click on **OK** after selecting a server, and then click on **Next**.

7. On the **Run As Accounts** page, click on **Add**, select **Run As account**, and then click on **OK** to add the account. When you finish adding the accounts, click on **Next** to continue and click on **Finish**.

Creating a tenant administrator role

The likely use for this scenario is in hosting environments with multiple customers, or in enterprise environments where you have multiple teams/branches and each one of them wants to have and manage their own environment.

Carry out the following steps to create the self-service user:

1. In the VMM 2016 console, in the **Settings** workspace, click on **Create User Role** on the ribbon.

2. In the **Create User Role Wizard** window, type the name (for example, `TenantA-admin`) and the optional description (for example, `Branch office at Voronezh`) and then click on **Next**.

3. On the **Profile** page, click on **Tenant Administrator** and then click on **Next**.

4. On the **Members** page, to add the user account(s) or group(s), click on **Add** and then click on **Next**.

5. On the **Scope** page, select the private cloud(s) (for example, **RLCLOUD**) that can be managed by this role, select **Show PRO tips** to allow performance and resource optimization management, and then click on **Next** as shown in the following screenshot:

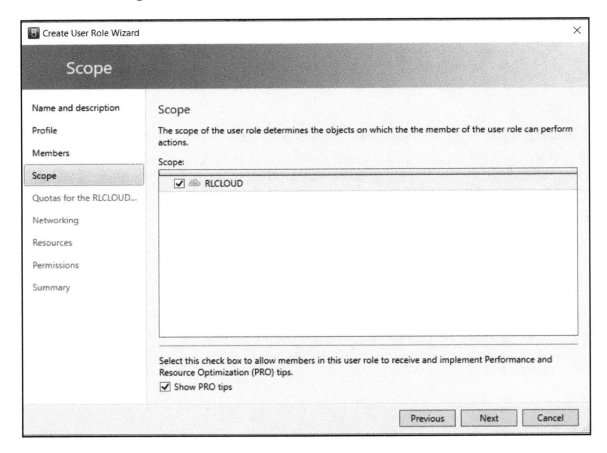

VMM must be integrated with SCOM to receive PRO tips for resources.

6. On the **Quotas** page, check the **Role level quotas** and the **Member level quotas** sections. If you need members of the user role to share quotas, add an AD security group instead of a user account:

Quotas for the RLCLOUD cloud

Role level quotas:

All members of this user role combined can use resources up to the specified limits.

Dimension	Available Capacity	Use Maximum	Assigned Quota
Virtual CPUs:	10	☑	10
Memory (MB):	24576	☑	24576
Storage (GB):	250	☑	250
Custom quota (points):	Unlimited	☑	Unlimited
Virtual machines:	Unlimited	☑	Unlimited

Member level quotas:

Each member of this user role combined can use resources up to the specified limits.

Dimension	Available Capacity	Use Maximum	Assigned Quota
Virtual CPUs:	10	☑	10
Memory (MB):	24576	☑	24576
Storage (GB):	250	☑	250
Custom quota (points):	Unlimited	☑	Unlimited
Virtual machines:	Unlimited	☑	Unlimited

7. On the **Networking** page, select the VM networks that can be used by this role and click on **Next**.

Click on **Add** to add the VM Networks.

8. On the **Resources** page, click on **Add** to select resources and click on **OK**, and then click on **Browse** and select the library upload data path.

9. Click on **Next**, and on the **Actions** page define the global permissions and permitted actions on the scope objects level (**RLCLOUD**, for example) and click on **Next** again, as shown in the following screenshot:

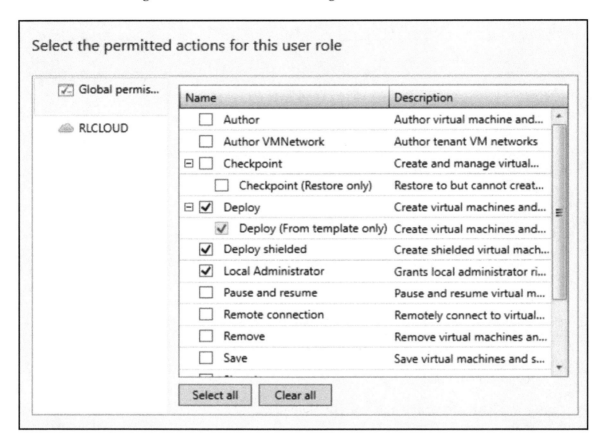

10. On the **Run As accounts** page (if it appears), add **Run as Accounts** that you want to share with role members to allow use of them when creating VMs and services.
11. On the **Summary** page, click on **Finish**.

To change **Members**, **Scope**, **Quotas**, **Resource**, and/or **Actions**, select the user role, right-click on it, and then select **Properties**.

Creating an application administrator (self-service user) role

Carry out the following steps to create the role:

1. In the VMM 2016 console, in the **Settings** workspace, click **Create User Role** on the ribbon.
2. In the **Create User Role Wizard** window, type the name (for example, BranchVRN-AppAdmin) and the optional description (for example, App Admin at Voronezh Branch Office) and then click on **Next**.
3. On the **Profile** page, click on **Application Administrator** and then click on **Next**.
4. On the **Members** page, to add the user account(s) or group(s), click on **Add** and then click on **Next**.

> To share a VM's ownership created by other members, use an ADD group for the user role or use the **Share** and **Receive** actions.

5. On the **Scope** page, select the private cloud(s) (for example, **RLCLOUD**) that can be managed by this role, select **Show PRO tips** to allow PRO management, and then click on **Next**.
6. On the **Quotas** page, enter the quota for each previously added private cloud(s), that is in the scope of the user, and click on **Next**.

> An individual page for each cloud will show whether more than one private cloud is assigned to the user.

7. On the **Networking** page, select the VM networks that can be used by this role and click on **Next**.

> Click on **Add** to add the VM networks.

8. On the **Resources** page, click on **Add** to select the resources (for example, hardware, OS, application and/or SQL profiles, VM templates, and/or service templates) and click on **OK**; then click on **Browse** and select the library upload data path.

9. On the **Actions** page, select the action(s) that the self-service users can perform and then click on **Next**.

 If you select **Author**, click on **Next** and select the **Run As account** that will be used to create the VMs and services, and click on **Next**.

10. On the **Summary** page, click on **Finish**.

Configuring self-service user roles to share and receive resources

Carry out the following steps to enable sharing and receiving resources between role members:

1. In the VMM 2016 console, in the **Settings** workspace, expand **Security** and click on **User Roles** on the left pane.
2. In the **User Roles** pane, select a user role, right-click on it, and then select **Properties**.
3. Click on the **Actions** page, select **Share** and **Receive**, and then click on **OK**.

See also

For more information, see the following references:

- Refer to the *Set up Self-Service in VMM* article available at: https://docs.microsoft.com/system-center/vmm/self-service
- Refer to the *Perform self-user tasks in VMM* article available at: https://docs.microsoft.com/system-center/vmm/self-service-tasks

Creating and deploying virtual machines

In this recipe, we will create a standard virtual machine that will later be used as a template. If you are seeking for detailed steps required to deploy shielded VMs, see the previous chapter.

Getting ready

Creating a VM is straightforward. You can create a new virtual machine using an existing virtual hard disk, or you can create a machine with a blank virtual hard disk and then install the OS using ISO media hosted in the VMM library or PXE resources.

VMM 2016 supports two VM generations. A newer one (Generation 2) was introduced in Windows Server 2012 R2 and it's now mainly used to provide the following benefits:

- Larger boot-volume-supported size
- Faster PXE boot using a synthetic network adapter
- Boot from SCSI controller (VHDX/DVD)
- Secure Boot
- UEFI firmware support

> You can only create Generation 2 VMs if deploying Windows Server 2012/Windows 8 and later. Check out the following article to understand the differences between Generation 1 and Generation 2 VMs: https://docs.microsoft.com/en-us/windows-server/virtualization/hyper-v/plan/should-i-create-a-generation-1-or-2-virtual-machine-in-hyper-v.

How to do it...

Carry out the following steps to create a virtual machine:

1. In the VMM 2016 console in the bottom-left corner, click on the **VMs and Services** workspace.
2. On the ribbon, click on **Create Virtual Machine** and then select **Create Virtual Machine**.

3. On the **Select Source** page, choose between the **Create the new virtual machine with a blank virtual hard disk** (the OS will have to be installed after the VM's creation) and **Use an existing virtual machine**, **VM template** or **virtual hard disk** options and then click on **Next**.

 You won't be able to use a Generation 1 VM as a source to create a Generation 2 VM.

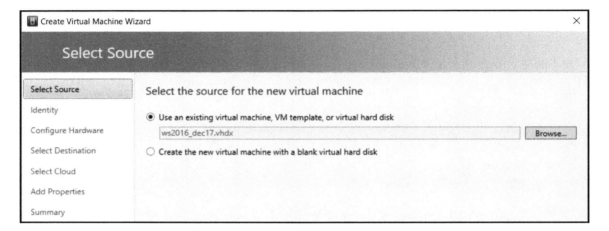

4. On the **Specify Virtual Machine Identity** page, type the virtual machine name (for example, W2016-DC01), a description (optional), select the VM Generation type (1 or 2) from the drop-down list, and then click on **Next**.

 The option **Turn on shielding support in the virtual machine after deploying it** is only available for Generation 2 VMs. Refer to the previous chapter to get more details about Guarded Fabric and Shielded VMs.

5. On the **Configure Hardware** page, provide the hardware settings or select a previously created hardware profile, and then click on **Next** as shown in the following screenshot:

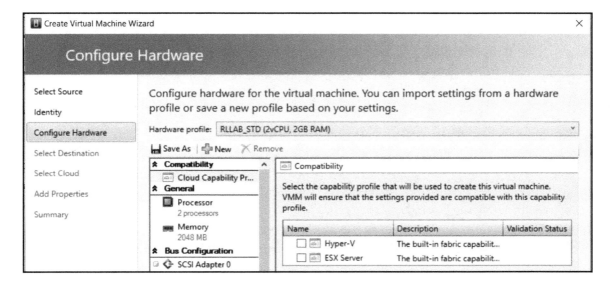

 For a VM Generation 1 to boot from the network (PXE Boot), in order to install an OS in the **Network Adapters** section, add a legacy network adapter type.

6. If you are creating a new VM from a blank VHD/VHDX disk, click on the **Bus Configuration** section; then click on **IDE Devices** for Generation 1 VM and on **SCSI** for Generation 2 VM and on the **Virtual DVD Drive** map within it, and select the ISO hosted in the VMM library or a CD/DVD drive with the OS media to be installed.

 To make the VM highly available, select **Make this virtual machine highly available** in the **Availability** section under the **Advanced** section.

7. On the **Select Destination** page, choose whether to deploy or store the VM (shown in the following screenshot) and click on **Next**:

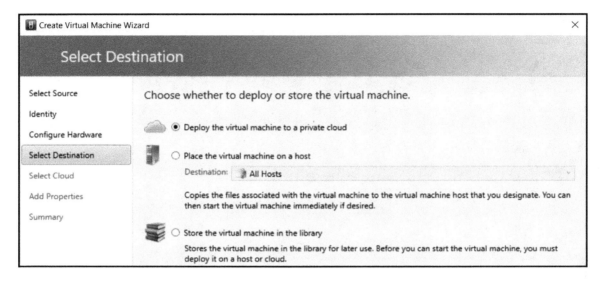

8. If you choose **Deploy the virtual machine to a private cloud**, select the cloud, confirm/modify the settings, and click on **Next**.

The recommendation of cloud placement is based on a star rating. Check out the following article, *Understanding Virtual Machine Placement and Ratings in VMM* at `https://docs.microsoft.com/en-us/system-center/vmm/provision-vms`, for more information about VM placement.

9. If you choose **Place the virtual machine on a host**, select the host and click on **Next and** on the **Configure settings** page, review/update the VM settings and click on **Next**.

10. If the **Select Networks** page appears, you can select the VM network, virtual switch, and/or the VLAN to be used by this VM and then click on **Next**.

11. If you choose **Store the virtual machine in the library**, select the library server and click on **Next**. Then, click on **Browse** to select the share location path to deploy the VM and click on **Next**.

12. In the **Add properties** page, select the automatic actions that need to be taken and OS to be installed.

13. On the **Summary** page, click on **Create**.

Once the VM is deployed, you can connect to the VM via Console (basic session) or RDP. In the VMM 1801 semi-annual channel release, you can also use an Enhanced Console Session (aka RDP via VMBus).

How it works...

This recipe guided you through creating and deploying VMs to a private cloud, to a specific host, or storing them in a VMM library. When **Create Virtual Machine Wizard** starts, select whether VMM will deploy the new VM either to the private cloud, directly to a host, or to a library. Once VMM knows that the VM is to be deployed to a cloud or to a host, a list will be provided and each one will be rated (check the **Rating Explanation** tab) for how well it will be able to handle the VM.

If a private cloud is configured, the options will differ depending on the user role and rights you are connected to.

When creating a VM in VMM 2016, you have the option to select the VM generation (Generation 1 or Generation 2). Both generation versions are also supported by service templates. VMM uses intelligent placement by analyzing the host's performance and rates them on a scale of one to five stars in order to choose the better host/cloud available for deployment. The following table indicates how the ratings are calculated:

Rating	Formula
CPU	[1 - (CPU utilization / (100 - CPU reserve))] x CPU weight
Memory (RAM)	[1 - (RAM used / (Total RAM - RAM reserve))] x RAM weight
Disk I/O capacity	[1 - (Disk IOPS / Max disk IOPS] x Disk weight
Network	[1 - (Network utilization / (100 - Network reserve))] x Network weight

For private cloud support, click on the **Cloud Compatibility Profile** menu option and select the capability profile (Hyper-V or ESX Server). VMM uses capability profiles to define the virtual machine's limits. By specifying the capability profile, VMM will determine how much maximum RAM, disk, and other resources can be assigned to a virtual machine.

If you have standalone hosts running different processor versions in the same family (Intel-to-Intel, AMD-to-AMD), to allow live migration between the hosts, select **Allow migration to a virtual machine host with a different processor version** in the **Processor** section.

You can use the **Save as...** option to save the hardware profile configuration.

If you are storing the VM in the VMM library before deploying it to a host, you need to use one of the default VMM library blank virtual hard disks on the **Select Source** page.

You can also use this recipe to create a VM template by running through the **Create a New Virtual Machine** wizard and selecting **Store the virtual machine in the library**. Name the file appropriately, for example, W2016 Datacenter.

 VMM will generalize the VM while running the **Create Virtual Machine Template** wizard from a deployed VM, but if you are creating a VM from an existing VHD file, make sure it has been generalized using the Sysprep tool or the VM will have the same ID as the source.

In VMM 2016, the **Select Cloud** and **Select Host** pages in the **Deployment and Transfer Explanation** tab will show information whether or not fast file copy, a VMM 2016 feature that uses ODX, can be used. For more information about ODX, check out the article *Windows Offloaded Data Transfers Overview*: http://go.microsoft.com/fwlink/p/?LinkId= 317143.

There's more...

If you are creating a VM from an existing VHD file, you need to generalize the guest OS.

Generalizing the guest OS using Sysprep

1. Start the virtual machine.
2. Go through the steps to install the OS.
3. Once the OS has been installed, configure the server roles and features if necessary. Normally, I also add the latest PowerShell DSC Resource Kit to use DSC in addition to/with VMM service templates to simplify domain services or SQL Server multiple deployments, for example.

PowerShell DSC Resource Kit is a collection of Desired State Configuration (DSC) resources to allow you to automate configuration of server roles or applications (Exchange, for example). Use the following to install the kit: `Find-Module -Tag DSCResourceKit|Install-Module -Force`. Here is a good example of DSC in action: `https://rlevchenko.com/2016/10/31/automate-exchange-2016-installation-and-dag-configuration-with-powershell-dsc/`.

4. Run the `sysprep` process (it is found at `C:\Windows\System32\sysprep`).

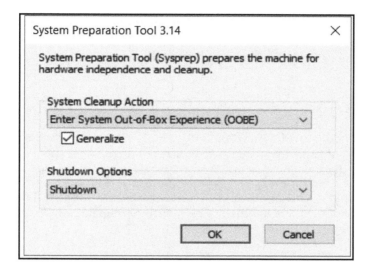

5. After the VM has shut down, copy the `SYSPREP VHD/VHDX` file to the library share, and then refresh the library if necessary.

See also

For more information, see the following references:

- Refer to the *How to clone existing VMs* article available at `https://docs.microsoft.com/en-us/system-center/vmm/vm-clone`
- Refer to the *What's new in Hyper-V 2016* article available at `https://rlevchenko.com/2015/05/24/what-is-new-in-hyper-v-windows-server-2016/`

- Refer to the *Switching dynamic IP to static in VMM* article available at: `https://rlevchenko.com/2017/09/01/switching-dynamic-ip-to-static-in-vmm/`

- See the FAQ: *Windows Server 2016 and Hyper-V Integration Services* article at `https://rlevchenko.com/2017/02/18/faq-windows-server-2016-and-hyper-v-integration-services/`

Creating virtual machine templates

VMM virtual machine templates are used to perform the automated installation and configuration of servers, dramatically reducing the time to release a server, and automating all these processes in a simple and uncomplicated deployment method.

Getting ready

Before you can create the virtual machine template, you need to create a new VM and install a vanilla OS (fresh Windows install) into it, which will be used as the basis for the template. See the *Creating and deploying virtual machines* recipe of this chapter.

To create a VM template, you can select the source for which the template will be created from an existing template: a virtual disk (VHD) with a preinstalled OS, or even a virtual machine that is being used in any host managed by VMM.

How to do it...

Carry out the following steps to create a VM template that is based on either an existing virtual hard disk or on a virtual machine template:

1. In the VMM 2016 console, click on the **Library** workspace, then on the ribbon, and then click on **Create VM Template**.
2. On the **Select Source** page, select **Use an existing VM template** or a **virtual hard disk stored in the library**.
3. Click on **Browse**, select a generalized Windows `Server.vhdx` file, then click on **OK**, and then click on **Next**.
4. Type the VM template name (for example, `W2016 General`) and click on **Next**.
5. If the selected source is a VHDX disk, the Generation box will show up. Select between **Generation 1** or **Generation 2 Virtual Machine format**.

6. On the **Configure Hardware** page, provide the hardware settings or select a hardware profile and then click on **Next**.

 To make the template highly available, in the **Availability** section, which is present under the **Advanced** section, select **Make this virtual machine highly available**.

7. On the **Configure Operating System** page, select a guest OS profile or provide the settings for it, and then click on **Next** as shown in the following screenshot:

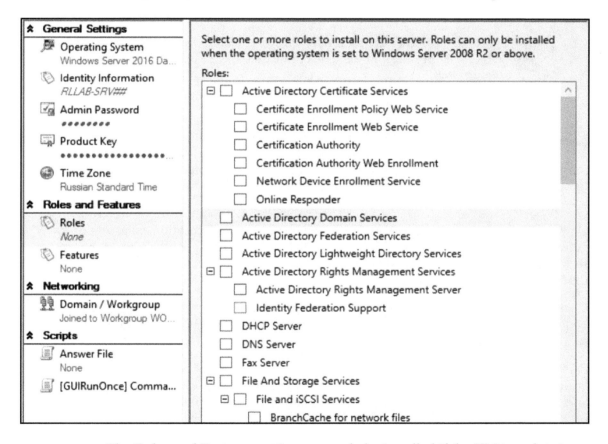

 The **Roles and Features** settings can only be installed if the VM template is used in a service template and the source virtual hard disk has Windows Server 2008 R2 or higher installed.

8. On the **Configure Applications** page, configure the settings or select an application profile, if any, and then click on **Next**.

9. On the **Configure SQL Server** page, configure the settings or select a SQL Server profile, if any, and then click on **Next**.

 Application and SQL Server deployment settings do not apply if the template is designated for standalone VMs that are not part of a service.

10. On the **Summary** page, click on **Create**.

 To verify whether the template has been created, in the **Library** workspace expand **Templates** on the left-hand side pane and then click on **VM Templates**.

How it works...

Start by selecting the source for which the template will be created. You can use an existing template, a virtual disk (VHD/VHDX) with a preinstalled OS, or even a virtual machine that is being used in any host managed by VMM.

On the **Configure Hardware** pane, specify the hardware configuration, such as a disk, network, memory, or processor, or select an existing hardware profile. In the **Advanced** section, you can specify settings for availability and checkpoint options, which will be discussed in the next chapters in detail.

Click on the **Cloud Compatibility Profile** menu option to select the capability profile to validate against the hardware profile for private cloud support. You can also use the **Save as...** option to save the hardware profile configuration.

On the **Configure Operating System** pane, specify the information for the Windows automated installation, such as computer name, product key, local administrator password, and OS. By using the # symbol, the virtual machine will be named based on a numeric sequence. To create random names use the * symbol. If the template used has a Windows 2008 R2 or later OS, you can use the **Roles and Features** option, which makes it possible to select the server roles and/or features that will automatically be installed.

In the **Configure Applications** option, you can add and configure applications and scripts to automatically be installed after the OS installation:

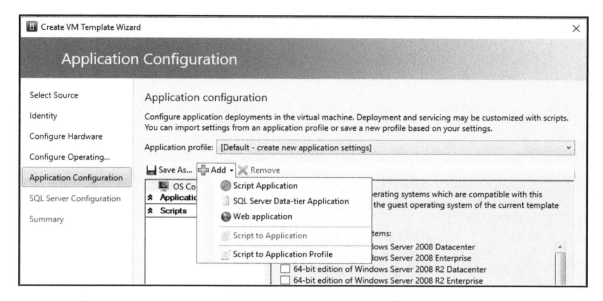

On the last screen in **Configure SQL Server**, you can also specify the SQL installation information and configuration.

 To use the same options provided for automating the creation of templates through PowerShell, click on **View Script**.

There's more...

Now that the VM template has been created, let's see how we can deploy it.

Deploying virtual machines from virtual machine templates

Carry out the following steps to create virtual machines from the virtual machine templates:

1. In the VMM 2016 console at the bottom-left corner, click on the **VMs and Services** workspace.
2. On the ribbon, click on **Create Virtual Machine**, then select **Create Virtual Machine**.

3. On the **Select Source** page, select **Use an existing virtual machine**, **VM template**, or **virtual hard disk** and click on **Browse**.

4. Select the template (for example, **W2016 General**), click on **OK**, and then click on **Next**.

 A message showing that the template settings will be ignored will appear if the template has roles or features configured, or application or SQL deployment settings.

5. In the **Identify/Specify Virtual Machine Identity** section, type the VM name (for example, `W2016-SRV01`), an optional description, and turn on shielding support if required, then click on **Next**.

6. On the **Configure Hardware** page, adjust the settings for the new VM and click on **Next**. In VMM 2016, you can also set a custom name for network adapters during the creation of VMs as shown in the screenshot:

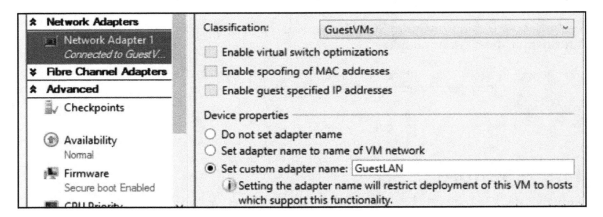

 When device naming for NIC is configured, VMM updates the **Hyper-V Network Adapter Name** advanced property with the provided value (`GuestLAN`, in the preceding example) during VM provisioning. Once the VM is deployed, you can use the following command to get a custom adapter name: `Get-NetAdapterAdvancedProperty | ? DisplayName -eq "Hyper-V Network Adapter Name"`

7. On the **Configure Operating System** page, provide the identity, network settings, and scripts (if any) for the new VM.

8. On the **Select Destination** page, choose whether to deploy the VM to a host or to a private cloud and click on **Next**.

9. If you choose **Deploy the virtual machine to private cloud**, select the cloud, and on the **Configure settings** page, review/update the VM settings and click on **Next**.

10. If you choose **Place the virtual machine on a host**, select the host, click on **Next**, and on the **Configure settings** page, review/update the VM settings, for example, select **Storage QoS policies** (if any), provide static IP/MAC, and check the deployment method as shown in the following screenshot:

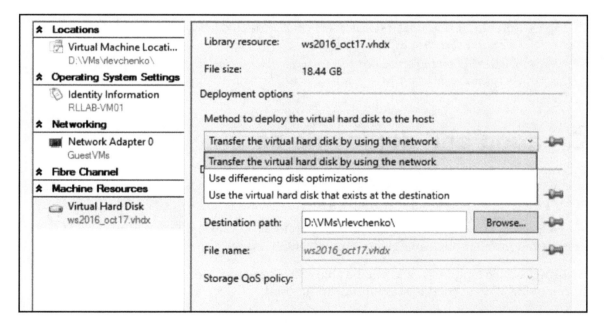

 If **Use differencing disk optimizations** is selected, you will need to provide the parent disk destination path or let VMM decide. These disks are typical for VDI deployments where pooled desktops use the same parent disk.

11. If you selected a cloud or a host, on the **Add properties** page select the automatic actions that are to be undertaken.
12. On the **Summary** page, click on **Create**.

> If you are placing the virtual machine on a host cluster, and if you click on **Browse** in the **Select Destination Folder** dialog box, the file shares will be listed under the **File Shares** node.

See also

For more information, see the following references:

- Refer to the *Creating a shielded VM template* recipe in Chapter 6, *Configuring Guarded Fabric in VMM*
- See the *Deploying a shielded VM from template* recipe in Chapter 6, *Configuring Guarded Fabric in VMM*

Creating and deploying service templates

In VMM 2016, a service is a set of VMs configured and deployed together and managed as a single entity. For example, the deployment of a three-tier business application, or a frontend web application with SQL Server running in the background.

A service template provides the ability to separate the OS configuration from the application installation, leaving you with fewer OS images.

By using service templates, you will be able to leverage variations in capacity, easily adding or removing VMs needed to support the application.

> It is the best practice to wrap even a single VM template in a service template as you, for example, scale it out.

Getting ready

Ensure the resources that you need in order to create the service are available. Review and document all the elements that the service needs to be up and running before starting. For example:

- What servers need to be deployed to support the service?
- Which existing VM template will be used?
- What roles/features should be installed? What applications or scripts need to be deployed?
- Have the needed VMM resources been created and configured?
- Which networking components are to be connected to?
- Who will use the service?

Take a look at a few important things you need to know:

- To install applications beforehand, have the installation files, scripts, and configuration made available
- To deploy a SQL Server instance on to a VM, make sure to have a VHD/VHDX file with a generalized SQL Server installation

How to do it...

Carry out the following steps to create the service template:

1. In the VMM 2016 console at the bottom-left corner, click on the **Library** workspace.
2. In the **Home** tab on the ribbon, click on **Create Service**, select **Create a service template**, and click on **OK**.
3. In the **New Service Template** dialog box, type the name for the service template (for example, AD_2Tiers).

By using PowerShell scripts, we will create a service template to deploy new domain infrastructure running root and secondary DCs.

4. Type the service template's release value for the version (for example, 1.0) in replacement for the new value .

 The release value is important for when you need to update the service. It helps identify the version of the service template.

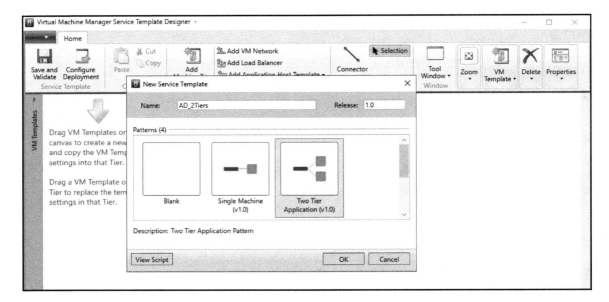

5. Select the number of tiers to create in the service template (for example, **Two Tier Application**, which creates blocks to be configured as VMs) and click on **OK**. Wait for the service to be created.

 Click on each machine tier and provide its name and optional description.

6. The best way to configure machine tiers is to use existing VM templates. Click on **Tool Window** in the ribbon and select **Templates**, then drag VM template(s) on to the canvas area. You can also click on **Add Machine Tier** in the ribbon and follow the wizard's instructions to create tiers from VM templates.

I will add two tiers using the previously created VM template: machine tier 1, named Root DC VM, and machine tier 2 , Second DC VM.

7. Double-click on the first machine tier (Root DC VM, in my case) and select the **General** page. As other tiers have dependencies from the Root DC VM(machine tier 1), we need to set **Preferred deployment order** and **Preferred servicing order** to value 1. Once VMM finishes Root DC tier deployment, customization of other tiers will be started depending on their servicing order values. For example, the following screenshot shows the settings for the second machine tier, which is used for deploying additional DCs:

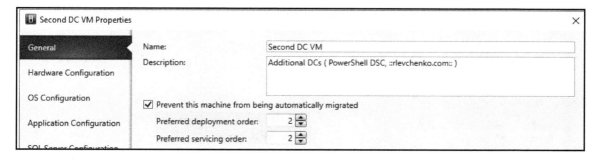

8. On the **Hardware Configuration** page, review the configuration and adjust settings if needed. For example, click on the **Network Adapter 1**, press **Browse**, select **Use a configurable service** setting, and type `@Network@`.

If configurable service settings are used, you will be asked to provide the *real* values for them during every service deployment (for instance, a VM network or a script's argument value).

9. On the **OS Configuration** page, check OS settings, including local administrator credentials, product key, time zone, and roles. In the following screenshot, you can see the configuration of one of my machine tiers. As one of my scripts uses AD and its PowerShell module, I asked VMM to install all required roles and features to make it work. Also keep in mind that the computer name format in the **Identity Information** should use asterisks (SRV-ADC###, for example). Otherwise, the service template won't scale out the machine tier.

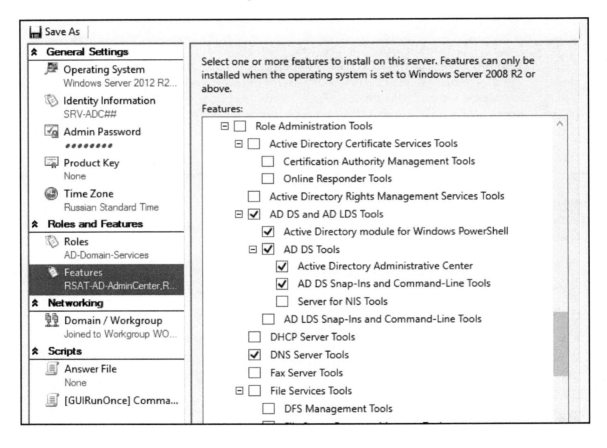

10. On the **Application Configuration** page, select an application profile or define a new one by clicking **Add** and selecting, for example, **Script Application**. Type the application name, specify the executable program (for example, `%windir%\System32\WindowsPowershell\v1.0\powershell.exe`) and its parameters (in my case, `-file .\secondDC.ps1 @password@ @domain@`), and then click on **Browse** and select a custom resource containing script files, for instance, as shown in the screenshot:

> Pay attention to timeout duration. If VMM does not receive an exit code during the timeout, VMM will mark the deployment as failed. I normally use a slightly higher value than actually required (depending on the application type).

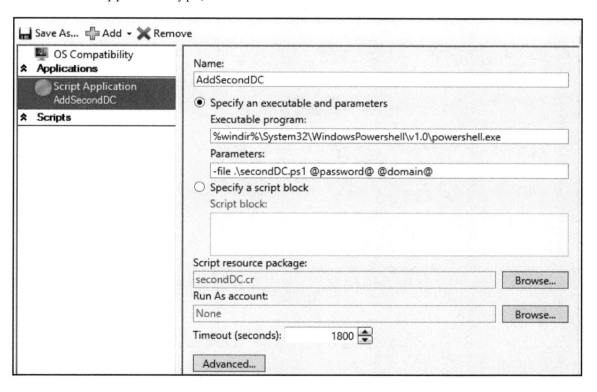

To simplify troubleshooting, define paths for output and error files. To do this, press the **Advanced** button, check **Write the standard output to a file on the guest operating system** and **Write the standard error to a file on the guest operating system**, then provide the file path, for example, `c:\scriptlogs\output.txt`.

11. Once you have finished configuring machine tier settings, including scripts and networking, click the **Save and Validate** button to check the template changes, and then click on **Configure Deployment** to start the service deployment. A sample of my service template configuration is shown in the following screenshot:

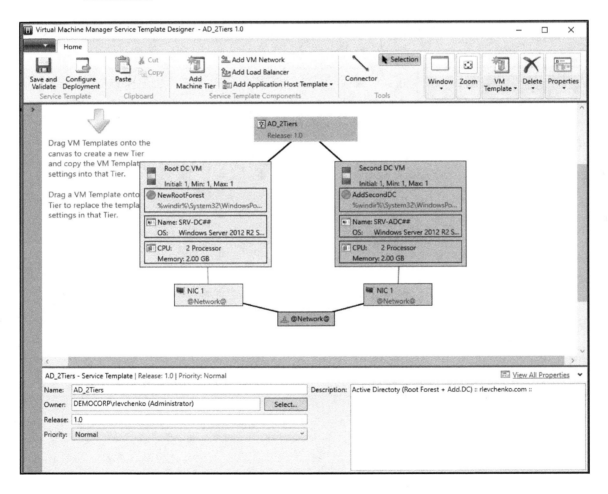

To view or change service configurable settings, double-click on the service template and in the **Service Settings**, check each setting and its properties.

Settings:

Name	Value	Mandatory	Encrypted
⊟ domain	rlevchenko.com	Yes	No
Root DC VM\NewRootForest\Script commands\Install\Parameters Second DC VM\AddSecondDC\Script commands\Install\Parameters			
Network		Yes	
⊟ password		Yes	Yes
Root DC VM\NewRootForest\Script commands\Install\Parameters Second DC VM\AddSecondDC\Script commands\Install\Parameters			

How it works...

A service template is a set of elements (for example, VMs, scripts, and networks) bonded to define the services' configurations.

To create a service template in the VMM console, click on **Create a Service** to open the **Virtual Machine Manager Service Template Designer** window.

You can use an existing VM template on a service template, which includes the VMs (deployed as a service), applications to be installed, and network settings.

After the service template is created, you can add/remove elements (for example, VMs, network, and apps), deploy it to a private cloud/host, and/or deploy the updated service template to a deployed service to update it as well.

 If you are changing a service template that is in use by a deployed service, a new release value will be required before saving.

After the service template has been saved, it will be located in the **Library** workspace on the service templates node. To open an existing one, click on the **Library** workspace, then in the designer select the service template. On the ribbon in the **Service Template** tab, click on **Open Designer**.

 To master VMM service templates, create a one-tier application and use the following script with an application profile to install Exchange 2016 server: `https://rlevchenko.com/2016/07/29/automating-exchange-2016-installation-with-desired-state-configuration/`.

There's more...

Now that we have created the service template, let's deploy it.

 If you have done a Network Controller (SDNv2) deployment described in Chapter 5, *Configuring Fabric Resources in VMM*, you can just skip this recipe. I'd recommend opening **Template Designer** and exploring **NC template machine tier** settings instead.

Deploying a service from the VMs and Services workspace

The **Deploy Service** window contains three panes. The left pane contains two tabs, namely **Services Components**, which lists the service tiers that will be deployed, and **Settings**, which shows the configuration that will be used for application deployment.

The center pane shows the service design with all instances that will be deployed as part of the service. The right pane is a **Minimap**, which contains a map of the service. This is illustrated in the following screenshot:

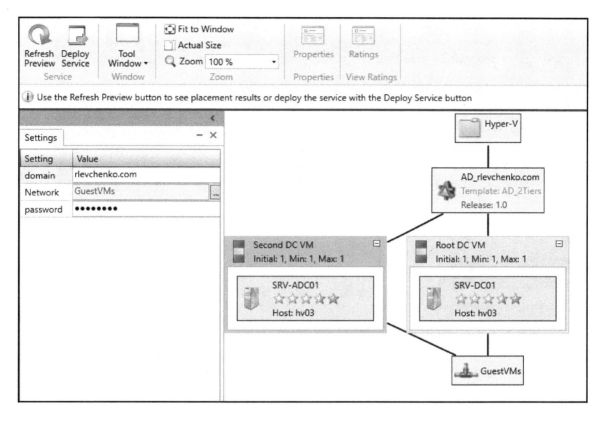

Carry out the following steps to deploy a service:

1. In the VMM 2016 console at the bottom-left corner, click on the **VMs and Services** workspace.
2. Select the private cloud or host group to deploy the service.
3. Under the **Home** tab on the ribbon, click on **Create Service**.
4. In the **Create Service** dialog box, click on **Use an existing service** template, then click on **Browse** and select the service template (for example, AD_2Tiers), and click on **OK**.
5. Type the service name and enter the location in the **Destination** list, and then click **OK**.
6. In the **Deploy Service** window, provide values for service settings and click on **Refresh Preview**, and then on **Deploy Service**.

VMM performs a placement check to determine the best location to deploy the service, and then opens the **Deploy Service** window. Follow the steps described to resolve any errors and warnings, and then deploy the service.

Scaling out a service in VMM

The scale out feature in VMM is useful if you are required to set up additional VMs on any tier of a deployed service; for example, to handle increased load on the IIS servers. The scale-out process creates a new VM identically configured to the other VMs in the tier, deploying OS roles and features and required applications.

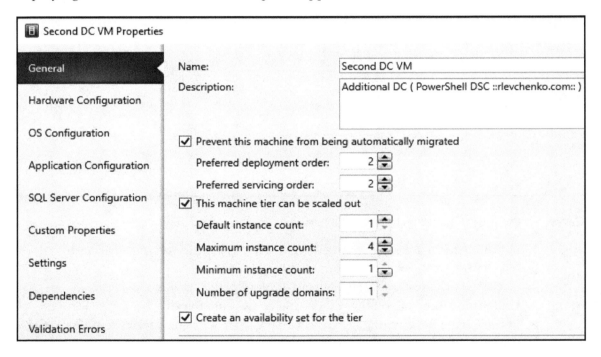

If you deploy a VM on a host cluster, you can create an availability set for the tier as shown in the preceding diagram. In that case, anti-affinity rules are applied to VMs (set members) and VMM will attempt to keep these virtual machines on separate hosts whenever possible to increase their availability.

Updating a service in VMM

To allow an update on a deployed service based on a service template, VMM retains the trail of which service template was used to deploy that service. (That is why you are required to update the release version before saving the new version.) To update a deployed service, you can use the following two methods:

- **Apply updates to existing virtual machines in-place**
- **Deploy new virtual machines with updated settings**

The following screenshot illustrates the use of these methods:

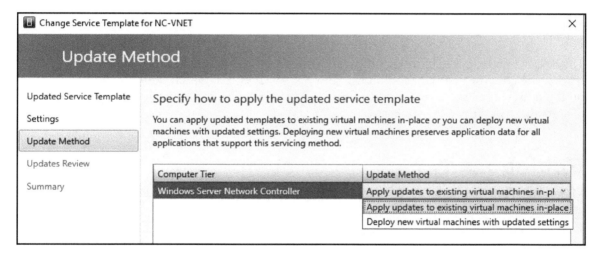

 In the VMM console, navigate to **VMs and Services**, select your deployed service, and then use the **Set Template** button in the ribbon to update the service.

See also

For more information, see the following references:

- *PowerShell DSC Overview* article available at: https://docs.microsoft.com/en-us/powershell/dsc/overview
- *How to Add Networking Components to a Service Template* article available at: https://technet.microsoft.com/en-us/library/hh410347.aspx

Rapidly provisioning a virtual machine by using SAN Copy

This recipe will guide you through the steps to rapidly provision a virtual machine by using the **Storage Area Network** (**SAN**) Copy technology (for example, snapshots and cloning).

Rapid provisioning can quickly create and deploy VMs, but to use a SAN Copy-capable template, the storage must support SAN Copy through cloning or snapshots.

 VMM 2016 supports ODX, which allows the provisioning of multiple VMs per LUN.

The SAN Copy-capable template allows VMM, when deploying a new VM, to create a read/write copy of the LUN containing the VHD/VHDX file, which then places the VM files on the new LUN assigned to a destination host/cluster. For this operation, storage transfer is used instead of a network transfer.

Getting ready

Make sure that the following prerequisites are met if you want to use the SAN Copy capability:

- Storage support for VMM storage management using SMI-S or SMP provider.
- Storage support for cloning or snapshots.
- Storage providers installed, configured, and accessible from the Hyper-V servers and VMM management server.
- If you are planning rapid provisioning, VMM should be managing the storage pool and it should be allocated to a host group. Also included are the following prerequisites:
  - The target Hyper-V hosts should be members of a host group and should use the same type of storage connectivity
  - The library server should be a member of the same host group and a Hyper-V host, if you are planning to create a SAN Copy-capable template from an existing VM and want to create and assign the LUN from a library server
- The **Multipath I/O** (**MPIO**) feature should be added to each host that needs a fiber channel or iSCSI storage array.

Making use of the **Microsoft Device Specific Module** (**DSM**), VMM automatically enables MPIO for supported storage. If you have already installed vendor-specific DSMs, they will be used to communicate with the storage instead. If, before adding the MPIO feature, you add a Hyper-V host to a VMM management server, you will be required to configure the MPIO or install vendor-specific DSMs manually outside VMM.

- If you are using fiber channel storage, each host that will access the storage array must have a **host bus adapter** (**HBA**) installed and should be zoned accordingly so that it can access the storage array.
- If you are using an iSCSI SAN, make sure that iSCSI portals have been added, the iSCSI initiator is logged into the array, and the **Microsoft iSCSI Initiator Service** on each host has been started and is set to **Automatic**.

How to do it...

You need to create an NTFS-formatted LUN beforehand and assign a drive letter from the managed storage pool. Carry out the following steps to configure the **Storage** for rapid provisioning in VMM:

1. In the VMM console at the bottom-left corner, click on the **Fabric** workspace. Expand **Storage** and click on **Arrays**, select the storage, right-click, then select **Properties**.
2. In the **Storage** properties window, click on **Settings**, select the snapshot type for SAN transfer, and click on **OK**.

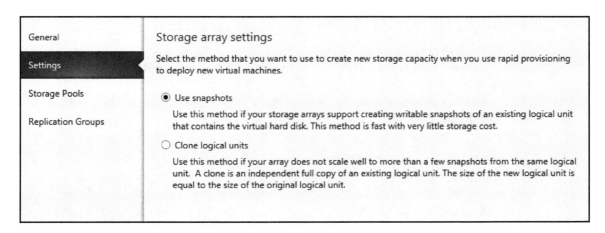

3. Now you need to create a **logical unit** from the storage pool. Under **Fabric** workspace, expand **Storage**, click on **Arrays**, click on **Create Logical Unit**, and then type the LUN name.

4. To allocate the created LUN to a host group, on the **Fabric** workspace, click on **Servers**, select the host group (for example, **Moscow**), right-click, select **Properties**, and then click on **Storage** in the left menu.

5. In the properties of the **Storage**, click on **Allocate Logical Units**, assign the **Available Logical Units** to **Allocated Logical Units**, and click on **OK**.

6. In the **Fabric** workspace, click on **Servers**, select the VMM Library host, right-click, select **Properties**, and then click on **Storage**.

7. On the **Storage** properties window, click on **Add** and select **Add Disk**.

8. For the logical unit, select the created LUN from the drop-down list.

9. Select **Format this volume as NTFS volume with the following settings** and check on **Perform a quick format**, type the volume label, and select mount in the following empty `NTFS` folder.

10. Select the `Template` folder under the library share and click on **OK**.

11. In the **Library** workspace, expand **Library Servers**, select the VMM library share, right-click, and select **Refresh**.

To create a SAN Copy-capable virtual hard disk on a host:

1. In the VMM console, click on the **VMs and Services** and select **Create Virtual Machine**.

2. On the **Select Source** page, click on **Create the new virtual machine with a blank virtual hard disk** and then click on **Next**.

3. On the **Specify Virtual Machine Identity** page, type the VM name (for example, `W2016-General`), specify the VM's generation and an optional description, and click on **Next**.

4. On the **Configure Hardware** page, review the hardware settings and click on **Next**.

5. On the **Select Destination** page, select **Place the virtual machine on a host** and click on **Next**.

6. On the **Select Host** page, select a host with the assigned LUN and click on **Next**.

7. On the **Configure Settings** page, click on **Virtual Machine Location**.

8. On the results pane, click on **Browse**, verify the text that the SAN (Migration Capable) field displays after the drive information, and select the drive (for example, `(E:\) [199.2 GB free of 200 GB, SAN (Migration Capable)]`).

9. Click on **OK**, and in **Machine Resources** click on **Virtual Hard Disk**.

10. In the results pane, click on **Browse**, select the same drive selected in *step 9* (that is, S), and click on **OK**.

11. Click on **Next** to continue.

12. On the **Select Networks** page, select the VM network, virtual switch, and/or VLAN setting.

13. On the **Add properties** page, select the automatic actions to be undertaken.

14. On the **Summary** page, click on **Create**.

> Once the new virtual machine is deployed, install and configure the guest OS, server roles, features, and applications. Generalize the image. See the *Generalizing the guest OS using Sysprep* subsection in the *Creating and deploying virtual machines* recipe of this chapter.

How it works...

Rapid Provisioning allows the deployment of VMs by using storage capabilities. VMM won't need to copy the VM from the VMM library to the Hyper-V host, alleviating I/O loads on the storage and network.

There are two methods to rapidly provision a LUN in VMM 2016 console: Snapshot copies and clones. You can also use PowerShell commands if you need finer granularity. Snapshot copies are provisioned almost immediately.

To use the SAN Copy capability, you must create and assign an empty storage LUN from a storage pool to the target host beforehand. You can either use VMM or the storage vendor management tools for this purpose.

The next step is to create a VM with a blank virtual hard disk (VHD/VHDX) file on that LUN. Then, install and customize the guest OS and applications and generalize the image by using Sysprep.

To finalize, using **New VM Template**, create a SAN Copy-capable template from the created VM. VMM will then transfer the files in the LUN from the host to the VMM library, through a SAN transfer.

> The library will index the new VHD/VHDX file during the next refresh.

There's more...

Now, let's create a SAN Copy-capable template and then deploy it.

Creating a SAN Copy-capable template

Carry out the following steps to create a SAN Copy-capable template:

1. In the VMM 2016 console, click on the **Library** workspace and click on **Create VM Template**.
2. On the **Select Source** page, click on **From an existing virtual machine that is deployed on a host**.
3. Click on **Browse**, select the VM (for example, **W2016-General**), click on **OK**, and then click on **Next**. In the warning dialog box, click on **Yes**.

> The virtual hard disks will be generalized. Therefore, any user data on the VM may be lost.

4. On the **VM Template Identity** page, type the VM template name (for example, **W2016-General-SAN**) and click on **Next**.
5. On the **Configure Hardware and Configure Operating System** pages, click on **Next**.
6. On the **Select Library Server** page, select the VMM library after verifying whether the **Transfer Type** column indicates SAN, and click on **Next**.
7. On the **Select Path** page, click on **Browse**. Select the path to store the VM files, click on **OK**, and then click on **Next**.
8. On the **Summary** page, click on **Create**.
9. In the **Library** workspace, expand VM templates, right-click on any column, and select **SAN Copy Capable**. Verify that the template you just created has the value **Yes** in the SAN Copy Capable column.

Create a new VM from the template if needed (refer to the *Creating and Deploying Virtual Machines* section in this chapter).

See also

For more information, see the following references:

- The Deploy VMs with rapid provisioning using SAN copy in the VMM fabric article available at: `https://docs.microsoft.com/en-us/system-center/vmm/vm-san-copy`

8
Managing VMware ESXi hosts

In this chapter, we will cover the following topics:

- Adding a VMware vCenter server to the VMM
- Adding VMware ESXi hosts or host clusters to VMM
- Configuring network settings on a VMware ESXi host
- Configuring host **Baseboard Management Controller** (**BMC**) settings
- Importing VMware templates
- Converting VMware VMs to Hyper-V

Introduction

This chapter includes recipes that will help administrators to use VMM 2016 to manage daily operations of VMware ESXi hosts and host clusters, such as the identification and management of hosts. In addition, it will provide you with the ability to create, manage, save, and deploy VMs on VMware ESXi hosts, all from the VMM console.

System Center 2016 relies on the concept of a fabric, which is made up of hosts, host groups, and library servers, as well as networking and storage configurations. This architecture abstracts the underlying infrastructure from the users, but lets them deploy VMs, applications, and services, irrespective of whether the infrastructure is running on Microsoft hypervisor technology or on a hypervisor from VMware.

As multiple hypervisors can be managed through a common console, we can deploy VMs and applications in a consistent manner and get the same capabilities from different hypervisors. We can choose to utilize a mix of hypervisors, aggregating one or more hypervisors' host groups into a private cloud without worrying about underlying hypervisor capabilities and limitations. Abstracting the hypervisor layer reduces complexity and makes it easier to perform common actions on heterogeneous environments.

Note that, in order to fully monitor and manage VMware environments, you will need the following System Center 2016 family components:

- **Virtual Machine Manager (VMM)**: This enables you to deploy and manage VMs and services across hypervisor platforms, including Hyper-V and VMware ESXi hosts.
- **System Center Orchestrator (SCORCH)**: This includes multiple built-in workflow activities to perform a wide variety of tasks. You can expand its functionality by installing integration packs; for example, the integration pack for VMware vSphere helps you automate actions by enabling full management. This pack is available at `https://www.microsoft.com/download/details.aspx?id=54099`.
- **System Center Operations Manager (SCOM)**: This helps in monitoring VMware environments by using third-party management packs, such as those from Veeam. For more details, see `https://www.veeam.com/management-pack-system-center-resources.html`, which will enable all Operations Manager functionalities, such as alerts on performance and events, integrated notifications, responses and automation, and detailed reporting and auditing for all VMware components (ESXi hosts, vCenter, and more).

Adding a VMware vCenter Server to VMM

In order to manage VMware hosts, you need to integrate the VMM with any existing VMware vCenter Servers. VMM supports the VMware vCenter Server virtualization management software for managing hosts.

The features that are supported when the VMM manages ESXi hosts are as follows:

Functionality supported by VMM	Notes
Private clouds	The ESXi host resources are available to a VMM private cloud when creating the private cloud from host groups with ESXi hosts, or from a VMware resource pool. VMM does not support or integrate with VMware vCloud.
Dynamic Optimization	VMM Dynamic Optimization features can be used for vSphere clusters.
Power Optimization	Using VMM 2016, you can turn vSphere hosts on and off.
Live migration	Live migration between hosts within the cluster is supported by VMM 2016 and uses VMware vMotion. Placing ESXi hosts into and out of maintenance modes can also be done from VMM.
Live storage migration	Supported by VMM 2016 and uses VMware Storage vMotion.
Networking	VMM identifies and uses the existing VMware vSwitches (it does not automatically create them) and port groups for VM deployment.
Storage	VMM supports and identifies VMware **Paravirtual SCSI (PVSCSI)** storage adapters and thin-provisioned virtual hard disks. VMware VMs with virtual hard disks connected to an **integrated drive electronics** (**IDE**) bus are not supported by VMM. Also, note that the storage connection for the VMware ESXi hosts should be configured outside VMM as the new VMM storage automation features are not supported on the ESXi hosts.
Library	You can organize and store VMware VMs, VMware **Virtual Machine Disk** (**VMDK**) files, and templates in the VMM library. You can create new VMs from templates or by converting stored VMware VMs to Hyper-V VMs. Note that: • VMware's thin-provision disk becomes thick when migrated to the VMM library. • VMM does not support older VMDK disk types. Supported disks are: VMFS and monolithicflat, vmfsPassthroughRawDeviceMap, and snapshots: vmfssparse.

VMM command shell	VMM PowerShell commands are common across the supported hypervisors.
Services	You can deploy VMM services to ESXi hosts, but bear in mind that VMM uses a different model than VMware vApp and the two methods can co-exist. VMM cannot be used to deploy vApps.

Getting ready

There are some prerequisites that need to be taken into account when integrating VMware vCenter with VMM 2016. The requirements are as follows:

- One of the following supported versions of VMware vCenter must be running:
    - VMware vCenter Server 5.1
    - VMware vCenter Server 5.5
    - VMware vCenter Server 6.0

 Considering release updates, always check for the updated supported version at the Microsoft official site at `https://docs.microsoft.com/system-center/vmm/system-reqs#vmware-servers-in-the-vmm-fabric`.

- An SSL certificate is required for communication between the VMM server and the VMware vCenter Server if encryption is being used, to verify the identity of the vCenter Server.
- You must create a Run As account that has administrative permissions on the vCenter Server. It is possible to use a local account or a recommended domain account (for example, `rllab\VMwareAdmin`). Either way, the account needs local admin rights on the vCenter Server.

How to do it...

Carry out the following steps to integrate the vCenter Server with VMM. If a self-signed certificate is being used, you can use the following steps, or you can import the certificate during the *Adding vCenter to VMM* section, as you will be prompted to.

Importing the VMware self-signed SSL certificate

For the integration to work, VMM needs to communicate with the vSphere infrastructure through vCenter over SSL. Carry out the following steps to import the self-signed SSL certificate:

1. Make sure you log on to the VMM server as a local administrator, or with a domain account with local administrator rights (for example, `rllab\vmm-admin`).
2. Open Internet Explorer and navigate to `https://vCenter.rllab.com/`.

> If you have logged in using an account that doesn't have local administrator rights, hold down the *Shift* key, right-click on the Internet Explorer icon, and then click on **Run as administrator**.

3. Click on **Continue to this web site (not recommended)** when you get a warning saying that the SSL certificate is not trusted.
4. Click on **Certificate Error** in the security status bar, select **View Certificate**, and click on **Install Certificate**.
5. On the **Certificate Import Wizard** window, click on **Place all certificates in the following store** and then click on **Browse**.
6. On the **Select Certificate Store** window, select the checkbox for **Show physical stores**.
7. Expand **Trusted People**, select **Local Computer**, and click on **OK**.

> If you don't see the **Local Computer** option under **Trusted People**, it means that you are logged in with an account that does not have sufficient permissions.

8. Click on **Finish** to complete the process of importing the certificate.
9. Click on **OK** when a window is displayed saying that the import was successful.
10. To verify the process, close Internet Explorer and then reopen it. Next, browse to the location of the vCenter Server (for example, `https://vCenter.rllab.com/`); if you do not receive a certificate error, the certificate was correctly imported and you can proceed to the next step.

Adding vCenter to VMM

Carry out the following steps to add VMware vCenter in VMM:

1. Open the VMM console and, in the **Fabric** workspace of the **Fabric** pane, click on **Servers** and then click on **vCenter Servers**, as shown in the following screenshot:

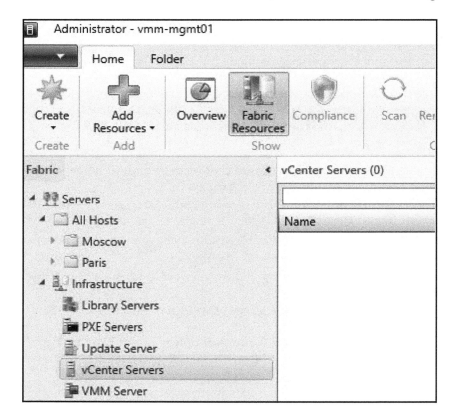

2. On the **Home** tab in the ribbon, click on **Add Resources** and select **VMware vCenter Server**.

You can also select **vCenter Servers** in the left-hand pane and then right-click on it and select **Add VMware vCenter Server**.

3. On the **Add VMware vCenter Server** dialog box, in the **Computer name** field, type in the name of the vCenter Server (for example, `vcenter.rllab.com`), that is, enter the NetBIOS name, FQDN, or the IP address.

4. On the **TCP/IP port** field, type in the port number that is required to connect to the vCenter Server (the default is `443`) or use the drop-down arrows.

5. For the **Run As account** field, click on **Browse...** and select a Run As account that has administrative rights on the vCenter Server; then, click on **OK:**

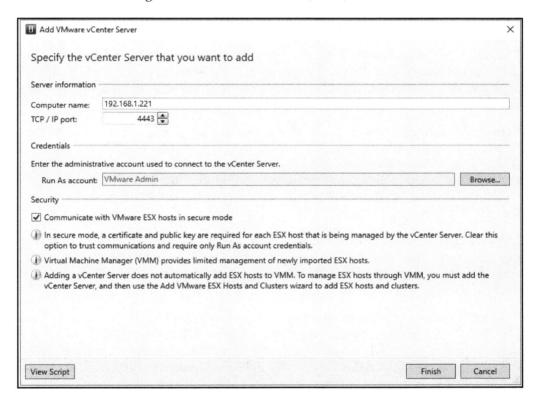

6. In **Security**, select **Communicate with VMware ESX hosts in secure mode** to use SSL encryption.

When **Communicate with VMware ESX hosts in secure mode** is selected (recommended approach), a certificate and a public key will be required for each vCenter host. If this option is not selected, you will only need the Run As account credentials for communication between VMM and vCenter.

7. Click on **OK** to finish and then verify that the Add Virtualization Manager job has the status of **Completed** in the **Jobs** workspace.

8. If you are making use of a self-signed certificate for vCenter, make sure you have first copied it into the Trusted People Certificates store on the VMM management server. Otherwise, click on **Import** in the **Import Certificate** dialog box to have the certificate added to the Trusted People certificate store.

How it works...

VMM has an abstraction layer that lets you manage multiple hypervisor platforms, including Hyper-V and VMware vSphere, making resources from these platforms available for datacenter and private cloud deployments by using a common user interface (VMM console and PowerShell).

In order to manage VMware hosts, VMM requires integration with the VMware vCenter Server. You can then use the VMM console to manage VMware ESXi hosts and host clusters, such as the discovery of these hosts and the ability to create, manage, save, and deploy VMs on them. Before integrating VMware vCenter with VMM, it is highly recommended that you create a Run As account with local administrative access rights on the vCenter Server.

In VMM 2016, on adding/integrating a VMware vCenter Server, VMM no longer imports, merges, or synchronizes the VMware tree structure. You will need to manually select and add ESXi servers and hosts to a VMM host group. Therefore, you will come across fewer issues during synchronization.

It is best practice to use secure mode communication to integrate VMM and VMware vCenter. To do that, you can import the self-signed SSL certificate from vCenter or you can use a third-party certificate. You can choose to use the self-signed certificate in addition to the vCenter certificate; in this case, you will be required to resolve the ESXi host's SSL certificates so that they are trusted, or you can choose to simply rely on the Run As account.

If you choose to use a public third-party certificate, you are not required to import the SSL certificate into the Trusted People Certificate store.

See also

- VMM system requirements: `https://docs.microsoft.com/system-center/vmm/system-reqs#vmware-servers-in-the-vmm-fabric`.

Adding VMware ESXi hosts or host clusters to VMM

Now that you've integrated vCenter with VMM, you can start adding the ESXi hosts that are to be managed by VMM.

Getting ready

The following is a list of some prerequisites and recommendations that need to be taken into account when adding VMware hosts to VMM 2016:

- The VMware vCenter Server that manages the ESXi hosts must already be configured and integrated with VMM.
- The host must be running a supported version of VMware vSphere. For more information, see `Chapter 1`, *VMM 2016 Architecture*.
- If encryption is required for communication between VMM and the vSphere hosts, a certificate and public key will be needed for each managed ESXi host.
- Although it is not a requirement, you can create a host group to organize the hosts (for example, `VMware`).
- As a best practice, create a Run As account with root credentials on the VMware ESXi hosts.

Although it is possible to create the Run As account when adding the ESXi hosts, as per VMM best practices, it is recommended to create it before the addition of hosts.

How to do it...

Carry out the following steps to add VMware ESXi hosts or clusters to VMM:

1. On the **Fabric** workspace in the VMM console, click on **Add Resources** on the **Home** tab; then, click on the **VMware ESX Hosts and Clusters** option:

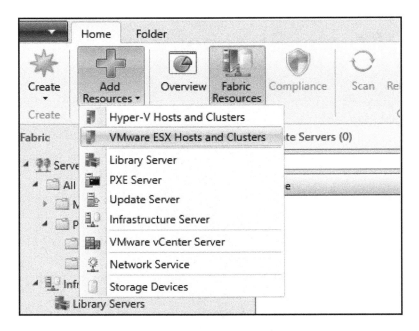

2. On the **Run As account** box in the **Credentials** page in the **Add Resource Wizard** window, click on **Browse** and select a Run As account with root credentials on the VMware ESXi host.
3. Click on **OK** and then click on **Next**.
4. On the **VMware vCenter Server** list in the **Target resources** page and select the vCenter Server (for example, `vcenter`).

The available ESXi hosts and clusters will be listed for the selected vCenter Server.

5. Select the VMware ESXi host(s) or host cluster to be added and click **Next**:

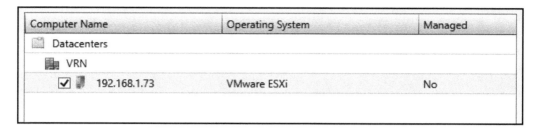

6. On the **Location** list in the **Host settings** page, select the host group to assign the hosts to and click on **Next**.

 You can change the placement path for these hosts if you want to.

7. On the **Summary** page, click on **Finish**.
8. After verifying that the job status of **Add ESX host** is **Completed**, navigate to the host group to which you added ESXi hosts and check its status:

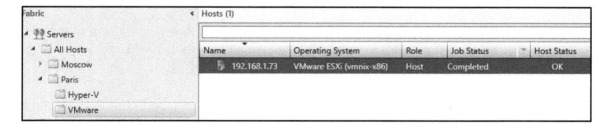

How it works...

The steps that need to be carried out to add VMware hosts or clusters are pretty straightforward. After integrating vCenter on the **Add Resources** wizard, select **VMware ESX Hosts and Clusters**, making sure you have created a Run As account that has root credentials on the ESXi hosts.

You can add one or more hosts, as well as VMware clusters. If you require encryption, you can either use the self-signed certificate that was created when you installed the VMware ESXi hosts, or a public, trusted certificate. Note that, if you decide to use the self-signed certificate, you are required to import it from each ESXi host to the VMM management server. You don't need to carry out this task if you are using an SSL certificate from a trusted certification authority.

There's more...

Carry out the following steps to verify that the ESXi host or host cluster was added correctly:

1. On the **Fabric** workspace in the VMM console, expand **Servers,** go to **All Hosts**, and then expand and select the host group where you had previously added the ESXi host/cluster (for example, VMware).
2. Verify that each host in the **Hosts** pane has a status of either **OK** or **OK (Limited)**.

If the status of the host shows **OK (Limited)**, it could indicate that the specified Run As account does not have the correct credentials (that is, it does not have the root credentials or the account does not have the requisite permissions) or that you have enabled the secure mode but did not import an SSL certificate and public key.

3. If the host status is **OK (Limited)**, you should correct the credentials or import the certificate for that host to enable management through VMM.

Updating the host status to OK

To update the host status to **OK**, follow these steps:

1. On the **Fabric** pane in the VMM console, expand **Servers** and then expand **vCenter Servers**.
2. On the **vCenter Servers** pane, select and right-click on the vCenter Server; then, click on **Properties**, confirm the secure mode setting, and click on **OK** to close.
3. For each VMware host that has the status **OK (Limited)**, right-click on the host and click on **Properties**.
4. Select the **Management** tab and confirm the Run As account.

5. Click on **Import** to claim the host SSL certificate and public key and then click on **View Details** to see the certificate.

6. Click on **Accept the certificate for this host** to confirm and then click on **OK**.

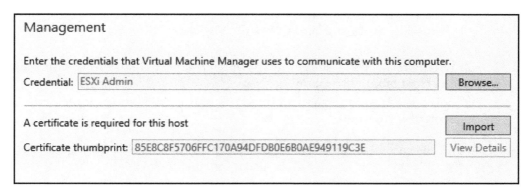

7. If the credentials of the secure mode are correctly configured, the host status will display **OK** in the **Hosts** pane.

8. Repeat these tasks for each host with the status **OK (Limited)**.

See also

- *Adding a VMware vCenter Server to VMM* recipe in this chapter

Configuring network settings on a VMware ESXi host

This recipe will guide you through the configuration of a logical network on the VMware host and show you how to view compliance data for the physical network adapters on that host. To make the host physical network adapters visible to the VMs that need external network access, you will need to assign them to logical networks.

Compliance data specifies whether or not IP subnets and/or VLANs allotted to a logical network are assigned to a host physical network adapter.

How to do it...

Carry out the following steps to associate logical networks with a physical network adapter:

1. On the **Fabric** pane in the VMM console, expand **Servers,** expand **All Hosts**, and then select the host group where the VMware ESXi host resides (for example, VMware).

2. On the **Hosts** pane, select the VMware ESXi host and then click on **Properties** on the **Host** tab in the ribbon.

3. Select the **Hardware** tab and select the physical network adapter to configure in **Network Adapters**.

> Be careful when selecting the logical network, as all the logical networks for this host group will be listed, not just the available ones.

4. On the **Logical network connectivity** list, select the logical network(s) that should be associated with the physical network adapter.

How it works...

To assign VMM logical networks with a physical network adapter, in the **Fabric** workspace, select the VMware ESXi host and then the physical network adapter under the **Hardware** section. Note that when selecting the logical network, all logical networks are listed.

By default, for each selected logical network, the IPs and VLANs defined for a host group or inherited through the parent host group will be assigned to a physical network adapter. If no IPs or VLANs show up in the **Available** or **Assigned** columns, no network site exists for the selected logical network that is defined or inherited by the host group.

If you're using VLANs, you will need to make use of VMware vCenter to configure the port groups with the VLAN for the corresponding network site.

There's more...

You can verify a VMware ESXi host's network settings and the compliance information in VMM. We'll see how to do this in the upcoming sections.

Verifying the settings for a virtual switch

Carry out the following steps to check the network settings for a virtual switch:

1. On the **Fabric** pane in the VMM console, expand **Servers**; under **Servers**, expand **All Hosts** and select the host group where the VMware ESXi host resides (for example, `VMware`).

2. On the **Hosts** pane, select the ESXi host; then, on the **Host** tab in the ribbon, click on **Properties** and click on the **Virtual Switches** tab.

3. On the **Virtual Switches** list, select the virtual network whose properties you would like to view.

4. In the **Logical network** list, check if the logical network is assigned to a physical network adapter:

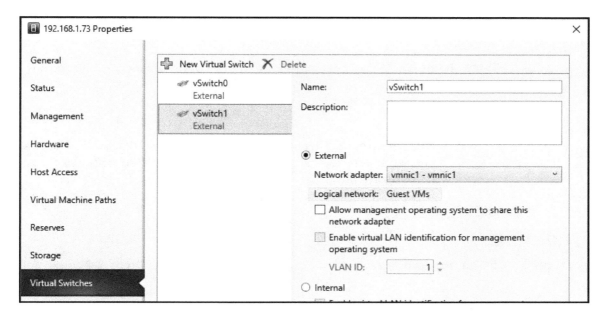

Viewing compliance information for a physical network adapter

Carry out the following steps to see the compliance information for a physical network adapter:

1. On the **Fabric** workspace in the VMM console, on the **Fabric** pane, expand **Networking**; then, click on **Logical Networks**.
2. On the **Home** tab in the ribbon, click on **Hosts**.
3. On the **Logical Network Information for Hosts** pane, expand the host and select a physical network adapter. The assigned IP subnets and VLANs for this network adapter will be displayed in the details pane.
4. On the **Compliance** column, the compliance status will show one of the following values:

   - **Fully compliant**: This status confirms that all the IPs and VLANs that are included in the network site are allotted to a physical network adapter.
   - **Partially compliant**: This indicates incomplete information. The IPs and/or VLANs that are in the network list and those assigned to a network adapter do not match.

 Check the reason for partial compliance in the **Compliance errors** section.

   - **Non-compliant**: This indicates that there are no IPs and/or VLANs defined for the logical networks that are associated with a physical network adapter.

See also

For more informatin, see *Adding a VMware vCenter Server to VMM* recipe in this chapter

Configuring host BMC settings

VMM 2016 supports dynamic optimization and power optimization on Hyper-V host clusters and on managed VMware ESXi host clusters that support live migration.

Power optimization, an optional feature of dynamic optimization, is enabled only if a host group is configured for live migration of VMs through dynamic optimization. To meet resource requirements and save energy, it shuts down hosts not needed by the cluster and turns them on only when they are needed.

There is a requirement that the servers must have a BMC that supports out-of-band management. In order to configure the host BMC, the installed BMC controller must support one of the following BMC protocols:

- **System Management Architecture for Server Hardware (SMASH)** version 1.0 over **Web Services Management (WS-Man)**
- **Intelligent Platform Management Interface (IPMI)** version 1.5 or 2.0
- **Data Center Management Interface (DCMI)** version 1.0

How to do it...

Carry out the following steps to configure the BMC settings:

1. On the **Fabric** pane in the VMM console, expand **Servers**; under **Servers**, expand **All Hosts**; then, in the **Host** pane, select the host you want to configure.
2. On the **Host** tab in the ribbon, click on **Properties**.
3. Select the **Hardware** tab and click on **BMC Settings** under the **Advanced** section; then select **This physical machine is configured for out-of-band (OOB) management with the following settings**.
4. Select the **BMC protocol** from the **Power management configuration provider** list (default is **IPMI**)
5. In the **BMC address** field, type the IP address of the BMC.

 VMM will automatically fill in the port number for the selected BMC protocol.

6. For the **Run As account** field, click on **Browse**, select the Run As account with BMC access rights, and click on **OK**.

How it works...

For power optimization to work, the servers must have a supported BMC controller. It is important to verify that your server has a supported BMC and that you have installed one of the supported protocols before carrying out the process to configure the BMC on each host, in order to benefit from power optimization.

By using a BMC, VMM can power the host on or off.

There's more...

Now that the BMC is configured, you can use it to turn the servers on or off.

Powering a computer on or off through VMM

Carry out the following steps to turn servers on or off through VMM:

1. On the **Fabric** pane in the VMM console, expand **Servers**; then, expand **All Hosts** and select the host that is to be configured in the **Host** pane.
2. On the **Host** tab, select one of the following available options—**Power On**, **Power Off**, **Shutdown**, or **Reset**.

> To view the BMC log information, select the **Hardware** tab in the host properties and, in the **Advanced** section, click on **BMC Logs**.

See also

- *Set up dynamic and power optimization in the VMM compute fabric*: https://docs.microsoft.com/system-center/vmm/vm-optimization

Importing VMware templates

This recipe focuses on importing VMware templates to VMM. In VMM 2016, the VMware virtual machine disk (.vmdk) file is not copied/moved to the VMM library while importing a VMware template. Instead, VMM copies the metadata associated with the VMware template and the VMDK file remains in the VMware datastore.

Employing this approach when using templates, VMM allows you to deploy VMs more efficiently and quickly. Moreover, VMM 2016 does not delete the source template.

> VMM 2016 is highly dependent on the VMware template that resides on the vCenter Server.

How to do it...

Carry out the following steps to configure the BMC settings:

1. On the **Library** workspace in the VMM console, on the **Home** tab in the ribbon, click on **Import VMware Template**.
2. Select the VMware template(s) to import and click on **OK**.
3. To confirm that the template(s) adding was successful, expand **Templates,** and click on **VM Templates** in the **Library** pane.

How it works...

In VMM, only the metadata associated with a VMware template is copied to the VMM library. The VM disk (.vmdk) file remains in the VMware datastore.

If the template is removed from vCenter Server, it will go into a missing state in VMM. On the other hand, if you convert it into a VM, make some changes, and then convert it back to a template, the ID will remain the same and VMM will set its state as OK instead of missing.

> When the VMware template is removed from the VMM library, it is not deleted from the VMware datastore.

See also

For more information, see *Adding VMware ESXi host clusters or cluster to VMM* recipe in this chapter.

Converting VMware VMs to Hyper-V

You can convert any VM running on a VMware ESXi host or stored in the VMM library, but VMM does not support **virtual-to-virtual** (**V2V**) conversion of a VMware VM that has an IDE bus.

The following versions of VMware ESXi are supported for V2V conversions by VMM 2016:

- ESXi 5.1
- ESXi 5.5
- ESXi 6.0

 Before you convert a VMware VM to a Hyper-V VM, you must uninstall VMware Tools on the source VM.

This recipe will guide you through the process of converting a VMware VM to a Hyper-V VM through the V2V conversion process.

How to do it...

Carry out the following steps to convert VMs:

1. On the **VMs and Services** workspace in the VMM console, on the **Home** tab in the ribbon, click on **Create Virtual Machine** and then on **Convert Virtual Machine,** as shown in the following screenshot:

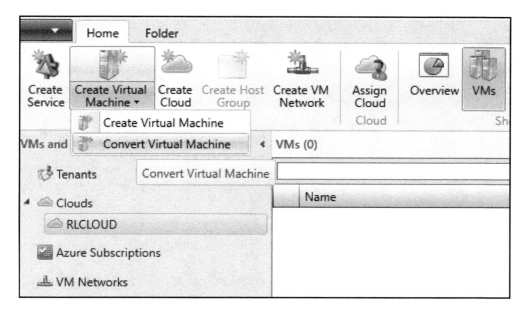

2. On the **Select Source** page in **Convert Virtual Machine Wizard**, click on **Browse** and select the VMware VM that is to be converted (for example, RL-VM01), as shown in the following screenshot:

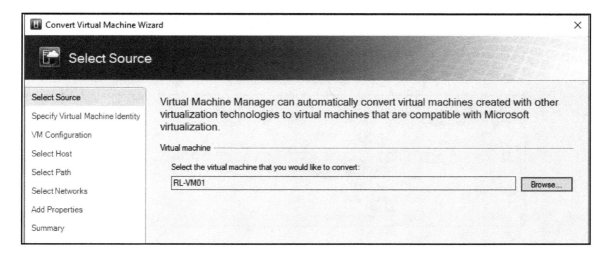

Online conversion is not supported. Power off the VM beforehand.

3. Click on **OK**; then, in the **Select Source** page, click on **Next**.
4. On the **Specify Virtual Machine Identity** page, confirm the VM name (you can change it if you want to), type in a description (optional), and click on **Next**.

The VM name does not have to match the computer name (the NetBIOS name), but as a best practice it is recommended that you keep both names the same.

5. On the **Virtual Machine Configuration** page, set the amount of processors and the memory, and click on **Next**.
6. On the **Select Host** page, select the target Hyper-V host, and click on **Next**.
7. On the **Select Path** page, specify the VM file's storage location.

The default VM paths on the target host will be displayed now. You can select a different path. Click on **Browse**, select the path/folder, and click on **OK**. Then, you can click on **Add this path to the list of default storage locations on the host** if you want this path to be a part of the default VM's path.

8. On the **Select Networks** page, select the VM network, logical switch, and VLAN (if applicable), and click on **Next**:

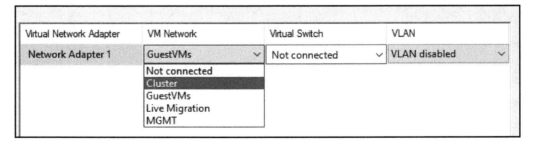

9. On the **Add properties** page, select your preferred actions from the **Automatic actions** list.

10. On the **Summary** page, click on **Start the virtual machine after deploying it**; then, click on **Create**.
11. Verify that the job status shows **Completed** and then close the dialog box.
12. To verify that the VM was converted, in the **VMs and Services** workspace, select the Hyper-V host that you had chosen earlier in this task.
13. On the **Home** tab, click on **VMs**; then, in the **VMs** pane, verify that the VM appears.

New-SCV2V cmdlet is used behind the scenes. So, you can automate all these tasks in the following way:

```
$VMHost = Get-SCVMHost -ComputerName HV03
$VM = Get-SCVirtualMachine -Name "RL-VM01"|where
{$_.VMHost.Name -eq "192.168.1.73"}
New-SCV2V -VM $VM -VMHost $VMHost -Path
"D:\VMs\rlevchenko" -Name "RL-VM01" -Description "My
first converted VM"-CPUCount 2 -MemoryMB 4096 -
StartAction TurnOnVMIfRunningWhenVSStopped -
DelayStartSeconds 0 -StopAction ShutdownGuestOS -
RunAsynchronously
```

How it works...

If you are running a supported version of a VMware VM, start by confirming that the source VM does not have an IDE bus, as VMM does not support it. Then, open the VMM console and click on **Convert Virtual Machine** on the ribbon. Carry out the steps given in the previous section, by first selecting the VM that you want to convert.

You can change the VM name when prompted for the VM identity and, optionally, you can type in a description for it. The VM name does not necessarily have to match the computer name (NetBIOS name), but as a best practice it is recommended that you keep them the same. On the VM's configuration page, you can change the number of allocated processors and the memory assigned while keeping the source configuration or changing it for the target VM. VMM creates a Generation 1 VM with the specified configuration on the host during the conversion process.

By default, the VM paths on the target host will be displayed when selecting the path for the VM, but you can specify a different one (if required) and make it the default path as well. Select the network you want the VM to be assigned to and configure the desired settings on the **Add Properties** page. Confirm all the settings on the summary page and click on **Create** to start the V2V machine conversion process.

At the time of writing, VMM 1801 semi-annual channel release introduced a conversion based on the firmware type. If the source VM is configured with EFI-based firmware and the guest OS supported by Generation 2, VMM will select Generation 2 for the VM. Otherwise, Generation 1 will be selected for the target VMs which don't meet Generation 2 requirements.

See also

For more information, see

- *How to customize a VMware ESXi image and install it in a Hyper-V VM:*
  `https://rlevchenko.com/2018/01/11/how-to-customize-a-vmware-esxi-image-and-install-it-in-a-hyper-v-vm/`

- *Adding VMware ESXi hosts or host clusters to VMM* recipe in this chapter

9
Managing Clouds, Fabric Updates, Resources, Clusters, and New Features of VMM 2016

In this chapter, we will cover the following topics:

- Cluster OS Rolling Upgrade
- Managing fabric updates
- Configuring Dynamic Optimization and Power Optimization
- Live migrating Virtual Machines
- Managing Linux Virtual Machines
- Configuring availability options and Virtual NUMA for VMs
- Standard and Production Checkpoints
- Configuring resource throttling
- Integrating with IPAM Server for IP Management
- Deploying Windows Azure Pack for cloud management
- Configuring Synthetic Fiber Channel

Introduction

In this chapter, we will take a closer look at the additional management and features provided by VMM 2016. We will also cover the Windows Azure Pack (which is the replacement of the App Controller) that will allow you to manage clouds.

 Windows Azure Pack should not be confused with Azure Stack (see Chapter 1, *VMM 2016 Architecture*). Azure Pack supports new features of Windows Server 2016 like Shielded VMs and some features of SDNv2, and its life cycle was extended to 2027.

In this chapter, we will continue to learn more about VMM management capabilities, such as cluster OS rolling upgrade, live migration, availability options, checkpoints, and virtual **Non-Uniform Memory Access** (**NUMA**).

 Although an integration with Azure is not covered in the book, keep in mind that VMM 2016 supports only management of classic Azure VMs. The latest VMM 1801 (semi-annual channel release) allows you to manage both Azure Resource Manager-based and classic VMs using management certificates or Azure AD Authentication. In addition, you can manage region-specific Azure subscriptions in VMM 1801. See the *Adding an Azure Subscription in VMM* article available at https://rlevchenko.com/2018/02/09/adding-an-azure-subscription-in-vmm/.

Creating Hyper-V clusters

This recipe will guide you to create a Hyper-V cluster using VMM. Using the steps provided here, you will be able to select the Hyper-V servers and join them to a cluster, configuring networking and storage resources in the process.

 Creating a hyper-converged S2D cluster is described in Chapter 5, *Configuring Fabric Resources in VMM*. See the *Deploying hyper-converged cluster with S2D and Hyper-V* recipe.

Getting ready

Before you start creating a Hyper-V cluster, there are some requirements that you need to look at. These are discussed in the following sections.

Prerequisites for cluster creation using VMM 2016

Make sure that the following prerequisites are met:

- You need at least two standalone Hyper-V servers, and they need to be under VMM management already (see the *Adding and managing Hyper-V hosts and host clusters in VMM* recipe in Chapter 5, *Configuring Fabric Resources in VMM*)
- The hosts should meet the requirements for failover clustering and should be running one of the supported operating systems (2012R2/2016)
- The OS is updated, and the required hotfixes have been applied
- The Hyper-V hosts must all be part of the same domain to be added as cluster nodes
- The VMM management server must either be in the same domain as the hosts or on a trusted domain
- If the Hyper-V hosts are configured with static IP addresses, make sure that those IP addresses are in the same subnet
- The Hyper-V hosts that are going to be added as cluster nodes need to be in the same host group
- Each Hyper-V host must have access to the storage array
- If you plan to create a cluster from bare-metal machines, ensure that your VMM fabric meet bare-metal deployment requirements

> See the *Provisioning a physical computer as a Hyper-V host: Bare Metal host deployment* recipe in Chapter 5, *Configuring Fabric Resources in VMM*).

- The **Multipath I/O** (**MPIO**) driver must be installed on each host that will access the fiber channel or iSCSI storage array.

If the MPIO driver is already installed (before the host is added to VMM), VMM will enable it for supported storage arrays using the Microsoft-provided **Device-specific Module (DSM)**.

If you installed vendor-specific DSMs for your supported storage arrays and then added the host to VMM, the vendor-specific MPIO settings will be used to connect with the storage arrays. If you added a host to VMM before installing the MPIO feature, you will need to manually install and configure the MPIO driver or vendor-specific DSMs to have the device hardware IDs added.

Prerequisites for fabric configuration

Make sure that the fabric configuration meets the following prerequisites:

- For VMM-managed shared storage:
    1. It is essential that the storage be added, configured, and classified in the **Fabric** workspace.
    2. The logical units need to be created and allocated to the target host group or parent host group and should not be provisioned to any host.
- For unmanaged shared storage:
    1. Disks must be made available to all the nodes in the new cluster.
    2. Provision one or more of the logical units to the hosts.
    3. Mount the cluster disk on one of the hosts and format it.

When working with asymmetric storage in VMM, you must configure each node of the cluster as a possible owner of the cluster disk. VMM is agnostic regarding the use of asymmetric storage.

When using a **fiber Channel Storage Area Network (FC SAN)**, each node must have a **host bus adapter (HBA)** installed with its ports correctly zoned.

When using an iSCSI SAN, make sure that the iSCSI portals have been added and the iSCSI initiator is logged in to the storage array. Likewise, make sure that the **Microsoft iSCSI Initiator** service on each host is configured to start automatically and is started.

Prerequisites for networking

Make sure that the following prerequisites are met:

- The Hyper-V hosts should be configured in the **Fabric** workspace, with at least one common logical network; if it has associated network sites, a network site should be defined for the target host group
- In addition, on each Hyper-V host, the logical networks should be linked with physical network adapters
- External virtual switches don't need to be created beforehand; if you do create them, make sure that the names of the external switches and associated logical networks are exactly the same on all Hyper-V hosts

 After creating the cluster in VMM, you can create and configure the external switches (virtual networks) on all the nodes of the cluster. You can also configure the virtual network settings for the cluster after it is created.

Check whether you have configured the fabric resources and deployed the Hyper-V servers (see `Chapter 5`, *Configuring Fabric Resources in VMM*) and whether the prerequisites are met.

How to do it...

Carry out the following steps to deploy a cluster in VMM:

1. Go to the **Fabric** pane in the **Fabric** workspace on the VMM console and click on **Servers**.
2. On the **Home** tab in the ribbon, click on **Create**; then, click on **Hyper-V Cluster**:

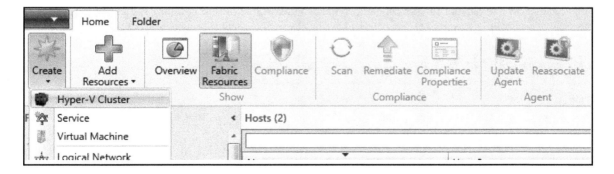

3. On the **Create Cluster Wizard** window, in the **Cluster name** box on the **General** tab, type in a cluster name (for example, `RLCL.rllab.com`), and in the **Host group** list, click to select the host that contains the hosts that are to be clustered (for example, `Moscow\Hyper-V`); then, click on **Next**.

The Hyper-V hosts that are to be clustered must all be in the same host group. In addition, they must meet the OS prerequisites in order to be displayed under **Available hosts**.

4. On the **Resource Type** page, specify a **Run As account** (recommended) or type in credentials for an account with local admin rights on all the servers that will be added to the cluster, in the format `domain\username` (for example, `rllab\host-admin`).

The domain for the account must be the same for the servers being added. In addition, the account needs the permissions **Create Computer objects** and **Read All Properties** in the container that is used for the server computer accounts in AD.

5. Select **Existing Servers running a Windows Server operating system** or **Physical computers to be provisioned.** If the second is selected, define a physical computer profile and BMC settings (**RunAs account**, protocol, and port) that will be used during bare-metal provisioning.

If you select **Skip cluster validation tests** (not recommended), the cluster will have no support from Microsoft as there will be no guarantee that the servers meet the cluster requirements.

6. On the **Select Hosts** page, in the **Available hosts** list, select a Hyper-V host that you want to add to the cluster or click on **Select All** if you want to create a cluster from all available hosts in the group. The following screenshot depicts the **Create Cluster Wizard**:

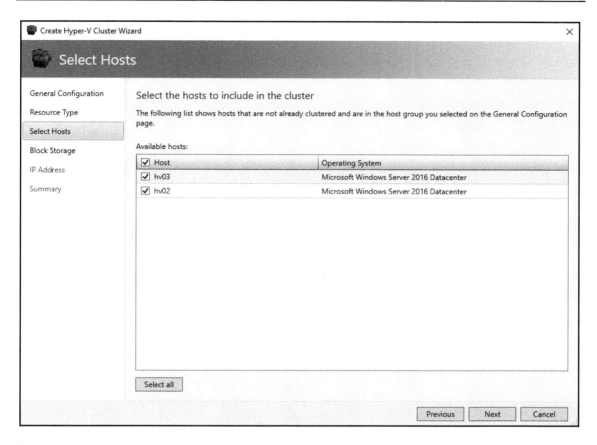

7. On the **BlockStorage** page, select the disk(s) to add to the cluster and then configure these options: **Classification**, **Partition Style**, **File System**, **Volume Label**, **Quick Format**, and **CSV**.

The list of available disks characterizes the logical units associated with the nominated host group. When assigning storage as out-of-band storage, as the disks are not managed by VMM, all disks will be selected and shown as available. You will not be able to change the selection. In addition, *do not select clustered file system disks for the cluster when using a third-party CFS*; if you do this, the cluster creation will be unsuccessful. If the number of selected hosts is even, the smallest disk (>500MB) will be automatically chosen as the witness disk and will become unavailable for selection.

8. The **IP Address** page of the wizard will be displayed if, among all the hosts, at least one physical network adapter is configured with a static IPv4 address, and there is a physical network adapter on all other hosts that are assigned to the same subnet.

VMM will display the list of associated networks for that static IPv4 subnet.

9. In the **Network** column, select the network(s) to allocate a static cluster IPv4 address to and then do one of the following:

- When no static IPv4 address pools are associated with the subnet, type in the IP address of the selected network in the **IP Address** column.
- When static IPv4 address pools are associated with the subnet, you can choose one of the following options:
  - In the **Static IP Pool** column, select an IPv4 address pool for VMM to automatically assign a static IPv4 from that pool.
  - In the **IP Address** column, type in an available IPv4 address within the same subnet and make sure not to select an IP pool in the **Static IP Pool** column. VMM will detect if you type an IPv4 address in the range of the IPv4 address pool and will not assign that to another host.

If any host has a physical network adapter configured with DHCP that falls in the same subnet, you don't need to set up a static IPv4.

10. On the **Virtual Switches** page, select a logical network that is to be automatically associated with the external virtual network when VMM creates it on each cluster node.

The logical network associated with a physical network adapter (including associated VLAN IDs) must be identical on all nodes. Logical networks already assigned to external virtual networks will not be displayed.

11. Type in a name and a description (optional) for the external virtual network.
12. If you want to allow the management of hosts through this network, select **Allow hosts to access VMs through this virtual network**.

It is recommended to have a dedicated physical network card for host management instead of sharing it with VM traffic.

13. If you need to communicate with the hosts over VLAN, select the **Hosts can access the VLAN ID** checkbox and then select VLAN (defined as part of the logical network).
14. Click on **Next** and verify the settings on the **Summary** page, and then click on **Finish**.

How it works...

During the cluster-creation process, VMM verifies whether the hosts meet the prerequisites, such as the required operating system versions and the domain; for each host, VMM enables the failover clustering feature, unmasks the selected storage logical units, and creates the external switches (virtual networks).

The setup continues; VMM runs the cluster-validation process, and then it creates the cluster with the quorum and enables **Cluster Shared Volume** (**CSV**) for each logical unit designated as CSV. When managing a logical unit assignment, VMM creates one storage group per host node by default. In a cluster configuration, it creates one storage group per cluster node.

In VMM, a storage group binds together host initiators, target ports, and logical units (which are exposed to the host initiators through the target ports). A storage group can have multiple host initiator IDs, that is, it can have an **iSCSI Qualified Name** (**IQN**) or a **World Wide Name** (**WWN**).

For some types of storage, it is ideal to use one storage group for the entire cluster, where host initiators of all nodes will be restricted to a unique storage group. For this configuration, use VMM PowerShell to set the `CreateStorageGroupsPerCluster` property to `$true`:

```
$StorageName = @(Get-SCStorageArray)[0]
Set-SCStorageArray -StorageArray $StorageName -
CreateStorageGroupsPerCluster $true
```

You can force the storage format using **Force Format**; on the **Storage** page, right-click on the column header and then click on **Force Format**.

 Use the **Force Format** option with extreme caution, as the current disk data will be overwritten during cluster creation.

When the cluster creation job is finished, verify the cluster status by clicking on the created host cluster and confirming that the host status for each node (in the **Host Status** column in the **Hosts** pane) is **OK**.

To view the detailed status information for the created host cluster (including the cluster validation test report), select the host and right-click on it, click on **Properties**, and then on the **Status** tab.

There's more...

Now, let's talk about some other options.

Adding a Hyper-V host as a cluster node

Carry out the following steps to add a Hyper-V server to an existing cluster:

1. In the **Fabric** workspace on the VMM console, in the **Fabric** pane, expand **Servers**, expand **All Hosts** and then highlight the cluster object, right-click, and select **Add Cluster Node**.
2. In the **Add Nodes Wizard** window, select a **RunAs account** (for example, `rllab\host-admin`) for an account with administrative rights on the host; then, select a resource type (**Existing servers running a Windows Server operating system** or **Physical computers to be provisioned**).

3. On the **Select Hosts** page, in the **Available Hosts** list, select the host to add to the cluster (for example, *HV02*); then, click on **Next**.

4. On the **Summary** page, review the settings and click on **Finish**. VMM will then add the node to the cluster. In the **Jobs** workspace, check the job status.

 You can verify that the cluster node was added by going to the **Fabric** pane, expanding **Servers**, expanding **All Hosts** and then locating and clicking on the host cluster. In the **Hosts** pane, confirm that the new node is displayed in the host cluster with a host status of **OK**.

See also

For more information, see the following references:

- *What is new in Failover Clustering in Windows Server 2016* at https://rlevchenko.com/2017/01/26/whats-new-in-failover-clustering-in-windows-server-2016/
- *Failover Clustering in Windows Server* at https://docs.microsoft.com/windows-server/failover-clustering/failover-clustering-overview

Cluster OS rolling upgrade

This recipe will guide you to upgrade a Hyper-V cluster using VMM. Using the steps provided here, you will be able to turn clusters from Windows Server 2012 R2 to 2016.

Getting ready

Cluster migration is usually a headache for administrators, as it could be the reason for huge downtime because we need to evict some nodes from old cluster, build a new one based on the evicted nodes or a new hardware and then migrate roles from the source cluster to the target. Consequently, in the case of overcommitment, we won't have enough resources to run migrated VMs. When everything is built around clouds, which are provided by **Cloud Solution Providers** (**CSPs**) under SLA policies defining service availability, a solution to reduce or even eliminate possible downtime is highly needed.

Cluster OS Rolling Upgrade (CRU) is a new feature in Windows Server 2016 that enables administrators to upgrade the operating system of the cluster nodes from Windows Server 2012 R2 to Windows Server 2016 without stopping the Hyper-V or the Scale-Out File Server workloads. It significantly simplifies the overall process and allows us to successfully upgrade existing nodes, reducing downtime and any costs required in the past. Because you can run both OSes during the cluster upgrade phase (a mixed mode), it's no longer necessary to create a new cluster or destroy/stop an existing one:

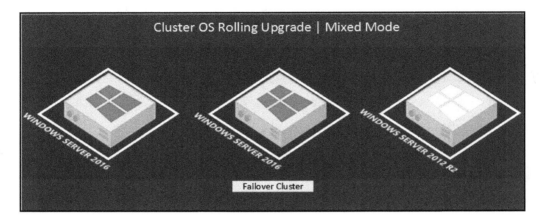

 CRU does not require any additional hardware. For example, you have evicted one node to upgrade, so the other nodes are still online, and they must have resources for workloads live migrated from the evicted node to achieve a zero-downtime. Otherwise, VMs will be stopped due to resource overcommitment.

Before you start upgrading your cluster, there are some requirements that you need to look at. These are discussed in the following section.

Prerequisites for cluster rolling upgrade using VMM 2016

Make sure that the following prerequisites are met:

- Each cluster that is going to be upgraded must be added to the VMM fabric (see the *Adding and managing Hyper-V hosts and host clusters in VMM* recipe in Chapter 5, *Configuring Fabric Resources in VMM*).

- Hyper-V and Scale-Out File Server clusters can be upgraded from Windows Server 2012 R2 to Windows Server 2016 without any downtime.

 Other cluster workloads can also be migrated. However, they will be unavailable during the minimal downtime, which is equivalent to failover time (for example, SQL Server with AlwaysOn FCI takes about five minutes).

- The cluster must meets bare-metal deployment requirements (see the *Provisioning a physical computer as a Hyper-V host: Bare-Metal host deployment* recipe in `Chapter 5`, *Configuring Fabric Resources in VMM*.

 VMM captures storage and network configs from each node, so it's not required to define these settings in the computer profile.

- Verify that the latest updates are applied in all cluster nodes. Also, make sure that there aren't any cluster errors/warnings in the event logs.

 It's recommended to have a backed-up cluster database with a system state backup to be able to restore cluster configuration if issues arise after upgrade.

- Make sure that you have a generalized image with Windows Server 2016 in the VMM library, and it's defined in the computer profile.

 Use a fixed disk for production servers to increase their performance. VMM converts dynamic disks to fixed type if the **Do not convert the VHD to fixed type during deployment** option is not enabled in the computer profile settings.

How to do it...

Carry out the following steps to cluster OS rolling upgrade in VMM:

1. Go to the **Fabric** pane in the **Fabric** workspace on the VMM console, exapnd **Servers**, and select the cluster object (*RLCL*, in this recipe).

2. On the **Host Cluster** tab in the ribbon, click on **Upgrade Cluster**, as shown in the following picture:

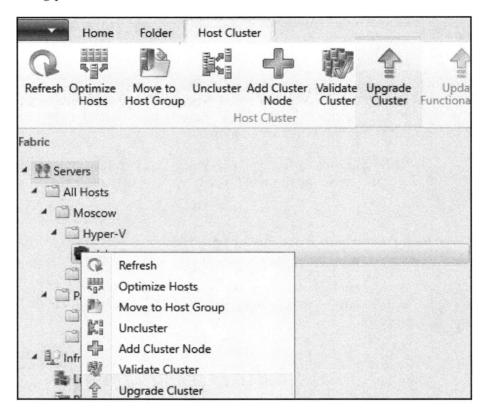

3. On the **Upgrade Cluster** window, select the cluster nodes to upgrade or click on **Select All** to cover all cluster nodes. In the **Physical Computer Profile** list, select the profile that will be used during bare-metal deployment (for example, *W2016-HyperV*) and then click on **Next.**

4. On the **BMC Configuration** page, click on **Browse** and select **BMC RunAs account** that has permission to access BMC, and then select the protocol and port used by BMCs, as shown in the picture:

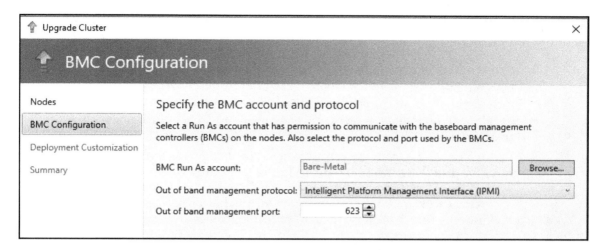

5. On the **Deployment Customization** page, wait while VMM gathers storage and network configurations from each node; then, review deployment options.

 In most cases, you don't have to change anything on this page. However, I would recommend to verify network configuration. For doing this, click on **Network Adapters** and check that they are configured with **Virtual Switches**. Also, make sure that at least one adapter is configured as a **Management NIC**.

6. Click on **Next** and verify the settings on the **Summary** page, and then click on **Finish**. In the **Jobs** workspace, wait while the **Upgrade Cluster** job is completed.

How it works...

VMM 2016 has a built-in support for a new Windows Server 2016 capability —Cluster OS Rolling Upgrade to sequentially upgrade clusters to Windows Server 2016 using a new concept of a **Mixed Mode**. This mode allows you to run 2012R2/2016 hosts in the same cluster during the upgrade.

 Keep in mind that it's recommended that you upgrade all nodes in the cluster within a month. A mixed-mode is not intended for permanent usage.

Because it's a Windows Server feature, you don't actually need VMM. However, VMM 2016 is highly recommended as it automates the entire process in the following way:

1. Starts a maintenance mode on the node and evacuates highly available VMs to the best possible node in the cluster.
2. Evicts the node from the cluster and removes the host from VMM by uninstalling virtual machine manager agent, guest agents, and DHCP virtual switch extension.
3. Creates a new host from the physical machine using bare-metal provisioning and computer profile, which you defined in the **Upgrade Cluster** wizard.

> During this step, VMM transfers the virtual hard disk containing Windows Server 2016 to the boot partition, creates system partition, and sets up boot from the VHD. VHD Native Boot is typical for bare-metal deployment.

4. Once OS is configured on the node, VMM enables Hyper-V and Failover Clustering server roles, adds MPIO feature, and installs VMM agent.

> If any scripts and drivers are defined in the computer profile, VMM will set up matching drivers and available scripts during the provisioning as well.

5. And now that the host has been added to the fabric, VMM changes properties of host network adapters and deploys virtual switch and its extensions.
6. Before adding the node back to the cluster, VMM connects Hyper-V host to cluster storage arrays, installs the failover cluster feature, and adds the host to the cluster, bringing the host out of maintenance mode and moving workloads back to it.
7. The earlier steps are the same for every node in the cluster. VMM upgrades them one by one, and once all nodes are running Windows Server 2016, cluster functional level update and cluster validation will be initiated.

In the Mixed Mode, cluster functional level is equal to 8 and new features such as VM Compute Resiliency, VM Storage Resiliency, or Cloud Witness are not available. Once you update cluster functional level to 9, the upgrade process can be considered completed and 2012 R2 nodes cannot be added to the cluster; so, there won't be a point of return. If you upgrade the cluster nodes before adding the cluster to the VMM and cluster functional level is not updated, select the cluster object and click on the **Update Functional Level** button on the **Host Cluster** tab in the ribbon.

When you have upgraded the cluster to Windows Server 2016, you can optionally update the VM's configuration level in order to enable and use new features of the latest OS. As shown in the following screenshot, there are multiple VM versions supported by host:

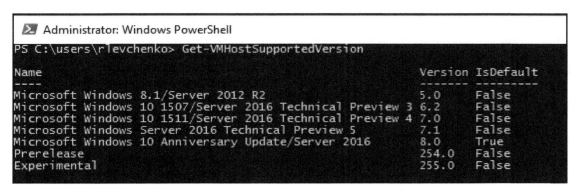

Using VMM GUI, you can select VMs and click on **Update Functional Level** on the **Virtual Machine** tab in the ribbon, as shown in the screenshot here:

This option is not shown for running VMs and VMs with the latest version.

To quickly update the version of all clustered VMs, you can use the following command:

```
$VMs=Get-SCVirtualMachine|? {$_.Version -ne '8.0' -and $_.IsHighlyAvailable
-ne "False"}
$VMs|Update-SCVMVersion
```

 You must stop VMs before upgrading their versions. So, plan a manteinance window and use `Get-SCVirtualMachine` cmdlet along with `Stop-SCVirtualMachine` or VMM GUI to stop a bunch of VMs.

See also

For more information, go through the following references:

- The *Perform a Rolling Upgrade of host cluster in the VMM* page at `http://docs.microsoft.com/system-center/vmm/hyper-v-rolling-upgrade`
- The *Step-By-Step: Cluster OS Rolling Upgrade in Windows Server* page at `https://rlevchenko.com/2015/04/29/step-by-step-cluster-os-rolling-upgrade-in-windows-server-technical-preview/`

Managing fabric updates

A VMM-managed fabric server comprises the following workloads: Hyper-V hosts and host clusters, the VMM library servers, **Pre-Boot Execution Environment (PXE)**, the **Windows Server Update Management (WSUS)** server, and the VMM management server:

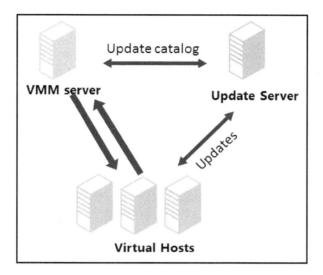

You can monitor the update status of the servers, scan for compliance, and update all or a set of the server's resources, as well as exempt resources from the installation of an update.

 To update Guest VMs, you can use SCCM configured with WSUS or even Microsoft **Operations Management Suite** (**OMS**), which is hosted in Azure.

You can also orchestrate update remediation on Hyper-V host clusters, in which VMM will place one node of the cluster at a time in the maintenance mode and install the updates. If the cluster supports live migration, the Intelligent Placement feature will be used to live-migrate the VMs off the node; otherwise, VMM will save the state for the VMs, and the host will start the VM after updating.

 After integrating the WSUS server with VMM, it is recommended that you manage it only through the VMM console (unless you have **System Center Configuration Manager** (**SCCM**) sharing the same WSUS server). Do not use the WSUS administration console to manage the integrated WSUS server.

Getting ready

In order to use VMM to manage the updates, it is recommended that you install a dedicated WSUS server, but you can use an existing one or install it on the VMM server if it is a small deployment.

As a prerequisite, install the WSUS administration console on the VMM management server before integrating WSUS with VMM (if the WSUS server is not installed on the VMM management server) and then restart the VMM service.

 It is neither a recommended approach nor a best practice to install the WSUS server on the VMM management server unless it is a lab, POC, or a small deployment.

How to do it...

The following sections detail the procedures to configure WSUS integration with VMM.

Installing WSUS for VMM 2016

Carry out the following steps to install WSUS for VMM:

 This step could be skipped if a WSUS server is already deployed in the network. Also, if you plan to use a WSUS server that is already configured with SCCM, make sure that the **Allow Update Server Configuration Changes** option is unchecked in the WSUS server properties in VMM (**Update Server | Properties | General**).

1. Install a WSUS role (which was covered in `Chapter 1`, *VMM 2016 Architecture*). You can use the following PowerShell commands:

   ```
   PS c:\>Install-WindowsFeature -Name UpdateServices, UpdateServices-Ui
   ```

   ```
   Administrator: Windows PowerShell
   PS C:\Users\rlevchenko> Install-WindowsFeature -Name UpdateServices, UpdateServices-Ui

   Success Restart Needed Exit Code      Feature Result
   ------- -------------- ---------      --------------
   True    No             Success        {Windows Server Update Services, WSUS Serv...
   WARNING: Additional configuration may be required. Review the article Managing WSUS Usi
    (http://go.microsoft.com/fwlink/?LinkId=235499) for more information on the recommende
   installation using PowerShell.
   ```

   Assuming `D:\WSUS` is the update content folder:

   ```
   PS c:\Program Files\Update Services\Tools> WsusUtil.exe PostInstall
   CONTENT_DIR=D:\WSUS
   ```

   ```
   Administrator: Windows PowerShell
   PS C:\Program Files\Update Services\Tools> .\WsusUtil.exe PostInstall CONTENT_DIR=C:\WSUS
   Log file is located at C:\Users\rlevchenko\AppData\Local\Temp\tmp3D63.tmp
   Post install is starting
   Post install has successfully completed
   ```

2. In the Windows Start menu, launch **Windows Server Update Services**, and in the **Configuration Wizard,** configure the following:

   - Microsoft Report Viewier 2008/2012 (not required if you installed the WSUS server on the VMM server)
   - Upstream Server
   - Languages
   - Proxy Server
   - Products (at least Windows OS, SQL, IIS, and System Center)
   - Classifications (at least Critical and Security Updates)
   - Sync Schedule (manual)

If you have installed the WSUS server on a server other than the VMM Management server (recommended approach), install the WSUS administration console on the VMM management server and restart the VMM service.

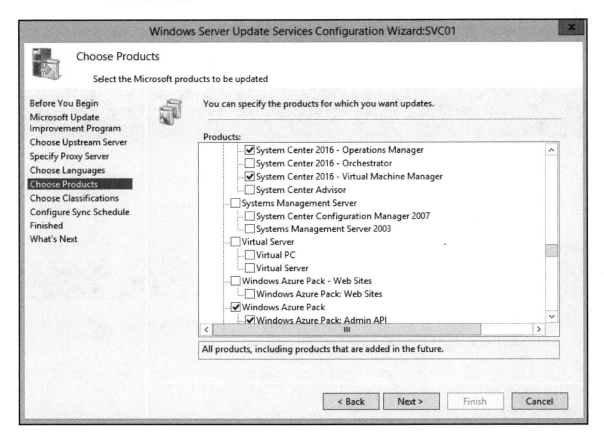

3. Click on **Finish** and then on **Synchronizations** in the navigation pane to confirm that the initial sync succeeded.

Integrating WSUS with VMM

Carry out the following steps to add WSUS to VMM:

It is not recommended to install WSUS on the same machine that you are installing VMM on. I would recommend a remote dedicated WSUS or a shared WSUS server with SCCM.

1. In the **Fabric** workspace on the VMM console, click on **Add Resources** on the **Home** tab in the ribbon.
2. Select **Update Server**, and on the **Add Windows Server Update Services Server** dialog in the **Computer name** field, type in the FQDN of the WSUS server (for example, `svc01.rllab.com`):

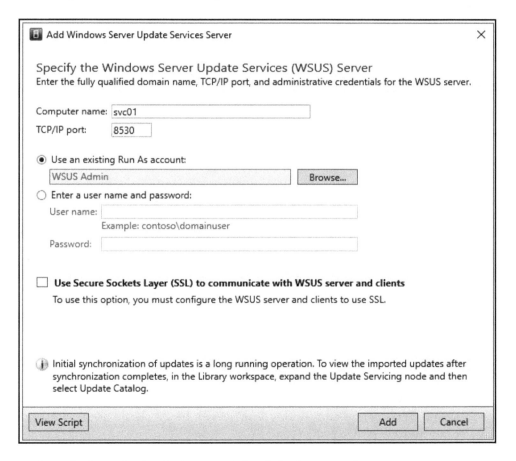

3. Specify the WSUS **TCP/IP** port (The default is `8530`).

4. Click on **Use an existing Run As account** and then on **Browse** to select the Run As account (in our case it is WSUS Admin, as per preceding screenshot), or click on **Enter a user name and password** and then type in the user credentials (in the format domain\username; for example, rllab\wsus-admin) for an account with administrative rights on the WSUS server, to connect to the WSUS server.

5. If required, select the **Use Secure Socket Layer (SSL) to communicate with the WSUS server and clients** checkbox and click on **Add**.

These steps will add the WSUS server to VMM, followed by an initial synchronization of a collection of updates. This operation can take a long time as it depends on a number of factors, such as the network, updates, and bandwidth.

If you get an error 444: your_vmm_server is a VMM management server. A VMM management server cannot be associated with another VMM management server, check whether you are deploying WSUS to a clustered VMM. Deploy WSUS to a dedicated remote VM and then integrate with VMM using the preceding steps.

How it works...

VMM uses WSUS to send updates to managed computers, but in a different way compared with the configuration manager. VMM provides two inbuilt update baselines that can be used to apply security and other critical updates to the servers in your VMM environment, but you must assign these baselines to host groups, clusters, or individually-managed computers before you start using them.

You can install WSUS on the same server on which you installed the VMM management server. Note that this is only recommended in small scenarios.

The WSUS administration console is required on each VMM management server.

To check whether the WSUS server was successfully integrated into VMM, in the **Fabric** workspace, expand **Servers** and click on **Update Server**. In the results pane, you should be able to see the configured WSUS server.

In the **Library** workspace, expand **Update Catalog and Baselines** and click on **Update Catalog** to see which updates were downloaded through WSUS synchronization.

Subsequently, you should configure the proxy server for synchronization by clicking on **Update Server** and **Properties** in the **Update Server** tab in the ribbon, and adjusting the update categories, products, and supported languages that will be synchronized by WSUS.

There's more...

You can assign computers to a baseline. To do that, carry out the following steps:

1. On the **Library** workspace on the VMM console, in the **Library** pane, expand **Update Catalog and Baselines** and click on **Update Baselines**.
2. In the **Baselines** pane, select the baseline (for example, **Sample Baseline for Critical Updates**).
3. On the **Home** page in the ribbon, click on **Properties** and then click on **Updates** on the baseline dialog box.

 You can add/remove baselines from those that are listed.

4. Click on **Assignment Scope** and then select the hosts, host groups, and/or clusters that are to be added to the baseline.
5. Select the computers symbolized by the roles they perform in VMM, or click on **All Hosts** to apply the baseline to all computers. Note that all the roles that the computer performs will be selected.
6. To confirm, click on **OK**. This will save the changes.

Scanning servers for compliance

You can scan computers to check their compliance status for a particular baseline. You will be required to scan the servers again if the server was moved from one host group to another, an update was added/removed from a baseline assigned to that server, or if it was just added to the scope of a baseline. To perform the scan, carry out the following steps:

1. In the **Fabric** workspace, go to the **Fabric** pane and click on **Servers**.
2. On the **Home** tab, click on **Compliance** and then check the compliance status in the results pane.

Until you scan the servers for compliance, the compliance status will show **Unknown** and the operational status will show **Pending Compliance Scan**.

3. In the **Compliance** view, select the servers to scan.

 You must perform and complete the updates successfully in the **Compliance** view.

4. In the **Home** tab, click on **Scan**.

 When the task is completed, the compliance status of each update will change from **Unknown** to **Compliant**, **NonCompliant**, or **Error**. The **Scan** and **Remediate** tasks are available in the **Fabric Resources** view as well.

Remediating updates for a standalone server in VMM

To make noncompliant standalone servers compliant, you will need to carry out the following steps in VMM:

1. In the **Compliance** view, select the servers to remediate:

 Click on a specific server to display the baselines checked for it.

2. Select an update baseline or a single update within a baseline that is **Non-Complaint**, and then right-click and click on **Remediate** or click on **Remediate** in the **Home** tab:

3. In the **Update Remediation** dialog, you can optionally select or clear update baselines or specific updates, to limit which updates are applied.
4. If the update requires a restart, select the **Do not restart the servers after remediation** checkbox to manually restart the server after the update is applied.
5. Click on **Remediate** to begin the remediation process.

Remediating updates for a Hyper-V cluster in VMM

To make noncompliant servers in a Hyper-V cluster compliant, you need to carry out the following steps in VMM:

1. In the **Compliance** view, click on **Remediate**.
2. In the resource list on the **Update Remediation** dialog, select the cluster to remediate.
3. If the update requires a restart, select the **Do not restart the servers after remediation** checkbox to manually restart the server after the update is applied.
4. Select **Allow remediation of clusters with nodes already in maintenance mode** to bypass maintenance mode for a particular node (which happens by default).
5. Select **Live migration** to move VMs before starting the process, or select **Save State** to shut the VMs down and then proceed with the updates.
6. Click on **Remediate** to begin the remediation process.

See also

For more information, see:

- The Set *up update servers in the VMM compute fabric* page at `https://docs.microsoft.com/system-center/vmm/update-server`
- The *Update infrastructure servers* page at `https://docs.microsoft.com/system-center/vmm/infrastructure-server`

Configuring Dynamic Optimization and Power Optimization

Dynamic Optimization (DO) is a VMM feature that initiates live migration of VMs that are on a cluster, to improve load balancing among cluster nodes and to correct any placement constraint violations.

 VM Load Balancer (Node Fairness), available in Windows Server 2016, will be turned off if dynamic optimization is enabled in VMM fabric.

It can be configured with a specific frequency and aggressiveness on a host group, which determines the amount of load discrepancy required to trigger a live migration through DO.

DO settings can be configured for the CPU, memory, disk I/O, and network I/O.

By default, VMs are migrated every 10 minutes with medium aggressiveness. You must take into consideration the resource cost (for example, the network) of extra migrations against the advantages of load balancing among cluster nodes, when setting the frequency and aggressiveness for DO.

 By default, a host group inherits DO settings from its parent host group.

Power Optimization (PO), a DO optional feature, is enabled only if a host group is configured for live migration of VMs through DO. It helps meet resource requirements and saves energy by shutting down hosts that are not needed by the cluster, and turns them back on only when they are needed.

PO settings comprise CPU, memory, disk space, disk I/O, and network I/O settings.

 For PO, the servers are required to have a **Baseboard Management Controller (BMC)** that supports out-of-band management. See the *Configuring host BMC settings* recipe in `Chapter 8`, *Managing VMware ESXi Hosts*.

The rules of thumb for PO are as follows:

- For clusters created outside VMM and then added to VMM:
    - One node can be shut down on a cluster with five to six nodes
    - Two nodes can be shut down on a cluster with seven to eight nodes
    - Three nodes can be shut down on a cluster with nine to ten nodes
- For VMM-created clusters:
    - One node can be shut down on a cluster with four to five nodes
    - Two nodes can be shut down on a cluster with six to seven nodes
    - Three nodes can be shut down on a cluster with eight to nine nodes

Then, for each extra one to two nodes on a cluster, one more node can be shut down.

Getting ready

In order to enable DO and PO, the VM must be running on a cluster. In addition, for PO, confirm the BMC-supported protocol. See the *Configuring host BMC settings* recipe in `Chapter 8`, *Managing VMware ESXi Hosts*.

How to do it...

We will carry out the steps in the following sections to configure settings for DO and PO:

Configuring settings for Dynamic Optimization (DO)

Carry out the following steps to configure DO:

1. In the **Fabric** workspace on the VMM console, expand **Servers**, expand **All Hosts** under **Servers** and then select the host group to configure.
2. Click on **Properties** on the **Folder** tab in the ribbon and then click on **Dynamic Optimization**.
3. If you don't want to inherit the parent host group settings, on the **Dynamic Optimization** page, deselect **Use dynamic optimization settings from the parent host group**:

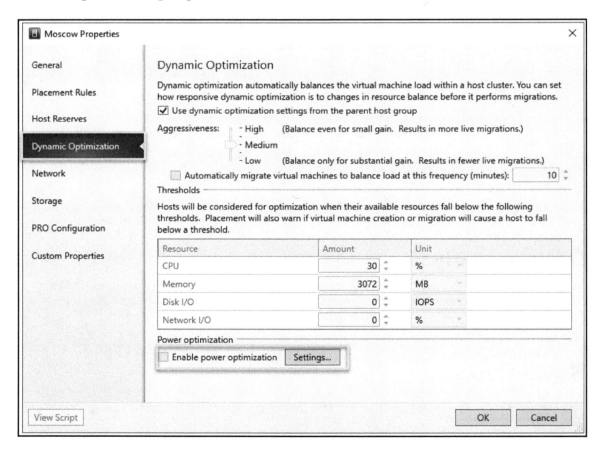

4. To set the **Aggressiveness** level, select either **High, Medium, Low,** or any value in between.

If you select a higher level of aggressiveness, the result will be more live migrations; on the other hand, if you lower the aggressiveness level, the end result will be fewer live migrations. The default value is **Medium**. Live migrations will happen based on the ratings determined by Intelligent Placement.

5. To run DO from time to time, select the **Automatically migrate virtual machines to balance load at this frequency (minutes)** checkbox and type in a value to specify how often it will run.

You can type in any value between 10 (default) and 1440 minutes (24 hours).

6. Click on **OK** to save the changes.

Configuring settings for Power Optimization

Carry out the following steps to configure settings for PO:

1. In the **Fabric** workspace on the VMM console, expand **Servers**, expand **All Hosts** under **Servers** and then select a host group to configure (for example, **Moscow**).
2. Click on **Properties** on the **Folder** tab in the ribbon and then click on **Dynamic Optimization**.
3. Select **Enable power optimization** to enable PO for the selected host group and click on **Settings**.

4. In the **Customize Power Optimization Schedule** dialog, configure the **CPU**, **Memory**, **Disk I/O**, and **Network I/O** resources settings or leave the default values as they are:

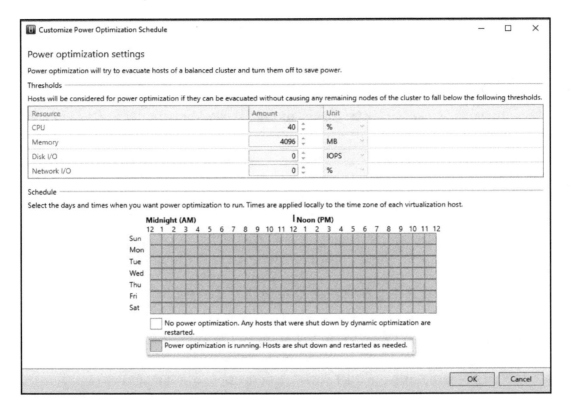

5. In the **Schedule** section, select the days and set the time you want PO to be performed.
6. Click on **OK** to save the changes and again click on **OK** to close the **Properties** window.

PO will be scheduled according to the time zone of each node in the cluster.

How it works...

DO can be enabled only for clusters with two or more nodes and will only be performed on the clusters that support live migration, have shared storage, and are not in the maintenance mode.

> If a host group comprises standalone hosts or clusters that do not support live migration, DO will not be performed on those hosts/clusters. Also, VMs that are not highly available are not migrated during DO.

DO on demand is also available for host clusters, without the need to configure DO on the host groups, which can be done using the **Optimize Hosts** task in the **VMs and Services** workspace. When DO is requested for a host cluster, VMM lists all VMs that will be migrated and then requests the administrator's approval.

In the DO settings, you can set the level of aggressiveness, which is a measure of how responsive DO is to changes in resource balance before it starts migrating VMs. Be cautious in balancing the resource cost of extra migrations against the benefits of balancing load among nodes on a cluster, and always check the effectiveness of DO in your environment for a certain period of time before increasing or decreasing the values.

When manually optimizing the hosts (using the **Optimize Hosts** option), for load balancing, VMM will suggest VMs for migration, with the current and target hosts indicated.

> The list excludes any hosts that are in maintenance mode and VMs that are not highly available.

By configuring PO for the host group to meet resource requirements, VMM will shut down hosts not needed by the cluster (migrating all VMs to other hosts in the cluster) and turn them on again when they are needed; VMM will perform the DO process to live-migrate VMs and balance load within the cluster.

> PO is only available when VMs are being live-migrated automatically to balance load, and the physical host has BMC settings configured.

PO settings specify resource capabilities that must be kept when VMM shuts down a node cluster. These settings make a buffer of resources available, to guarantee that oscillations in resource usage in the course of usual operations do not end in VMM powering the nodes of the cluster on and off unnecessarily.

It is possible to schedule the time (in hours and days) at which PO can be performed, according to the time zone of each host.

By default, PO will be run continuously if the feature is enabled.

There's more...

Now that we have enabled DO, let's take a look at how it is performed on a cluster.

Performing DO on the host cluster

Carry out the following steps to perform DO on a cluster:

1. In the **Fabric** workspace on the VMM console, expand **Servers**, expand **All Hosts** under **Servers** and then select a host group.
2. On the **Folder** tab in the ribbon, click on **Optimize Hosts**. Click on **Migrate** to start the DO process within the cluster.

VMM will perform DO assessment to decide whether a VM should be live-migrated to improve load balancing in the cluster.

See also

For more information, check the following reference:

- The *Set up dynamic and power optimization in the VMM compute fabric* page at https://docs.microsoft.com/en-us/system-center/vmm/vm-optimization

Live migrating virtual machines

Live migration is a feature that got a huge improvement back in VMM 2012 SP1 version due to the following Windows Server 2012/R2/2016 capabilities:

- Live migration between two isolated Hyper-V servers (with no shared storage).
- Live migration within clusters nodes.
- Live migration between nodes of two different clusters.
- Live storage migration: You can migrate the VM files (for example, VHD/VHDX, ISO, and VFD files) to update the physical storage, or to address bottlenecks in storage performance. Storage can be added to either an isolated Hyper-V host or a Hyper-V cluster and then the VMs can be live-migrated (moved) to the new storage.
- Live VSM: You can use live system migration (VSM) to migrate both the VM and the storage in a single action.
- Concurrent live migration: You can perform multiple concurrent live migrations of virtual machines and storage. The limit of concurrent live migration can be manually configured; the live migrations will be queued if the number of live migrations exceeds the specified limit.

 Note that the network usage for live migration might create a bottleneck.

Getting ready

Before you start performing live migrations, there are some requirements that you need to look at. These are discussed in the following sections:

Requirements for Live migration

The following are the requirements that need to be met before live migration can be performed:

- Two or more Hyper-V servers with processors from identical manufacturers (either all Intel or all AMD). This is because it is not possible to live-migrate from AMD to Intel processors and vice versa.

- VMs should be configured to use virtual hard disks or virtual fiber channel disks and not pass-through disks (physical disks).
- A dedicated private network for live migration network traffic (recommended).
- Source and destination Hyper-V servers on the same domain or on trusted domains.
- If the source or destination VM VHD has a base disk, it should be in a share available to the target host as well, as live migration does not usually migrate the base disk.
- Live migration among clusters is only supported for hosts running Windows Server 2012/R2/2016 with the failover cluster service and the CSV feature installed and enabled.
- If the source and destination Hyper-V hosts use shared storage, all VM files (for example, VHD/VHDX, snapshots, and configuration) must be stored on an SMB share with permissions to grant access on the share to both source and target computer accounts.

Requirements for Live storage migration

The following are the requirements for live storage migration:

- Live storage migration moves VM images (VHD, VFD, and ISO files), snapshot configurations, and data (saved state files)
- Storage migration is for virtual machines
- Storage migration does not migrate parent (base) disks, except for snapshot disks

Requirements for Live system migration

The following are the requirements for live system migration:

- The VM must exist in a location that is not visible to the destination host
- For individual Hyper-V Windows 2012/R2/2016 hosts, the migration can happen among local disks or SMB 3.0 file shares
- For Hyper-V Windows 2012/R2/2016 clusters, the VM can be migrated (moved) to either a CSV or SMB 3.0 file share on the target (destination) cluster

Although Windows Server 2012 has been mentioned above, keep in mind that is no longer supported by VMM 2016. Use a Hyper-V/Clustering Manager instead.

How to do it...

Carry out the following steps to perform a live migration of a VM between two standalone Hyper-V Servers:

1. In the **VMs and Services** workspace on the VMM console, in the **VMs and Services** pane, expand **All Hosts**.
2. In the **VMs** pane, select the VM to migrate (for example, **RL-LM01**).

 As this is a live migration, the virtual machine is running.

3. On the **Virtual Machine** tab, click on **Migrate Virtual Machine** to open the **Migrate VM Wizard** window:

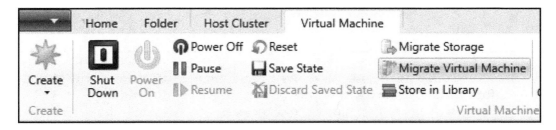

4. In the **Select Host** section, a list of possible destination hosts and their associated transfer types will be displayed:

If both the Hyper-V hosts can access the same SMB 3.0 file share, the transfer type will display **Live**.

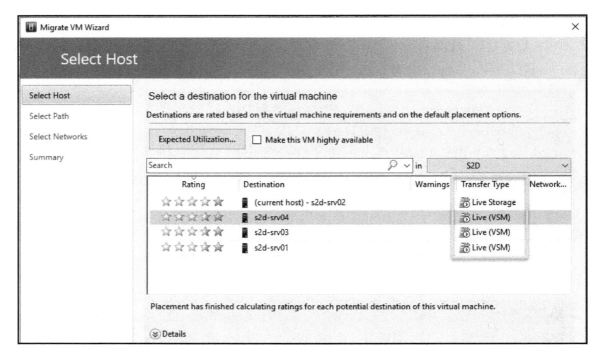

5. Select a destination host that shows a better rating and **Transfer Type** Live (for example, **s2d-srv04**) and click on **Next**. Click on **Move** on the **Summary** page to start the migration process.
6. The **Jobs** workspace will open, showing the tasks being performed.

How it works...

There are a number of ways in which live migration can be used. You can live-migrate a **virtual machine** (**VM**) from one Hyper-V host to another, keeping the VM files (VHD/VHDX, ISO, and VFD files) and configuration files at the same shared location (a CSV storage, an SMB share, and so on), move the VM files and the virtual machine together (live VSM), or move only the storage (live storage migration).

VMM reviews and validates the configuration settings of the target Hyper-V host before initiating the migration.

If the VM is running, the storage migration option enables you to live-migrate the storage from one location to another without stopping/breaking the workload of the VM. Storage migration can also be used when you need to move, provision, maintain, or upgrade storage resources, or to move a standalone or cluster VM to another location.

Live-migrating a VM does not necessarily move the VM files (VHD/VHDX, ISO, and VFD files); keeping that in mind, you can perform the following actions:

- Configure the VM files to run on a file share that has access from both source and target Hyper-V hosts and then run a live migration
- Run a live VSM, which is a combination of live migration and storage migration, but in a single action
- Run a separate live storage migration

There's more...

As we have seen before, there are many types of live migrations available, especially with the SC 2016 version. Let's see how we can perform each one of them.

Performing live migration of a VM between hosts in two clusters

Carry out the following steps in order to perform live migration of VMs between hosts in two different clusters:

1. In the **VMs and Services** workspace on the VMM console, in the **VMs and Services** pane, expand **All Hosts**.
2. In the **VMs** pane, select the highly available VM to migrate (for example, **RL-LM02**).
3. On the **Virtual Machine** tab, click on **Migrate Virtual Machine** to initiate the **Migrate VM Wizard** window.

4. In the **Select Host** section, review and select a destination cluster node that shows a better rating and the transfer type **Live** (for example, **s2d-srv03**) and then click on **Next**.

> To see the detailed rating, click on the **Rating Explanation** tab in the **Details** section.

5. Click on **Next** and then click on **Move** in the **Summary** section.
6. To track the job status, open the **Jobs** workspace.
7. To check the migration status, on the **VMs and Services** pane in the **VMs and Services** workspace, select the destination host; in the **VMs** pane, you should see a VM status of **Running**.

Performing live storage migration between standalone hosts

1. In the **VMs and Services** workspace on the VMM console, in the **VMs and Services** pane, expand **All Hosts**.
2. In the **VMs** pane, select the VM for which you want to perform storage migration (for example, **RL-VM01**).
3. On the **Virtual Machine** tab in the ribbon, click on **Migrate Storage** to open the **Migrate VM Wizard** window:

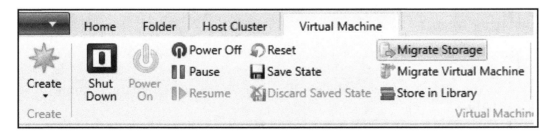

4. In the **Storage location for VM configuration** field in the **Select Path** section, select the default storage location or click on **Browse** to select the storage destination; then, click on **OK**.

 To specify path for each disk connected to the VM, select **Allow VHDs to be placed individually** and then click on **Browse** and select location.

5. Select the **Add this path to the list of default storage locations on the host** checkbox if you would like to make this the default path for the VM's storage.

 Make sure that you specify the FQDN of the destination file server in the share path if you specified an SMB 3.0 file share in the storage location field (for example, **w2016-fs02.rllab.com\vms**).

Migrate VM Wizard is shown in the following screenshot:

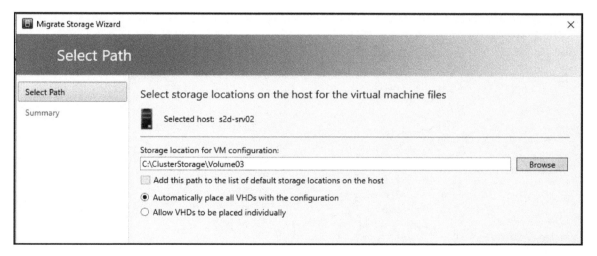

6. Click on **Next** and then click on **Move** in the **Summary** section.
7. Check the job status in the **Jobs** workspace.

Performing concurrent live migrations

When you perform more than one live migration per host at a time, VMM runs it concurrently. On the VMM console, it is not possible to select multiple VMs at the same time for the live migration wizard; instead, you will need to start the multiple live migrations one by one.

 VMM considers live VSM as one live migration and one storage migration.

Carry out the following steps to view the concurrent migration settings:

1. In the **Fabric** workspace on the VMM console, select the Hyper-V host.
2. Right-click and select **Properties**, and then click on **Migration Settings**:

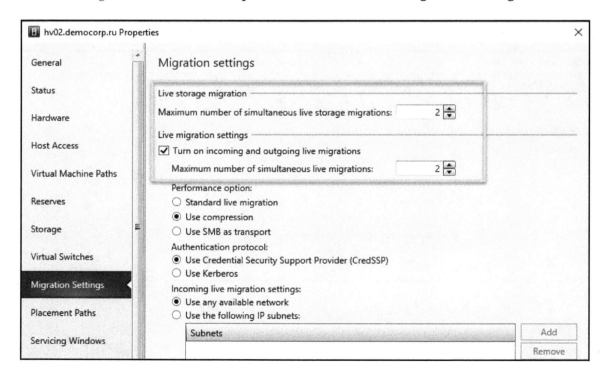

3. Change the concurrent live migration settings accordingly.

4. Click on **OK** to save.

You need to perform this operation for every Hyper-V host.

See also

For more information, see:

- The *Live Migration Overview* page at `https://docs.microsoft.com/en-us/windows-server/virtualization/hyper-v/manage/live-migration-overview`

Managing Linux virtual machines

Linux-based VMs are fully supported since VMM 2012 SP1, when hosted on a Hyper-V Server. This gives you the ability to add Linux-specific settings, such as OS specialization, when creating a Linux VM template, and additionally, the ability to add that template to a service template that deploys a multitier application or service.

Getting ready

Before deploying Linux VMs, check whether **Linux Integration Services** (**LIS**) is installed on the VMs. VMM does not check whether a VM meets the LIS requirement. However, if these requirements are not met, the VM will fail to deploy.

Some Linux distributions include LIS by default. But if LIS is not included, you must manually install it.

How to do it...

Carry out the following steps to install the VMM agent for Linux on a Linux VM:

1. Log in to the VMM management server with administrative rights.
2. Click on the Windows key and type `cmd`. Right-click on **cmd** and select **Run as administrator**.
3. Type in the following command in the command prompt:

   C:\>cd "\Program Files\Microsoft System Center 2016\Virtual Machine Manager\agents\Linux"

```
Administrator: Command Prompt

c:\Program Files\Microsoft System Center 2016\Virtual Machine Manager\agents\Linux>dir
 Volume in drive C has no label.
 Volume Serial Number is FC6E-E823

 Directory of c:\Program Files\Microsoft System Center 2016\Virtual Machine Manager\agents\Linux

10/25/2017  11:21 PM    <DIR>          .
10/25/2017  11:21 PM    <DIR>          ..
07/05/2016  04:00 AM             9,209 install
07/05/2016  04:00 AM         4,014,080 scvmmguestagent.1.0.2.1075.x64.tar
07/05/2016  04:00 AM         3,522,560 scvmmguestagent.1.0.2.1075.x86.tar
               3 File(s)      7,545,849 bytes
               2 Dir(s)  16,988,225,536 bytes free
```

4. Copy the agent installation files to a new folder on the Linux VM and then open it on the Linux VM.
5. If your Linux VM is a 32-bit version, run the following:

   #./install scvmmguestagent.1.0.2.1075.x86.tar

6. If your Linux VM is a 64-bit version, run the following:

   #./install scvmmguestagent.1.0.2.1075.x64.tar

How it works...

When creating a VM with Linux as the guest operating system, if the Linux distribution does not already have LIS, you must install it; after the machine starts, you will need to install the VMM agent for Linux as well.

The following will be created on the virtual hard disk when installing the VMM agent for Linux:

- A configuration file (`scvmm.conf`) containing the location of the log file
- An installation log file (`scvmm-install.log`)
- The log file (`scvmm.log`) that will be generated at the next VM boot when the program starts automatically
- A default log folder (`/var/opt/microsoft/scvmmagent/log`)
- A default installation folder (`/opt/microsoft/scvmmagent/`)

See also

For more information, see:

- The *Supported Linux/FreeBSD VMs for Hyper-V 2016* page at
  `https://docs.microsoft.com/windows-server/virtualization/hyper-v/supported-linux-and-freebsd-virtual-machines-for-hyper-v-on-windows`
- The *Supported guest operating systems for Hyper-V 2012 R2 VMs* page at
  `https://docs.microsoft.com/previous-versions/windows/it-pro/windows-server-2012-R2-and-2012/`

Configuring availability options and virtual NUMA for VMs

Since VMM 2012 SP1, you can configure availability options for VMs that are deployed on Hyper-V host clusters, which include:

- **VM priority**: By configuring these settings, the host clusters will be instructed to start orp place high-priority VMs before medium- or low-priority VMs, ensuring that (for better performance) the high-priority VMs are allocated memory and other resources first.

- **Preferred and possible owners of VMs**: These settings influence the placement of VMs on the host cluster nodes. By default, there is no preferred owner, which means that the possible owners include all cluster nodes.
- **Availability sets**: By placing VMs in an availability set (to improve continuity of service), VMM will attempt to keep those VMs on separate hosts whenever possible.

You can also configure NUMA, which is a memory architecture that is used in multiprocessor systems. NUMA tries to reduce the gap between the speed of the CPU and the memory usage; its benefits include avoiding slow processor performance that is caused when various processors attempt to access shared memory blocks. A NUMA node is identified as a group of CPUs for each block of dedicated memory. For more NUMA concepts, see `http://msdn.microsoft.com/en-us/library/ms178144(v=sql.105).aspx`.

How to do it...

Carry out the following steps in order to configure priority for a VM or a VM template on a host cluster:

1. Open the VMM console and execute one of the following options:
    - To configure a deployed VM, on the **VMs** pane in the **VMs and Services** workspace, select the VM, right-click on it, and click on **Properties**
    - To configure a VM stored in the VMM library, in the **Library** workspace, select the stored VM, right-click on it, and click on **Properties**
    - To configure a VM at the time of creation, click on the **Configure Hardware** section
    - To configure a VM template, in the **Library** workspace, expand **Templates** in the left-hand side pane, click on **VM Templates**, right-click on the VM template in the templates pane, and click on **Properties**

2. On the **Hardware Configuration** (or **Configure Hardware**) section, select **Advanced** (you will probably have to scroll down to see this option) and click on **Availability**:

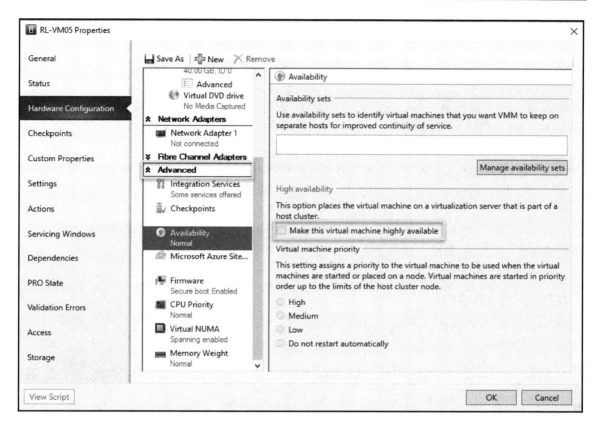

3. Select **Make this virtual machine highly available**.

 On a deployed VM, this setting cannot be selected, as it depends on whether the VM is running on a host cluster or not.

4. On the **Virtual machine priority** section, select the VM priority as either **High**, **Medium**, or **Low**. However, if you want the VM to always start manually and never preempt other VMs, select **Do not restart automatically**.
5. Click on **OK** to save the settings.

How it works...

Availability options allow you to configure VM priority, preferred and possible owners of VMs and availability sets. These options are configured by the VM and will allow you to refine the VM high-availability settings by prioritizing resources such as CPU and memory as well as by influencing the placement of VMs in cluster nodes, all to improve performance and the continuity of service.

In the case of a node failure, if high priority VMs (the VMs for which you selected the priority level **High**) do not have the necessary resources to start, lower priority VMs will be taken offline to free up necessary resources. The preempted VMs will later be restarted in the order of priority.

You can also use PowerShell for Failover Clustering to configure the **Availability sets** setting (**AntiAffinityClassNames**).

There's more...

Let's have a look at more configuration options.

Configuring availability sets for a VM running on a host cluster

On the VMM console, do the following:

1. For a deployed VM, on the **VMs and Services** workspace in the **VMs and Services** pane, expand **All Hosts** and then select the VM in the **VMs** pane.
2. For a stored VM, in the **Library** workspace, in the library server where the VM is stored, select the VM.
3. Right-click on the selected VM and then click on **Properties**.
4. On the **Hardware Configuration** tab, click on **Availability**.
5. Make sure to select **Make this virtual machine highly available**:

On a deployed VM, this setting cannot be selected as it depends on whether the VM is running on a host cluster or not.

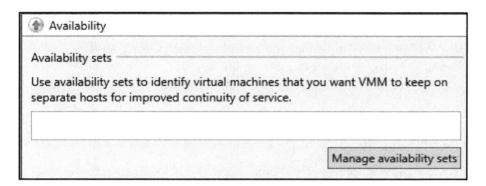

6. In the **Availability sets** section, click on **Manage availability sets**:

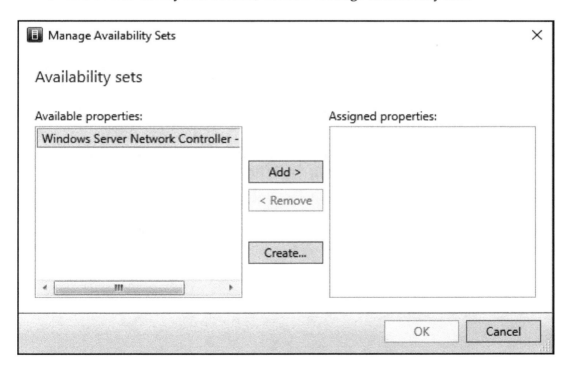

7. Click on an availability set and either **Add** or **Remove**.

To create a new availability set, click on **Create...**, type the set name, and click on **OK**.

8. In the **Manage Availability Sets** dialog, click on **OK** to confirm.
9. In the VM properties sheet, click on **OK**.

Configuring preferred and possible owners for a VM

Carry out the following steps to configure the preferred owner for a virtual machine:

1. In the **VMs and Services** workspace on the VMM console, in the **VMs and Services** pane, expand **All Hosts**; then, select the VM in the **VMs** pane.
2. Right-click on the selected VM and select **Properties**.
3. Click on the **Settings** tab and then do the following:
   - Configure the preferred owners list if you want to control which nodes in the cluster will own the VM regularly
   - Configure the possible owners list and do not include the nodes that you don't want as owners of the VM if you need to prevent a VM from being owned by a specific node
4. Click on **OK** to confirm.

Configuring virtual NUMA in VMM 2016

Virtual NUMA projects NUMA topology onto a virtual machine, which allows guest operating systems and applications to make intelligent NUMA decisions, aligning guest NUMA nodes with host resources. Carry out the following steps to configure virtual NUMA:

1. In the **Advanced** section of the VM properties, click on **Virtual NUMA**:

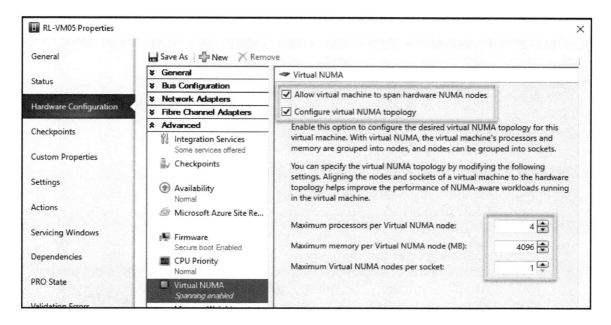

2. In the **Maximum processors per Virtual NUMA node** field, specify the maximum number of VPs on the same VM that can be used simultaneously on a virtual NUMA node.

3. In the **Maximum memory per Virtual NUMA node (MB)** field, specify the maximum amount of memory that can be assigned to a single virtual NUMA node.

4. In the **Maximum Virtual NUMA nodes per socket** field, specify the maximum number of virtual NUMA nodes that are allowed on a single socket.

To enable maximum bandwidth, configure different NUMA VMs to use different NUMA nodes.

5. To enable spanning, select the **Allow virtual machine to span hardware NUMA nodes** checkbox. Deselect the checkbox to disable NUMA spanning.

> Even if NUMA spanning is not enabled, based on the physical host topology, virtual nodes can still allocate memory from the same or different host NUMA nodes.

Configuring checkpoints in VMM 2016

Using checkpoints, you can create point-in-time images of virtual machine. These images then can be used to restore the VM to the previous state. There are two checkpoint types available in VMM 2016:

- Standard checkpoints (formerly known as snapshots) pause a virtual machine, create copies of the VM configuration files, configure the VM with a differencing disk (AVHDX), run the VM, capture a vCPU activity, and then save content of the VM's memory to the disk. As a result, a complete image of the VM's state, data and configuration will be created.
- Production checkpoints, introduced in Windows Server 2016/Windows 10, rely on a backup technology and use a **Volume Shadow Service (VSS)** in the VM via integration services to create data-consistent checkpoints. Unlike standard snapshots, they don't include information about running applications. If your application is VSS-aware, production checkpoints would be the best choice. This checkpoint type is the default in Hyper-V/VMM 2016.

> Keep in mind that checkpoints are not substitutes for backups.

Carry out the following steps to configure checkpoints:

1. In the **Advanced** section of the VM properties, click on **Checkpoints**.
2. Select either Production checkpoints (by default) or Standard checkpoints. If you choose **Production Checkpoints**, select **Create standard checkpoints if it's not possible to create a production checkpoint**. Otherwise, no checkpoint will be taken:

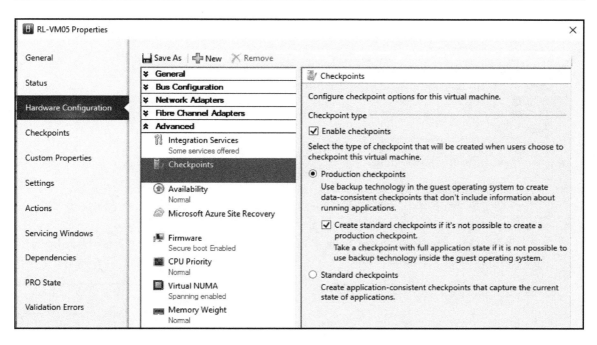

3. To disable checkpoints, clear the **Enable checkpoints** checkbox.
4. On the **Checkpoints** tab, you can manage VM checkpoints. To create a new one, click on **Create**, type a checkpoint name and its optional description, and click on **Create**:

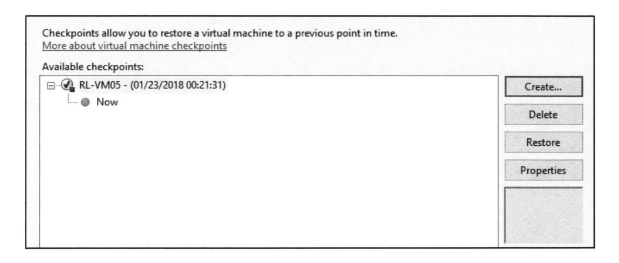

Adding a virtual adapter to a running VM in VMM 2016

Starting with VMM 2016, you can add/remove a vNIC to/from a running VM.

 Only Generation 2 VMs are supported by this feature.

Carry out the following steps to add/delete a virtual adapter to/from VM:

1. For a deployed VM, on the **VMs and Services** workspace in the **VMs and Services** pane, expand **All Hosts** and then select the VM in the **VMs** pane.
2. Right-click on the selected VM and select **Properties**.
3. On the **Hardware Configuration** tab, click on **New** and select **Network Adapter**, as shown in the screenshot:

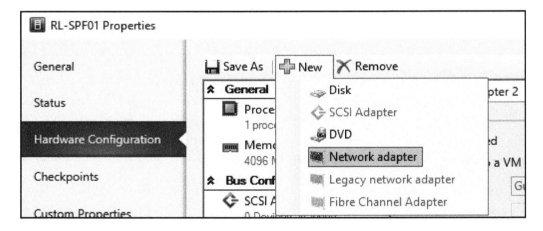

4. Verify the connectivity settings and associate the virtual adapter with the VM network and logical switch if necessary and then click on **OK**.
5. To remove the network adapter, double-click on the selected VM, open the **Hardware Configuration** tab, select the network adapter, and click on **Remove** and then click on **Yes**.

The following commands add vNIC using PowerShell:
```
$VM = Get-SCVirtualMachine -Name "RL-SPF01"
$vNetA = Get-SCVirtualNetworkAdapter -VM $VM
Remove-SCVirtualNetworkAdapter -VirtualNetworkAdapter
$vNetA
```

Managing static memory on a running VM in VMM 2016

Now it's possible to modify the memory configuration of a running VM that uses static memory. This feature helps in eliminating workload downtime due to increasing or decreasing memory allocation. Unlike for dynamic memory, you should use PowerShell to change VM's static memory on a running VM:

```
PS C:\Users\rlevchenko> $VM=Get-SCVirtualMachine -Name RL-SPF01
PS C:\Users\rlevchenko> $VM|ft Memory,VirtualMachineState
PS C:\Users\rlevchenko> Set-SCVirtualMachine -VM $VM -MemoryMB 4096
```

```
Windows PowerShell - Virtual Machine Manager
PS C:\Users\rlevchenko> $VM=Get-SCVirtualMachine -Name RL-SPF01
PS C:\Users\rlevchenko> $VM|ft Memory,VirtualMachineState

Memory VirtualMachineState
------ -------------------
  2048            Running

PS C:\Users\rlevchenko> Set-SCVirtualMachine -VM $VM -MemoryMB 4096

VMCPath                                    : D:\VMs\rlevchenko\RL-SPF01\RL
```

See also

For more information, go through the following references:

- The *NUMA Concepts* section on the page at
  http://msdn.microsoft.com/en-us/library/ms178144(v=sql.105).aspx

- The *Manage Virtual Machine Settings* page at
  https://docs.microsoft.com/system-center/vmm/vm-settings

Configuring resource throttling

The additional features provided with the resource throttling feature in VMM 2016 include enhanced CPU (processor) and memory-throttling capabilities, which ensure that CPU and memory resources are allocated and used effectively. The ability to set the **virtual processor** (**VP**) weight to provide it with larger or smaller shares of CPU cycles ensures that VMs can be ranked when CPU resources are overcommitted.

Memory throttling helps to rank access to memory resources in situations where memory resources are constrained.

How to do it...

Carry out the following steps in order to configure processor-throttling:

1. On the VMM console, execute one of the following:
    - To configure a deployed VM, on the **VMs** pane in the **VMs and Services** workspace, select the VM, right-click on it, and click on **Properties**
    - To configure a VM stored in the VMM library, in the **Library** workspace, select the stored VM, right-click on it, and click on **Properties**
    - To configure a VM at the time of creation, click on the **Configure Hardware** section
    - To configure a VM template, in the **Library** workspace, expand **Templates** on the left-hand side pane, click on **VM Templates**, right-click on the VM template in the **Templates** pane, and click on **Properties**

2. In the **Hardware Configuration** section, select **Advanced** (you will probably have to scroll down to see this option) and click on **CPU Priority**:

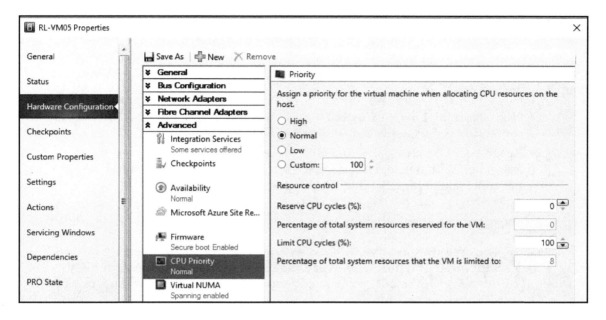

3. Select the VM priority, which specifies how the CPU resources will be balanced between VMs:

VMM Priority	High	Normal	Low	Custom
Relative weight value in Hyper-V	200	100	50	between 1 and 10000

4. In the **Reserve CPU cycles (%)** field, type in the percentage of the CPU resources in one logical processor that will be reserved for a VM.

A zero value indicates that there is no reserve.

5. In the **Limit CPU cycles (%)** field, type in the maximum percentage of CPU resources in one logical processor that the VM will consume.

How it works...

In the **Advanced** section of the **CPU Priority** settings of the virtual machine, you can configure the weight of a VP to make a share of CPU cycles available to it. You can configure the following settings:

- **High**, **Normal**, **Low**, or **Custom**, which defines how the CPU is shared when contention occurs, with VMs defined as **High** being allocated CPU resources first
- **Reserve CPU cycles (%)**, which defines the percentage of CPU resources associated with one logical processor that should be reserved for the virtual machine; useful for CPU-intensive applications
- **Limit CPU cycles (%)**, which defines the maximum percentage of resources on one logical processor that the VM can consume

 The options to reserve CPU cycles and limit CPU cycles are only supported in Windows Server 2012 Hyper-V hosts and later. For highly intensive workloads, you can add more VPs, particularly when a physical CPU is near its limit.

There's more...

You can also configure the memory-throttling feature, which will help rank access to memory resources in situations where they are constrained, meaning that VMs that have a priority of **High** will be given memory resources before VMs with lower priority.

Note that defining a VM as one with a priority of **Low** might prevent it from starting when the available memory is low.

The memory priority settings and thresholds can be set to **Static**, allowing you to assign a fixed amount of memory to a VM. They can also be set to **Dynamic**, where you can define the following settings:

- **Start-up memory**: This is memory that is allocated to the VM when it starts up. The value will be adjusted as required by **Dynamic Memory** (**DM**).
- **Minimum memory**: This is minimum memory required by the VM. It allows a VM to scale back the memory consumption below the start-up memory requirement (in case the VM is idle). The unbound memory can then be used by additional VMs.
- **Maximum memory**: This is the memory limit allocated to a VM.

- **Memory Buffer Percentage**: This defines the percentage of spare memory that will be assigned to the VM, based on the amount of memory required by the applications and services running on the VM. The amount of memory buffer is calculated as the *amount of memory needed by the VM/(memory buffer value/100)*.

Configuring memory throttling

Carry out the following steps to configure memory throttling:

1. In the properties of the VM, in the **Hardware Configuration** section, select **General** and then click on **Memory**:

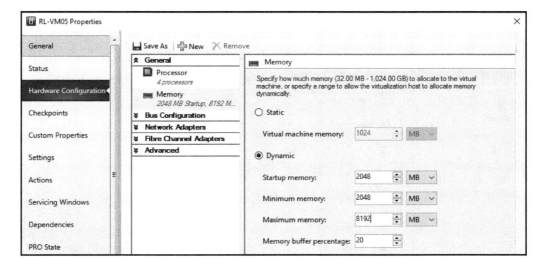

2. Click on **Static** to define the fixed memory that should be allocated to the VM.
3. Click on **Dynamic** and then do the following:
   - In the **Startup memory** field, specify the memory for the VM for when it starts up.
   - In the **Minimum memory** field, specify the minimum memory that the VM can run on.
   - In the **Maximum memory** field, specify the maximum memory that can be allocated to the VM. For Windows Server 2012/R2/2016, the default value is **1TB**.
   - In the **Memory buffer percentage** field, specify the available memory that will be assigned to the VM (if it is needed).

Configuring memory weight

You can give priority to a VM when memory resources reach the limit. Configuring the VM with **High** will give it higher priority when allocating memory resources. On the other hand, if you set the VM priority as **Low**, the VM will not be able to start if the memory resources are reaching the limit.

To configure the memory weight for a VM, on the properties of the VM in the **Hardware Configuration** section, click on **Advanced** and then click on **Memory Weight** and configure the priority:

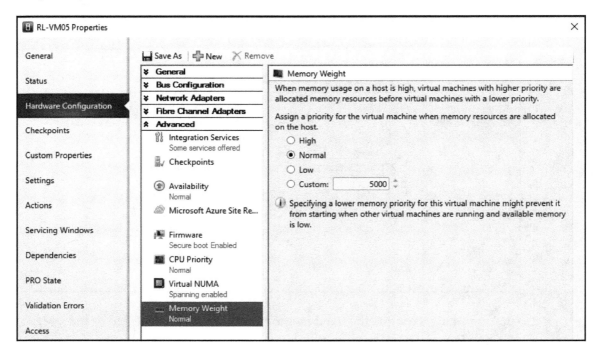

See also

For more information, see the following:

- *Configuring availability options and virtual NUMA for VMs in VMM 2016*

Integrating with IPAM Server for IP management

Since VMM 2012 R2, **IP Address Management (IPAM)** can be integrated with VMM, which allows a consolidated management of the IP address space on a corporate network and in Microsoft-powered cloud networks.

After integrating VMM with IPAM, the IP address configuration associated with logical networks and VM networks created in VMM will be synched with the IPAM server, which can detect and prevent IP address conflict, duplication, and overlaps across multiple instances of VMM 2016 (when deployed in large-scale data centers).

As VMM administrator, you can use IPAM GUI to configure and monitor logical networks and their associated network sites and IP address pools. However, VMM tenants need to use VMM server, not IPAM server GUI, to configure VM networks that use network virtualization.

Getting ready

This chapter does not cover the installation of IPAM Server, which must be installed on a Windows 2012 R2/2016 domain member server, and it must meet the requirements that are described at `https://docs.microsoft.com/previous-versions/windows/it-pro/windows-server-2012-R2-and-2012`.

You can use the IPAM Server to delete a logical network, keeping the VMM synchronization correct, by deleting the IP address subnets associated with that logical network and not deleting the name associated with the VMM logical network field on the IPAM Server. By deleting the name associated with the VMM logical network on the IPAM server, in the VMM console, the correspond network site and logical network must be deleted as well, in order for the deletion process be completed.

Also, make sure of the following:

- Create a domain service account with the password set to never expire and ensure to add it to: **IPAM ASM Administrators** and **Remote Management Users** on the IPAM Server
- Confirm time synchrony on IPAM Server and VMM

How to do it...

Carry out the following steps in order to configure IPAM integration in the VMM management server:

1. In the **Fabric workspace** on the VMM Console, click on the **Fabric Resources** and then on the **Fabric** Pane.

2. In the Home tab, click on **Add Resources** and then select **Network Service**.

3. In the **Add Network Service Wizard Name** window, type the Network Service name (for example, **IPAM**) and an optional description.

4. Click on **Next**.

5. In the **Manufacturer and Model window**, select **Microsoft** as a Manufacturer, select **Microsoft Windows Server IP Address Management** in the Model list, and click on **Next**:

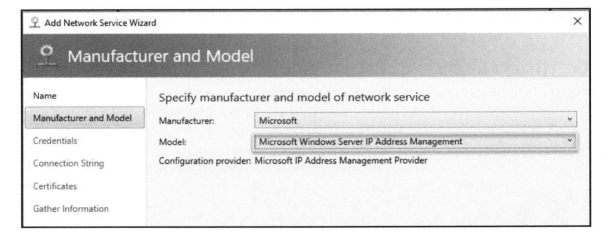

6. In the **Credentials** window, select the Service Account by clicking on **Browse**, then on the Select a Run As Account dialog box, click on **Next**.

 You can click on **Create Run As Account** to create a new Run As account with the required permissions.

7. In the **Connection String** window, type the **connection string**, which is the **Fully Qualified Domain Name** (**FQDN**) of your IPAM server (for example, ipam.rllab.com) and then click on **Next**.

If the IPAM server is not using a default port (`48885`), you should specify the FQDN followed by colon and the port number (for example, `ipam.rllab.com:48620`).

8. On the **Gather Information** page, click on the **Scan Provider** button and then check that **Is Network Data Manager** property is **True**:

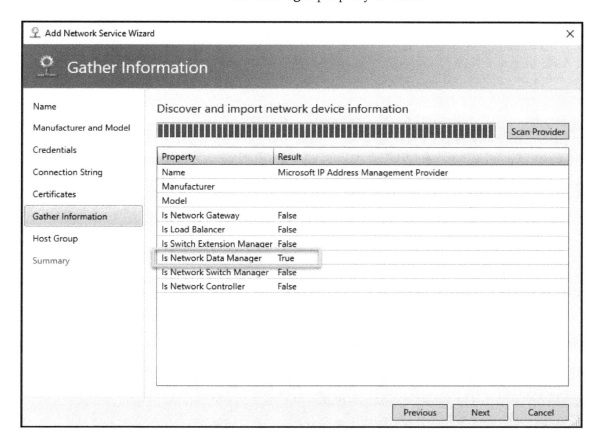

9. In the **Host Group** window, select **the host group(s)** that will support the IPAM integration.
10. In the **Summary** window, confirm the configuration.
11. Click on **Finish** and confirm whether the IPAM server is listed under Network Services.

To update the latest configuration to/from the IPAM server, right-click the IPAM server and then click on **Refresh**.

How it works...

Deploying Windows IPAM server means that you don't need to rely on Excel spreadsheets to keep track of the server's IP anymore, as the IPAM service will take care of that for you. IPAM integrates with Directory Services (Active Directory), DNS and DHCP as well with System Center 2016 VMM, to keep its database up-to-date.

As IP addresses can be under no control, especially in `test/lab/stage` environments and production environments where scalability is a must-have, as well as when providing **Infrastructure as a Service (IaaS)**, IPAM can be the solution to automate the process to keep track of the IP address assignments.

Although back in VMM 2012 SP1 we had the option to feed info into IPAM running on Windows 2012, in VMM 2012 R2 and Windows Server 2012 R2, Microsoft enhanced the integration between VMM and IPAM Server to provide a full IP address management.

There's more...

Now that you've integrated IPAM with VMM, there are some other things to consider.

IPAM and VMM Time Synchrony

Making sure of the time synchrony of the IPAM server and the VMM server is a requirement for the integration. If such a task cannot be achieved, the permissions on the IPAM server must be added/updated in order to the VMM provider to query the current time setting on the IPAM server.

Carry out the following tasks in order to update the permissions on the IPAM server console:

1. Right-click on the Windows start button on the Desktop and click on **Run**.
2. Type `wmimgmt.msc` to open the **WMI Control (Local)** and right-click on **WMI Control (Local)**
3. Select **Properties**, and on the **Security** tab, navigate to **Root\CIMV2** and then click the **Security** button
4. Click on **Add** for the addition of the Service Account created previously
5. Click on **Remote Enable** on the **Permissions for Authenticated Users** and select **Allow**:

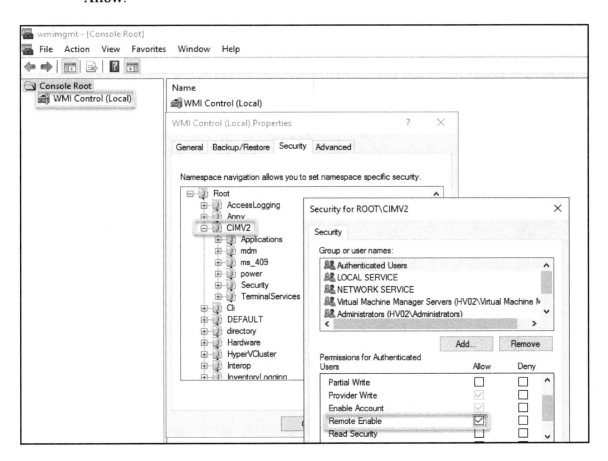

Deploying Windows Azure Pack for cloud management

Windows Azure Pack is a replacement of the App Controller. However, it is far from being just a replacement. It enables integration and management of VMM 2016, and cloud services, which means that you can provide management portals and authentication services for both tenants and administrators to enable self-service cloud supporting different integrations scenarios, including public cloud services, billing systems, or security solutions.

 For example, Azure Pack can be integrated with public Azure cloud using an Azure Pack Connector available at `https://github.com/Microsoft/Phoenix`.

Getting ready

Windows Azure Pack (**WAP**) can be deployed in two different ways: express and distributed. In the express deployment, you install all WAP components on one machine, and it's recommended only for test or demo environments. If you plan to use WAP in your production, you should use distributed deployment, which requires WAP main and optional components to be installed on multiple physical or virtual machines.

 Depending on the deployment size and system load, you may need to configure load balancing for Windows Azure Pack services. Refer to the samples of WAP architecture available at `https://technet.microsoft.com/en-us/dn296433`.

Before installing WAP, ensure that the system meets the hardware and software requirements. Actually, WAP installation wizard deploys software prerequisites automatically; therefore, you need to just verify that your OS and hardware/VM's configuration meet requirements (see `Chapter 1`, *VMM 2016 Architecture* and the *Specifying the Correct System Requirements for a Real-world Scenario* recipe*).

 WAP is fully supported on Windows Server 2016 and also supports many Windows Server 2016 features (for example, Shielded VMs).

In this recipe, we will go through the steps required by WAP express deployment. WAP VM is configured with 8 Gb RAM and runs Windows Server 2016. Also, make sure that you have already deployed a supported SQL Server version to store WAP databases.

How to do it...

Carry out the following steps to deploy Windows Azure Pack:

1. Log in to the server if you plan to install WAP with administrative rights (for example, *RL-WAP*), download and start the Web Platform Installer from `http://go.microsoft.com/fwlink/?LinkId=327966`.

2. In the **Web Platform Installer** window, type *Azure Pack* in the search box, and click on **Add** next to **Windows Azure Pack: Portal and API Express** and then click on **Install**:

WAP software requirements and other additional components will be
added to the items to be installed as well.

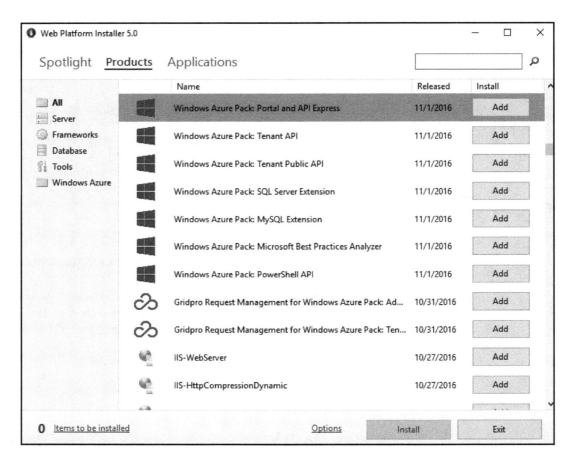

3. In the next window, review the license terms and accept them by clicking on the **I accept** button. Then, select **Use Microsoft Update when I check for updates (recommended)** and click on **Continue.**

 Wait while wizard downloads and installs WAP components. It takes
about 5-10 minutes depending on the network bandwidth and server
performance.

4. On the **Configure** page, click on **Continue** to launch the WAP configuration site. Review the installation logs on the **Finish** page in the Web Platform Installer, and click on **Finish** to close the wizard.

 You can open the WAP configuration page at any time by browsing `https://<wapservername>:30101` (for example, `https://rl-wap01:30101`).

5. On the **Database Server Setup** page, type the SQL Server name and instance (for example, *RL-SQL01\WAP*), select the authentication mode and, if SQL Server authentication is selected, provide SQL administrator name and password, and enter configuration store password, as shown in the screenshot:

Ensure that you write down the passphrase. If you forget or lose this passphrase, there is no way to recover it.

6. Click on **Next** twice and press **Complete** button to set up WAP features.
7. After the WAP is successfully configured, click the check mark in the bottom-right corner of the **Features Setup** and then press **Yes** to close the **Internet Explorer** tab.
8. Run **Internet Explorer** as an administrator and then go to `https://localhost:30101`. Verify that the **All Features are configured** message is shown at the WAP configuration site:

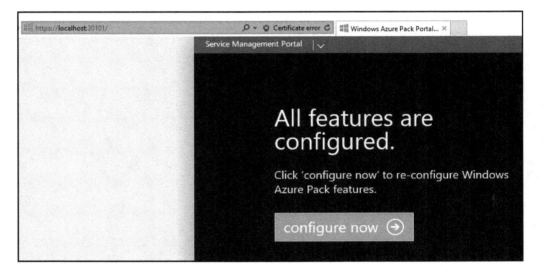

 Windows Azure Pack shortcuts for PowerShell module and portals are stored at `<systemdrive>:\ProgramData\Microsoft\Windows\Start Menu\Programs\Management Service`.

9. Right-click on the **Start** button, select **Search**, and type *Azure Pack* in the search box. Select **Windows Azure Pack Administration site**, provide credentials, and verify that site is working. We will use it to integrate WAP with VMM later in this recipe:

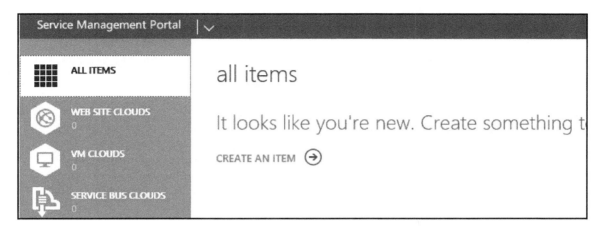

 To check the WAP tenant site, open Windows Azure Pack Tenant Site that uses port `30071` (`https://<wapservername>:30071`).

10. Using Web Platform Installer, you get the latest version of Windows Azure Pack. However, you can check the WAP version. For doing this, open the administration site and press *CTRL+ALT+A*. Check the **Portal Version** value as shown in the following screenshot:

Diagnostics Info

UTC Time:	2018-01-24 23:12:26Z
Browser:	Mozilla/5.0 (Windows NT 10.0; WOW64; Trident/7.0; .NE
Language:	en-us
Portal Version:	3.37.8196.0 (rd_auxsmp_stable_v2_gdr.161031-2132)
PageRequestId:	ddfcf03d-dfa9-47fb-a270-fd34f178a8b6
Email Address:	DEMOCORP\rlevchenko ({1})
Subscriptions:	

How it works...

Before you begin the installation of the Azure Pack, ensure that you have checked all the prerequisites, as per the page at https://technet.microsoft.com/en-us/dn296442.

Also, decide which deployment type meets your requirements: express or distributed. If you choose distributed deployment, multiple virtual or physical machines will be required.

 Although WAP express deployment is targeted to test and demo environments, it's not unusual to see such deployments at enterprises (just a fact). However, it's always better to divide public-facing from privileged Azure Pack services (API, Admininistration site, and Management Database) at least.

In order to install the Azure Pack, you must download and start Web Platform Installer available at http://go.microsoft.com/fwlink/?LinkId=327966 and then select WAP components.

During the process, you will be required to provide the database connection, authentication type, and passphrase to encrypt and decrypt data.

 Make sure that you configured SQL Server firewall ports and network protocols for desired instance. Use the *netstat -a* command to verify listening ports on the SQL.

At the end of the installation process, you have the option to start the WAP portals, including configuration, tenant, and administration sites.

 You might have to log out of your system and log back on before you can access the management portal for administrators.

There's more...

Now that you've installed Windows Azure Pack, you can integrate it with VMM.

Windows Azure Pack: integrating with VMM 2016

After you deploy and configure the base components of Windows Azure Pack for Windows Server, you can add and configure the services that you want to make available to your customers/tenants. Out of the box, you can use optional cloud services such as VM Clouds, websites, or databases providing IaaS, PaaS, and DBaaS cloud models, respectively. In this recipe, we will integrate WAP with VMM 2016 to use VM Clouds service (for example, to create a VM in the VMM cloud using WAP interface).

Before we start, ensure that the following requirements are satisfied:

1. As VM Cloud service in WAP builds on the **Service Provider Foundation** (**SPF**) API to enable self-service IaaS, you need to install and configure SPF 2012 R2/2016 beforehand. SPF is bundled with SC Orchestrator.

> See the installation guide at `https://rlevchenko.com/2014/10/29/step-by-step-installation-of-service-provider-foundation-2012-r2/`.

2. In the underlying VMM server that you plan to use with the SPF endpoint, you must have created a cloud and its associated components, such as VM Templates, Hardware Profiles, and virtual networks. See the *Creating Private Clouds* recipe in `Chapter 7`, *Deploying Virtual Machines and Services*.

3. In the underlying VMM Server, you must have created virtual templates that can be used by tenants to provision standalone virtual machines using VM Clouds.

> Make sure that you do not select any of the cloud capability profiles and that the Guest OS profile is not set to **None**. You should specify a valid value for Guest OS.

Carry out the following steps to integrate WAP with VMM:

1. On the SPF server (for example, `rl-spf01`), right-click on the Start button and select **Run**, then type `inetmgr.exe` and press *Enter* to open **Internet Information Services** (**IIS**) Manager.

 Make sure that you have installed IIS Manager. To add it, use the following command: `Install-WindowsFeature Web-Mgmt-Console`

2. In the IIS manager, navigate to **Application Pools** and note identities for VMM, Usage, Admin and Provider application pools (they are all with **spf- prefix**, in this recipe):

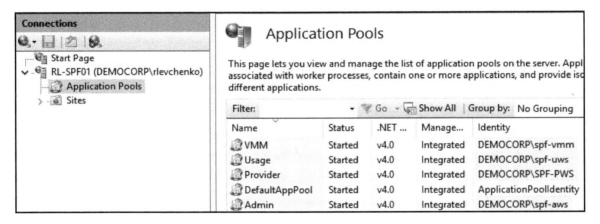

3. Open **Local User and Groups** by running the MSC file `lusrmgr.msc` and then add VMM application pool identity to the **Administrators** and **SPF_VMM** groups.
4. Make the identity of Provider application pool (`spf-pws`, for example) a member of **Administrators**, **SPF_VMM**, **SPF_Admin**, **SPF_Provider** groups.
5. Add the identity of Usage application tool (`spf-aws`, for example) to the **Administrators** and **SPF_Usage** group on the SPF server.
6. The identity of Admin application must be added to the **Administrators** and **SPF_Admin** groups.

You can automate the last four steps using the following commands:

```
#Pool Identities
$VMMpool='democorp\spf-vmm'
$Provider='democorp\spf-pws'
$Usage='democorp\spf-uws'
$Adminpool='democorp\spf-aws'
#VMM Pool
net localgroup administrators
$vmmpool /add
net localgroup spf_vmm
$vmmpool /add
#Provider Pool
net localgroup spf_provider $provider /add
net localgroup spf_vmm $provider /add
net localgroup spf_admin $provider /add
net localgroup administrators $provider /add
#Usage Pool
net localgroup spf_usage $usage /add
net localgroup administrators $usage /add
#Admin Pool net localgroup spf_admin
$adminpool /add
net localgroup administrators  $adminpool /add
```

7. Create a new local user (for example, `spf_wap`), and make the user a member of all groups starting with `SPF_` (`SPF_Admin`, `SPF_Usage` and so on). This user will be used to register SPF with WAP.

By using these accounts, VMM manages tenants, user roles, virtual machines, networks, and other fabric elements belonging to the cloud.

8. Open the VMM console, click on **Settings**, select **User Roles**, and double-click on **Administrator**.

9. In the **Administrator Properties** window, select the **Members** tab and then click on **Add...** , type VMM and Admin application pool identities (`spf-vmm` and `spf-aws`, in this recipe), and click on **OK**.

10. Now we are ready to register SPF with WAP. For doing this, open a management portal for administrators, go to **VM Clouds**, and click on **First you must register your System Center Service Provider Foundation**.

11. In the **Register System Center Provider Foundation** dialog box, provide the Service URL (for example, `https://rl-spf01:8090`), username, and password of the account created locally on the SPF server and which was added to the SPF groups at step 7, as shown in the following screenshot:

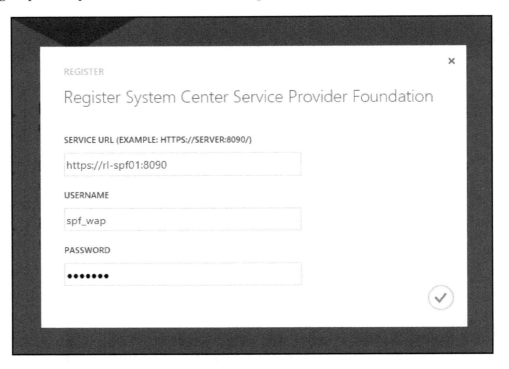

12. Verify that registration has been successfully completed. Check the status under the **Register System Center Service Provider Foundation**, as shown in the following screenshot:

13. Once the SFP is registered, in the **VM Clouds**, go to **Clouds** and then click on **Use an existing Virtual Machine Cloud Provider to Provision Virtual Machines,** as shown in the screenshot:

14. Type the VMM management server name (for example, vmm-mgmt01), optional port and remote desktop gateway FQDN, and click on **Register.**

 Remote Desktop Gateway provides an ability to connect to virtual machines using the VM console. It's useful when they are not available via RDP. See https://blogs.technet.microsoft.com/keithmayer/2014/ 05/14/windows-azure-pack-configuring-remote-desktop-gateway-for-vm-console-access/.

15. Once the VMM server is registered, you can see all available VMM clouds under the VMM server in **Clouds**, as shown in the screenshot:

16. To verify our integration, we need to create a hosting plan that defines cloud resources available to tenants, which we will also create later. Navigate to **Plans** and then click on **New**. In the new dialog box, type a friendly name of the plan (for example,RLCLOUD), select **Virtual Machine Clouds** as an offered service in this plan and click **Complete** button.

17. On the **Plans** page, verify that the new plan shows in the list and click on the plan; then, select **Virtual Machine Clouds**.

18. On the **Virtual Machine Clouds**, select the VMM management server (for example, vmm-mgmt01) and virtual machine cloud (rlevchenko.com, in this recipe), add networks, hardware profiles, and templates, and set additional settings (for example, console, checkpoints, and VM states); then, click on **Save** at the bottom of the page:

19. On the **User Accounts** page, click on the **Create a New User** or **+NEW** button and then enter an email address and account password, and choose a desired plan for the account. Click on **Create** to add a new user account and its subscription.

 This account will be shown under **User Roles** in the VMM Console too.

20. On the **User Accounts** page, click on a just create user account (for example, consumer@rlevchenko.com) and make sure that it has **Active** status, as shown in the screenshot here:

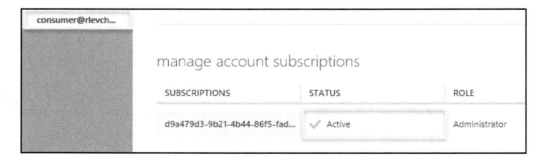

If **Status** shows **out of sync**, make sure that SPF web service accounts are properly configured on the SPF and VMM servers. In addition, check that SPF, VMM, and WAP have the latest updates.

21. Open the WAP tenant site, type the user account mail address and password and click on **Submit** to enter the tenant's portal.
22. Click on **Create an item**, select **Standalone Virtual Machine** and then **Quick Create.** Type a name for the VM (for example, `My1stCloudVM`), choose a template that you associated with the cloud, and enter password that will be used for local administrator on a guest OS, and then click on **Create VM Instance.** Check that the VM is shown under **Virtual Machines.**
23. In the VMM Console, go to **VMs and Services** and click on the cloud (`rlevchenko.com`, for example); then, select **VMs** on the **Home** tab in the ribbon. Make sure that the new VM is shown, and you can track its creating process, as shown in the screenshot:

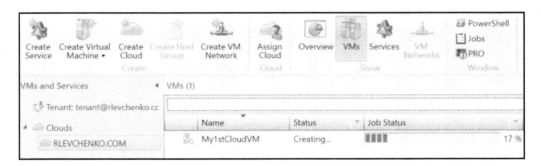

24. Once the VM is created, go back to the WAP tenant site, open **Virtual Machines**, and verify that the VM is running.

See also

For more information, see the following references:

- The *Windows Azure Pack Architecture* page at
  `https://technet.microsoft.com/en-us/library/dn296433.aspx`

- The *Reconfigure portal names, ports, and use trusted certificates* page at https://blogs.technet.microsoft.com/privatecloud/2013/12/10/windows-azure-pack-reconfigure-portal-names-ports-and-use-trusted-certificates/
- The *SPF Installation Guide* page at https://rlevchenko.com/2014/10/29/step-by-step-installation-of-service-provider-foundation-2012-r2/
- The *Account Subscription is Out of Sync* page at https://rlevchenko.com/2014/11/11/the-portal-cannot-load-management-data-for-this-resource-type-and-account-subscription-is-out-of-sync/
- The *Windows Azure Pack: How to add and troubleshoot VM Clouds* page at https://rlevchenko.com/2015/05/22/windows-azure-pack-how-to-add-and-troubleshoot-vm-clouds-2/
- The *Adding an Azure Subscription in VMM* page at https://rlevchenko.com/2018/02/09/adding-an-azure-subscription-in-vmm/

Configuring Synthetic Fiber Channel

Since VMM 2012 R2, Synthetic Fiber Channel has been added to support Guest Fiber Channel in Hyper-V.

The VMM feature, which makes use of the SMI-S provider, allows you to assign a Virtual Fiber Channel Adapter in the guest VM with cut-down zone management.

Virtual Fiber Channel supports single/multiple storage arrays connected to single/multiple fabrics.

Multiple storage arrays connected to multiple fabrics would provide dual-redundant paths to storage arrays.

Getting ready

In order to be able to use Virtual Fiber Channel, confirm that the following are in place:

- SAN, Fiber Channel switches, and HBA NIC's firmware and drivers are up to date
- SAN are configured to present logical units (LUNs)
- SAN SMI-S provider is installed and configured

- NPIV are configured and enabled on the Fiber Channel switches and HBAs
- Hyper-V Servers must be running Windows Server 2012 or newer
- You are logged with an account that is member of the VMM Administrator or a member of the Delegated Administrator user role in VMM Console
- You have created a **Run As Account** with permissions to access the SAN SMI-S provider

How to do it...

After confirming all the preceding prerequisites, carry out the following tasks to configure Guest VM direct access to the SAN:

Discover and add the Fiber Channel fabric and assign classifications to it:

1. In the VMM Console, in the **Fabric** workspace, **Fabric** pane, click on **Storage**.
2. Click on **Add Resources** at the **Home** tab and then select **Storage Devices.**
3. In the **Select Provider Type** page, select **Fiber Channel fabric discovered and managed by a SMI-S provider** and click on **Next:**

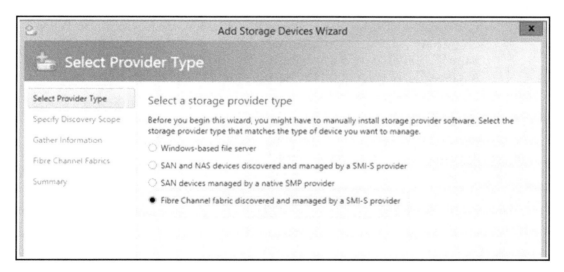

4. In the **Specify Discovery Scope** page, enter the following information:
   - IP address or the FQDN of the storage provider
   - Port number used to connect to the storage provider
   - Run As account that has access to the storage provider

 If required, select **Use Secure Sockets Layer (SSL) connection** to enable HTTPS in order to communicate with the storage provider.

5. In the **Gather Information** page, VMM will automatically discover and import the fiber Channel fabric information.

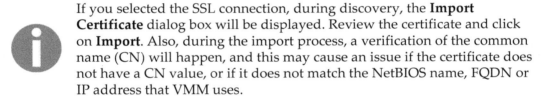 If the process succeeds, the fabric name, switches *and* **World Wide Node Names** (**WWNN**) will be displayed on this page. To retry the discovery process for an unsuccessful attempt, click on **Scan Provider**.

6. Click on **Next** to continue.

 If you selected the SSL connection, during discovery, the **Import Certificate** dialog box will be displayed. Review the certificate and click on **Import**. Also, during the import process, a verification of the common name (CN) will happen, and this may cause an issue if the certificate does not have a CN value, or if it does not match the NetBIOS name, FQDN or IP address that VMM uses.

7. On the **fiber Channel Fabrics** page, select the Fiber Channel in the **Storage** column and select the **Classification** and then click on **Next**.

8. On the **Summary** page, click on **Finish**.

How it works...

A **virtual Storage Area Network** (*vSAN*) is a collection of physical *fiber Channel* **Host Bus Adapter** (**HBA**) ports on a physical Hyper-V server in which a virtual machine connects to in order to access fiber Channel storage.

 One or more vSANs can be created for each physical server, but vSAN's can only have HBAs from the same fabric.

Virtual Host Bus Adapters (**vHBAs**) symbolize the virtualization of the fiber Channel HBAs, which are then used by virtual machines to connect to a vSAN.

Each vHBA has its own unique WWNN. Windows 2012 R2/2016 Hyper-V *NPIV* capability allows a physical HBA to have many associated vHBAs. You can add or remove HBA ports assigned to a vSAN as required.

 As a recommended best practice when working with Virtual Fiber Channel, make sure that you update firmware and drivers throughout the entire stack: Servers, Switches, Storage, HBAs, and OS. Also, confirm that each Hyper-V host is configured identically. Templates or bare-metal host provisioning can help you with that. Otherwise, if you're PowerShell-ready, there is DSC in 4.0 and later.

There's more...

After discovering, adding, and classifying, you will be able to perform storage operations.

Creating virtual SANs

Carry out the following steps to create a *vSAN*:

1. Click on the **Fabric** workspace, and in the **Fabric** pane, select the Hyper-V server, right-click and then click on **Properties**.

2. Click on the **Hardware** tab, click on **New Virtual SAN**, and provide a name and description for the vSAN:

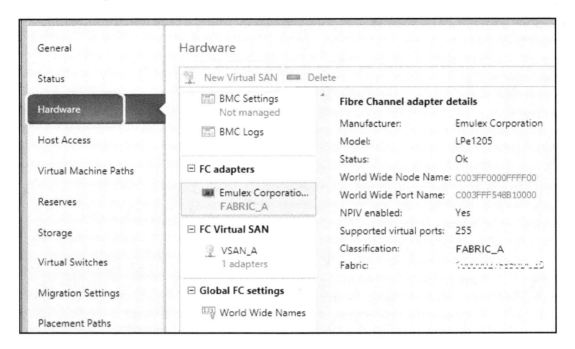

3. Below **fiber Channel adapters**, select the HBAs that will be assigned to the vSAN and click on **OK**.

4. Create the **Zones** and activate or inactive *zone sets*.

 Zones tie each Server or Virtual Machine *vHBA* to a storage array.

5. In the **VMs and Services** workspace, **Services** pane, select the Virtual Machine, right-click and then click on **Properties**.

6. Click on the **Storage** tab, click on **Add** and then select **Add fiber Channel Array**.

7. In the **Create New Zone** window, provide the Zone Name, select the Storage Array, Switch, the relevant *WWPM port(s)* and then click on **Create**.

You can view the available *zone* aliases by clicking on **Show aliases**. To change an existing *vHBA* port configuration or to apply a new setting, you will need to recreate the port by removing it and adding it again.

8. Now, create the storage LUNs and register them for the Hyper-V servers, virtual machines or service tier as required. For more info, check the *Creating logical units (LUN)* recipe of `Chapter 5`, *Configuring Fabric Resources*.

9. For step-by-step instructions, see *Managing Storage LUNs for Virtual fiber Channel*: `http://technet.microsoft.com/en-us/library/dn458364.aspx`.

10. Create a VM template, and for each virtual fiber Channel adapter (vHBA) that is created, specify dynamic or static WWN assignments and select the fabric classification. The fabric classification is used to connect a vHBA to a storage fabric. For more information, see *Creating a VM or a VM Template with Virtual fiber Channel*: `http://technet.microsoft.com/en-us/library/dn458371.aspx`.

11. Create a VM, select the destination host to deploy the VM to, zone a fiber Channel array to the VM, add a disk to the VM, create a LUN and then register (unmask) the LUN to the VM. For more information, see *Creating a VM or a VM Template with Virtual fiber Channel*: `http://technet.microsoft.com/en-us/library/dn458371.aspx`.

12. Create a service template, add VM templates to it, and for each virtual fiber Channel adapter (vHBA) that is created, specify dynamic or static WWN assignments and select the fabric classification. For more information, see *Creating a Service Tier for Virtual fiber Channel*: `http://technet.microsoft.com/en-us/library/dn458367.aspx`.

13. Create and deploy the service tier, zone a fiber Channel array to the service tier, add a disk to the service tier, create a LUN, and register (unmask) the LUN to the service tier. For more information, see *Creating a Service Tier for Virtual fiber Channel*: `http://technet.microsoft.com/en-us/library/dn458367.aspx`.

Creating a VM or VM Template with virtual fiber Channel

The next step is to create a VM or a VM Template with a vHBA. Follow the steps described in `Chapter 7`, *Deploying Virtual Machines and Services*, and then:

1. In the **Configure Hardware** page, add a new **fiber Channel adapter**.
2. Assign Dynamic or Static WWPN and choose the fabric **classification** for every created *vHBA*.

When placing and deploying the VM Hyper-V host, make sure that it contains a vSAN that ties with the storage. For more information, see `Chapter 7`, *Deploying Virtual Machines and Services.*
After the virtual machine is deployed to a Hyper-V host, the HBA can be zoned to that VM and then a LUN can be created for the array and registered to the VM.

Editing vSAN port assignments

Carry out the following steps to modify the Hyper-V HBA ports assigned to a *vSAN*:

1. In the **Fabric** workspace, **Fabric** pane, select the Hyper-V host, right-click and select **Properties**.
2. Click on the **Hardware** tab and then below **FC Virtual SAN**, check/uncheck the listed HBA ports.

Removing a vSAN

Carry out the following steps to remove a *vSAN*:

1. In the **Fabric** workspace, **Fabric** pane, select the Hyper-V host, right-click and select **Properties**.
2. Click on the **Hardware** tab and then below **FC Virtual SAN**, select the *vSAN* click on **Delete** and then click on **OK**.

Adding a new vHBA

Use the following procedure to add a virtual fiber Channel adapter (vHBA) and assign it to a vSAN.

1. Open the **Fabric** workspace.
2. In the **Fabric** pane, right-click the applicable host and then click **Properties**.

3. On the **Properties** page, click on the **Hardware Configuration** tab and click on **New**, then on **fiber Channel Adapter** and then do the following:

  - In the **Virtual SAN name** box, select a *vSAN* from the drop-down list to assign to the vHBA
  - If you want to dynamically assign the range of port settings for the vHBA, click on **Dynamically assign World Wide Names**
  - If you want to statically assign port settings for the vHBA, click on **Statically assign World Wide Names** and then enter primary and secondary WWNN and WWPN port settings for the vHBA
  - When completed, click on **OK**

Editing vHBA WWNN and WWPN Dynamic Settings

Carry out the following steps to modify the port settings that can be assigned to a vHBA:

1. In the **Fabric** workspace, **Fabric** pane, select the Hyper-V host, right-click and select **Properties**.
2. Click on the **Hardware** tab and then below **Global FC settings**, provide **the World Wide Node Name** and the *lowest* WWPN and *highest* WWPN port settings and then click on **OK**.

See also

For more information, visit the article *Managing Virtual fiber Channel in VMM* at `https://docs.microsoft.com/en-us/system-center/vmm/storage-fibre-channel`.

10
Integration with System Center Operations Manager 2016

In this chapter, we will cover:

- Installing System Center Operations Manager 2016
- Installing management packs
- Managing Discovery and Agents
- Configuring the integration between Operations Manager and VMM
- Enabling reporting in VMM

Introduction

This chapter provides tips and techniques to allow administrators to integrate **Operations Manager (OM)** 2016 with VMM 2016 to monitor the health and performance of virtual machine hosts and their virtual machines, as well as to use the OM reporting functionality.

In a hybrid hypervisor environment (for example, Hyper-V, VMware), using OM **management packs** (**MPs**) (for example, Veeam MP), you can monitor the Hyper-V hosts and the VMware hosts, which allows you to use only the System Center Console to manage and monitor the hybrid hypervisor environment.

You can also monitor the health and availability of the VMM infrastructure, management, database, and library servers. The following screenshot will show you the diagram views of the virtualized environment through the OM:

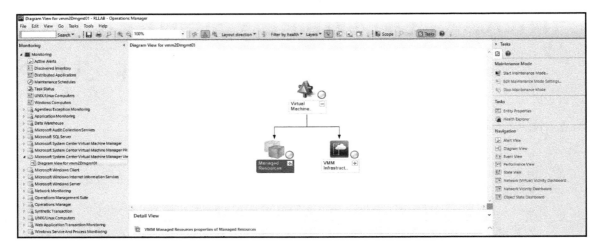

Installing System Center Operations Manager 2016

This recipe will guide you through the process of installing a **System Center Operations Manager** (**SCOM**) for the integration with VMM.

OM has an integrated product and company knowledge for proactive tuning. It also allows the user to compute the OS, applications, services, and out-of-the-box network monitoring, reporting, and many more features' extensibility through management packs, thus providing a cross-platform visibility.

The deployment used in this recipe assumes a small environment with all components being installed on the same server. For data centers and enterprise deployments, it is recommended to distribute the features and services across multiple servers to allow for scalability. For a complete design reference and complex implementation of SCOM 2016, follow the Microsoft Operations Manager deployment guide available at `https://docs.microsoft.com/system-center/scom/deploy-overview`.

 When planning, use *Operations Manager Planning Guide* (`https://docs.microsoft.com/system-center/scom/plan-overview`) to determine the hardware requirements.

Getting ready

Before starting, check out the system requirements and design planning for SCOM 2016 at `https://docs.microsoft.com/system-center/scom/plan-system-requirements`

 In this recipe, SCOM will be installed on the separate VM with Windows Server 2016. SQL Server 2016 (DB services, Full Text and **Reporting Services (RS)** in native mode) is already configured on another VM. All machines are members of the same domain.

How to do it...

Carry out the following steps to install OM 2016:

 As SCOM 2016 requires many prerequisites to be installed beforehand, I would recommend to automate complete installation by using PowerShell. See the simple script available at `https://rlevchenko.com/2018/01/16/automate-scom-2016-installation-with-powershell/`.

1. Browse to the SCOM installation folder and click on **Setup**.
2. Select **Download the latest updated to the setup program** and click on **Install**. Once the wizard has checked available updates, the next page will be shown.

3. On the **Select the features to install** page, select the components that apply to your environment, and then click on **Next,** as shown in the following screenshot:

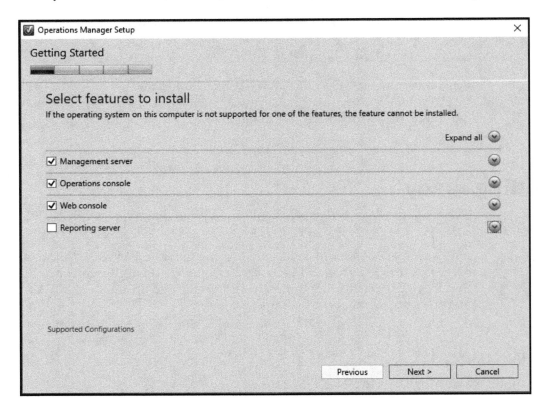

The recommendation is to have a dedicated server, but it all depends on the size of the deployment. You can select all of the components to be installed on the same server for a small deployment.

4. Type in the location where you will install OM 2016, or accept the default location and click on **Next**.

5. The installation will check if your system has passed all of the requirements. A screen showing the issues will be displayed if any of the requirements are not met, and you will be asked to fix and verify it again before continuing with the installation, as shown in the following screenshot:

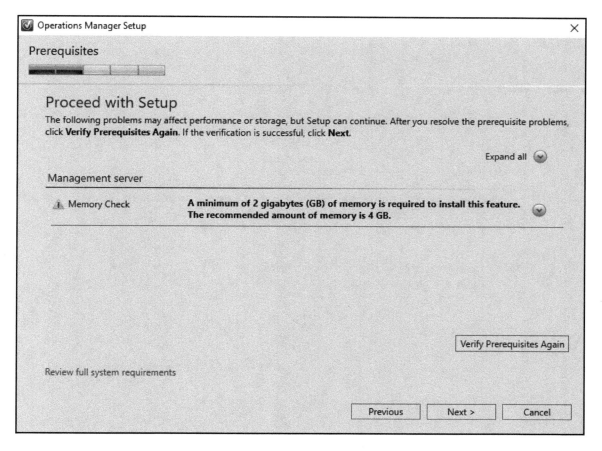

6. If all of the prerequisites are met, click on **Next** to proceed with the setup.

7. On the **Specify an installation option** page, if this is the first OM, select the **Create the first Management Server in a new management group** option and provide a value in the **Management group name** field; otherwise, select the **Add a management server to an existing management group** option, as shown in the following screenshot:

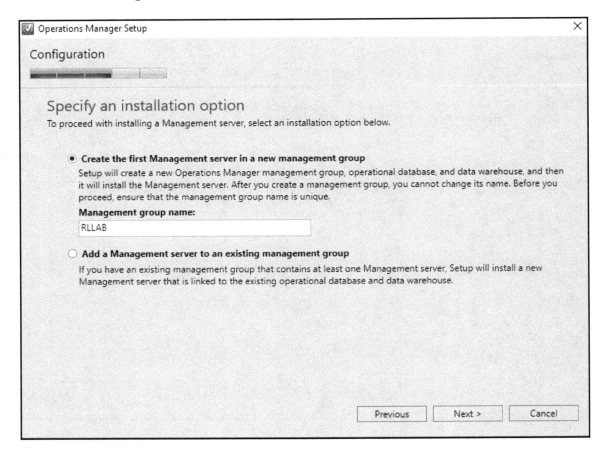

8. Click on **Next** to continue, accept the **end user license agreement (EULA)**, and click on **Next**.

9. On the **Configure the operational database** page, provide the SQL Database **Server name and instance name**, **Server port**, **Database name**, **Database size (MB)**, and **Data file folder**, as shown in the following screenshot, then click on **Next**:

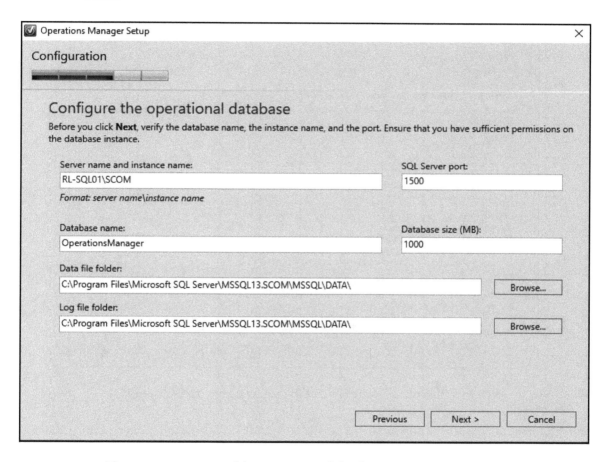

If you create a named instance on a SQL Server, it's best practice to define a custom port on the instance using SQL Server Network Configuration in the SQL Server Configuration Manager (`SQLServerManager13.msc`). In this recipe, dynamic ports are disabled on all SQL Server interfaces and custom port `1500` is set.

10. On the **Configure the data warehouse database** page, provide the SQL Database server for the data warehouse: SQL Database **Server name and instance name**, **SQL Server port** ; **Database name**, **Database size (MB)**, and data file folder, as shown in the following screenshot:

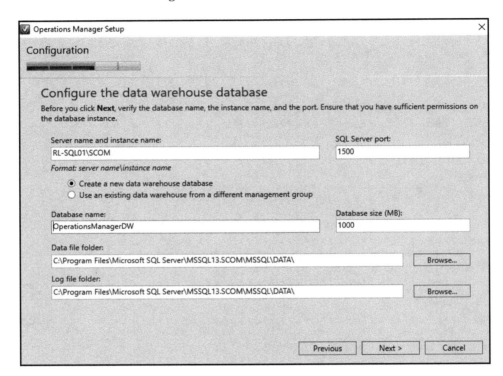

 The installation account needs DB owner rights on the database.

11. On the **Specify a Website** page, leave the **Default Web Site** selected and optionally select **Enable SSL**, then click on **Next**.
12. Select an authentication mode for use with the Web Console and click on **Next**.

 For intranet scenarios, select **Mixed Authentication**.

13. If **Reporting server** had been selected, on the **SQL Server instance for Reporting Services** page, select the instance where you want to host the RS.

 Make sure SQL Server has the **SQL Server Full-Text Search and Reporting Services (Native)** component installed.

14. On the **Configure Operations Manager accounts** page, provide the domain account credentials for the Operations Manager services, as shown in the following screenshot:

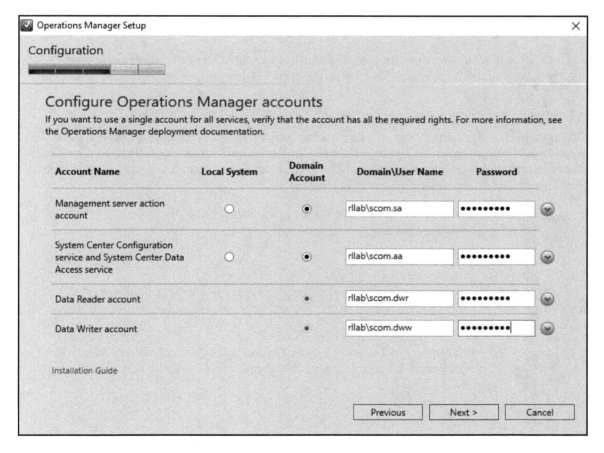

15. On the **Installation Summary** page, review the options and click on **Install**, and then on click **Close**. The **Operations Manager** console will open.

How it works...

When deploying Operations Manager 2016, it is important to consider the placement of the components. Work on the OM design before implementing it. See the *Operations Manager Planning Guide* ;available at `https://docs.microsoft.com/en-us/system-center/scom/plan-overview`

On the **Configure Operational Database** page, if you are installing the first management server, a new operational database will be created. If you are installing additional management servers, an existing database will be used.

On the **SQL Server instance for reporting services** page, make sure you have previously configured the RS at SQL setup using the **Reporting Services Configuration Manager** tool, and that the **SQL Server Agent** is running.

> I would recommend deploying the reporting server to another server when deploying OM in a production environment.

During the OpsMgr setup, you will be required to provide the **Management Server Action Account** credentials and the **System Center Configuration service and System Center Data Access service** account credentials too. The recommendation is to use a domain account so that you can use the same account for both services.

> The setup will automatically assign the local computer `Administrators` group to the OM administrator's role.

The single-server scenario combines all roles into a single instance and supports the following services: monitoring and alerting; reporting; audit collection; agentless-exception management; and data.

> If you are planning to monitor the network, it is recommended to move the SQL Server `tempdb` database to a separate disk that has multiple spindles.

There's more...

To confirm the health of the management server, carry out the following steps:

1. In the **OpsMgr** console, click on the **Administration** workspace.
2. In **Device Management**, select **Management Servers** to confirm that the installed server has a green check mark in the **Health State** column.

See also

For more information, you can visit the following links:

- *Automate SCOM 2016 installation with PowerShell* article/script: `https:// rlevchenko.com/2018/01/16/automate-scom-2016-installation-with- powershell/`

- *Deploying System Center 2016 – Operations Manager* article: `https://docs. microsoft.com/system-center/scom/deploy-distributed-deployment`

Installing management packs

After installing OM, you need to install some management packs and agents on the Hyper-V servers and on the VMM server.

This recipe will guide you through the installation, but first make sure you have installed the Operations Manager – **Operations console** on the VMM management server.

You need to import the following management packs for the VMM 2016 integration:

- Windows Server Operating System Library
- Windows Server 2016 Operating System (Discovery)
- Windows Server Internet Information Services 2016
- Windows Server Internet Information Services Library
- Microsoft Windows Internet Information Services 2003
- Windows Server 2008 Operating System (Discovery)
- Windows Server 2008 Internet Information Services 7
- SQL Server Core Library

Getting ready

Before you begin, make sure the latest version of PowerShell is installed on both SCOM and SCVMM servers. Open the PowerShell command and type:

```
PS \> $PSVersionTable
```

Alternatively, you can type `Get-Host`.

How to do it...

Carry out the following steps to install the required MPs in order to integrate with VMM 2016:

1. In the OpsMgr console, click on the **Administration** workspace on the bottom-left pane.
2. On the left pane, right-click on **Management Packs** and click on **Import Management Packs**.
3. In the **Import Management Packs** wizard, click on **Add**, and then click on **Add from catalog**.
4. In the **Select Management Packs from Catalog** dialog box, for each of the following management packs, repeat the steps 5 to 7:
   - Windows Server Operating System Library
   - Windows Server 2016 Operating System (Discovery)
   - Windows Server Internet Information Services 2016
   - Windows Server Internet Information Services Library
   - Microsoft Windows Internet Information Services 2003
   - Windows Server 2008 Operating System (Discovery)
   - Windows Server 2008 Internet Information Services 7
   - SQL Server Core Library

The Windows Server 2008 and IIS 2003/7 MPs are required by VMM 2016 even though you are installing it on a Windows 2016 server. There are numerous management packs for SCOM. You can also use this recipe to install other SCOM MPs using the catalog web service.

5. In the **Find** field, type in the management pack to search in the online catalog and click on **Search**.

6. The **Management packs in the catalog** list will show all of the packs that match the search criterion. To import, select the management pack, click on **Select**, and then click on **Add,** as shown in the following screenshot:

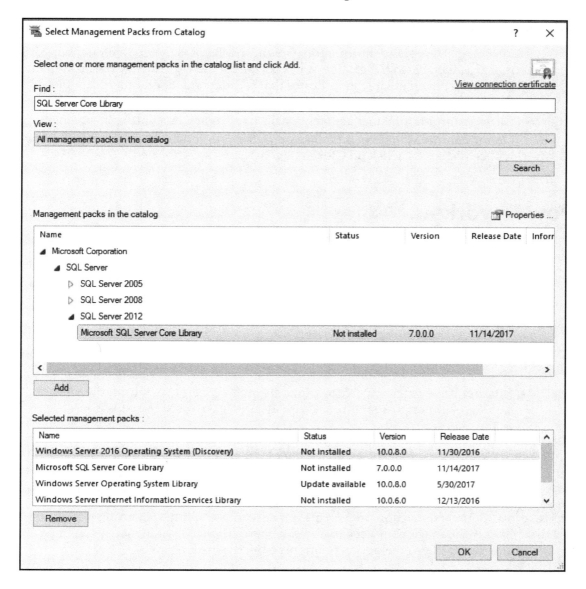

In the **View** section, you can refine the search by selecting, for example, to show only those management packs released within the last three months. The default view lists all of the management packs in the catalog.

7. Click on **OK** after adding the required management packs.
8. On the **Select Management Packs** page, the MPs will be listed with either a green icon, a yellow icon, or a red icon. The green icon indicates that the MP can be imported. The yellow information icon means that it is dependent on other MPs that are available in the catalog, and you can fix the dependency by clicking on **Resolve**. The red error icon indicates that it is dependent on other MPs, but the dependent MPs are not available in the catalog.
9. Click on **Import** if all management packs have their icon statuses as green.
10. On the **Import Management Packs** page, the progress for each management pack will be displayed. Click on **Close** when the process is finished.

How it works...

You can import the management packs available for Operations Manager using the following:

- **OpsMgr console**: You can perform the following actions in the **Management Packs** menu of the **Administration** workspace:
    1. Import directly from Microsoft's online catalog.
    2. Import from disk/share.
    3. Download the management pack from the online catalog to import at a later time.
- **Internet browser**: You can download the management pack from the online catalog to import at a later time, or to install on an OpsMgr that is not connected to the internet

While using the OpsMgr console, verify whether all management packs show a green status. Any MP displaying the yellow information icon or the red error icon in the import list will not be imported.

If there is no internet connection on the OpsMgr server, use an internet browser to locate and download the management pack to a folder/share. Then, copy the management pack to the OpsMgr server and use the option to import from disk/share.

See also

For more information, refer to the following:

- The *Installing System Center Operations Manager 2016* recipe

Managing discovery and agents

After installing the Operations Manager, you need to deploy the agents and start monitoring servers, network devices, services, and applications.

We also need to install the agents on the VMM management server and on all Hyper-V servers. This is required in order to integrate VMM with Operations Manager.

How to do it...

Carry out the following steps to install the OpsMgr agent on a Windows OS by using the **Discovery Wizard** tool:

1. On the OpsMgr console, click on **Administration** on the left, right-click and select **Discovery Wizard...**, as shown in the following screenshot:

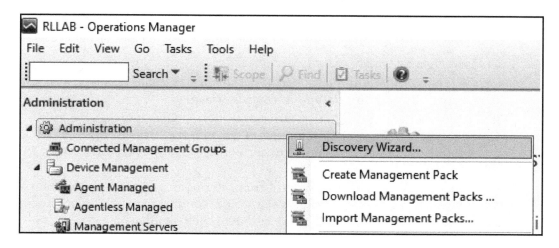

2. On the **What would you like to manage?** page (shown on clicking the **Discovery Type** tab), click on **Windows computers** and then click on **Next**.

3. On the **Auto or Advanced?** page, select either **Automatic computer discovery** (to scan all of the Windows computers on the domain) or **Advanced discovery.**

4. If you have selected **Advanced discovery**:
   - From the **Computer and Device Classes** drop-down list, select either: **Servers and Clients**, **Servers Only**, or **Clients Only**
   - From the **Management Server** drop-down list, select the OpsMgr management server or the gateway server

   This is shown in the following screenshot:

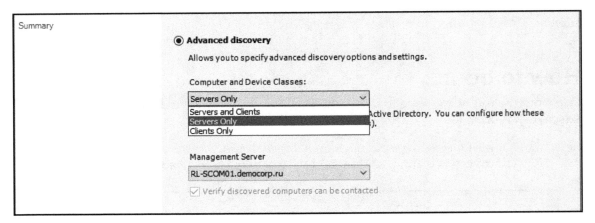

5. Click on **Next** to discover.

6. On the **Discovery Method** page (show in the next screenshot), select **Scan Active Directory** or **Browse for, or type-in computer names**.

7. If you have selected **Scan Active Directory**, click on **Configure**. In the **Find Computers** dialog box, in the **Computers** tab or in the **Advanced** tab, provide the information of the search criteria and click on **OK**. Then, select the domain from the **Domain** list.

8. If you selected **Browse for, or type-in computer names**, click on **Browse**, provide the computer names separated by a semicolon, comma, or a new line character (for example, **HV03**, **vmm-mgmt01**), and then click on **OK**:

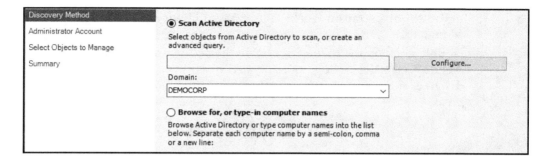

9. Click on **Next** and then on the **Administrator Account** page. Select **Use selected Management Server Action Account** or **Other user account** and provide the **User name** value, **Password**, and the **Domain** value (from the drop-down list).

Click on **This is a local computer account, not a domain account** if it is not a domain account.

10. Click on **Discover**, and on the **Discovery Results** page, select the computers on which you want to install the agent and be monitored by OpsMgr, or click on **Select All** and in **Management Mode**, select **Agent** and then click on **Next**.

Do not select any virtual cluster node to be managed.

11. On the **Summary** page, confirm the installation path and in the **Agent Action Account** section, select either **Local System** (default) or **Other**. In either case, you will need to provide the **User name**, **Password**, and **Domain** values.

If you choose a path different from the default, make sure you create the root of the path on the target computers, or else the agent installation fails.

12. Click on **Finish**, and in the **Agent Management Task Status** dialog box you will see the agent **Status** column changing from **Queued** to **Success**. This indicates that the computers are ready to be managed. Lastly, click on **Close**.

13. In the **Administration** workspace, expand **Device Management** and then **Agent Managed.**

14. Double-click on the managed host in the right pane, and in the **Security** tab of the **Agent Properties** dialog box, select **Allow this agent to act as a proxy and discover managed objects on other computers**. Repeat this step for each of the hosts.

> To automate the last two steps and enable agent proxy, use the following command:
> ```
> Get-SCOMAgent | where {$_.ProxyingEnabled.Value -eq
> $False} | Enable-SCOMAgentProxy
> ```

How it works...

In this recipe, as we are targeting the VMM server and the Hyper-V hosts, select **Servers Only**. You can use the same steps to install the agents on any Windows OS computer.

Note that if the AD does not contain the computers' names, you need to select the **Servers and Clients** option, and then select the **Verify discovered computers can be contacted** checkbox.

Discovery is the process in which OpsMgr searches the environment for all manageable objects and deploys an agent to monitor it. You can use the discovery process at any time to add the newly-installed computers or roles/features to be managed.

For the OpsMgr agent to be installed, the account used to run the process requires local administrator rights on the target computer.

You can manually install the agents, or you can embed the agent in the host image of the monitored computer.

See also

For more information, refer to the following:

- The *Planning Agents deployment* article available at https://docs.microsoft.com/system-center/scom/plan-planning-agent-deployment.

- The *Install Agent on UNIX and Linux Using the Discovery Wizard* article available at https://docs.microsoft.com/system-center/scom/manage-deploy-crosspla t-agent-console</a>
- The *Install Agent Using the MOMAgent.msi Setup Wizard* article available at https://docs.microsoft.com/system-center/scom/manage-deploy-windows-agent-manually

Configuring the integration between Operations Manager 2016 and VMM 2016

This recipe will guide you through the process of configuring the connectivity between VMM and SCOM.

By integrating VMM with Operations Manager (OpsMgr), you can use the OpsMgr console to monitor the health and availability of the VMs and Hyper-V servers, VMM management and database servers, library servers, and diagram views of the virtualized environment.

In order to establish a connection with VMM, you need to configure the Operations Manager servers to work with VMM. This configuration is done on the VMM console.

The VMM management pack supports up to 400 hosts with up to 8000 VMs.

Getting ready

Before starting, make sure that you do the following:

- Install the Operations Manager console on the VMM management server as it is required for the integration between VMM and Operations Manager
- Install the required OpsMgr management packs, as discussed in the *Installing management packs* recipe in this chapter

How to do it...

Carry out the following steps to set up the integration between Operations Manager 2016 and VMM 2016:

1. If you installed the Operations Manager on a separate server (recommended), install the Operations Manager agent on the VMM management server.
2. In the VMM console, in the **Settings** workspace to the left of the window, click on **System Center Settings**, and then right-click on **Operations Manager Server,** and then select **Properties,** as shown in the following screenshot:

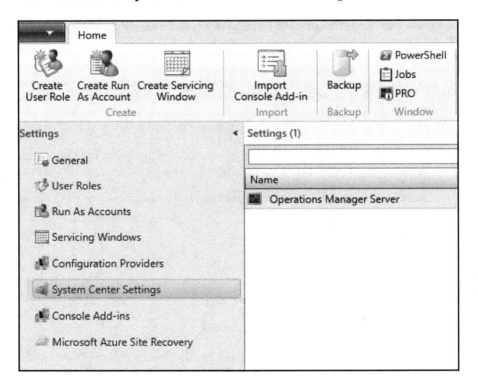

3. On the **Introduction** page, click on **Next**.
4. On the **Configure connection from VMM to Operations Manager** page, in the **Server name** field, type the OpsMgr management server name (for example, `rl-scom01`).

5. Select the account that is a member of the Operations Manager Administrators role. You can use the VMM server service account or specify a Run As account, as shown in the following screenshot:

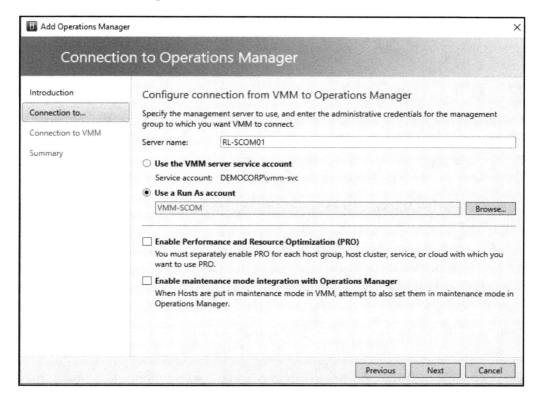

Do not select **Enable Performance and Resource Optimization (PRO)** and **Enable maintenance mode integration with Operations Manager** at this point, or else the operation will not succeed and will show the following error: Operations Manager discovery failed with error: **Exception of type 'Microsoft.VirtualManager.EnterpriseManagement.Common.Discovery DataInvalidRelationshipSourceExceptionOM10** was thrown.

6. Click on **Next**, then type the account credentials for Operations Manager to connect with the VMM management server (for example, `rllab\scom-vmm`), and then click on **Next**.

This account will be added to the administrator user role in VMM.

7. On the **Summary** page, click on **Finish**.

How it works...

The process consists of registering the Operations Manager on the VMM management server using the VMM console.

During the connection process, the account informed to connect Operations Manager to VMM will be added to the administrator user role in VMM.

To verify that the VMM to OpsMgr integration was completed, open OpsMgr and select the **Monitoring** workspace. In the navigation pane, confirm that you see:

- **Virtual Machine Manager**: This includes the health and performance information for virtual machines, hosts, and VMM servers
- **Virtual Machine Manager View**: This displays diagrams for the managed systems

Note that the OpsMgr diagrams will not be displayed right after the connection is established. It may require several hours to get updated.

Do not enable the PRO or maintenance mode at the integration setup. Enable both later, after the connection is completed.

In case of any warnings during the integration, you may need to remove the existing connection and try to set it up again. To remove the connection, use the following:
`Remove-SCOpsMgrConnection -Force`

There's more...

Now that you have enabled the integration with Operations Manager, let's see what more you can do.

---

[520]

Enabling PRO tips and maintenance mode integration in VMM 2016

Performance and Resource Optimization (PRO) is a feature supported since VMM 2012 when integrated with Operations Manager. Carry out the following steps to enable the PRO tips in VMM:

1. In the VMM console, in the bottom-left pane, open the **Settings** workspace.
2. Click on **System Center Settings**, select and right-click on **Operations Manager Server**.
3. On the **Details** page, select **Enable Performance and Resource Optimization (PRO)**.
4. Select **Enable maintenance mode integration with Operations Manager** and then click on **OK**.

> When in maintenance mode, the OpsMgr's agent suppresses alerts, notifications, rules, monitors, automatic responses, state changes, and new alerts. It also automatically places VMs in the maintenance mode when they are moved to the VMM library.

5. On the **Properties** window, click on **Test PRO**.

> Allow some time for the task to complete before clicking on **Test PRO** and after setting up PRO.

6. Confirm the results either in the VMM console (the **Jobs** workspace) or in the Operations console in Operations Manager.

> Note that Dynamic Optimization is now performed and configured in VMM in place of the host load balancing that was performed by PRO in VMM 2008 R2. VMM does include PRO monitors to monitor a VM's **dynamic memory (DM)** allocation and maximum VM memory aggregations on Hyper-V hosts.

See also

For more information, go through the following:

- The *Configuring Dynamic Optimization and Power Optimization in VMM* recipe in Chapter 9, *Managing Clouds, Fabric Updates, Resources, Clusters and New Features of 2016*
- The *Installing System Center Operations Manager 2016* recipe

Enabling reporting in VMM

After integrating VMM with Operations Manager for monitoring, you can also enable the integration to provide reporting, which will give you the ability to create and view reports related to Hyper-V servers, VMs, and VMM-related components (for example, the management and library servers).

 Operations Manager only supports **SQL Server Reporting Services** (**SSRS**) in the native mode.

Getting ready

In order to enable the reporting, you will need to have **SQL Server Analysis Service** (**SSAS**) preinstalled on the Operations Manager Reporting server (for example, `rllab\rl-sql01`).

You also need to install **Analysis Management Objects** (**AMO**) on all of the VMM management servers for the SQL Server you have installed. For SQL 2012 SP1, see `https://www.microsoft.com/en-us/download/details.aspx?id=35580` (`SQL_AS_AMO.msi`).

How to do it...

Carry out the following steps to configure the SSAS in VMM:

1. Open the VMM console. On the bottom-left pane, click to open the **Settings** workspace, and then in the **Settings** pane to the left, click on **System Center Settings**.
2. Select and then right-click on **Operations Manager Server**.
3. In the **Operations Manager Settings** dialog box (shown in the following screenshot), click on the **SQL Server Analysis Services** tab on the left pane.
4. Select **Enable SSAS**:

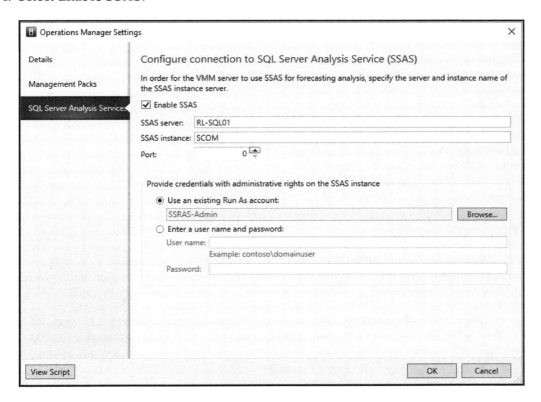

5. Type the **SSAS server**, **SSAS instance**, and **Port** values.

Ensure that SQL Server Browser Service UDP 1434 and TCP 2382 ports are unblocked. If you use a default SQL Server instance, also open the TCP 2383 port.

6. On the **Provide credentials with administrative rights on the SSAS instance** page, select **Use an existing Run As account**, click on **Browse**, and provide the Run As account, or select **Enter a user name and password** and provide the username (for example, `rllab\ssas-scom`) and password.
7. Click on **OK** to confirm.

How it works...

The process to set up the SSAS integration with VMM requires a VMM administrator user role. The account must belong to the **Operations Manager Report Security Administrator** profile.

On the setup wizard, provide the SSAS instance name, which must be the same as that of the SSRS. You need to type the instance name even if it is already the default instance: **MSSQLSERVER**. The default port is 0.

Also, make sure that SSRS allows report access by using the default HTTP port 80.

There's more...

You can view reports in the Operations Manager console's **Reporting** workspace or by browsing through the OpsMgr report server (for example, as a named instance is used in this recipe, browse to `http://rl-sql01.rllab.com/reports_SCOM`).

Use **Reporting Services Configuration Manager** to check and configure Web Services/Portal URLs (to enable SSL for Web Services, for example).

You can choose from the predefined reports or create your own:

- **Host Group Forecasting report**: This calculates host activity based on history
- **Host Utilization report**: This shows the number of VMs running, plus their usage (CPU/memory/disk)

- **Host Utilization Growth report**: This shows the percentage change in resource usage and the number of virtual machines that are running on selected hosts during a specified time period
- **Capacity Utilization report**: This specifies the detailed usage for hosts and other objects, as shown in the following screenshot:

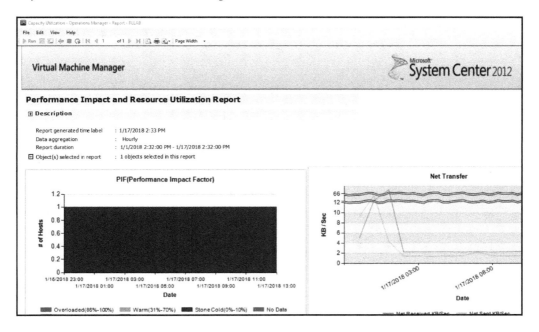

- **Power Savings report**: This shows summary/detailed information about the power saved for each host in a host group
- **SAN Usage Forecasting report**: This calculates the SAN usage based on history
- **Virtual Machine Allocation report**: This shows information about a VM's allocation
- **Virtual Machine Utilization report**: This shows information about resource utilization by VMs
- **Virtualization Candidates report**: This helps identify the physical computers that are good candidates for conversion to VMs

Other Books You May Enjoy

If you enjoyed this book, you may be interested in these other books by Packt:

Microsoft System Center 2016 Service Manager Cookbook - Second Edition
Anders Asp, Andreas Baumgarten, Steve Beaumont, Steve Buchanan, Dieter Gasser

ISBN: 978-1-78646-489-7

- See a practical implementation of the ITSM framework and processes based on ITIL
- Deploy and configure the new Service Manager HTML5 Self-Service Portal along with Service Catalog design and configuration
- Get to know about Incident, Problem, and Change Management processes and configuration
- Get to grips with performing advanced personalization in Service Manager
- Discover how to set up and use automation with and within Service Manager 2016
- Work with Service Manager Data Warehouse
- Find out what Security Roles are and how to implement them
- Learn how to upgrade from SCSM 2012 R2 to SCSM 2016

Deploying Microsoft System Center Configuration Manager

Jacek Doktor, Pawel Jarosz

ISBN: 978-1-78588-101-5

- Install ConfigMgr servers and the necessary roles
- Design and scale ConfigMgr environments
- Configure and administrate essential ConfigMgr roles and features
- Create software packages using .msi and .exe files
- Deliver detailed reports with an automatic patching process
- Apply proper hardening on your deployment and secure workstations
- Deploy operating systems and updates leveraging ConfigMgr mechanisms
- Create high-availability components using the built-in mechanism for backup and recovery

Leave a review - let other readers know what you think

Please share your thoughts on this book with others by leaving a review on the site that you bought it from. If you purchased the book from Amazon, please leave us an honest review on this book's Amazon page. This is vital so that other potential readers can see and use your unbiased opinion to make purchasing decisions, we can understand what our customers think about our products, and our authors can see your feedback on the title that they have worked with Packt to create. It will only take a few minutes of your time, but is valuable to other potential customers, our authors, and Packt. Thank you!

Index